Hidden Hands

DUCKWORTH EGYPTOLOGY
Series Editor: Nicholas Reeves

Burial Customs in Ancient Egypt
Wolfram Grajetzki

Court Officials of the Egyptian Middle Kingdom
Wolfram Grajetzki

**Hidden Hands: Egyptian workforces in
Petrie excavation archives, 1880-1924**
Stephen Quirke

**The Middle Kingdom of Ancient Egypt:
history, archaeology and society**
Wolfram Grajetzki

Performance and Drama in Ancient Egypt
Robyn Gillam

HIDDEN HANDS

Egyptian workforces in
Petrie excavation archives
1880-1924

Stephen Quirke

Duckworth

First published in 2010 by
Gerald Duckworth & Co. Ltd.
90-93 Cowcross Street, London EC1M 6BF
Tel: 020 7490 7300
Fax: 020 7490 0080
info@duckworth-publishers.co.uk
www.ducknet.co.uk

A catalogue record for this book is available
from the British Library

ISBN 978-0-7156-3904-7

Typeset by Ray Davies
Printed and bound in Great Britain by
CPI Antony Rowe, Chippenham and Eastbourne

Contents

Djedi nim min
    senu bin
    inentu m djerdjeru r metet net ib

Who can I speak to today?
    Brothers are evil,
    they fetch for strangers for advice of the heart
                        From 'Dialogue of a man with
                            his soul', 1850 BC

Preface

The Great Pyramid has aroused in viewers from different cultures the same mixture of awe at its scale and geometric perfection, and horror at the human cost in labour. Yet few commentators seem to return their gaze to their own societies. In the present state of our knowledge, it seems that the pyramids were built by a system that, however harsh (we do not know), was not a slave economy, whereas most later historians have come from social strata that depended on slave labour: ancient Greek and Roman, modern European and American up to the later nineteenth century. The same contradiction continues to affect twenty-first-century reactions: awe at size and architectural perfection, horror at an assumed despotism, indifference to current labour and social relations.

Archaeology has incorporated this fusion of admiration, revulsion and indifference into the foundation of its practice. Excavations and surveys typically involve inserting outsiders, in theory selected for their expertise, into a landscape targeted for its traces of the past, with no relevance to or for the people already in that landscape. For evidence on the construction of that peculiar indifference, this book explores the formative phase in the history of archaeology as a profession and a university discipline, the late nineteenth and early twentieth centuries. At that time, the land of the pyramids suffered direct British military occupation, from the 1882 invasion to formal independence in 1922, with troops staying on until their ejection in the Suez crisis of 1956, after the 1952 revolution.

With the British being the occupying power in Egypt, the most prominent London-based archaeologist in the country, Flinders Petrie, is a key figure in this history. Born in a London suburb in 1853, Petrie worked in Egypt from 1880 to 1924. As a direct result of restrictions placed on foreign expeditions by the post-1922 government in Cairo, he left to work and live in Palestine, and died in Jerusalem in 1942. In 1892 Petrie became the first Professor of Egyptian Archaeology in England, at University College London, where he amassed a vast teaching collection including tens of thousands of objects and some ten thousand photographic negatives, along with two hundred Notebooks from the excavations he directed or helped fund. Petrie achieved two main objectives in his career: he trained the next generation of English archaeologists to work in Egypt, and he published a large number of scientific research books on Egyptian archaeology, with reference catalogues of objects by type, as well as excavation reports. Many of these works have been superseded, and his dig records do not match later standards, but they had a profound impact on the formation of archaeology in Egypt. The Petrie-led excavations in Egypt from 1880 to 1924 yielded a distant product in London: a collection of objects; series of published books; dig documentation; and pictorial archive. Next to none of this is in Arabic: a rigid exclusion, the result of colonial rule that already operated in Egyptology at the time Petrie first landed in Alexandria. Each subsequent generation of archaeologists, of all nationalities including Egyptian, has recreated that exclusion. If things are to change, archaeology needs to examine its own history critically to understand how this way of working came into force.

In this spirit, I propose an approach to the history of London-based excavations in Egypt, 1880-1924, on the model of a survey and an excavation layer by layer (the stratigraphic method that Petrie adopted at Tell Hesy in Palestine in 1890, but never in Egypt). My first chapter surveys the current profile of Egyptology as knowledge-production, and the historical background to the Egypt Petrie knew, with the political developments that took place there during his career. The excavation of the formative discipline begins in Chapter 2 with a study of references to Egyptians, with or without names, throughout his publications, introduced by his manual for excavation, *Methods and Aims in Archaeology* (1904). Beneath the publications, a second stratum comprises the semi-public 'Journals', the name given by Petrie to circulars that he sent to a small group of supporters up to 1900, together with later more private correspondence from both him and his wife Hilda. Chapter 3 collects the references to named Egyptians in the Journals, while the fourth chapter considers instances where names were omitted. The third, final layer explored in his writing is the collection of almost two hundred pocket Notebooks, containing miscellaneous notes and records from surveys and digs directed or funded by Petrie, the subject of Chapter 4. These sources are more difficult than the published narratives and letters, because they tend to be written for their writer, not a reader. Furthermore, they have previously been scoured for archaeological data missing from the summary publications, rather than for modern historical or economic evidence. The analysis of the Notebooks represents, then, a new departure, and I hope that this acts as an invitation to non-archaeological historians to consider them as primary sources for more elusive aspects of modern history, the rural desert margins, and the interface between archaeology and politics (as in the essays for Trumpler 2008). Chapter 5 presents the numerous miscellaneous references to Egyptians in the Notebooks, from security, politics and law, to working conditions of health, pay and accommodation. Chapter 6 collects all instances where finds of single items or site features are ascribed to a named Egyptian, while Chapter 7 covers all finds of object-groups, which at this time replaced the single find as the foundation for studying the past in professional archaeology. Finally, challenging the focus on the named individual in disciplinary histories, the Notebooks offer a different resource: the great name-lists by which Petrie recorded pay costs in his employment of literally hundreds of men, boys and, in Delta excavations, girls, between 1883 and 1914. Hundreds more employees never entered the lists, as Petrie changed his recruitment methods and payment arrangements. Nevertheless, the pay-lists provide us with the names of several hundred excavators omitted from histories of archaeology. Chapter 8 records the names in the Anglicised forms found in the Petrie Notebooks, with separate indices for each main period of his work. Parallel to the paper archive, the ten thousand negatives and prints from Petrie work offer a parallel vein of evidence, outlined in Chapter 9 under the same guiding questions, where do Egyptians appear with name, and where without?

The aim of the first chapter is to encourage study of this history in full awareness of our own prejudices concerning the recent past. However terrible the impact of previous generations, it is ourselves and our own time that present the greater threat to the world. Therefore, rather than just easy condemnation of past archaeologists, the archive offers opportunities to chart an alternative future. To that end, the book closes with a summary biography of some famous and some overlooked names in the history of Egyptian archaeology, as one means of rejecting the established life of the discipline, and its established boundaries of practice and theory, and replacing them with new ways of discovering, and relating to, the past.

1

Setting a stage

From their uncertain birth between science and university politics, all disciplines live out a crisis of identity. Archaeology in Egypt exposes this historical question of existence with particular force. If the discipline is perceived at its sites of work as a western study of the past, it may have little future in lands without western populations (Meskell 1998). Although excavating and surveying teams are immersed for weeks or months every year in intensely local relationships, their aims have been sealed against local involvement so hermetically that it seems too late to declare an interest in them now. The division between archaeologists and those inhabiting archaeological landscapes is not geographically confined; it operates as a universal structuring principle of the profession (Wilmore 2006). Historically, the rupture may derive from practices created during its formation under imperialism, and so arguably, to some extent at least, 'within' our past. Yet a history is not in itself reassuring, if the problematic practices remain, not just active, but normative in the present.

Most archaeological fieldwork requires a manual labour force, and archaeologists have traditionally recruited this labour from among the low-paid or destitute. Although urban and industrial archaeology are now fully established in universities as parts of the discipline, throughout the world archaeology still often operates in marginal rural environments, where local soil conditions and sparse populations have combined to give archaeological remains a better chance of survival. In such conditions, archaeological employment could be, and has been, considered social welfare, as Henry Wellcome proposed explicitly to the British colonial authorities in 1910 for his digging in central Sudan (Addison 1949: 1-2: 'welfare work'; 'Archaeology, in short, was the handmaid of philanthropy'). Excavation does not necessarily, on that view, amount to an ethically flawed practice, and might even be regarded as socially benign. However, nearly all fieldwork, including that carried out in nominally worker-oriented countries, enacts a systematic division between skilled and manual labour, performed across a temporal axis; the axis is defined as from excavation to post-excavation, and materialised as presence and absence. By this division, archaeology denies its own workforce any professional presence. Even during the phase of manual digging, field-directors ensure that unskilled labour leaves no autographed signature in documentation. In publication, archaeological writers strategically excise the individual identities, in their very names, and the collective presence of the workers.

The main trace of their activity may be confined to colour photographs, in public-information web-sites, magazines and brochures, often oriented toward fundraising. By this stroke of excision, archaeology is denying itself its own right to exist, or, in practical terms, its prospects to continue existing.

Late twentieth-century developments within the discipline include the founding of the World Archaeological Congress and the growth of a sub-discipline of Public Archaeology (cf. Ascherson 2000, Shackel and Chambers 2004). With external public funding pressures for accessibility, archaeologists are already heavily engaged in the processes of change (e.g. Mapunda and Lane 2004). The premise of this book is that the early twenty-first century offers opportunities for more concerted and theoreti-cally-engaged strategies of change. Theoretically, as part of a public sphere, archaeology ought to be capable of encouraging its own structural transformation, and so solving its crisis of legitimacy concerning the issue of consent. The same should be true for any part of the chains of study of material from the past, from the disciplines formed around ancient writing and language (Assyriology, Egyptology) to the entire scholarly, public and commercial enterprise of display (Museum Studies). In such a wide range of often mutually hostile institutions of knowledge, many approaches must be available. The approach tested in this book is to explore archaeology archives, focussing on a case-study from past London-based direction of work in Egypt, in order to help future researchers identify structural elements open to transformation.

'Public sphere': Egyptology as a print readership

Print publication of word and image has accompanied and sustained the historical experience of European global colonisation so efficiently that economic exploitation can seem almost secondary to printing, as perhaps in the Benedict Anderson thesis of 'print capitalism' (McInerney 2000). As twin domains of publicity, the print-production and circulation of adver-tising and 'news' both respond to and generate a 'public sphere' of informed readers, positing them(selves) as active, as the agents in and of history. Habermas explored this production from the northwest European experi-ence in his 1962 *Habilitation*-dissertation *Strukturwandel der Öffent-lichkeit* (English translation published as *Transformation of the Public Sphere* in 1989; German re-issue with new foreword by Habermas 1990). However, Habermas silently equated several separate categories: the public square; the print readerships active in modernity; and the liberal political definition of 'democracy'. Intellectual elites globally have tended to follow him in conflating these three (cf. Bakhtin, in Hirschkop 1999: 260-1). The equation with democracy is achieved only by ignoring the unwanted noisy masses (Montag 2000). Specifically, the equation requires a pathological amnesia brought into effect by a law of discipline with two clauses. First, we must forget all the extreme violence necessary to support the 'public sphere' or 'democracy' on which western European journalism prides itself. Secondly, any residual sub-consciousness of that violence must be shifted from our present to the other in space and time – or, as the 'Orient', both (Said 1978). A public sphere is, then, never natural, but always legalised for 'standard opinion' (*senso commune* in Gramsci, see Crehan 2002: 110-15), and, like the law, always sustained by police: by the threat and practice of violence. If we remove that political tactic of forgetting the violence, the thesis on the public sphere regains its force; Habermas charts the contemporary contours of mass communication, as well as the existence of a history for those contours (Hirschkop 1999: 30-4). If our conditions for communicating are not as inevitable or natural as they may seem to us, but instead historical, then another transformation no longer seems a political impossibility.

Given the pace of innovation in media since the 1980s, radical change in the form of the digital revolution is being experienced and studied today. Two centuries of European hegemony in communication technology may not yet be over, but, in an age of electronic media, the printing-presses perfected by the early nineteenth century already belong to the past. The 'moment' of the print revolution when Johannes Gutenberg produced his printed Bible (1452-54) might be seen as the inaugural triumph of that technology. However, early printing produced editions that varied widely in content – more, in fact, than carefully revised manuscripts. The new printing-press technology and earlier systems of editorial control needed another three and a half centuries before they combined to achieve mass-production of printed editions in which each item was identical in content and form (Cerquiglini 1989: 17-29). These developments took place within the socio-economic formation of early capitalism in its western European heartland, so print production was perfected for the scripts of that region, derived from Latin. Today, digital technology is again transforming the relations between different script worlds. The changes promise to overturn a hierarchy ensconced by nineteenth-century colonisers, one that set Europe above all of Asia and Africa, including on the front line the Arab world. In retrospect, manuscript traditions of Arabic script and philosophy seem disadavantaged by the Latin-based script of the print revolution; Eurocentric historiography routinely interprets late adoption of printing as a sign of inertia or decline. Against this view, Timothy Mitchell has argued that the Arabic-writing and -reading world of knowledge consciously avoided the new technology, because the more fixed post-1800 printed books in Latin-based scripts locked words with a military precision alien to a classical Arabic philosophy of authorship – and, arguably, to the way words work in any human language (Mitchell 1988: 150-4). The 1798 French expedition against Ottoman Egypt brought Cairo the printing-press in its newly perfected form, at a time when the material economy of print (raw materials, production, authors, readership, circulation, retail-outlets) served the ascendant colonising West European centres of capital. In 1800 those main centres of finance and war had long been London and Paris, one step removed from the Italian, Flemish and Dutch production centres of both paper and books which had dominated the early modern stage since the fifteenth century (Bloom 2001).

Cheaper paper and the permanence of printed words proved to be West European assets in the history of science and industry, for they created unpredecedentedly stable objects of reference. It is less easy to predict the winners in new, more flexible electronic communicative environments. The dominant web monoglossia can seem a cruelly close reflection of Euroamerican military power, warning us how internet freedoms tend to be exaggerated (McDavid 2004; Goldsmith and Wu 2006). Yet the changes are also taken as opportunities in countries outside the English-speaking world (Armbrust 2003). Earlier twentieth-century artists and writers in Cairo embraced new visual media to establish Egypt as a centre for radio and cinema throughout the Arab world, and that history remains a forceful model for contemporary action (Armbrust 1996). Print-space might, then, give way to more open fields. Strong vested interests still block radical structural transformation: interests of class within Egypt as well as multi-national interests beyond it. As the geographical meeting-point of the three Old World continents, Egypt has undergone bitter competition among the English, French and American colonising forces, analysed by Said (1978), with contributions from almost all of Europe, south and east as well as north. There are no innocents in this history. In their upriver extension into Sudan, Egyptians joined Englishmen as colonisers, and colonial period agreements enable both Sudan and Egypt to block Ethiopian rights to Nile water (Tvedt 2004). Detailed histories can demonstrate how the vulnerable did not merely submit, in any country. Their resistance may offer the only legitimate foundation for future study of the past.

Egyptology in the twenty-first century

For study of the Egyptian past, a nineteenth-century West European tradition has been naturalised as dominant. Yet its contemporary configuration disconnects segments of that past in curiously random patterns that would surprise observers outside the disciplines. The starkest disjuncture is that between Egyptology and Archaeology, in the professional self-definition of both. Egyptology is part of Archaeology in the public eye, but the two are separated in their histories, university practice and interests. In universities, most study of the past is institutionalised as the disciplines of History and Archaeology, assigning past writing as evidence for judgement by historians, and past material without writing as evidence for judgement by archaeologists (Sauer 2004). Yet Egyptology belongs to neither History nor Archaeology, because it deals not with Egypt as a whole, but only with its ancient writing; as one particular category in reception, this written record stands outside defined European horizons (Gosden 1999: 25, cf. Iversen 1961). In the Western tradition, most colonised terrain was denied history, because the observable history exposes too painfully the barbarism of the colonising Europeans. The colonised present was handed to Anthropology, and the study of its less tangible past, as Prehistory, to Archaeology and evolutionary Physical Anthropology. As Egyptology covers areas with writing to the south and east of Europe, it has instead been broadly categorised under the university grouping that, since Said, has lost the power of its name, Oriental Studies. On these lines, Europeans have assigned ancient Egypt to Asia, implicitly or explicitly under the label of Oriental Despotism (Pope 2006). As with western Asia, the study of Hellenic or Hellenising material from Egypt throughout the millennium between Alexander the Great and the arrival of Amr (332 BC to AD 640) fell largely to Greek studies (cf. Alcock 1994: 171-3); tens of thousands of Greek manuscripts from Egypt are assigned to a specially-created sub-discipline, Papyrology, with a focus on Greek rather than Egyptian history, and so privileging Greek papyri over those in Egyptian scripts (cf. Clackson 2004: 21 with nn. 2-3). The prehistory of Egypt, when included in study anywhere, hovers between Egyptology, treating the fifth to fourth millennia BC retrospectively as an ancestral phase, termed 'predynastic' (cf. Wengrow 2006: 72), and Prehistoric Archaeology, with coverage under other names, such as 'lower Nile' or 'northeast Africa'. In sum, the Egypt of Egyptology is not the geographical space of the nation-state, but an historical surface inscribed by Egyptian hieroglyphs (in use 3000 BC to AD 400). Efforts to place this restricted 'ancient Egypt' in the context of its continent, Africa, have been largely ignored when written by Africans, most notably Cheikh Anta Diop and Theophile Obenga (Howe 1998: 194). The same efforts, when inscribed within the Anglo-American 'Academy', have again, generally, not gained special attention within disciplinary Egyptology, although they have activated heated debate from academics studying ancient Greece (Bernal 1987; rejection by Lefkowitz and Rogers 1996; response Bernal 2001).

In most universities offering the discipline at undergraduate or graduate level, Egyptology is taught as a combination of Egyptian history 3000-1000 BC, covering enough ancient Egyptian language and script to enable a student to read and comment on select passages of ancient writing, and examples (though little in the way of theory) of visual art and architecture. Courses generally omit direct contact with the relevant disciplines of history, art history and comparative literature and linguistics, with few overlaps in reading-lists or lecturers, despite the growth in multi-lecturer courses. Under higher education time constraints, Egyptology course reading-lists also generally steer clear of training in archaeological theory and fieldwork, or in anthropological theory or, more broadly, cultural studies. This pattern may explain in part why Egyptologists have rarely cited Edward Said's *Orientalism* in the three decades since it was published. In some countries, these omissions could have been corrected by opportunities for second subjects (German *Nebenfach*) or student-centred degrees combining one- and two-year programmes (e.g. non-Egyptological Part One, Egyptological Part Two in the 1970s to1980s at Cambridge) or courses across different disciplines (such as the North American modular system, increasingly applied in England from the 1980s).

National disciplinary tradition may dictate the options on offer to learners. Anglo-American students may pursue archaeological fieldwork training, and, outside select centres, avoid Egyptian language advanced courses; Dutch, French, German and Italian students almost invariably follow philological study, often to the exclusion of archaeological fieldwork and theory. At universities offering a degree in Egyptology the library would be equipped with around a dozen core journals still being produced in the discipline:

Publishing institution	Name of journal (abbreviated)	First year	Country
Humboldt University, Berlin	*Zeitschrift (ZÄS)*	1863	Germany
Supreme Council of Antiquities	*Annales (ASAE)*	1900	Egypt
French Institute, Cairo	*Bulletin (BIFAO)*	1901	France
Egypt Exploration Society	*Journal (JEA)*	1914	England
Scuola di Papirologia Milan	*Aegyptus*	1920	Italy
Egyptological Society Brussels	*Chronique (CdE)*	1925	Belgium
German Institute, Cairo	*Mitteilungen (MDAIK)*	1930	Germany
University of Paris	*Revue (RdE)*	1933	France
American Research Centre	*Journal (JARCE)*	1962	USA
Society for the Study of Egyptian Antiquities	*Journal (JSSEA)*	1970	Canada
University of Göttingen	*Miszellen (GM)*	1972	Germany
University of Lille	*Cahiers (CRIPEL)*	1973	France
University of Hamburg	*Studien (SAK)*	1974	Germany

Depending on local tradition, a library might add 'oriental' periodicals such as the *Journal of Near Eastern Studies* (Chicago 1942-), *Journal of the Economic and Social History of the Orient* (Leiden 1958-), *Orientalia* (Rome 1932-), *Welt des Orients* (Göttingen 1947-), *Wiener Zeitschrift für die Kunde des Morgenlandes* (Vienna 1887-), and *Zeitschrift der Deutschen Morgenländischen Gesellschaft* (Leipzig 1847-). Older centres would store discontinued series such as *Kemi* (Paris 1928-71) and *Proceedings of the Society for Biblical Archaeology* (London 1870-1919). Often journals have been re-named, or experienced gaps in issue. The *Annales du Service des Antiquités de l'Egypte* succeeded a short-lived *Musée Egyptien*; the *Revue d'Egyptologie* succeeded the *Revue de l'Egypte Ancienne*, itself a successor combining the *Recueil de Travaux* (Paris 1879-1923) and *Revue Egyptolo-*

6

gique (Paris 1880-1920). Similarly, the *Journal of Near Eastern Studies* is the name adopted in 1942 for the old *American Journal of Semitic Languages and Literatures*, previous to 1895 called *Hebraica* (founded 1884). Each new name, birth and death of a journal expresses the juncture of academic activity with political and economic history, to be investigated as a collective history. Training restricted to the disciplinary base outlined above could provide a learner with the philological basis for university employment, in the reproduction of the discipline. This career can be built on a narrow base of knowledge; after six years, a student may, for example, have acquired familiarity with a particular period-specific corpus of economic sources or of literary writing, but have little grasp of the rest of even the written record from the same period, let alone the rest of its material culture, or relevant current archaeological fieldwork.

Beyond philology and basic empirical knowledge of art and history, any move to the outside – to the museum, or to archaeological fieldwork – requires additional training. Most often, this has not been acquired by supervised formal training. As philologist in a museum, from 1989, I was introduced to the use of museum resources such as registers or conservation reports, not from Egyptology, Archaeology or Museology courses, but from direct contact with those resources and from colleagues at work in my employment within a museum. Similarly, under current regulations of the Supreme Council of Antiquities in Egypt, an archaeologically-untrained philologist may, as representative of university Egyptology, receive an official permit to excavate, and must then learn 'on the job'. Despite many substandard examples, and against the claims of the disciplines in their institutions, the results of informal (self)-training can be highly productive, yielding new data to acceptable standards of documentation. Evidently disciplinary borders are not enough to condemn processes of non-formal training. Moreover, the quantity of specialised literature must be measured against the number of reading hours in a three- or even six-year course. On that basis, arguably, any area-study like Egyptology is bound to remain multi-disciplinary, and to require informal, extra-disciplinary acquisition of skills. However, in probing such prosaic reasons for disciplinary practice, processes in producing knowledge of the past suddenly lose the aura of superior expertise. Specifically, in the international context, if European Egyptologists are walking on such thin ice, then those processes should easily be transferable to non-European practitioners, for example, the local inhabitants. Threateningly, if excavating can be learnt in the practice of fieldwork, the dividing-line between expert and other could be an illusion.

The question arises whether archaeological skills-acquisition is different inside and outside Egyptology. According to a recent frank account of a career within Archaeology itself, rather than Egyptology, fieldwork skills were acquired precisely not in the classroom but from the first encounter with the ground, as self-training (Ucko 2007). These considerations could be taken further by compiling a list of specific skills and categorising them according to need for formal classroom training, for apprenticeship (as Petrie learnt survey techniques, from his father), and informal or self-training. This inventory of skills can also contribute to the institutional and wider public spaces in which the results of fieldwork are communicated and developed – results including, for example, philology from inscribed material, or art-historical analysis of figurative expression.

In England, transformation of Egyptian archaeology may be a harder task, inasmuch as archaeologists there have come to caricature Egyptology as a stock example of bad practice in both fieldwork and theory. The most famous find in archaeology can act as a paradigm for the informal but pervasive way in which professional archaeologists may dismiss Egyptology as treasure-hunting: the 1922 discovery of the tomb of Tutankhamun by a team led by Howard Carter. In this world-famous event, the team strode self-consciously into the public sphere, manipulating media relations through an exclusive relationship with *The Times* of London, which infuriated both Egyptian nationalism and the rest of the foreign media (Colla 2007: 172-226). Already too hands-on and untrained for academic colleagues, and now, even more sinfully, too popular, Carter became the figurehead in creating 'the hegemonic press image of an excavation' (Ascherson 2004: 145). Yet, against accusations of unscientific gold-digging, despite the bluntly colonial exclusion of Egyptians, and even despite the evidence of theft by Carter and the dig-sponsor Carnarvon (Hoving 1978), the archaeological archive illustrates how the Carter team maintained exemplary documentation throughout a cautious clearance lasting a full six years, with four more to complete conservation (Reeves 1990: 56-67). Whatever the political failings and personal flaws, the archaeological record from 1922 matches professional standards.

In the relations between academic disciplines, good and bad practice prove less of an issue than the need to create evaluative hierarchies of disciplinary space in order to secure contested resources. All sides may suffer from the historical accident that disciplines such as Art History, Philology and Archaeology developed separately from one another. In English-speaking countries, Archaeology can rarely extend to formal training in art-historical theory on the visual arts and monumental architecture. Similarly, unlike its often twinned discipline Anthropology, university Archaeology generally excludes training in the languages of the subjects of its study. In the case of Philology, opposition may be easy to justify on the grounds of philological narrow-minded positivism; yet, if it ejects that tradition of detailed study of writing, Archaeology may reinforce the absence of the past subjects by excluding their languages. In their absence, the 'agent' in archaeological theory risks expressing only the cultural home of the discipline, in a comfortable world with nuclear family and private property (cf. Shanks and Tilley 1989: 123 on 'methodological individualism', also contested in Callinicos 1987, e.g. pp. 36-8 on constraints on individual action). Archaeology and Philology would work best as complementary investigations rather than antagonistic disciplines (Dialismas 2004). This requires impersonal, structural changes, which may not be possible under present conditions. Sour relations between disciplines in university faculties develop out of something more strategic and structural than mere personal dislikes. Disciplinary struggles have been said to express and reinforce a need for competing partners in the political economy of a capitalist society with global ambition (Bourdieu 1984). Petty interdisciplinary strife may be structurally crucial in creating distance between the disciplinary arena and all other social worlds. Realistically, we must be aware that the removal of interdisciplinary hostilities may not be an option.

Fabian coevality: ethics in ethnographies of fieldwork

Anthropology and Archaeology share a genealogy within European imperialism, which allotted them the essential ideological tasks of colonising space and time respectively. Colonial anthropology tended to follow a model of political liberalism in the imperialist Foreign Office, echoing the methods and attitudes of the earlier short-term princely embassy. Well before Malinowski instituted London social anthropology (Gosden 1999: 40-52), the ethnographic fieldworker ventured into foreign territory more or less alone, immersed himself (usually, at that time, him) in a foreign society, learning the language as well as observing customs, and returning to file a full report. With perhaps the one major exception of Gordon Childe after 1935 (Trigger 2006: 344-53), Archaeology tended instead to follow a model of political conservatism, adopting the methods and attitudes of the military colonisers in the imperialist Ministry of War (as it was called before its Orwellian renaming as Ministry of Defence). Archaeological fieldworkers adopted, not uninterrupted ground-war on the modern pattern, but rather a seasonal campaign along lines of pre-modern warfare, with groups of Europeans deploying large-scale forces at each newly targeted battle-site, and no knowledge of local language or customs beyond the needs of manpower recruitment. Both fieldwork types may have been treated by all imperialist government ministries as weird but useful for intelligence, delivered to a relatively low budget, when not self-financed.

The conscience of some disciplines in some instances allows periodic redefinition of roles in changing worlds. Decolonisation after the Second World War had little immediate impact on research in Western Archaeology and Anthropology, beyond complicating Euro-American access to decolonised lands. The most substantial review of the history of archaeological theory concluded that 'over most of Africa, colonial archaeology seems to have been followed, not by national, but by neocolonial archaeology' (Trigger 2006: 276). By contrast, movements culminating in the upheavals of 1968 fostered radical self-critique among anthropologists, reflecting on their relation with imperialist power (papers in Asad 1973). From a survey of its history in England, Stephan Feuchtwang confronted Social Anthropology with a list of research agendas that it had decided not to pursue, including 'real participant observation' and 'the study of imperialism as a system' (Feuchtwang 1973: 100). In research published in 1983, Johannes Fabian investigated the use of the present tense in Anthropology, finding it a consistently deployed stratagem for removing from Euro-American presence the subjects of its ethnographic fieldwork. Fabian argued that anthropologists need to combat this disciplinary tradition, and ensure against it a time constantly shared between the academic practitioners and the subjects of their disciplinary work. He used the term coevality to express the time-sharing that would dismantle barriers between ethnographic observer and observed (Fabian 1983). More critically, around the same time, from the perspective of a Palestinian in American English literary studies, Edward Said suggested that, despite the best intentions, ethnographers could never achieve fair representation for peoples who had suffered colonisation, and he questioned the survival of the discipline of anthropology (Said 1989). Fabian defended ethnography as best a radical anthropologist could, asking what would fill a space vacated by the more well-intentioned reporters (Fabian 1992).

Although archaeology may have generated little or no explicit reception of Fabian theses, recent decades have seen increased concerns over the ethics of the discipline, in its history under colonialism, in its fieldwork, and in barriers between professional and public interest. The conventional stance of apolitical academic neutrality ended in the debates over apartheid, with the founding of the World Archaeological Congress (Ucko 1987). Greater social responsiveness led to the emergence of the sub-discipline Public Archaeology, demonstrated, in London, by the journal of that name (Ascherson 2000). The ethical scrutiny of fieldwork has grown most strongly from intense efforts to end the destruction caused by the antiquities trade (Brodie *et al.* 2006). In the spirit of Public Archaeology, the debate now extends to self-critique on issues such as the removal of knowledge-production as well as material culture from local landscapes (cf. Cooper 2006, on epistemic inclusion, and Holowell 2006: 85, 88, 92 on involving those living in the archaeological landscape in knowledge-production). Short of the name, and specific thesis, coevality seems a live issue in archaeology, and the time may have arrived for its fuller impact on fieldwork and publishing practice.

Any archaeological department benefits from self-critical reflection, in Egypt as well as in England; postcolonial has meant neocolonial in Eurocentric (re-)production of knowledge, as Feuchtwang found for anthropology thirty-five years ago (Feuchtwang 1973), and as Freire recalled from a warning of Pope John XXIII on the economy a decade earlier (*Mater et Magistra*, cited in Freire 1996 [1970]: 121 with n. 14). Currently, inside Egypt, both Egyptian and foreign expeditions continue to enforce labour regimes established in the late nineteenth century before industrial relations had outlawed extreme exploitation. Manual work-forces are expected to play no part in excavation beyond the removal of soil and delivery of finds. Most workers are assumed to be archaeological illiterates, to the extent that they are not even entrusted with the marking of finds, a first essential step in documenting material as it is discovered in the ground, let alone surveying, planning or photography (cf. Wynn 2008). This division of labour is exactly as Petrie prescribed in his manual for excavating in Egypt or in England or elsewhere, over a hundred years ago (Petrie 1904, see Chapter 2 below). Prolific monument-surveyor and field-archaeologist in England, Egypt and Palestine, Flinders Petrie is an essential part of this story for several reasons, not least his timing. His career in Egypt began in 1880 during a period of nationalist government under Ottoman Turkish suzerainty; two years later, an English army occupied the country. He continued working there, interrupted only by the First World War, until 1924, when nationalists dominated Parliament in a nominally independent but still English-occupied Egypt. Petrie was a staggeringly hard-working and practical campaigner, who voiced his scorn of armchair or gentlemanly colleagues, and exhorted archaeologists to follow his example in hands-on experience of the dirty work of archaeology. With the missionary zeal of a rescue archaeologist, he excavated at thirty sites of widely varying type during the formative years of institutionalisation for both Archaeology and Egyptology as distinct university subjects. He occupies a central place in the history of those institutions, as first holder of the first university Professorship in Egyptian Archaeology and Philology, the Edwards Chair (from 1893). Over the same half-century, from 1880s to 1930s, and in part through his writings and practice, disciplinary archaeology was developing its rules of combat. Petrie made impact in his time by a voluminous output in excavation reports, typological collection catalogues, and articles on every aspect of ancient and prehistoric Egypt (cf. for the monographs alone Drower 1985: 466-9). He achieved all this without university education, non-existent in England for the subject in his youth, and starting at a time when he had almost no rivals in England for the title of Egyptologist (cf. Maspero 20 May 1882 letter, cited in Drower 1982: 309).

If print publication underpins a public sphere defined as a joint reader-ship, Petrie was rivalled in imperialist Britain only by his arch-enemy, the avowedly armchair Egyptologist Wallis Budge, Keeper of Egyptian and Assyrian Antiquities at the British Museum from 1891 to 1924 (on relations between Budge and Petrie, see Drower 1985: 105, 211). In exhibition display and popular publication, Budge was an unsurpassed publiciser, matching any modern standards of access (Morrell 2002; Bierbrier 1995: 71-2 for publications list). However, apart from an early stint of recording at Aswan in 1887, he seems to have pursued no original research, and to have visited Egypt only to arrange purchases for his department. In this,

Budge differed from many others at the British Museum, where Petrie was on good terms both with the Departments of Coins and Medals and Greek and Roman Antiquities, and with other staff in the Department of Egyptian and Assyrian Antiquities (cf. Petrie 1930, a sympathetic obituary for a later leading figure there, Henry Hall). In contrast to Budge, Petrie spent half his life working the ground, the other half revealing and reviewing the results, and refusing either to limit himself to the aesthetic, or to exclude it for being beautiful. In 1894, at desert-edge sites near the villages of Naqada and Ballas, Petrie introduced into Egypt a statistically useful scale of quantitative recording, new in archaeological method even in Europe (Drower 1985: 216). Instead of recording only a few of the best-preserved or most extraordinary finds, with three European assistants he documented three thousand burials cleared by a team of Egyptian men and boys for the recording. By this manoeuvre, Petrie freed Egyptian archaeology from its self-limitation to highlights, the monumental, the inscribed, and the displayable. In his report that year to excavation sponsors, subscribers to his Egyptian Research Account, he announced:

> This Research Account fills a place as yet unoccupied, without any interference with existing institutions ... For the present the scope of it is in the most unoccupied field, that of scientific excavation for recording the social and racial history of Egypt. (Petrie 1895; [1])

As a result, his own collection and dozens of others formed of finds from his fieldwork constitute not art galleries, but presentations of social history. Here, as a fuller reflection of all Egyptian life, unwritten answers may be found to the questions that modern viewers of ancient Egyptian monuments may ask – what did the people we call 'the ancient Egyptians' eat, how long did they live, what did they wear, what did they look like, what did they cherish and what did they throw away?

No other individual worked more physically on innovative methods than Petrie, or made greater impact in the formation of the public sphere called Egyptian archaeology, a joint readership of many of those interested in the past of that one land. For these reasons, the Petrie records deserve particular scrutiny in the contemporary struggle to transform the structure of that public sphere, now again on the faultlines of history. The difficulty for writer and reader is to set dry structural analysis of a discipline in place of an enthralling biographical narrative of one man, to turn an easy critique of the past into the more radical task of self-critique in our present.

Reading Petrie: history and reception

Out of context, a Petrie script becomes illegible to a twenty-first-century readership; above all, for English readers reading Petrie in his own language, in English, false senses of kinship obscure revolutions in accepted 'common sense'. Most twenty-first-century London newspaper-readers may quite readily accept ideas that would have been anathema to many an 1880s reader, such as the idea of Egyptian, Indian or Irish independence (for a political outline of the decade, see Wilson 2002: 437-536). Conversely, rural child labour or peasant illiteracy might not have struck every 1880s English middle-class reader as problematic. On these issues, a reader today may too easily imagine that all 1880s readers of the same paper shared similar opinions – for example, that they all voted against the Liberal Party then led by Gladstone. Any family biography could correct such generalisations, and the family of Flinders Petrie is no exception; his wife Hilda had a sister Maud of whom his biographer notes, 'In her political sympathies she went against the family tradition, voted Liberal and supported the Boers' (Drower 1985: 231). On a topic such as the rights of women to vote or to receive university degrees, the views of Petrie as well as his early patroness Amelia Edwards were more liberal than many Establishment figures of the time, considering the late date at which women were granted the vote in England (1918 limited; extended in 1928, see Holton 2003, Smith 2007). When a political issue is linked to a named individual, it is difficult not to respond with personal feeling as if in hand-to-hand combat. Taking written content at face-value as individual self-expression, a readership may be liable to heroise and demonise as left- or right-wing without historical reflection. Outside its literary domain, a biographical reading may unwittingly promote the unthinking reproduction of existing world-views. Given this risk, a shift to structural and social-historical approaches in reading can help to overcome the barrier between a subject of high imperialism 1880-1924 and a subject of its successor world order a century later.

In structural context, Petrie can be read, not innocently, but more fairly, as he writes to differentially defined circles of readers, that can be classified in generalised manner as four groups occupying broadly separate strata in the accumulation of his written words: (1) a broad public targeted in his continual fundraising for excavation resources; (2) the academic readership, not yet disciplinarily limited, addressed together with (1) in the introductory pages of his excavation reports, and without (1) in more detailed paragraphs and articles; (3) a restricted circle of perhaps five to ten people, to whom he sent letters for circulation with details of his working life, most regularly in his bachelor years of fieldwork 1880-1895; (4) a circle, still more restricted in practice, of scientific research colleagues, implicitly addressed in the pocket-Notebooks underpinning his fieldwork publications. Over time, the fourth group, readers of the Notebooks, might in theory amount to the same academic readership as the second. Yet, item by item, they are limited to the rare individuals who might on one specific day consult archives for a particular speck of data, rather than rest with the publication. At the moment at which each note was written, its audience is even more restricted, being addressed only to the writer him- or herself.

Academic researchers and research institutions have often claimed autonomy from their social and political environments, but such protestations of innocence are undermined by their as frequent protests against the impact of economic conditions on their work. In excavating the four strata for different topics, as loci across the published and unpublished Petrie word-world, any reader must consider the multidimensional historical contexts for each of the original target audiences. An archaeological or Egyptological reader in particular needs to learn to encounter as foreign worlds both England and Egypt at the time of Petrie. Before praising or damning, in London or in Cairo, a twenty-first-century reader of a Petrie comment needs first to recall, for example, the full range of political opinion among Petrie contemporaries, and in both cities. Beside the liberal and conservative political parties alternately governing in London, newspaper reports even in *The Times* would have made present to Petrie too the extra- and anti-parliamentary forces in nationalism and socialism, again in both lands. Sometimes he would have had personal links to these alternative views. His biographer records how he introduced one young Egyptologist, the Canadian Charles Currelly, to a famous neighbour and friend of his father in Bromley, the exiled prince Peter Kropotkin, one of the main theorists of anarchism (Drower 1985: 298). From his excavations after 1900, whenever his funds covered packing and transport costs, Petrie sent most of the better-preserved groups of human remains to the UCL anthropometric/eugenic research collection, managed by a Fabian liberal, his UCL colleague Karl Pearson. In his fifties, and in common with his own archaeological idol Lane (Lane Fox Pitt Rivers), Petrie expresses himself forcibly enough in print from the conservative end of the spectrum of political opinion, opposing trade unionism in his *Janus in Modern Life* (1907). That book accompanied or led to his entry into right-wing groups: the British Constitution Association, which elected Petrie its president in 1914 and fought welfare state measures introduced by the Liberal Government; and the more self-explanatory Anti-Socialist Union (Drower 1985: 342-3). Yet his political opinions are useful for the present work only in delineating the space claimed by one main player in the formation of a discipline, and they need be cited only in order to specify possibilities for transformation of our present public sphere. Personal strengths or flaws, and disagreements of opinion, are of limited structural interest compared to the present obstacles that lie in the way of achieving a locally-embedded archaeology. Among the greatest obstacles are European and Euroamerican ignorance (outside disciplinary History): on the one side, of nineteenth-century radicalism in Europe, and, on the other, of any political history in Egypt.

Egyptian 'public spheres' in the
late nineteenth century

From 1517 to 1914 Egypt was formally a province of the Ottoman Turkish Empire, with a governor appointed from Istanbul. The early Ottoman Sultans maintained the existing power structure, under which a military elite reproduced itself by importing enslaved youths, *mamluk* in Arabic, from the Asian and south Russian steppes, while leaving some provinces to the control of a steady stream of bedouin nomads from both Arabia and north Africa (Holt 1961). Mamluks had ruled Egypt since they terminated the Ayyubi dynasty of Salah al-Din in 1250; they spoke Turkic languages rather than Arabic, and constituted a visibly and audibly foreign presence on the Nile, despite a certain Arabising trend (disputed: see Hathaway 1994: 300). They have been condemned as a parasitical drain on urban and rural resources, a charge that can be levelled at any oligarchy; their monuments offer an entirely different history, against most Eurocentric writing (Behrens-Abouseif 2008). Over the long term, the Mamluk and Ottoman Periods of Egyptian history witnessed both a substantial fall in population and the demise of important industries such as paper-making. Select economic down-turns and the failures of nineteenth-century Ottoman finances have allowed European historians their impression of 'oriental' stagnation, against which a revisionist pro-Ottoman historiography continues to struggle (Crabbs 1990). In fact, Cairo remained a vibrant international mercantile city, which continued to thrive into the late eighteenth century on the coffee and spice trade through Mecca and other principal markets for Egypt, almost all within the internal trade of the Ottoman Empire (Raymond 1974).

Imperial Ottoman interests in Egypt may have been limited principally to tribute in currency or kind, trade route control, and, perhaps most crucial, manpower for wars against European powers and against Shiite Iran. Out of this variable interest, a high degree of Egyptian autonomy was obtained in the eighteenth century by Ali Bey (Crecelius 1981), and again, after French Republican occupation 1798-1801, in the early nineteenth century by Muhammad Ali (Marsot 1984). An officer from the European territories of the Ottoman Empire, Muhammad Ali eliminated the Mamluk upper stratum, but continued to employ mainly Turco-Circassian courtiers and army officers, with increasing numbers of Christian Egyptians and Syrians, and Europeans, in his administration. He was succeeded by members of his family; under this dynasty, still formally subject to Ottoman Turkey, Egypt was integrated into the global European-dominated economy, echoing developments at Istanbul. In cultural policy, these modernising rulers created the Antiquities Service and Egyptian Museum in Cairo, as first recommended in 1835 by Rifaa al-Tahtawi from the studies of the previous decade by Jean-François Champollion in Paris (Reid 2002). When Egyptian armies invaded Syria and threatened

15

Turkey itself, English forces joined the Ottomans to defeat the military ambitions of Muhammad Ali, confining him to Egypt, with a reduced army, by the 1840 Treaty of London (Ufford 2007). The ensuing redirection of reduced national resources brought advantages to some areas, such as regional health provision (Chiffoleau 1997: 31-2, 35). Yet, with the loss of the main military client, schools and factories closed, and the shrinking of the state also seems to have left the museum of Rifaa al-Tahtawi, the Antikakhana, moribund (Colla 2007: 116-20). Europeans readily occupied the public spaces vacated by the new Egyptian state, above all in agricultural production and finance. During the mid-nineteenth century, English and French capital became dominant in Egyptian cultivation of cash crops, notably cotton, and in capital infrastructure projects, above all the construction of the Suez Canal, which eventually left the Khedive Ismail in thrall to London and Paris (Hunter 1984: 179-89). In 1875 the Khedive was forced to sell his share in the Canal to the English, and over the next four years Europeans became formally the financial rulers (Owen 2004: 96). When Khedive Ismail resisted, he was removed, and replaced by the younger Tawfik. The European presence antagonised Egyptian opinion, which was also becoming more demonstratively hostile to the privileged Turco-Circassian class in the army. Towards the end of the 1870s, nationalist feeling crystallised around the Egyptian officer Ahmad Urabi, creating unprecedented internal pressures on the debt-burdened Tawfik court (Schölch 1972; Cole 2000).

Over the course of the nineteenth century and into the twentieth, Egyptian society had to adapt to the modernising programmes of its rulers, the conversion of the economy from Ottoman global trade to European global capitalism, the massive intrusion of foreign capital, and a steady rise in population to pre-Byzantine levels. According to the 3-4 May 1882 census carried out under the management of Albert Boinet, one of the European financial 'advisers' at the court of the Khedive, and published at the recommendation of another European, Colvin, the total population of Egypt was then 6,806,381, including 98,196 bedouin still living a nomadic life (Boinet 1884: introduction, xxvii, xxix). A higher number of bedouin had settled, but in villages separate from the main population, and kept customs distinct from the Egyptian rural population (Boinet 1884: section 6, v-vii). The number of Europeans in Egypt before the English occupation remained low; the largest community was the Greek, calculated at 0.55% of the total population, followed by Italian and French communities half that size, and smaller numbers again of Austro-Hungarian and British citizens (Boinet 1884: section 2, viii). The Egyptian rural population made up the overwhelming majority, and, as Kenneth Cuno writes (1988: 133):

> Egypt's peasantry were not a homogeneous mass. At the beginning of the nineteenth century, village society comprised economic strata ranging from 'large' landholders of 50 faddans or more, to smallhold fallahin and the landless.

1. Setting a stage

Gabriel Baer identified two major changes in the countryside by 1882: the rise of a rural class of owners of medium-sized estates, and the growth of a class of landless tenants and agricultural labourers (Baer 1982: 240-2). He notes that the landless now had no rights of residence, in contrast to eighteenth-century practice, and that their presence, albeit undefined, is implicit in earlier references to *al-fallahun wa'l-battalun*. These three elements among the population – bedouin, smallhold farmers, and land-labourers – are the Egyptian hosts of archaeologists like Petrie. Their presence in image and reported speech may be one of the greatest benefits of archaeological archive, still to be mined by social historians of the nineteenth century.

Illiteracy would seem the principal block to any contribution by farmers and landless to cultivating knowledge, intensifying the need for a more precise social demography. Against considerable odds, including rapid population growth, literacy rates have increased steadily over the course of the twentieth century, to an estimated 51.4% in 1995 (Adams 2003: 22-4), but were only 13% for men and 1% for women in 1907 (Gorman 2003: 36). Yet the divide in part-literate societies allows far more flexibility than the census statistics record: the geographical and social distribution of the literate can touch a higher proportion of even rural populations for whom reading and writing may have remained more substantially separate skills than a bare percentage can reveal (on the separable history of reading, Chartier 1992). Research is always required before assessing the contours of literacy and its impact in each individual locality; middle-class writers have tended to make unwarranted assumptions concerning working-class access to writing (Rose 2001). The links between poverty and illiteracy may be strong, and strategically manipulated by government educational policy in one direction or another. However, in the following chapters it will be seen that the bedouin and Egyptian farmers recruited by Petrie for archaeological labour did include writers, and did have access to circulation of correspondence. Evidently, the assumption of peasant illiteracy is as contestable as the myth of peasant submissiveness (Baer 1969). Again, archives of excavators may be useful to social historians as a resource for a history of writing and reading in rural Egypt during the nineteenth and early twentieth centuries.

The principal Egyptian 'public spheres' of writing and debate lay elsewhere, in urban life, both regional and metropolitan. Following Delanoue, nineteenth-century Egyptian reflective output may be located not so much in two spheres over-readily glossed as 'tradition' versus 'modernity', as on two reflective planes which are not exclusive to one another, but use different expressive terms to capture foci distinct in their relation to time and existence (Delanoue 1982: xii-xiii). On one plane, proponents of *tamaddun* 'civilising' came to the fore in the nationalist movement around Urabi, and the metropoleis Cairo and Alexandria became their principal centres for generating new magazines and newspapers in the 1870s. Here belong not only government officials and supporters of modernisation, but also politically radical thinkers such as Gamal ad-Din al-Afghani, Muhammad Abduh, Abdallah al-Nadim, and the Syrian Christian Adib Ishaq. Even before the 1882 English military occupation of Egypt, these men were attacking European hegemony with a vocabulary still vibrant today in Arab World protests against American imperialism. As example of this simultaneously modernising and anti-European nationalism, in the first issue of *Misr al-Qahira*, 24 December 1879, the 23-year-old Ishaq denounces the English colonial trick of claiming a humane and civilising mission that is only a mask for imposing *al-khusuna wa'l-istibdad* 'brutality and tyranny' (cited Tomiche 1982: 310). Ishaq aims for an Arab nationalism that builds on its ancient past, on Nineveh and Memphis, as well as on the glories of the Islamic Period. Modernisers such as these participated in the *nahda*, the nineteenth-century renaissance in Arabic literature, which adapted even such essentially European institutions as theatre to Cairo society (Armbrust 1996: 42-3). Anyone doubting the potential for importing a European institution such as archaeology into Egypt, should consider popular successors of Arabic theatre in film and television (Nasrallah 2007).

The second reflective plane is more embedded in worlds of knowledge rooted in Egyptian history over the longer term. Its best-known and most self-conscious representatives are the *ulama* 'scholars' of Islam and their equivalents in the clergy and monastic orders of eastern Christian churches. However, to a substantial degree, and with considerable overlap, this knowledge circulated and developed also among the traders and craftsmen and -women based in regional as well as metropolitan centres (Hanna 2003). These people outside the religious institutions are less eminent and so less often cited by historians, but as prominent in the production and circulation of knowledge and books, printed and manuscript, throughout the Ottoman Period. Among the senior representatives, Delanoue counts three nineteenth-century writers of printed books: Jabarti, Rifaa al-Tahtawi, and Ali Mubarak (Delanoue 1982). All three are familiar with, and comment on, European knowledge, and Rifaa contributes in particular to nineteenth-century Egyptian engagement with the newly accumulating knowledge of the ancient Egyptian past (Reid 2002). The same writer can appear on both reflective planes; Rifaa figures among the main modernising forces for changes in education during this period (Mitchell 1988: 74-5, 77, 88-9, cf. Gorman 2003: 13). Such ambivalence complicates a division of modern from traditional as much for the nineteenth century as for today (Zaman 2002). That Weberian division comes to seem a product of a peculiarly north European insistence on exclusive binary categories, perhaps foundationally the pair public/private (cf. Bannerji 2001: 51).

Outside the larger metropolitan centres, this second reflective world can seem more elusive, because it found less opportunity or, more importantly, reason to adopt the foreign printing-press technology available in Cairo (Mitchell 1988: 133-4, 153-4). Manuscript copying and circulation has so far attracted less research than the early history of printing in Arabic, and most manuscripts have yet to be published; a recently published regional history by a Petrie contemporary, Muhammad al-Maraghi al-Girgawi (1865-1942), may be characteristic of a nineteenth-century output still outshone by printed books (Gran 2004). Gran notes that Upper Egyptian regional scholarship flourished in the nineteenth century at Asyut and Tahta, in succession to centres such as Girga and Qus (Garcin 1976). In 1897 Petrie would encounter, and learn from, a scholar in this tradition named Umran Khallil (Petrie 1898: 2), in a rural environment not far from Bahnasa, a town which had been until early Ottoman times a prominent regional centre (still centre for a governorate, see Shaw 1962: 16, listing only Minya, Manfalut and Bahnasa, between Girga and Giza). The second reflective plane is sometimes said to culminate in Jabarti at the start of the nineteenth century (cf. Gorman 2003: 12 'the finest and final product of the classical tradition'). Such assessments relate in the main to printed works; manuscript sources could offer a different picture. For the future of locally-embedded knowledge, with its existing traditions of studying the past, this second reflective plane holds greater potential than the nationalist print tradition which is more accessible and more familiar outside Egypt. The same observations apply to the circulation of knowledge in the second religious community of modern Egypt, Coptic Christianity. On its own terms, as a parallel world to print, the two religious traditions may not require print publication and familiarity to outsiders. In the twenty-first century, their use of electronic media carries the potential for redistributed centres of communication, overturning the dominance of print-based knowledge-systems.

Petrie and other English in Egypt, 1880-1924

Nationalist ministers were in government, and nationalist newspapers were prominent in 1880 when Flinders Petrie arrived in Egypt, at the age of 27, to survey the Great Pyramid at Giza. He achieved his goal with the help of Ali Jabri, ten years his senior, one of the Najama bedouin settled at the site. At this time Auguste Mariette was still in service, but died in 1881, to be succeeded by his fellow countryman, Gaston Maspero (David 1999: 78-83). Maspero allowed Petrie to conduct limited excavation at Giza in order to complete his survey, technically as a member of Egyptian Museum staff. After two seasons, Petrie returned to London to write up his first great publication of work in Egypt, *Pyramids and Temples of Giza* (1883). A few weeks after his departure, in the summer of 1882, the British Liberal Prime Minister Gladstone had sent a British navy to bombard Alexandria, and to land the army that occupied Cairo in September and the rest of Egypt soon after, all nominally under the rule of Tawfik for the

Ottoman Sultan (Schölch 1972). Egypt would not be free of English troops again until after the Egyptian Revolution removed the monarchy in 1952-1953, with the resolution of the 1956 Suez crisis under Gamal Abdel Nasser.

In the spring of 1882, after several years of effort, the writer Amelia Edwards spurred London academics and dignitaries to found a new society, the Egypt Exploration Fund, to raise money for excavations in Egypt by public subscription in England (Moon 2006: 160-71). Writing in January 1880 to enlist the support of an unenthusiastic Samuel Birch, Keeper of Egyptian and Assyrian Antiquities at the British Museum, Edwards argued for her cause 'You see, excavations in Egypt cost very little – labour is so cheap' (Moon 2006: 163). Two weeks after Petrie had left Egypt for England, Maspero was writing to the new Fund Committee; dated 20 May 1882, his letter reveals the force of nationalist opinion on Egyptian archaeology and specifically on the prospect of foreign excavations. The contents demonstrate how the public sphere of archaeology in Egypt, though vacant, was not free for foreigners before the English occupied. Maspero had proposed to Edwards that a young English Egyptologist be assigned to him as assistant, and that the finds from a British-funded excavation might be displayed in a special room in the museum in Cairo. As no young English Egyptologist currently existed, Maspero is forced to suggest instead a student of Oriental Studies. Then, in strong terms, he advises the new Committee against its own existence, against the principle of founding for Egypt any new society on the model of the Palestinian Exploration Fund, which promoted research into Syria-Palestine:

> I do not imagine that anyone in England is thinking of forming a Society dedicated to the exploration of ancient Gaul: Egypt is somewhat in the conditions in which Gaul finds itself – not at all the conditions in which Syria finds itself. In Syria there is no antiquities service, no guardians of monuments, no museums: in Egypt all that exists as in France. Let me present to you the current view of the Egyptian government. This government says: we spend every year a sum of X for the maintenance and discovery of monuments. Doubtless this sum is inadequate, but what would be the adequate amount for the exploration of a country like Egypt? You may tell me that the gulf between the allotted sum and the needs of the service is so great, that the monuments cannot be maintained, and perish. Who destroys the monuments? The foreigners who scour the country year-in, year-out, buy antiquities, remove blocks of stone for the Louvre and the British Museum: they carry out here what they would not do in Germany, or England, or Spain, or France, or Italy. This is not an imaginary conversation that I am inventing for you: I am only repeating to you conversations that I have had with all the successive ministers in office since I have been in Egypt. (Drower 1982: 309, my translation)

The Maspero document overturns twenty-first-century Eurocentric assumptions of a disinterested nationalist Egypt in 1882. Evidently, the nineteenth-century nationalist agenda would not accommodate foreign expeditions, even if the head of the Antiquities Service was himself a foreigner. Everything could have been, and be, different. Seven weeks later, on 11 July, the British bombardment of Alexandria began.

In 1883, the Committee had selected Petrie as its excavator, and he returned to a now English-occupied Cairo. At Giza, he enlisted the help of Ali Jabri and his kin once more, to start on Delta excavation for the Fund. Three seasons later, having excavated Tanis, Nabasha and Dafanna in the Eastern Delta, and published the discovery of Naukratis in the western Delta, he abandoned the Fund in 1886, citing their lack of attention to small finds and their delays in publishing results. Over the next year Amelia helped him find two private sponsors in England, Jessie Haworth and Martyn Kennard, and public support in Philadelphia, Pennsylvania (Moon 2006: 215-16). With this backing, Petrie resumed his work under the aegis of the Antiquities Service, then under the direction of the meticulous, and less Anglophile, Eugène Grébaut. The next five years were among his most productive, with excavation at Hawara, al-Lahun, and Madinat al-Ghurab in the Fayum, Maydum nearby, and at Amarna in Middle Egypt. For this work, Petrie relied heavily initially on Muham- mad abu Daud from Giza, from the wider family of Ali Jabri, and recruited his workforce at Madinat al-Fayum and Lahun. Ali Suefi from Lahun became his right-hand man, and continued to work under his successor Guy Brunton in the 1920s.

When Amelia Edwards died in 1892, her will allotted the resources, including her collection and library, to create the first Chair in Egyptian Archaeology and Philology in England (Moon 2006: 240-1). A strong feminist, she had made her first choice University College London, then still the only English university awarding degrees to women students (Moon 2006: 213-14 for an 1886 letter on her intentions; Harte 1979, Dyhouse 1995: 12-13 on 1870s degrees for women). Amelia was hostile to Wallis Budge at the British Museum, and so her will declared her wish that the Professor could not be a serving member of staff of that institu- tion, and should be under 40; Petrie was 39, and duly became the first Edwards Professor. In his inaugural lecture, on 14 January 1893 (repro- duced Janssen 1992: 98-102), Petrie announced a new Egyptian Research Account, to bring students from England to train on site as the next generation of archaeologists, alongside his own excavations still funded from 'private friends' (Janssen 1992: 99-100). In fact, the agreements with Kennard and Haworth expired and the ERA became his own funding channel. For the jointly-funded 1893 dig, he selected the ruined temple and town-site at Qift in Upper Egypt, bringing James Quibell, an Oxford graduate in chemistry and Greek (Drower 1985: 206, 208). Here he found the earliest monumental sculpture from Egypt; here too, he recruited the team of 'Quftis' who remained his core workforce for the remainder of his career. In his first year after the Qift season, the ERA funded his excavation at Naqada, where, for the first time, hundreds of burials of an entire cemetery were not only excavated but individually planned and their finds marked for study, and for future generations to check. In quantity and method, the Petrie expedition at Naqada marks the opening of a mathematical scientific archaeology in the Nile Valley. Here Petrie found the prehistoric culture from which the ancient Egyptian state grew, but he initially mistook the material as evidence for a foreign invasion. From the rapid Petrie publication, the then Director of the Antiquities Service Jacques de Morgan immediately identified the finds as part of a range of newly emerging evidence for the prehistory of Egypt (de Morgan 1896-1897: the Naqada finds are listed in the series of sites vol. I: 67-89, under the name of another settlement in the area, Tukh). Fortunately, Petrie had documented this excavation so thoroughly that he was able to revise his findings from the dig records. In combination with 1898-1899 work at Hu, he used the finds to establish what is still accepted as the detailed time-sequence for the development of the Nile farming societies 4000-3000 BC, through the thousand years to the formation of the Egyptian state (Hendrickx 1996). His research account functioned alongside the Egypt Exploration Fund, to which he was reconciled in 1897, working for the Fund at new sites, notably the tombs of the first kings at Abydos, until 1905.

Petrie fell out with the Fund a second and final time over the failure to publish the archaeology as well as the copies of inscriptions from his 1904-1905 season at Sinai (Petrie 1906a: vi-vii). In 1905 he created his own new British School of Archaeology in Egypt, its Patron the British governor in Egypt, Evelyn Baring, by then 'al-Lurd', Lord Cromer (Petrie 1906b: 1). This School provided for the rest of his excavating career (1906-1914 and 1919-1924 in Egypt, 1926-1937 in Palestine). Over the same decades Egypt moved steadily towards its liberation from English rule. Nationalism gave the colonial authorities no respite, particularly after the hanging of Egyptian villagers from Dinshawai for the death of an Englishman after an aggressive English hunting-party in 1906 (Shaw 1984 [1907]: 39-52). The episode marked the start of an alliance between different classes against British military occupation (Berque 1967: 242; conversely, for the foreign working-class component in the Egyptian movement, see Gorman 2007). At the outbreak of the First World War, England declared Egypt a 'protectorate', to remove any threat from Ottoman Turkey, ally of the German enemy (McKale 1997: 23-4). A new influx of foreign troops required large-scale diversions of labour, livestock and food for both, leading to a marked increase in malnutrition in the countryside (Goldberg 1992: 270-1). Abroad, the convulsions of the war included, within a few weeks in 1917, the Stockholm Peace Congress, attended by Pan-Islamic delegates (Kramer 1986: 58-9; Skovgaard-Petersen 2003), the Russian Revolution, and the Balfour declaration in London favouring 'establishment in Palestine of a national home for the Jewish people' without consulting the then ninety per cent Palestinian Arab population of the territory (Pappé 2003: 84).

1. Setting a stage

In Egypt after the war, during nationalist uprisings against British occupation, excavation workforces too went on strike, although not, reportedly, the core Qufti workforce (Drower 1985: 349). In 1922, acting unilaterally in its own interests, England declared Egypt a kingdom, still under the descendants of Muhammad Ali. The world had changed against them, and against foreign control of local archaeology (Goode 2007; Colla 2007). England was forced to accept elections that would produce a nationalist parliament in Cairo. By an apparent act of fate, that same year Howard Carter revealed to the world the tomb of Tutankhamun; the integral preservation of the tomb contents in Egypt became a topic of international political debate. In fear of losing the right to a major share in excavation finds from his own work, Petrie withdrew from Egypt and moved to Palestine (Drower 1985: 355-7). In the First World War, Arab nationalists had helped Britain defeat Ottoman Turkey, but, against wartime promises to the Arab allies, London assumed direct control of Palestine by a 'mandate' from the new Euroamerican international order (Kapitan 1997: 16-17; Safty 2009: 49-69). In 1933, Petrie retired from University College London and left England too behind, to live in Jerusalem. In 1938, now 85 years old, he was forced to give up his life of digging not so much by age, as by the fall-out from the January 1938 murder of his dig director James Starkey, mistaken by a local nationalist for a Jewish settler, and the destruction of the expedition house at Tell el-Ajjul near Gaza (Drower 1985: 415-16). Violence was flaring over English-endorsed displacement of Palestinian Arabs by Jewish immigration, at a time when the Nazis were attacking the property and lives of European Jews in Germany and Austria. As the Second World War peaked, Petrie was confined to a hospital bed in Jerusalem, where he died in 1942. His body was buried in the Protestant Cemetery, except for the head, by his wish removed for the teaching collection of osteology in the Royal College of Surgeons in London (Ucko 1998).

Seeing Petrie: an Orientalist view

Before we embark on an exploration of his words, an aestheticised image of Petrie can serve to illustrate how far we need to change our views. In 1896, the English painter and collector Henry Wallis visited the archaeologist during excavations at the Ramesseum, a ruined temple of Ramses II in a rural environment on the desert edge at Qurna, anciently the west bank of the city called Waset by Egyptians and Thebes by Greeks (Drower 1985: 219). Here he depicts Flinders Petrie as nineteenth-, twentieth- and twenty-first-century European tradition visualises the archaeologist, as Hero, against a background that provides an accurate view of the landscape. For informed 1890s English audiences, the Ramesseum probably evoked Shelley's poem 'Ozymandias', deftly capturing European dismissal of a despotic timeless 'Orient', intentionally or not (Colla 2007: 67-71).

1.1. Excavating in Egypt: Professor Petrie at Thebes, watercolour by Henry Wallis, 1895.

Unlike Wallis, the poet never saw the site, and wrote his lines casually for a prize. Despite this prosaic origin, archaeologically and in the history of public reception of archaeology, 'Ozymandias' can rest on two colossal sculptures of the Ramesseum: the fallen thousand-ton stone colossus still on the site, and the upper half of a colossal statue that more than any other single object established ancient Egyptian sculpture as Art against the neo-classical tendency newly turning from Rome to Greece (Jenkins 1992; Moser 2006). The statue head came to be known as the Younger Memnon, from the Greek term for western Theban monuments collectively as the Memnoneia. It arrived in the British Museum in 1817, removed from Egypt by official permission, under the supervision of the Italian engineer Giovanni Battista Belzoni, and at the behest and budget of the Swiss adventurer Jean-Louis Burckhardt and Henry Salt, English representative at the court of Muhammad Ali. Although other colossal statue heads removed by Belzoni for Salt entered the Egyptian Sculpture Gallery in 1821, none have gained a nickname, arguably reflecting lesser impact in their European reception (on the removal and, in detail variable, reception of the sculpture, see Colla 2007: 24-66). Eighty years later, in radically different political conditions, a London viewer of the Wallis depiction might have felt personal kinship with the site, internalising through poetry and gallery a colonial military occupation of the ancient landscapes.

False proprietorial self-confidence would have fed on the strategic arrangement of the human figures in the foreground. Echoing, presum-

ably unwittingly, ancient Egyptian rules for senior figures in a composition, Petrie stands just marginally higher than anyone else; the only
European depicted, he is the most clothed, surrounded by some startling
rear exposures (cf. Ballerini 1993). For a Victorian audience, his working-
cap and clothing establish him as a practically active participant. His role
as controlling force, the agent of archaeology, is further indicated by his
military upright poise, against the languidly reclining figures expected in
London of Ottoman men (Erdogdu 2002). Ignoring practical rules of object-
handling in favour of the aesthetic pose of an art connoisseur, the artist
depicts Petrie holding, by the base, with one hand and, for dramatic effect,
at arm's length, an inscribed ancient jar. The pose contrasts with the way
Petrie advocated engagement in the dirty work of archaeology in his 1904
manual (see next chapter); Wallis seems to be projecting more his own
relation to excavated material. For, by 1896, the painter had visited Egypt
often, and had become a collector with particular connoisseurship in
ceramic arts (Wallis 1898, 1900, cf. Wilson 2002). Yet there is a kinship
between the worldviews of the older artist and younger excavator. The
work that had made Wallis famous in London was *The Death of Chatterton*
(1856), celebrating a poet who had committed suicide over the lack of
appreciation of his poetry. A year later, Wallis produced a pendant, *The
Stonebreaker*, depicting a labourer destroyed by work; this was exhibited
in 1858 with a quotation from its literary inspiration, *Sartor resartus* by
Thomas Carlyle (1834). The passages adjacent to the quoted lines juxtapose creative and manual labour with no hesitation over the hierarchy:
'Two men I honour, and no third. First the toilworn Craftsman that with
earth-made Implement laboriously conquers the Earth and makes her
man's ... A second man I honour, and still more highly ... we can name him
Artist; not earthy Craftsman only, but inspired thinker' (as cited and
discussed in Werner 2005: 131-2). These pre-Victorian gendered and
class-bound oppositions form the ground to the outlook of both generations, Wallis and Petrie, even without the reinforcement of race. The 1896
depiction then raises the 'inspired thinker' and demotes the foreign toiler
to passivity. Wallis has constructed the antiquity in the hand of the
discoverer as the focal point, both of the composition as viewed externally,
and, within it, of the gaze of the onlooking workers, as if they too appreciate
what the London viewers feel, that only the archaeologist can read the
inscription and assign the vessel its place in time. In effect the pose combines
genres of history painting and devotion, delivering Petrie as campaign-leader
and as the angel of a scientific Annunciation. This painting depicts not an
individual so much as an abstracted power of European knowledge, trium-
phant in a land that is unable, according to imperialism, to rule itself. Today,
the same attitudes continue to feed daily on news reporting, and on required
consumerist rituals of tourism (MacDonald 2003). Overcoming this ignorance
is part of the potential in archaeological archives.

Labour and name in the Petrie publications

Petrie's *Method and Aims*

In 1904 Petrie published his manifesto for a new formation of his discipline, *Methods and Aims in Archaeology*, one of the few explicit and
systematic statements of intentions from those working in Egypt. At many
points its language and attitude seem close to twenty-first-century concerns, and disarmingly candid. The self-assured tone may reflect the
degree of control enjoyed by an established university professor in London
at the height of its imperialism. However, Petrie had displayed this
self-confidence well before his first visit to Egypt, in his programme of
surveying archaeological sites in England (Drower 1985: 22-4). In *Methods
and Aims*, names of workers are included only incidentally, none with the
images of work-crews and individual Egyptians. Nevertheless, the book is
a useful introduction to Petrie and his work in his own words, raised as a
standard to be followed, and so freer for assessment. In the following
account, page numbers in brackets refer to Petrie 1904.

The volume opens with the programmatic statement:

> Archaeology is the latest born of the sciences. It has but scarcely struggled
> into freedom, out of the swaddling clothes of dilettante speculations. It is still
> attracted by pretty things, rather than by real knowledge. It has to find
> shelter with the Fine Arts or with History, and not a single home has yet
> been provided for its real growth. (vii)

The headings of the short, well-illustrated chapters in the manual convey
the programme for action: I the excavator, II discrimination (how to tell
the difference between sites, dates, styles), III the labourers, IV arrangement of work, V recording in the field, VI copying (making squeezes, casts,
drawing, inscription hand-copies), VII photographing, VIII preservation of
objects, IX packing, X publication, XI systematic archaeology (aims of
excavation), XII archaeological evidence, XIII ethics of archaeology, XIV
the fascination of history.

Several of these chapter titles already demonstrate an exceptional
degree of practicality that distinguishes Petrie from most of the rest of the
field, although this distinction can be overstated. Twenty-first-century
fieldwork-trainers would doubtless also include in their courses and hand-
books the details of on-site photographic technique. Within
nineteenth-century and early twentieth-century Egypt, photography, a

crucial element in the production of archaeological knowledge, seems initially limited to foreign production and tourist consumption (cf. Mardam-Bey and El Hage 2007, Sheehi 2007). Among the constituents of later archaeology, it is important to consider the role of imaging (both photography and draughtsmanship) along with survey, printing, and the creation of posts for historical disciplines in universities. If we are to understand how archaeology developed in excluding Egyptians, all these ingredients will need to be assessed in their specific historical contexts.

Twenty-first-century practitioners would also recognise the urgent need for skills in conservation of every type of material. Petrie sounds modern in his insistence that 'to expose things only to destroy them, when a more skilful or patient worker might have added them to the world's treasures, is a hideous fault', and that, therefore, 'some familiarity with chemistry and physics and properties of materials, is one of the first requisites for an excavator'. However, today most archaeologists might forget or take for granted that 'all this applies in a lesser degree to the difficulties of transport, which is also part of the preservation of the antiquities' (85). Petrie may still be alone among field-directors in not just recognising, but giving extended print-space to the manual labour of packing, with illustrated guidance on different forms of crate. If he wrote today, a century later, Petrie would still have to argue hard against the worst practices, of 'digging merely for profitable spoil, or to yield a new excitement'; he comments on the ethical dimension, 'Gold digging has at least no moral responsibility, beyond the ruin of the speculator; but spoiling the past has an acute moral wrong in it' (1). Intermittently, in this way, Petrie provides a full commentary on his contemporaries: 'to attempt serious work in pretty suits, shiny leggings, or starched collars, would be like mountaineering in evening dress, or remind one of the old prints of cricketers batting in chimney-pot hats. The man who cannot enjoy his work without regard to appearances, who will not strip and go into the water, or slither on slimy mud through unknown passages, had better not profess to excavate' (7). His ideal is 'solid, continuous work, certain, accurate and permanent' (3). In themselves, these exhortations are inspiring, but declarations of industry can serve other strategic ends, as nineteenth-century Arab nationalist journalists such as Ishaq were already so aware. Specifically, the rhetoric of industry may purchase space for the social relations of superiority in relation not only to colleagues, perhaps rivals, but also to all other participants in the action of archaeology. In the background lies the English self-image of productivity, even if, statistically, England was already on its steep descent in industriousness, in contrast to the rising American and German competition (for one account of English preference of rural to industrial, see Wiener 1982). Consciousness of national self-delusion over work and leisure can help set in context the comments, and actions, of the London professor. Petrie opens his book with separate chapters on excavator and labourers, already naturalised as explicitly distinct categories, setting between them 'discrimination'; re-reading of these first three chapters can help to unveil the artifice in that principal division.

The *Methods and Aims* excavator

The ideal excavator attributes in chapter I conjure up the stereotypical Hero of European imperialism as disseminated in print by travelogues and illustrated magazines (Fabian 2000: 24). He – Petrie talks from p. 1 of 'man' and 'he' – must be already experienced in archaeological work, hard-working, imaginative, with brains not (just) money, historically informed, able to read all scripts in a locality, skilled in organisation, conservation and photography (3-6). An excavation director cannot possess all these skills, but all must be present in his team of archaeologists. The reader is advised that 'the spoken language of the country should be fluently acquired', not to appreciate the country, but 'for simple purposes, so as to be able to direct workmen, make bargains, and follow what is going on. To be dependent on a cook, a dragoman, or a donkey boy, is very unsafe, and prevents that close study of the workmen which is needed for making the best use of them' (6). The first chapter establishes the primary relation of director with workforce as insecurity, a fear of losing control.

In a chapter separating this collective superman from his labourers, Petrie introduces in clear and practical terms the quality that justifies that division: 'discrimination'. The first half of chapter II covers ability to identify sites and their nature: temple, town, cemetery. For example, 'Prehistoric camp sites are noticed by the difference of tone of the ground in walking over them; the ashes holding so much air that the reverberation to the foot-step is quite different from that on ordinary desert' (13). Up to this point, some possible readers in 1904 – some Fabians in their London clubs, as well as more radical social democrats of the Second International – might have asked why experience of terrain would grant only to directors an ability to discriminate, and how rural inhabitants could be second to urban directors. Justification is provided in the second half of chapter II, where the contents turn to human-made finds: 'The first requisite acquirement of a digger – his archaeological experience – consists in discriminating and distinguishing the differences between products of various dates' (14), above all beads and, the 'essential alphabet of archaeology in every land' (16), pottery. The more detailed version of this talent is discrimination of style: 'in a trained observer a long series of experience should result in an unexpressed – almost intangible and incommunicable – sense of the style of each country and each age, such that a piece of work can at once be referred to its proper place, though not a single exact comparison can be quoted for it', citing as example central Asian bronzes, and contrasting the eclecticism of 'the modern designer' (18, anticipating perhaps a contrast between archaeological evidence and modern 'mass ornament' by Siegfried Kracauer, cf. Schwartz 2005: 137-44). Here a decent dose of mysticism strengthens the task of closing the door on any prospect for non-elite participation, but this task has to be completed with an assertion of domination: accordingly, beside skill in general and specific discrimination, a director must also possess 'visual memory'. As if to avoid the risk that anyone else might be privileged by possessing such a memory, this third discriminatory talent is cited only in relation to 'the master'. As a turning-point in this presentation, locking out any prospect of equality, and as a rare instance of naming, the passage needs to be read in full:

> A visual memory of the site and excavations should be constantly in mind; the master should be able to go over the whole site, and every man at work on it, entirely from memory; he should be able to realise at once, on seeing the place next day, exactly how every one of fifty different holes looked the day before; and know at once where the work stood, and what has been done since, so as to measure it up without depending on any statements by the workmen. If a boy comes with a message that Ibrahim or Mutwali needs direction, the master should be able to visualise the place, inquire what has been done, and how each part now stands, and then give sufficient temporary direction entirely from memory of the site, and memory of what he expected to do, or to prove, or to find, from that particular hole. (18-19)

Direction stands opposed to dependency; control is still the main aim here (cf. Foucault 1975 on the *panopticon* devised by Jeremy Bentham in late eighteenth-century London). Discrimination, acquired essentially simply by experience, proves far too fragile a basis on which to build the structure of domination that the archaeologist requires. The unstated element is violence, judicial and extra-judicial, under the colonial military occupation with its varied local alliances.

The *Methods and Aims* workforce

Chapter III 'The Labourers' begins with 'supply' and 'selection', and throughout its recommendations concern industrial relations (cf. Owen 2004: 357-8 for the effective ruler of the time, Evelyn Baring, considering Egypt as a malfunctioning factory, with himself as the manager to put it right). Its tips could be applied as readily to the cotton mills of Lancashire (Hutton and King 1981), the dockyards of Liverpool (Milne 2000), or the silk factories of Mount Lebanon (Khater 1996), as to the archaeology of Egypt, Greece and England. Some supply factors are beyond colonial control; Petrie records that girls can be recruited in Syria and the Nile Delta, but not in Upper Egypt (23). From the start, the director of work must confront resistance to work, which is called, as is usual in hegemonic comments, laziness and stupidity (analysed as 'Weapons of the Weak' in Scott 1985: xvi). The director must strive against the odds to secure from the labour force 'rational regular hard work'; he can achieve this in Egypt, less readily in Syria(-Palestine), and not at all in Greece (20). Even in Egypt, though, a workforce cannot be relied upon to submit, and must be checked at every opportunity. Petrie seems continually on his guard to ensure that he is not being cheated. One opportunity for deceiving the director arises with tools, because labourers owned some of the means of production under the archaeological regime: 'the workers are always expected to provide their own picks and baskets in Egypt; while ropes, crowbars, and other tools only occasionally wanted are provided by the master' (33). The baskets 'need to be looked at for size, especially those of local boys'; 'a fair size of basket should be insisted on as a condition of employment', with dismissal for any day on which the basket was too small. Another practice earns its own sub-heading, 'Substitution': 'the fact of being chosen is worth something; and the worker will try to sell his place to a substitute, and then get in again soon after on the plea of being an old hand', often to introduce much younger boys 'so that the fellow who was 14 or 16 at first, dwindles imperceptibly until he can hardly carry a basket' (24). These tricks imply a live field of manipulation in which both sides played their cards.

Overseers can be employed to assist in overcoming worker resistance, but they might themselves threaten the work in various ways, extorting a wage-share from workers, or striking private deals with local shops (25). A good overseer is particularly dangerous: 'The more indispensable they seem, the less desirable is it to have so to trust a native' (24-5). Beside these remarks lurks an unstated threat to the 'master', that of a skilled deputy taking over his work. The manual recommends against employing overseers, but concedes a need for some subalterns, distributing authority among men still working, to prevent a rival concentration of authority, as well as any 'idleness' (26). Petrie compares conditions in Greece and England, a reminder that the same general structure of labour relations applied across Europe as well as in Egypt:

> In England about as much work may be done per man as in Egypt, but at about five or six times the cost. Hence the number employed is not so large, twenty or thirty being a large gang, instead of 150 or 200 as in Egypt. As they can follow directions tolerably, an overseer or foreman is not needed, the best of the workers usually taking the lead. (27)

The manual also provides practical tips for the director on enforcing discipline more directly, combining observation with the threat of group dismissal:

> It is impossible to be known to be away, as then no work will go on effectively. An air of vigilant surprises has to be kept up. A sunk approach to the work behind higher ground is essential; and, if possible, an access to a commanding view without being seen going to and fro. A telescope is very useful to watch if distant work is regular. At Tanis the girls in a big pit were kept by

the men walking up and tipping baskets at the top; but the telescope showed that the baskets were all the time empty. The immediate dismissal of fourteen people was the result. (28)

Paying by results, 'piece work', can save the time wasted on directorial spying required by 'day work', but takes time in calculating the rate. The manual summarises pay rates current on a (Petrie) dig in Upper Egypt: 2½ to 3 piastres (6d to 7d) per day for a man, 1½ to 2 piastres (3½ to 5d) 'for a boy, of fit and proper quality'; and for piece work ½ piastre to 1 piastre per cubic metre, depending on the hardness of the ground (29).

Dismissal is also the disciplinary strategy recommended for controlling the youngest workers, keeping them to time and attaining the prize of 'regularity':

> The local boys should all give the names of their villages on enlistment, and be kept in lists according to villages, so as to group them for payment in gold. In case of any serious theft or trouble due to boys from one village, all the rest from that village can be dismissed as a warning. (31).

On the issue of age, the manual tends towards the specificity of a census, providing information rarely printed elsewhere. Facing p. 20, two photographs show a boy and girl (fig. 13), and three boys (fig. 14), together captioned 'workers at Tanis' (their names are given in the archives: see Chapter 9 below). The accompanying text reveals that these children are supplementary to a main corps of teenage workmen:

> The best age for diggers is about 15 to 20 years. After that many turn stupid, and only a small proportion are worth having between 20 and 40. After 40 very few are of any use, though some robust men will continue to about 50. The Egyptian ages early; and men of 45 would be supposed to be 65 in England. The boys are of use for carrying from about 10 years old; and they generally look mere boys till over 20. The ornamental man with a good beard is quite useless and lazy; and the best workers are the scraggy under-sized youths, with wizened wiry faces, though sometimes a well-favoured lad with pleasing face will turn out very good (fig. 13). In choosing boys the broad face and square chin are necessary tokens of stamina; and the narrow feminine faces are seldom worth much. (20-1)

Child labour is not always an option, not quite for the legal reasons we might expect: 'In European countries this use of boys is scarcely possible owing to the national education. In Greece as in England the boys are required to go to school, and their holidays there are not at a time suitable for excavating, while in England the holidays are occupied by the harvest' (32).

As in Chapter I for the director, in keeping with a dominant social Darwinism, Petrie uses the category of character to frame his account of labourer selection. He seeks 'honesty, shown mostly by the eyes, and by a frank and open bearing; next, the sense and ability; and lastly, the sturdiness, and freedom from nervous weakness and hysterical tendency to squabble' (21). Then, 'the education of the workers begins', and Petrie encourages his archaeologist with promises of unexpected results. This passage too is required reading for any twenty-first-century understanding of the structures to be transformed:

> Often some oafs who will not understand any directions, and have no sense to work unless encouraged by watching, may yet be brought up in a few months to be good workers if associated with a skilful man. And almost every boy and man will greatly improve by steady work and control. The effect of selection and training is astonishingly seen on comparing some old hands, who have had five or ten years at the business, side by side with new lads. There is as much difference between their capacities as there is between the fellah and an educated Englishman. (21-2)

Here Petrie is emphasising distance between Egyptian farmer (Arabic *fallah*) and educated westerner; he cannot use the keyword 'school', because he too was not educated at school, and so he needs nationality to explain the gap. Yet, in drawing a line in those terms, Petrie is effectively abolishing it at the same time:

> A gang of well-trained men need hardly any directions, especially in cemetery work; and their observations and knowledge should always be listened to, and will often determine matters. The freshman from England is their inferior in everything except in recording; and at least a season's experience is needed before any one can afford to disregard the judgment of a well-trained digger. (22)

For all the tactical shoring-up, the 'hardly', 'except' and 'at least', the structure of domination is here exploded from within: the only defence is to stop the worker recording. A humanitarian impulse drives Petrie to this self-destruction of his power, and it opens the door at once to an acknowledgment of difference, if not quite equality.

> The better class of these workers are one's personal friends, and are regarded much as old servants are in a good household. Their feelings and self-respect must be thought of, as among our own equals, and they will not put up with any rudeness or contempt. A man with landed property and cattle, and an ancestry of a couple of centuries, can afford to look down on most Englishmen who would bully him. (22)

Despite its paternalism, these lines give space to an Egyptian point of view, one that Petrie knows more intimately and more sympathetically than most of his liberal critics could.

Yet the dominant colonial nationalist rivalries of the time encroach here, despite the official Anglo-French Entente Cordiale of that same year (for its Egyptian section, see Owen 2004: 322-4). These deflect the logical consequences of this passage; 'such workers are of course entirely above going into the usual Government or French work, where the lash is used; and their good service and skill is only given for friendly treatment' (22). Employment conditions under the French-directed Antiquities Service of the Egyptian government are used a second time in the chapter, to demonstrate the essential fairness of the English director: 'Mariette's overseers used to go to a village with a Government order for so many men, and demand the best men they could venture on claiming. These bought themselves off, each at a few shillings a month, and lower men were taken, until most of the villagers were paying heavy tribute' (25). Auguste Mariette, the director of the Egyptian Antiquities Service, died in Cairo in 1881, the year before the British army occupied Egypt. The 1904 manual on archaeology remains in a simultaneously Francophobic and orientalist tradition of attacking economic and political rivals as ethical tyrannies. This description evokes the work of Mariette as a dark age, from his reliance, as government official, on the corvée (obligatory project-based) labour that terrorised the Egyptian rural population. It does not mention a principal grievance against Mariette, that he refused access to Egyptian sites to any archaeological expeditions other than those of the government Service, nor does it acknowledge that Mariette was unfunded or at best underfunded over the two decades in which he headed the service, or that he had managed to sustain a longer-term reality out of the Cairo Egyptian Museum created two generations earlier by Rifaa al-Tahtawi (David 1994).

In evoking the harsh measures in other archaeological work, Petrie is declaring his own work pure of unjust violence, but not of all violence, for he reverts at once to the theme of Control, the immediately following sub-heading, beside the words: 'Yet there is a danger in letting control slip away' (22). In print, Petrie claims that control can be maintained by dividing among several men prized services such as shopping and carrying things for him, on the imperialist rule Divide and Conquer: 'if there be two parties – as from opposite sides of the Nile – always keep them well balanced in your consideration. Each will then keep a sharp lookout on the opposition' (23).

Few would contest the legitimacy of one part of the directorial concern for control: protection of sites from theft. In his battle with antiquities dealers, the archaeologist seems ethically unassailable, as defender of the national heritage. Local networks of dealers existed before the development of archaeology, and the struggle against the trade was hard. Perhaps the only possible response is to enlist the police resources of the state. Yet, when that response is recorded in the manual, the ethics become complicated by the intersection of an ethical good (defending ancient sites and knowledge) with an ethical evil (the colonial military occupation):

> The dealer and the spy are a constant plague. No man must be allowed to loaf about the work, or to lie watching it from a look-out point. And any

troublesome men are best dealt with by taking shoes or head-shawl from them, and offering to send the clothes to the man's sheikh to be returned to him. To get them he must give his name, and the name of his sheikh; and that no man will do, as he can then be dropped on by the police in future. (38-9)

A reading as comedy may be intended, but these motifs of humiliation and police invoke physical violence on behalf of foreign archaeologist against local inhabitant. Archaeological ethics are not so much compromised, as bankrupted by imperialism.

Petrie argues at length for fair treatment, implemented by a system that would not be acceptable under later conditions, and that caused controversy even in his time (Shaw 1999: 279-80), but which was in his eyes the only effective and responsible policy: paying the workers the local value of their finds (33). Petrie uses the term *bakhshish* for this additional remuneration, and asserts that 'the extra payments secure willing workers', attracted by the prospects of sporadic higher pay, and that this 'is by no means only as a safeguard to honesty', as it encourages diggers to be more careful not to break finds, and to report even smaller items – 'Nothing can ensure care better than paying for it' (35). Similarly attentive to the feelings of the workers, Petrie insists on transparent accounts in forms accessible to those who cannot read, using a tally system on sheet zinc (37-8), and on spending time in hearing complaints, giving way in cases of reasonable doubt (36-7). He is also a concerned field doctor: 'A stock of medicines, and some care in applying them, are necessary in any excavations' (38). If his role in archaeology is that of industrialising capitalist, he is among the most humane. This, with his intense practicality, makes him all the more interesting as a subject, in the overarching question, why did archaeology exclude its workers?

Assessing *Methods and Aims*: modernisation as a change in mode of production?

A nationalist historiography might consider that British imperialism explains expressions in *Methods and Aims*. Not Petrie, but the British Empire would be responsible for the way in which Egyptians are treated in the text. However, the Petrie manual is for use in England and Greece, as well as in Egypt; 'Orientalism' as the dehumanisation of the other starts at home. Moreover, Egyptian as well as European archaeologists all continue to exclude their workforce in the twenty-first century, fifty years after Nasser nationalised the Suez Canal. The persistence of the structure of social relations in an excavation would seem to invalidate the nationalist account. A transnational theory seems required, such as the modernisation thesis of Max Weber in *The Protestant Ethic and the Spirit of Capitalism*, the first part of which was also, coincidentally, published in

1904 (Giddens 1971: 124-7). Since Lenin and Luxemburg, both also writing at the time of Petrie, a Marxist historiography has combined elements both from the nationalist resistance to Empire, and from the economic and political theses by Marx and Weber on industrial modernisation. The experience of Egypt under, first, European credit, and then British occupation is among the examples cited by Luxemburg in her 1913 monograph *The Accumulation of Capital* (cf. Davis 2001: 103-5). According to the analysis by Lenin, *Imperialism: The Highest Stage of Capitalism*, published between the two 1917 Russian revolutions, imperialism functions with militarised racism, as resisted by nationalists, but with the vital difference from mainstream nationalist writing, that Empire is considered an aspect of class war, and the European empires a particular historical form of capitalism (Labica 2007; Losurdo 2007). Transferring the focus to social class, this history-writing would account for the existence of the same struggles and structure within both Egypt and Europe, as well as between them (for the complicating transnational element, in Egyptian Marxist histories of foreigners resident in Egypt, see Gorman 2003: 181-4). Beside nationalist and Marxist historiography, there remains the biographical narrative option of accepting Petrie as Hero in a history of ideas, and replying to the challenge to authority by asking what precisely is going to take its place. A defence of authority may sound conservative, but it is not necessarily exclusive to the right of the political spectrum. Marxist writings include a short sharp article by Engels 'On Authority' (first published in the Italian newspaper *Almanacco Repubblicano* in 1874, as 'Dell'Autorità'), as well as the Lenin pamphlet of 1920, *The Infantile Disorder of 'Leftism' in Communism*, directed against anarchic trends in communism after the defeat of revolution by military force and rising fascism in Italy, Hungary and Germany (Lorimer 1999). Simpler labels by nation, or left and right, seem ineffective, perhaps too abstract, for unravelling these overlaps. Greater specificity is needed in frame and method.

Both Marx and Weber offer a socio-economic vocabulary for understanding what in idealist history would be the transformation of public spheres. Weber uses the language of rationalisation, translating social class into a matter of 'ranks', while Marxist historiography applies the vocabulary of the mode of production, with its transformation of feudal into capitalist anchored in European history. The Eurocentric horizon of both approaches is controversial, and can only be defended as overtly political and redemptive, if they seek to explain why European, rather than Asian or African, military-commercial empires smothered the globe (Amin 1973). The reason for shifting from idealist to more socio-economic frames, is to bring the target of this study into sharper focus. In its institutional history of university chairs and courses, in 1904 the discipline of Archaeology is undergoing its formative stage (Gosden 1999: 53 for the institutions at Cambridge in 1851, fully salaried from 1927, Liverpool in 1904, Oxford in 1906, Edinburgh in 1926). According to Marxism, at this time the global landscape is adjusting from local, often feudal social relations to a world entirely dominated by the capitalist mode of production. The hero in this history is bourgeois revolution; the *Communist Manifesto* praises capitalism for its demolition of feudal conditions (Marx and Engels 1848). Thus the contrast drawn by Petrie between Mariette and himself can still be expressed as heroic progress, but with greater precision over what constituted the forward drive, and greater realism over its economic root and human impact. At the time of Mariette, the only archaeology permitted is national, foreign-directed, employing Mamluk-Ottoman methods of recruitment, with a mixture of local Egyptian and foreign overseers. These excavations might be said to display late feudal relations; global capital is penetrating Egypt, and its traditional ruling class promotes self-colonisation (or self-capitalisation) in response (Mitchell 1988). In the person of Mariette, foreign-directed nationalisation of excavating arrives with, and via the same international framework as, the Suez Canal debt (Reid 2002: 100). By 1904 the working regime can no longer be so ostensibly feudal, since global capital installed its military in 1882. During a policed economic re-regulation by English bureaucrats trained from colonial service in India, the archaeological expedition undergoes its Weberian transformation from pre-modern mass to modern regiment. The prescripts of *Methods and Aims* echo this fuller transition to capitalism at the rural marketplaces of archaeology, in England, in Greece and in Egypt. Petrie expresses the new condition of archaeology during a shift in the mode of production. Something similar occurs within nineteenth- and earlier twentieth-century capitalist control of working practice, moving from more informal Taylorist to more mechanised and depersonalised Fordist management style (for migrant labour in Egypt from this perspective, see Toth 1999).

As a part of a public sphere governing views of the past, or more generally of time, archaeology may be expected to reproduce the relations of domination which apply in the environment which Weber calls a rationalised economy, and Marx a capitalist mode of production. The name Mariette represents the beginnings of transition to industrial capitalism. The name Petrie represents a more developed phase, for which Lenin uses the term imperialism, to provoke resistance and revolution, and Weber the less traumatic, more nostalgic term, 'disenchantment'. Since social relations lie at the heart of the change, the personal name offers an appropriate category for investigation. Therefore, the specific method that I propose for investigation of archaeology as a public sphere, and of the possibilities for its structural transormation, is the indexing of occurrences of the personal name at each level of writing in the encounter between the excavation director and the workforce. In *Methods and Aims* itself, the following modern personal names appear:

Prof. Perry p. 3 for 'the engineering training of mind and senses'.
Dr. Birch p. 4 for the request for pottery fragments from sites to date the
  pottery from the known history of the sites 'so complete was the
  ignorance of archaeology a quarter of a century ago' (Samuel Birch was
  Keeper of Egyptian and Assyrian Antiquities).
Professor Ernest Gardner p. 186 (proposal for a state register of works of
  art).
Messrs. Hogarth and Welch p. 158 (article in *Journal of Hellenic Studies*
  21, 1901, 78).
Ibrahim and Aly p. 40 local practice of taking share of wages (generic
  examples).
Ibrahim or Mutwali p. 19 'needs direction' (generic example).
Mariette p. 25 (harsh methods of his overseers).
Mr. Myres p. 158 (discoverer of a particular pottery style on Crete).
Schliemann p. 35 (method of daily payment of workers).

In addition, the name Saleh Muhamed appears in Arabic and English on
the 'account-card for native wages' illustrated on p. 38 as fig. 21.

Far more often, explicitly in 'I' and 'my', more often hidden behind
impersonal verb forms, Petrie is naming himself (cf. Drower 1985: 280,
identifying the *alter ego* as the philologist-director of excavation Edouard
Naville). The Freudian *ich* can be considered here its harsher English
translation as imperialist Ego, the name that conceals itself. In this 1904
publication, the name is otherwise a precious, rare resource, European or
Egyptian, and it reveals just four national identities in play, in three
different roles: the British and (Schliemann) German, as scientific inves-
tigators and discoverers; the French, representing a foreign and unwanted
presence, tainted for Petrie by an alliance with oriental tyranny; and the
Egyptian, as generic presence where Ibrahim and Aly, and 'Ibrahim or
Mutwali' play type-roles to provide a stage-name for a narrative episode.
Compared with the national stereotypes on the European side, reduction
of Egyptian name to cypher seems strategically dehumanising. How did
this happen to the humane Petrie? A first source for clues is the remainder
of his immense publication record, above all, the swiftly-issued excavation
reports.

Losing individuals: references to names in
Petrie publications, 1880-1930

Forty-four publications resulted from the excavations directed or spon-
sored by Petrie, from his 1883 report on the Giza survey to the final
publications of Egyptian work by his later institution, the British School
of Archaeology in Egypt. Already within his first seasons of Delta work,
printed references range from praise for named individuals to a dehuman-
ised anonymity in his published excavation reports. Petrie pays tribute to

his Egyptian excavation supervisors in his report on the 1885-1886 excavations for the Egypt Exploration Fund at Nabasha:

> I must not conclude this without acknowledging what is a necessary part of my facilities for work, the characters of my overseers. By continual selection and weeding, I have now three or four men whom I respect and trust more, the better I know them. The three brothers – Mahajub, Said, and Muhammed – abu Daud el Gabri have proved unequalled for sturdy independence, unceasing goodwill and kindliness, obedience, and readiness for any service, asked or unasked; while Tulbeh, their little cousin, promises to be quite their equal. Though they never stand between me and my workers in any matter, yet it would be impossible to maintain such a good spirit and straightforwardness in the work with men inferior to my good friends. (Petrie 1888: 3)

By contrast, at Naukratis in the western Delta, in the very same years of work, Petrie makes no reference to workforce conditions or Egyptian names. Only an anonymous mass 'all the workmen' appears, once, in the description of systematic removal of earth by an advancing line (Petrie 1886: 12). Given the twin tracks of anonymity and naming within a single year, a broader span of time offers a more useful unit for analysis of his practice across the five decades of work in Egypt.

The archaeological career of Petrie can be divided into five phases by institutional filiation and financial support:

I. His 1880-1882 survey at Giza, independent, with status as Antiquities Service official for the limited excavation at the site.
II. His 1883-1886 Nile Delta excavations for the Egypt Exploration Fund.
III. 1887-1892 self-directed excavations under the Antiquities Service in Fayum province, nearby at Maydum, and at Amarna in Middle Egypt.
IV. Excavations in Upper Egypt after his appointment as Professor at University College London, with his Egyptian Research Account from 1893 and then in combination with the Egypt Exploration Fund from 1897.
V. Excavations for his British School of Archaeology in Egypt, from 1905.

If we read the publications against his institutional history, it emerges that Petrie identified Egyptians by name when he was embarking on a new phase; the only time he names an Egyptian in an excavation report during his final, most established phase of work, it is to acknowledge a local landowner, rather than anyone in the workforce (Petrie *et al.* 1910: 38). The other two post-1900 references are both to Ali Suefi, and in both instances from an Englishman publishing the first excavation in his own name (Engelbach 1915; Brunton 1927). The space for the name seems provided by the insecurity of the 'master' on the new terrain.

2. Labour and name in the Petrie publications

Work Phases	Publications	Names of Egyptians
1880-1882	Petrie 1883	Ali Gabri, 'slave' Muhammed, nephew Muhammed, Shekh Omar, Abu Talib, Ibrahim, guard Abdallah
1883-1886	Petrie 1888	Muhammed (same as below), his cousin Tulbeh Mahajub, Said, Muhammed abu Daud el Gabri
	3 other books	no references to Egyptians by personal name
1887-1892	Petrie 1889	Muhammed (same as above)
	Petrie 1890	overseer of fishermen at Lahun bridge M'haisin
	Petrie 1891	worker 'the lad Mekowi'
	Petrie 1892	worker from Maydum Handawi
1893-1905	Petrie 1894	no references to Egyptians by personal name
	Petrie 1896b	Ali Suefi 'best lad' from Illahun
	Petrie 1897	Ali (= Ali Suefi) dealer Muhammed Mohassib (good) dealer Abd er-Rasul (bad)
	Quibell 1898a	dealer Mohammed Mohassib (good) 'dealer friend' Girgis
	Petrie 1898	'native scribe' Umran Khallil (exceptional)
	10 other books	no references to Egyptians by personal name
1906-1930	Petrie et al. 1910	Sheykh Muhammed Abeyd of Mitraheneh
	Engelbach 1915	Aly es-Sweyfy
	Brunton 1927	Ali es Suefi
	17 other books	no references to Egyptians by personal name

In sum, whereas most of the Giza bedouin who worked for Petrie at Giza itself and in the Delta are named by him in the 1883 and 1885 publications, for the remainder of his career just two Fayum workers are named, Mekowi and Ali Suefi, and one Maydum worker, Handawi. Nor is their place left vacant. Regularly, from 1889, these same publications do speak of the 'workers', but these are now defined by name or implicitly as men and women who were foreigners in Egypt like Petrie himself. From 1892 to 1930, Petrie and his European co-archaeologists refer only to Ali Suefi or to Egyptians who are not digging – two antiquities-sellers, one land-owner, and the local *katib* 'scribe' Umran Khallil who so fascinated Petrie in the 1897 report.

One publication is not included in the tabulation above, coming at a career turning-point and standing out against this trend: the report on work in Sinai (Petrie 1906a, with chapters by Currelly). Sinai presented a greater logistical challenge than other work in Egypt, because the terrain was so inhospitable and sparsely inhabited. Although farmers and Ababda bedouin were recruited from his core workforce at Qift, Petrie depended on local Sinai bedouin supply routes. In this context he recorded much that was novel to him, in comparison with work conditions in the Nile Valley and Delta. Here extensive sections, including the whole of chapter 2, 'The Bedawy and the Desert', are devoted to narrative accounts of the adventurous expedition into the Sinai desert, with ethnographic and character descriptions, and correspondingly more names. Petrie seems more in love with the desert and its inhabitants than Currelly, who states blankly in his narrative 'I found the Bedawyn of Sinai mean, thieving, and lying' (in Petrie 1906a: 236). Yusuf 'the son of the Ababdeh sheikh' is mentioned by both authors (Petrie at p. 22, Currelly at pp. 229 and 241), but otherwise Petrie refers mainly to men providing camels or security: the camel-men 'varied' but 'the best of them was Salah Abu Risq' and the party was joined on its way by 'the wily Khallyl Itkheyh', while 'the most distinguished of our men was M'teyr' (Petrie 1906a: 6). Khallyl is cited again on pp. 21-2, where there is also reference to another trader Abu Qudeyl and 'our former guard, Selameh'. However, the fullest description is of 'old Abu Ghaneym, the sheykh of the Wady Maghareh and Serabit el Khadem' (the two sites with the most abundant ancient Egyptian inscriptions). The 'old' man was not much older than Petrie, with a 'rather younger' brother Ra'abiyeh; he had known a previous Sinai explorer, Major Macdonald, whom he remembered as 'Mazhur' with his boy 'Willem' (Petrie 1906a: 22, 24-5, 30, 42, 53). Here, glimpsed in European writing, Abu Ghaneym seems less the 'other', and more himself, looking at, judging, and remembering the European.

The Sinai volume was published in exceptional circumstances, marking the final break between Petrie and the Egypt Exploration Fund. The Fund would publish only the inscriptions, not the other archaeological material or historical conclusions. Petrie decided to publish that essential material himself, and to raise all the funds for his own future work; to achieve this, he founded the British School of Archaeology in Egypt. In his publications under the new arrangement, in contrast to his practice at Giza and Nabasha thirty years earlier, he names only one Egyptian, Sheykh Muhammed Abeyd, the landowner facilitating his work at Mit Rahina (the site of Memphis). Against the ellision of Egyptian by European personal names in the paradigmatic slot for acknowledging co-workers, these publications provide more information on a collective level; these references to collectives amass a further stock of evidence for the archaeological view of the inhabitants of archaeological landscapes, and deserve to be considered before probing the archaeological archives.

Egyptians without personal name in
Petrie publications, 1880-1930

As the Sinai narrative demonstrates, Egypt present as well as past attracted the ethnographer in Petrie, and this fascination allowed him occasional print-space to refer to the present Egypt, even in his accounts of the work on recovering the past. It is important to remember that his archaeological publications were addressed to a specific combination of informed archaeological and historical colleagues, and a broader public from whom Petrie hoped to raise funds for following seasons of work.

2. Labour and name in the Petrie publications

These books are not places to expect views outside the mainstream of moneyed British 'public opinion'. Here, though, we find out what an English reader of printed archaeological reports could know of the people inhabiting the country in which archaeology claimed its interest.

Ethnicity

Petrie uses several collective designations for the labour force: 'natives' (e.g. Petrie 1894: 2, referring to the local inhabitants at Amarna, and perhaps also to five men and boys recruited in Fayum province for the Amarna work), 'Arabs' (e.g. Petrie 1885: 2, perhaps only Giza bedouin supervisors on the Delta work), 'Egyptians' (e.g. Petrie 1896a: 2, on inhabitants of Qift), and 'fellahin', Arabic for farmers (e.g. 1896b: viii, on the workforce at Naqada, comprising mainly men and boys from Qift, some from Fayum province). In some localities, outside the workforce recruited, Petrie also refers to bedouin, the Arabic word for desert nomads (e.g. 1888: 2). In nineteenth-century usage, the word 'Arabs' denoted the bedouin population; generally their identity was maintained in opposition to that of the Egyptian 'fellahin' farmers, despite a bedouin tendency to settle down and eventually to merge with local population (Schölch 1976-1977).

Place-names: specific points of recruitment, different sites of work

For his work in the 1880s across the Nile Delta, and again for his Fayum work, Petrie recruited supervisors from the men he had known at Giza (Petrie 1888:2; 1889: 3), while the main labour force was local. 'I arrived in due course at Medinet el Fayum, and settled on the side of the great mounds, hard by a mill, once more living free in a tent ... I soon got together some men from the village of Menshiet Abdallah at the end of the mounds; and they went with me afterwards to Hawara' (Petrie 1889: 1).

Evidently, local is a relative term. Petrie deliberately limited his recruitment of the very nearest inhabitants of a site, declaring great advantage in moving the workforce away from their homes:

> I then moved over to Hawara, and all my men and boys were anxious to go with me; I picked over sixty of them, and they went altogether with my baggage, and settled as a camp along the canal bank by the pyramid of Hawara ... It is a great advantage also to have the workmen by themselves: they are always ready to begin work; they are regular in coming every day, and can be depended on; they are much less liable to take anything found to their homes, or to bring out things to the work; there is no trouble with shekhs or guards interfering; and, above all, there are no loafers getting in the way and stopping business by coming and talking. I believe it is always the best to draw the workers from a distance, and to have a few of the people of the place in order to keep touch with them; then both parties are afraid of being dismissed, and they know that if they are troublesome they will only drive you into employing the opposite side. (Petrie 1889: 3)

41

The avoidance of the nearest inhabitants in an archaeological landscape constitutes a crucial step in separating ancient past from modern population. Moreover, by mixing workers from different places, Petrie was creating a worker hierarchy with 'older hands' brought across a distance, over more local labour:

> I began by going over to my old quarters at Illahun to fetch my baggage, and engaged two or three dozen of my old workmen, who were all willing to go with me. They, and others of my older hands from near Medinet, used to walk over sixteen or eighteen miles with a sack of dried bread, work for ten or eleven days, and then walk back for fresh supplies, thus returning every fortnight. These men and boys were as honest and pleasant fellows as I wish to see; they camped in rough huts by my tent, and served as guards by night and workmen by day. ... I also employed many men from Medum and the villages near; and some of them were splendid workers. (Petrie 1892: 1-2, on the season at Maydum)

> I then fetched five of my old workers from Illahun and reached Tell el Amarna on 17th Nov. 1891. A few days were occupied in building huts and looking over the ground; and on the 23rd November I began work ... We settled to live at the village of Haj Qandil, fixing at the north-east of the houses, and building a row of mud-brick huts as we needed them. (Petrie 1894: 1, on the season at Amarna)

Occasionally, Petrie gives more specific comments on inhabitants of specific place-names. From his 1885 work he refers to fugitives from conscription, a regular feature of Egyptian life, although this may be a fear of new, foreign requisitions, in the years immediately after the occupation by the English: 'All the marsh ground of the north Delta is more or less inhabited by men who have fled from the conscription, and two of my stoutest workers were men of Zagazig, who had thus saved their liberty by settling on the borders of the inhabited land near Defenneh' (Petrie 1888: 2).

His most famous recruiting and training was at Qift (Koptos):

> The Kuftis proved to be the most troublesome people that I have ever worked with. The pertinacity with which the rascals of the place would dog our steps about our house, and at the work, was amazing. And the regularity with which a fresh spy was set on every morning, to try and watch our doings, was most irritating. Among this rather untoward people we found however, as in every place, a small percentage of excellent men; some half-dozen were of the very best type of native, faithful, friendly, and laborious, and from among these workmen we have drawn about forty to sixty of two following years at Negadeh and at Thebes. They have formed the backbone of my upper Egyptian staff, and I hope that I may keep these good friends so long as I work anywhere within reach of them. Beside these I had living with me at Koptos four of the Illahunis from the Fayum; and some of the former workers from Tell el Amarna came also, but did not prove satisfactory. (Petrie 1896a: 1)

Recruits from earlier seasons were skilled enough in the labour of archaeology to take on the role of trainer: 'Every workman was carefully educated
by myself or our older hands. I brought with me my best lad, Ali Suefi, who
has been kindly rescued from conscription by the Sirdar, for the interests
of archaeology; and I also had two or three other old hands from Illahun.
The bulk of the men were the picked workers from Koptos, selected from
the year before' (Petrie 1896b: viii, on the season at Naqada). The division
of skilled from unskilled labour becomes especially fragile in this worker-
to-worker training.

Age and gender

Workers could be young, sometimes very young, who again express the
fear that Petrie is anxious to deflect: 'I saw every labourer at least twice,
and often four times, a day. Thus I knew everyone about the place, and
kept up a friendly intercourse with them all, so that the smallest children
were not afraid; while at the same time I held to necessary discipline, by
means of dismissal for a longer or shorter time' (Petrie 1885: 2-3).

As noted in *Methods and Aims*, girls might work alongside the men and
boys in the Nile Delta, but there is no mention of adult women: 'When at
last I started, we formed a procession of about forty, with two baggage
camels of mine; the men with bundles of bread on their backs – for no food
can be bought in the desert, – the boys with the hoes, and the girls with the
baskets on their heads, with a few *kullehs* and utensils.' (Petrie 1888: 2)

Ideal working life

In the passage immediately following the camel-train extract, Petrie
extols isolation from modernity as his ideal working and living environment, showing how he attained this goal already early in his career, in the
more isolated work at the north-eastern fringe of the Nile Delta:

> This settlement at Defenneh was a sort of experiment I had often wished for;
> I went with only my faithful *reis* Muhammed – a lad of about twenty, – and
> his younger cousin, a fine, sturdy boy named Tulbeh; the rest were all stray
> workers whom I had never seen till a short time before. We had no soldiers,
> no police, no shekhs, no guards, nor any of the usual machinery of Egyptian
> rule; there was no authority to be invoked under several hours' journey. The
> experiment answered better than I could have supposed; though I had up to
> seventy people there, far from all dwellings, in the desert, I never had the
> least trouble with any one, and I never heard a squabble between them
> during the whole two months. They worked as well as I have ever known
> them work, they obeyed completely, and a thoroughly contented and happy
> spirit was always seen. Not only so, but the Bedawin around, who used to
> hunt for stray antiquities and weights, were as quiet and respectful as could
> be wished; our camp used to be left without any guard, and only a pin in the
> flap of my tent, while we were half a mile away; yet nothing was ever
> disturbed, nor had we any complaint to make. I never spent two months more

smoothly than while heading our desert camp. Yet the people had not much to content them; they came without any shelter, and nothing but what they wore; they had dry bread to eat, and brackish water to drink; and they worked for sixpence a day, most of them for but five days of the week, as they had to walk twenty-five to forty miles to fetch their food. (Petrie 1888: 2)

It is instructive that, even under English military occupation, the evils of police authority can be ascribed here to 'the usual machinery of Egyptian rule'.

Constructing separate shared space

In that description of ideal working life, as later in *Methods and Aims*, Petrie prides himself on living with and working with workmen, in explicit contrast to hotel-based, separated excavation directors. He takes pleasure in the simplicity even in the construction of his dig-house, as in the economies from its dismantling at the end of a season:

> Such rooms can be built very quickly; a hut twelve feet by eight taking only a few hours. The bricks can be bought at tenpence a thousand; the boys make a huge mud pie, a line of bricks is laid on the ground, a line of mud poured over them, another line of bricks is slapped down in the mud so as to drive it up the joints; and thus a wall of headers, with an occasional course of stretchers to bind it, is soon run up. The roof is made of boards, covered with durra stalks to protect them from the sun; and the hut is ready for use, with a piece of canvas hung over the doorway. Such a place is far better than a tent to live in; and on leaving we found that every native was so afraid that we might give away the materials to some one else, that we had offers for all our bricks, boards, and straw, at nearly the new price. (Petrie 1894: 1)

However, three descriptions of the detailed arrangements for living-quarters indicate that this was not quite full sharing.

> For the first fortnight I lived in a tent, close by the village of San; but afterwards I moved up to a room that I had built on the top of the mounds, some sixty feet above the river level; and, gradually completing my house there, I had at last a little block of buildings of a defensible form, with only one outer door, and comprising six rooms around a courtyard; the rooms being about six by eight feet each, and four of them serving for me and the stores and finds, while the other two housed my overseers. From my room I could see the temple through the open doors, so as to watch the workers, with a telescope, when I needed to be up in the house. (Petrie 1885: 2)

> I cleared a space along the north wall of the temple of Set, and built a row of huts, one for each of our English party, and two large ones for our men. There we lived as a community all the time, with the most complete sense of security in our good friends from Koptos, many of whom we heartily liked and esteemed. Mr. Quibell built huts for himself and his sister, Miss Quibell, at his work at Ballas to the north, and had likewise a colony of picked men to live beside him. (Petrie 1896b: vii)

The next gallery contained about sixty workmen and boys, with very often half a dozen donkeys and an occasional camel; and another short gallery served for my best man Ali and his family, and the mother of another of the men. (Petrie 1897: 1)

Labour skill: what archaeologists would not train workmen to do

Petrie assured his readers that even his senior workers are without archaeological skills (Petrie 1885: 2):

The only duty of my Arab overseers was to watch the men, see that they kept to work, observe what was found, and make any little changes needed from hour to hour; but I saw every labourer at least twice, and often four times, a day.

Gardner drew the dividing-line between Egyptian and European on the grounds of trust, commenting on supervision of the workforce by Petrie, Griffith and himself in early Nile Delta work (Gardner 1888: 10):

As many as this were kept in the work while Mr. Petrie was still with me; after he had left, I found 120 to 150 was as large a number as I alone could keep under proper supervision. For though our overseers were excellently trained by Mr. Petrie, and thoroughly trustworthy, it was of course most undesirable to leave any site where excavation was going on for many hours without a visit. At first, however, as there were three of us to direct the labourers, we were able to make a division of the work.

This lack of trust, and training, is confirmed by Petrie in his introduction to the lengthy account of his great 1894 innovation at Naqada, the recording of site features on a massive scale. This quantitative leap seems exactly the point at which it would have made most sense to train up larger numbers of recorders. In order to justify the illogicality of the division, Petrie falls back on a xenophobic prejudice:

In researches such as are described in this volume, the exactness of the information is the very essence of its value; and as the manual work of excavating was mainly performed by Egyptians, who have ordinarily no idea of exactness, it is needful to give a full account of the mode of securing the information, and the way of working. Some credentials are certainly needed before asking any person to take on credit the details of minute arrangements of bones or of vases in tombs excavated by the *fellahin*. (Petrie 1896b: viii-ix)

Marking finds is also done by the foreign supervisors, not by the workers. Indeed, until the 1960s, none of the hundreds of thousands of excavated objects distributed outside Egypt bears a letter or numeral in Arabic script: 'When the grave was finished the last matter was to mark the number of the grave on every jar that was kept; the bones were generally put into a large jar to go to the huts; and there every pot and every large bone was numbered with black varnish' (Petrie 1896b: ix). Permanent marking of material is described as a stage of work after the workforce has been paid and left: 'At noon and in the evening all the workers assembled at our huts, standing in a row along the outside of the dwarf wall of the courtyard, some seventy feet long. Each placed on the wall before him his baskets of pottery and bones; each lot was looked at, and the bakhshish assessed which I should give them, sometimes a halfpenny or a penny, sometimes a dollar or a pound, and duly entered against their names in the wages-book. Then came the long work of the permanent marking of everything, and putting it away' (Petrie 1896b: ix).

In this, his longest description of method in a published report, Petrie refers to his own work as 'skilled labour' and 'skilled record', more or less as antonym of 'native labour' (Petrie 1896b: ix). The specific line of the great divide can be identified as an assumed illiteracy.

Labour organisation: payrates and productivity

A fair amount of work was got out of them; a man ordinarily cutting, in good ground, about 200 cubic feet, or seven and half cubic yards, a day for his wages of 6*d.*; and three or four children, at fifteen or twenty pence a day, will carry this quantity about twenty yards in baskets on their heads. (Petrie 1885: 3)

These men and boys were as honest and pleasant fellows as I wish to see; they camped in rough huts by my tent, and served as guards by night and workmen by day ... If constantly encouraged they will earn surprising amounts, by work so hard that any person would cry shame if they were forced to do it. To tempt such people by constantly giving them opportunities of stealing or cheating is extremely wrong; but by guarding against this, and letting them feel that they are always kept in hand and noticed, they prove admirable and industrious workers. Of course so far as possible all my work was piece-work; and though the rate was only from ½ to 1 piastre the cubic metre, or 1*d.* to 1¾ *d.* the cubic yard, according to the hardness of the ground, yet they usually earned 18*d.* to 2*s.* a day for a man and boy, double the best native wages; 15 to 20 cubic yards <p. 2> was a common discharge for a couple. (Petrie 1892: 1-2)

The engagement of each man, allotting the work to him, keeping account of his time, and paying him, was attended to by myself; thus there was no opening for native favouritism, bakhshish, or cheatery. (Petrie 1885: 2)

This cutting or this carrying is about equal to three quarters of a day of an English labourer with spade and wheelbarrow; so that a gang of a man and children, costing about two shillings a day, will do as much as an English labourer in a day and a half. (Petrie 1885: 3)

Either these opportunities for pay, or the working conditions, or the unusual activity itself, stimulated a demand for work: 'Long before I went there, my people at Nebesheh were all clamorous to go with me, and the questions about my intentions were more pressing as time went on' (Petrie 1888: 2); 'I then moved over to Hawara, and all my men and boys were anxious to go with me' (Petrie 1889: 3). In the clamour and anxiety, we might read a thirst for work, or the more sinister pressure of a hunger for work. Yet, however hungry his workforce might be for work, Petrie stated it necessary that he impose order, and in these statements the motif of fear reappears, however jocular his tone:

> In the first place, strict discipline was maintained among the men, and new comers were carefully allotted with old hands, so as to be educated. Carelessness in breaking up skeletons was punished, sometimes se-verely. At one part of the work, where a friend of mine was not accustomed to the men, the skeletons came often to grief. So I announced that the next man who broke bones would be dismissed, and closely worked every grave myself. A rather good man was the unlucky one, and when I found two fresh fractures, he was paid up at once, and sent off. Every lad trembled in his hole after that, and was terrified if I came on even a snapped rib. (Petrie 1896b: viii)

Labour resistance

Sometimes, even in the printed pages, labour resists. In recruitment, other work may come first: 'During the harvest, of course, they had to work in their fields, and I had but thirty children left' (Petrie 1885: 2). In other instances, resistance takes on the features recurrent in class antagonisms, vilified in the vocabulary of the dominant by motifs from idleness to theft, as in the achievement of avoiding passing 'loafers' in the account of work at Hawara cited above (Petrie 1889: 3, cf. again Scott 1985: xvi). The vocabulary of class is glossed here with the difference between writer (with readers) and 'native': 'The difficulty was to avoid overstocking; as, in that case, so little attention could be given to each that they would not feel kept in hand, and would deteriorate, and become lazy. The engagement of each man, allotting the work to him, keeping account of his time, and paying him, was attended to by myself; thus there was no opening for native favouritism, bakhshish, or cheatery' (Petrie 1885: 2). In an episode in 1884, Petrie used the technique and language of an industrialist: 'So much did they dread losing work, that once dismissing the whole of the gang for half a day because they persistently came late, completely cured them; I never had a man late after that' (Petrie 1885: 3)

A missing category in archaeological
reports: social class

In all these comments, as much the archaeological focus as contemporary ideas of race and Empire might obscure for the English print-reader the specific social and economic realities of the people recruited. Presumably, imperatives of economy would encourage the foreign-investigator-turned-rural-employer to recruit a seasonal workforce from the lowest socio-economic group in order to minimise pay. Yet, in particular in the 1880s work, supervisors earned more, and Petrie emphasises the attractiveness of his conditions – above all in the system of paying finders for the local market value of their finds. More than one group is present in the countryside, and literacy, though rarer than in towns, is present nonetheless. Returning to the comments by Cuno on the demography of the village in nineteenth-century Egypt, we can ask, what are the precise local social networks in play? For into these Petrie and other European excavators arrive, more or less disruptively. These social fields enable local inhabitants to take advantage of the new arrivals. For this issue, the printed books need to be supplemented by an examination of the archive of manuscript papers behind, or below them. It is time to excavate the archaeologist.

3

Names in the Petrie Journals

The correspondence Petrie called his Journals presents a highly hetero-
geneous corpus of material, but follows a historical development of its own,
clear in the publication of major extracts by his biographer Margaret
Drower (Drower 2004). The original letters are preserved at the Griffith
Institute, Ashmolean Museum, Oxford, and copies are available for research at the Petrie Museum, UCL: I cite from the Petrie Museum copies,
stating where extracts are in Drower 2004, and I am indebted to the
Griffith Institute for permission to use these citations. In his earlier
seasons (phases I-III of his career as defined by his institutional affili-
ations), Petrie regularly sent home long letters containing details of his
progress, more or less every week. These Journals were circulated among
a small number of colleagues counted as close friends, interested in his
scientific work. In one letter from his first season for the Egypt Exploration Fund, he uses the term 'periodical' and proposes to separate his
reports of finds from the overall progress, as in the two main works of the
first-century AD Jewish historian Josephus, 'Ant.' (*Antiquities of the Jews*)
and 'Bell.' (*Jewish War*):

> As from an 'unofficial communication' it seems requisite to somewhat alter
> the arrangement of this periodical, I may as well say somewhat about it. I
> have slipped into putting more of antiquities into this, as I can record thus
> how things go from day to day, without waiting till I know the whole of each
> subject so as to be able to really report on it. I look on a report as serious, it
> is (for the time) a final summing up and judgement on a point; and I scarcely
> like to write thus about things here where my knowledge is growing and
> opinion changing from day to day. ... As it now seems that the transient notes
> of these pages may be utilized as informal reports, I will alter the arrange-
> ment into putting all matters of antiquities on to separate sheets, though
> still noting them from day to day, without pinning myself to the final
> accuracy of what I note down. Like Josephus: Ant. et Bell. (5.5.1884)

Although he did not follow this plan, he continued to comment on his form
of communication. In 1885, he writes in mock complaint (2.2.1885): 'So I
am to do my journal in triplicate it seems; a pity I can't set it up in type
and receive subscribers names for it if it is to go on at this rate. I only hope
it will be sufficiently legible, but I must lay on hard.' A year later, he chides
himself: 'I must really begin some account of my proceedings, for I have
been going on day after day, in rather an irresponsible way. In order to

save double writing, I shall make this a record of various details which may interest Mr Poole and Miss Edwards, outside of my regular reports on sites' (1.2.1886). By the end of the 1880s, they had become semi-official circulars, and from their contents he drew much of the record for the published reports. In a sense, the early Journals provide the first subterranean stratum of the archive underlying the 1883-1896 publications, and a next opportunity for uncovering the development and practice of the almost total exclusion of Egyptians of all classes from the history of archaeology in Egypt.

During phase IV of his career, by 1900, the letters had shortened, as Petrie transferred much of the logistics of expeditionary work and life to his European co-workers, above all, from the time of his marriage in 1896, his wife Hilda. She wrote a number of the later Journals, in a different vein but not without her own general account of archaeological work, as Petrie notes: 'As I find that Hilda does the general account of things with far more freshness than I do, I shall in future describe the discoveries more fully and leave the rest to the better hand' (weeks starting 22.12.1897). Increasingly, Hilda is journal author. In his Araba (Abydos) years 1899-1903, Petrie protests that he is simply too busy recording, but, evidently conscious of failing his readers, he apologises more than once:

> It is a scandalously long time since I sent any journal, but every evening is so occupied with drawing that I never seem to have a minute to spare. (12.2.1900, Drower 2004: 155)

> This season is not favourable to journal writing; there is a crowd of drawing work to be done, and seldom any great prize or excitement to describe. (1.2.1901)

Perhaps more tellingly, Petrie expressly considered these circulars a form of entry into a public sphere, partly reflecting a marginally larger readership by this stage: 'Journal has been long in abeyance as we have not wished to publish our good things until Maspero could be informed' (26.2.1901). The gap between journal and book was closing, and with it the reason for writing collective letters home.

In the final stage of his career in Egypt (1906-1924), the material filed as Journals seems to comprise only occasional regular private letters to single correspondents. Perhaps his mother had been the mainstay of the earlier practice, but the letters had continued as fuller Journals after her death in 1892. Marriage in 1897 evidently transformed dig life and its time-tables. Yet, beside these personal factors, the work-regime also changed as archaeological recording intensified, the reason given by Petrie himself for not writing: from the late 1890s, the construction of typologies involved more systematic recording of vastly greater quantities of finds, notably pottery and, at Araba, stone vessels. Moreover, in the institutionalisation of the discipline, the Petrie British School of Archaeology in Egypt, with a structure including periodic meetings, replaced earlier informal circles of interested friends. The gap is partly filled by letters between Hilda and Petrie, on the relatively rare occasions when they were not working together, or from Hilda (mainly) to their children, John, born in 1907, and Ann, born in 1908 (Drower 2004: 188, 190).

This history of development favours again a banded chronological approach to the Journals, with an exploration of context and themes within each phase of his career.

Phase I. Giza survey and limited excavation, 1880-1882

Summary of names
Names in publications: Petrie 1883: Ali Gabri [Jabri], slave Muhammed, nephew Muhammed, Shekh Omar, Abu Talib, Ibrahim, guard Abdallah. Additional names in Journals 1880-1882: sheikh Ibrahim, Abu Saud son of Ali Gabri, Smyne, Abdurrahman brother of Ali, chief of village guards, Mahmoud Issy Egyptian astronomer.

Introduction to Ali Jabri, and 'Pyramid Arabs'
Arriving for the first time in Cairo, Petrie goes directly to Dr James Grant, the Aberdeen physician who provided an introduction into the social networks of Europeans in Cairo and, more importantly for Petrie, of the inhabitants of the archaeological destination, Giza. Of his first dinner with Grant, on Saturday 18 December 1880, Petrie records:

> He considers it quite safe to go and settle in with Ali Gabri (not Dobree as C.P.S. writes it) as head-man, giving the shekh occasional bakksheesh fully £1 a month, but no great lump at last: they are too much head to mouth to do that. He says, as Highet said, and Baedecker also, that there is no chance of a raid, still less of personal violence, that even nothing large would be ventured on, or any regular stealing, but only appropriation of trifles and attempts at imposition; and that Ali would be above that, as C.P.S. says. He told me that some of the Pyramid Arabs are nearly every day in Cairo; so often, that it is not worth while to go out there to find Ali, as he might be out; I therefore, as he recommended, went to the Oriental Hotel and to Shepherd's and asked the door attendants to send any of the Pyramid Arabs they might see to Dr. Grant; and he will get Ali Gabri over to his house, and there make a personal settlement with him and me.

Petrie may be less fearful than his readers over the dangers of the desert; part of his reassurance rests on the authority of Dr Grant, part on the regular appearance of the 'Pyramid Arabs' in urban Cairo. No more information is given on the identity of these 'Arabs'; just as he assumes that his readers already know 'C.P.S.', Charles Piazzi Smyth, Petrie assumes prior knowledge about the inhabitants, perhaps specifically from the publications by Smyth.

Petrie gives a quick character sketch from his first encounter with the man who would help him through the next five years of his work:

> there stood Ali Gabri with a card from Mr. Grant, saying that if I would come with him to the Dr's we would settle matters. So off I started, and chatted to Ali on the way; he speaks very fair English, and though no beauty he has a very pleasant and trustworthy face, looking calm, simple, decided and straight forward, a man whom I would trust without a recommendation; and considering the excellent character given him by C.P.S., Weyman Dixon, Mr. Gill, and Dr. Grant, I felt every confidence in him. (20.12.1880, Drower 2004: 13-14)

Grant acts as interpreter in drawing up an agreement:

> I had written out all that I thought necessary to settle, and Dr. G. took my paper and talked over each point with Ali Gabri in Arabic. Ali saying that regular Bakhsheesh to the shekh was quite unnecessary, only giving when any special service was required. Having settled it all, and engaged Ali at £1 per week from that time forward, (he saying that he did it for love of Mr. Smyth and Mr. Gill and not for the sake of money) we then left.

Later that evening, Petrie completes his character sketch and defines starting-terms:

> I then looked over his testimonials, which he was anxious I should see; they speak of him in even higher terms than I had heard before; C.P.S., Dixon, Watson, and Gill, and another traveller who took him up the Nile, all agree in his great intelligence, scrupulous honesty and protection of his travellers from any imposition, and his gentlemanlyness and companionability. From my talk with him this evening over coffee, I can only say that his manners are those of a perfect nature's gentleman, and one feels that the same delicacy and politeness is due to him that one would use to any gentleman. I gave him 5 fr. as a starting baksh: we settled that I should join him about 6 ½ tomorrow, and see the things, off, then overtake them by donkey and get an hour or so to look over the tombs before they get there.

Defensive comments to his English Journal-readers suggest continuing surprise over the qualities of his host: 'I then came back home to supper, and had a chat as usual to Ali. We talk on astronomy, navigation, constitutional government, etc, in a fashion that would make anyone laugh' (23.12.1880). The scene might not have looked or sounded quite as Petrie describes or an English-reader receives, considering relative age and language of host and guest. According to the 1883 publication of the Giza survey, Ali Jabri was then about 46, Petrie nineteen years younger. With a report from one side only, the reader must decide if the laughter comes from, or is directed at, one, or both, during, or after. This learning did not extend to literacy, as a later episode reveals: 'Ali had not appeared while

I was getting up, so I could not tell him where I was gone, as he cannot read even a word of Arabic; in fact he does not know it from English when he sees it' (25.2.1881, Drower 2004: 26). However, at the end of the season, when Petrie begins to refer to Ali's son, it is clear that the next generation had different opportunities and attitudes; Petrie mentions obtaining in Cairo 'an Arabic-English alphabet for Abu Saud (who asked me for it on the way, and who seems anxious to pick up all he can)' and soon after he notes 'abu Saud reading over his alphabet again, which I gave him last night. Ali is rather against his acquiring such infidel knowledge' (1.4.1881).

In his description of the start to his new life, on the morning of 21.12.1880, Petrie reveals a detail on the village, that it had moved within the previous generation (Drower 2004: 14):

> We reached the Pyramid about 10; a lovely morning with delicate mare's tail sky, and the pyramids, one side warm with sunshine, the other grey blue with slight haze. I then looked over all the tombs available; the Arab village has been moved since C.P.S. was here, and his tomb is no longer to be had. Weyman Dixon's is however all ready to go into, Ali having the key and door and 2 windows perfect. So I decided to take that, at least for the first.

The 1882 census confirms this feature of settled life, with swift relocations of populations locally, from the ease of building and demolishing mud-brick houses; this internal mobility is used to explain a striking statistic that 12.9% of 1,084,384 buildings recorded are uninhabited (Boinet 1882: Section 5, xii-xiii). However, in the case of Giza, the move of the village could reflect a local impact of archaeology. Under Mariette, the Antiquities Service conducted excavations in the area and a village built around rock-cut tombs might have been considered an obstacle and a threat; in modernising, preservation may be given precedence over the local living, as with Qurna village in Upper Egypt during the twentieth and twenty-first centuries (Gamblin 2004). The formally pre-colonial and post-colonial histories of Pyramid and Qurna villages exemplify the complications that arise when the past has been excised from the present, or vice versa. These villagers are not passive or innocent, as the patronising sentimentalist view of the Romantics might imply, but history reveals how vulnerable their lives are to national and global forces.

The arrival of Petrie on the Giza pyramid plateau can readily be consumed as an adventure in European exploration of unknown lands, but the Journals reveal more thickly than the 1883 book how he enters not a human desert but a web of pre-existing social networks, including the commerce in supplying antiquities to outsiders. After a month of Giza life, Petrie records details of that social network, struck by its distinction from kinship ties, and unknown to any 'Frank', the Arabic *frangi* denoting any European:

Ali explained the regulations of the community. Any traveller paying the regular fees to the shekh (or anything the shekh may get from me publicly) the money is divided, ¼ to the shekhs, and the rest equally among all the Arabs. Then, if by pestering, the guides can get extra bakhsheesh, that is divided among the guides 'family'; not family of relationship, but family of guides, they forming brotherhoods of about 4 each, who equally divide the surplus spoils which any of them get. And a social regulation is that the guides to a party must be taken out of different 'families', or comradeships, so that extra bakhsheesh may not fall too much into one party's hands. This is all far more complex and communistic than I had imagined; I rather think hardly any Frank knows of it; I know the Grants, who know more than most people, are quite in the dark about it. (13.2.1881, Drower 2004: 25)

Petrie moved very literally into the midst of this trade: 'One of the three conjoined tombs is but small, and is full of antiquities of Ali's, but I stuck my jars in there for lack of room elsewhere, and a skull of some old Egyptian gazes at me from behind them as I stand in my other two tombs' (23.12.1880). The trades of Giza include, then, that of antiquities-seller, in a tradition echoing, but not necessarily directly descended from, the medieval guild of the *mutalibin*, the Seekers who unearthed tombs and monuments for their treasure (El Daly 2005). These medieval seekers may turn out to be looters after economic gain, as they must seem in the eyes of archaeologists in rich countries today, but their quest would be worth exploring from their own words, if they can be found. The reflex of the university discipline would probably be to identify the Seekers as ancestors of the modern, appallingly and increasingly destructive antiquities trade, rather than of archaeology, but this assumption needs checking by medievalists, particularly within the reflective plane of Islam as a religion enjoining a quest for knowledge (El Daly 2000).

A further complication in the traditionally pure genealogy of archaeology is the direct and enthusiastic involvement of its heroes in the antiquities trade. In his second autobiography, *Seventy Years in Archaeology*, Petrie himself placed the start of his life in archaeology as an eight-year-old fascinated by coins, developing into a coin-collector selling to the numismatics department of the British Museum (Petrie 1931: 9). These practices form a bond of interest between Petrie and Ali Jabri at the start of their work together:

I overhauled a batch of coins of Ali's this evening; they were all Imperial Alexandrian, a lot of Nero, and the bulk of Probus, some Aurelian and Diocletian, and two of Tacitus whom I have not got. He is accustomed to get fearful prices for them; ½ or ¼ franc, for what would sell for 1d to ½ d in London. (24.12.1880)

After breakfast (during which I sorted over many hundreds of Alexandrian coins of Ali's without finding one prize) .... (25.12.1880)

At breakfast Ali brought in a lot (101 he said) of Ptolemy, only two types, and nearly all large. He wanted 1 ½ fr. for large and ½ fr. for small, or 7 ½ d each for whole lot. I offered 10/- for the pick dozen, as I think they are worth more; but I would not go in for all; he talked of them as belonging to a mysterious 3rd party, whom I was quite willing to believe in, whether he existed or no as it allowed me to say they were very dear more freely: but he left them so decidedly, that I have no doubt the 3rd party will acquiesce; probably my offer was only just over his price, so that Ali will have no guilt on the transaction. They are very fine. (6.1.1881)

When Petrie begins to survey, with limited excavation to clarify points for the survey, he seems dependent on the knowledge and the resources of Ali and others in the neighbourhood. He cites Ali as witness to the rarity of his early finds, and names him a finder of specific items of significance:

Beyond sundry basalt hammers and an old whetstone, my main haul was a bottom corner casing stone [sketch] from one of the little pyramids in black basalt, a substance hitherto unknown I believe in casing, and Ali had never seen such before. The angles are close to 52°, and there seems no doubt on the matter. Ali brought in a big top corner of a casing stone 7 ins & 9 ins long from the angle, a large bottom corner of about 8 and 6 ins on the faces he secured also this morning. (2.2.1881)

Two other local notables seem to assist him in proceeding with the work:

So on going out I interviewed Shekh Abu Talib (the one who was impudent to Ali before) and Shekh Ibrahim also joined up immediately. ... Abu Talib was remarkably subdued and polite and scarcely smiled, Ibrahim on the other hand tried to take the matter up by shaking hands, and assenting to everything I said. (3.2.1881)

A few other Pyramid villagers are introduced by name into the Petrie narrative, mainly in relation to the purchase or inspection of antiquities:

I saw Smyne who showed me his testimonials, and wanted to know if I required a cook; also an old sheikh Omar about whom Ali shakes his head; he has some testimonials, but he is of no authority here, and only hovers about to deal in antiquities, both genuine and largely otherwise. (21.12.1880: in the 11.5.1881 journal, Smyne appears again, more clearly in relation to antiquities purchases, and identified as 'brother' of Ali Jabri)

Ali's brother, Abdurrahman, the chief of the village guards, brought up all his remainders of the stock of antiquities. (17.5.1881)

One more prominent individual in the first season Journals is initially identified by race as 'the negro' (22.12.1880, Drower 2004: 16), but soon after by name as Mohammed (25.12.1880), and is variously called 'servant' (21.12.1880, Drower 2004: 15) and 'slave' (22.12.1880, Drower 2004: 16) of

Ali Jabri. The exact character and legal status of this domestic servitude cannot be determined from these records. Gabriel Baer states in his summary of social relations that only bedouin had juridically enslaved workers down to the mid-nineteenth-century, when, for two generations, the largest estates of landowners used enslaved Egyptian farmers, usually related to the ruling family (Baer 1982: 243). The category of agricultural enslavement that blighted modernising Egypt in the mid-nineteenth century seems closer to the colonial evils in Europe and the Americas than the domestic servant, without excusing the latter form of servitude. At his first appearance, Muhammad seems to have the role of a childhood companion for the son of Ali Jabri, though the age of neither is estimated: 'Then after supper on ship biscuit eggs and chocolate, during which Ali's son and negro servant came in and I gave them a taste of the biscuit, the hardness of which amused them (all with the view of shewing them that I had not luxuries and expensive things) Ali bid me good night leaving his negro to sleep inside the tomb door as a night guard, and I now hear the said fellow fast asleep breathing most curiously hard and quick (32 per minute) about double my rate.' Petrie gives brief notes on the language and appearance of Muhammad: 'at 6 ½ was woke up by Ali's slave calling on the "khawagha" (sounded "khkaghka") to get up, and on looking out from my curtain his negro face gave a broadly smiling salute; he belongs to the tribes who slash their faces, and has three orthodox furrows in each cheek. … The negro and a nephew (?) of Ali's sleep together in the next tomb, with only a thin rock between.' Petrie did not share their taste in music: 'Mohammed and his friends had a musical evening last night, which I was obliged to stop at last at 11.0; 3 fearful reeds screeching Arab monotonous drones for over half an hour' (7.3.1881).

At the end of his first week, Petrie raised the question of payment to Muhammad: 'At breakfast paid Ali his weekly £1, and asked him about Bakksheesh to Mahommed the negro, who always sleeps as nightguard, and goes to Cairo if wanted and does odd jobs, fetching water, etc.; as he is Ali's slave, of course as Ali said, if you give him nothing he has nothing to say about it; but still Ali thought 4/- a week would be fair to him under the circumstances, as all he does is extra work' (27.12.1880). A little later, Petrie says that he has found out that the money was being taken by Ali (17.1.1881), to Petrie an example of infamy, to Ali perhaps a score in the game of negotiating with the foreigner or the wealthier.

In the second season at Giza, Petrie refers by name only to Ali Jabri, and, on one occasion of clearance work, to three others (20.10.1881, Drower 2004: 36): 'Ali had got six on the work, a man to dig and a chain of five to pass the baskets up the passage, among whom were Abu Saud, Muhammed, the negro, and little Muhammed; so it is almost a family affair.' On Ali, Petrie mentions two more points in passing:

N.B. This is not Africa, by native reckoning; Ali talks of going to and coming from Africa, as from Europe or other foreign countries. (5.12.1881)

Ellis and Ali both so sleepy that they could hardly work, but I did all the readings, and took care against mistakes. (9.4.1881)

The first displays a rather modern and defensive interest in the relation between continental geography and identity. More research on the Arabic of the Najama at Giza would be needed to determine whether Ali was in fact talking of Tunisia as Ifriqiyya. The second validates results against the lower standards of work by one European and one Egyptian co-worker, much as Petrie affirms the reliability of his results at Naqada in the 1896 publication. In defending himself on this point, Petrie raises the suspicion that Ellis and Ali would also take readings, when less sleepy. Petrie has stated that Ali is illiterate, but he might not be innumerate or unable to mark off readings. At the very beginning of the division of skilled from unskilled archaeological labour, the claim of illiteracy also obscures a strategic choice, not to employ a reader – or rather, in the case of local young reading-enthusiast Abu Saud, to employ them only for manual labour and not to train them in the two skills that Petrie was adding to his archaeology, surveying and recording.

Egyptians know more
Outward bound in October 1881 for his second season, Petrie recorded an encounter that points to a history that might have been, with European employed by Egyptian, though not in archaeology. Petrie is in the company of a certain Colonel Haigh:

Shewed him the rough plan I had of the P. triangulation; and an Arabic gentleman whom I had just spoken to before stepped over and asked to look at it to my great surprise. A passenger to whom he was talking then called me to explain some points; and I found the Arab knew all about it; still more surprising. At last it came out he was Mahmoud Issy (the Egyptian Astronomer) and he ended by saying they were going to reorganise their astral survey, and wanted surveyors accustomed to triangulation, and he wished to know what salary I should require. This was as Frankie D. says, 'quite sudden and unexpected', so I replied it would probably be best if I was to assist for a month or so, and for me to see what they wanted. This he approved of; so we exchanged cards, and I suppose before we land I shall make some definite arrangement as to doing some trial work. (8.10.1881)

Nothing came of the arrangement, as they did not find time to discuss the idea further (13.10.1881). However, the episode indicates how the pieces that formed European archaeology were in place without Europeans at the start of 'scientific archaeology' in the Nile valley. A survey was evidently not an unthinkable prospect either to an Alexandrian customs official in 1880 or to pre-occupation Egyptian government officials in 1881. At the same time, the immediate inhabitants of the archaeological landscapes included people who knew the sites and the material emerging from them, and some of whose children were learning to read and write in Arabic and in European script and language. This does not change the course of history, that the elements did not gell before an Englishman Petrie organised the survey at Giza, and, the essential point in his breakthrough, published the results. Yet, the existence of the elements within Egypt has been overlooked in the telling of that story in archaeology. Even the determining feature in the Petrie storyline, the publication, was by then at home in Cairo. In the same quarter as the Egyptian Museum, at Boulaq, the government had its own printing-press, where the May 1882 census would be published in one French and one Arabic volume in 1884, two years after the catastrophe of English bombardment of Alexandria and occupation of Egypt.

Phase II. Nile Delta excavations for the Egypt Exploration Fund, 1883-1886

Summary of names

Names in publications: Petrie 1888: three 'brothers' Mahajub, Said, Muhammed abu Daud el Gabri, their cousin Tulbeh.

Additional names in Journals 1883-1886 (in order of appearance): Ali Gabri, Ibrahim, Khallil, Abd el Halim, Mursi (1883-1884), Khalifa, three Abd el Wahab 'brothers' (Suleiman, Sueilim, Salim), Yusif Salim, Wusif Salim, Medallallah, reis Muhammed, Abd er Rahim, Abu Saud, Said abu Daud, Abd es Salam Abdallah, antiquities-seller Suleiman, Agub Pasha, Muhammad Berish, Suleiman Khatab, Abdullah Saidi, Auad Umad, Mukhtar Ali, sheikh Muhammad Jabri, Midani, Mursi (1885-6), antiquities-seller Yusuf.

With Ali Jabri to Nile Delta margins

Petrie arrived in November 1883 in occupied Egypt to excavate for the Egypt Exploration Fund in the Delta. The greatest concentration of monuments lay at San al-Hagar (ancient Egyptian Djanet, Greek Tanis); there, the Antiquities Service under Mariette had continued clearance work and sculpture-removal that had started in the 1820s by agents of Bernardino Drovetti, representative of France at the court of Muhammad Ali. In the 1880s, archaeology still operated within the Mariette map of sites with monumental architecture, and so it was natural for Delta work to mean work at San. Maspero seems to have considered Petrie an extension of the Antiquities Service, and asked him to wait for his return to Cairo for official permission to work. As soon as this was done, Petrie went to recruit help from his Egyptian 'friends' (1.1.1884): 'Off to the Pyramids to see Ali and settle matters. Saw all my old friends there, and had a long talk with Ali. When I asked him whether he would go with me as I had proposed to him he replied, "Well, I not go for money, but if you want me go, I go; I know you, I not care to go for any man, but I know you take care for me, and I take care for you. Yes, when you wanting me I go to you". Such was our agreement …'. The reserve in Ali's tone seems echoed in the lack of success in securing other assistants, despite initial promises from an Ibrahim and a Khallil: 'Coming back Khallil to my great disgust said that he would not go to San. I was quite reckoning on the boy, he was so intelligent and good, but San frightens him, and no persuasion that he should have full man's wages, live in a brick house, and be with Ali Gabri, would induce him to go. Little Abd el Halim I also lost, because his father was just going up the Nile, reis of a boat, and took him; so I am left without anyone but Ali.' Ibrahim, Khallil and Abd el Halim do not reappear identifiably in these records.

At San al-Hagar, Petrie found Ali Jabri an indispensable ally in the removal of opposition from local sheikhs to the work conditions and terms:

> One of the shekhs was up here talking to Ali today, saying that I should pay more than 2 ½ piastres. Ali replied: 'Why you should see the lots of people that are here in the morning, from other places, all waiting for work, and willing to go for 2 piastres rather than leave here.' 'Then' said the Shekh, 'I shall not let those people from other places stop in the village'. 'No matter', replied Ali, 'we shall build a big house up in the temple for all the other people, and have so many of them.' So the shekh shut up, finding that his interference would only make matters worse for his friends. I enjoy having got him at my mercy, in this way; the people are quiet enough themselves, and I have too many strangers here now for any row to be made about it. (11.2.1884)

The local objections to the intrusive new methods did not subside at once, and Ali remained the source of information for Petrie:

> Ali has heard more of the backhanded doings of the village. The shekhs tried to stop the people from working, because they did not get the money through their hands; but the people are so glad to get regular pay without any deduction that they say they intend to work, shekhs or no shekhs, as long as there is pay to be had. The Mamur (who was so friendly up here) told the shekhs that they should all desert the village, and leave me without men; of course hoping that I should need to appeal to the authorities at Zagazig, and give them bakhsish to restore order. But as the shekhs know that would only result in my having a colony of new men from the surrounding country, they don't cut their noses off to spite their faces. One of the shekhs grumbling to Ali about the money not going through their hands, he plainly said: 'I'm nearer him than anyone else, and yet he never lets me do with the money or say who's work.' In fact, I have the two ends of the chain; the people themselves, who, so long as they are paid regularly, defy anything short of open violence to stop them; and at the other end the European authority of Cairo, before which no one can oppose me only. Hence all the spongy links between find that they cannot absorb as usual. (13.3.1884)

Ali complicated the picture by his role in the antiquities trade, as Petrie noted at the most remarkable find of this season, a Roman Period building with an extraordinary range of material, one of the most important assemblages of that date found in Egypt:

> There is about 50/- worth, according to London sale value; I give about 8 per cent of such value, and nearly squabble about it with Ali, who insists that about 4 per cent is plenty. I reply that it is not a matter of money more or less, but of doing whatever will best secure getting the things, and preventing dealing elsewhere. I rather think there is a little professional feeling in this, as he fears I shall raise the market in one of the favourite hunting-grounds of the petty dealers, or as he says 'all spoil business if you do like that'. If I can but get a name in the neighbourhood for giving rather more than they are accustomed to get from other people it will be worth anything to me, and I shall be sure to get all that is found. (20.3.1884)

The antiquities trade gave Ali strong local interests even so far from the pyramids, and he turned out to have personal connections: 'Two men that Ali knows have turned up here, one from Gizeh direct, the other a Gizeh man settled near here, and addicted to <u>antika</u> hunting. This increased our party to 6 men in all' (15.2.1884). Evidently Ali had not been the only one to leave Giza, and Petrie words his team as follows a week later: 'Happily, beside Ali, Muhammed and Mursi, an old reis of Mariette's has turned up and a son of another; both are from Gizeh but settled near here after the work, and have spent the last 25 years in plundering the district of antikas, so I hope to get a lot of information about sites when I can move about across country in the dry weather. The nephew is my messenger to Fakus as he lives between here and there' (22.2.1884). In his description of the old reis in the same Journal, Petrie reveals his understanding of the continuity and rupture between archaeology under Mariette and his own new methods, and enacts the colonial combination of claiming to end violence and retaining it in practice:

> The old reis is a fine figure, with a commanding voice; always with a large black wrapper over his head, and falling down around him; wearing a pair of huge black goggles, which with a nose and a grey beard are all that I have seen between the edges of his overall wrap; he always, sitting, or standing, or walking, carries a long stick bolt upright, ready to smite the wicked. The people were scared at seeing him come up to inspect, as they remembered his former doings under Mariette, but Ali assured them that he would not be allowed to go on in that way now. One man that was refractory about carrying a big stone from work for my house, he gave a fearful whack to the other night, and Ali had to come in as moderator. It is very well to have such a man here, he will serve as a ferocious sheep-dog, who would bite if he dared; the Arabs will appreciate mild treatment all the more, and I can let him exercise himself if occasion requires. He cannot do harm so long as engagement, dismissal, & the money-bag, are all in my hands, and any one can complain to me at once. I mainly want him for the sake of knowing

exactly where things were found, and what ground has been worked; and he may easily double my results in this way.

Although Petrie is not specific, this is presumably the 'old reis Muhammed' named five weeks later (2.4.1884). Similarly, the nephew at Fakus is named almost in passing: 'Tomorrow Khalifa when he takes this to Fakus is to hunt for another' (22.2.1884).

Petrie distinguishes between his own 'mild' exercise of authority and the harsh practices he found in Egypt, noting 'the idea of the rights of an inferior seems nowhere' even for Ali, 'a favourable specimen of an Arab' (15.3.1884, Drower 2004: 55-6). However, his account in that journal of the exchanges between supervisors and supervised exposes the dangers of reading at face value with a presumption of despotism. Here local reality turns out to be a matter of negotiation, not entirely serious on either side:

> Khalifa, who is the most energetic driver that I have, has given the tone to the working, which is copied by Muhammed and Mursi; all day the trenches echo to the shouts of 'Ya ibn el kelb! Ishtaghal Istaghal, ya bint! Hawafi, ya shekh, hawafi! Ent ze hamir!' ('Oh, son of a dog! Work, work, oh daughter! Gooday, oh shekh, good day! You are like donkeys!' This *hawafi* is new to me; Ali says it is 'goodday', but he cannot explain the particular value of such a remark, and it seems to be equal to 'I've got my eye on you'). To all of which the reply contentedly, and even cheerfully, is 'Hader, ya sidi hader.' ('Ready, oh my lord, ready'). What a realization this is of the old words in the tomb of Ti to the workmen: 'You are like apes', and their reply: 'Your order is executed, the work is well done.' (15.3.1884, Drower 2004: 52)

In his naming practice, Petrie rarely moves beyond the immediate circle of his supervisors to the two hundred men, boys and girls in the workforce, and then usually only to illustrate general procedure rather than to introduce an individual, as in his account of pay-day in the 22.2.1884 Journal:

> I begin to learn their names tolerably, particularly if they are distinctive; but what with Hassanen Ali, Ali Ibrahim, Ibrahim Muhammed, Muhammed Hassan, Ali Hassan, Ibrahim Ali, Ali Muhammed, etc, etc, etc it is rather puzzling; and such distinctions as Riani, Dafani, Shergawi, Adib, and Gandur are refreshing changes. They regard the weekly payment as a sort of sign of respectability and 'nahar es sebt' – seventh day – is generally added on by the children to their names 'Muhammed Hassan Dahabieh nahar es sebt andak' is run out all in a string (andak = 'you have it' = it is booked so) and one says proudly to another 'ana maktoub' – I am written.

Here he also gives a rare quotation from Ali Jabri, on asking about a girl with the name of a man:

> Among the boys one girl came and gave name as Muhammed Hassan. So I asked Ali how it was a girl had such a name. 'Oh they think you not take a

girl for work, so that call her father's name'; 'Did they think I could not see it was a girl' I asked. 'Oh time Mariette work here, so many girl, they dress in white, and send work for boys'. (mem. girls and women wear dark blue, and boys and men white & brown).

Petrie has an ethnographic eye in attention to local custom, following the model of Lane in the paths of orientalism (Said 1978). More in the tradition that would be called physical anthropology, he records unusual appearances among some new recruits:

> The new boys that have come are a wild-looking lot, creatures of an undecipherable sort of age, lean and scraggy, with long lank black locks hanging from their half-shaved heads. The Sanites are thought to be wild, but they seem highly respectable citizens beside these beings, who come from I-don't-know-where. Their very names seem barbarous, three brothers are Suleiman abd el Wahab, Sueilim abd el Wahab, and Salim abd el Wahab; the two others Yusif Salim and Wusif Salim. (24.3.1884)

The only more personal reference concerns a sick girl, of whom no more is heard in later reports: 'Another child ill today: little Medallalah, a fragile-looking girl who always reminds me of Mabel Vivian' (2.4.1884).

Supervisors

Supervisor violence seems to present Petrie with a dilemma, to judge from his comments on an incident where one Abd er Rahim beats one of the boys: 'It is rather a pity to have to weaken the authority of the reises in this way; but it has the counter-advantage of removing the people further from collusion with the reises, and making them more at one with myself' (27.5.1884). Petrie had less qualms in settling other difficulties with supervisors, starting with Mursi:

> Mursi I have sent away; he has been rather careless and troublesome; used to stay out half the night at fantasias with the villagers, and made rather too free a use of Ali's property. Besides this, the young gosling was fascinated with a widow down in the village, to Ali's great disgust; and unbidden, and unwished for, his father had turned up, a helpless old fellow, loafing about the place, whom I knew, sooner or later, I should be plagued to take on for work. So I cut the whole affair short by calling Mursi in the evening before he should have his week's pay, handing him the money, telling him I should not want him any further, and that I gave him the following day to disappear in. And he disappeared accordingly. Ali knew a few days before that I was intending to do this, and had apparently imparted the news to Khalifa, for just the evening I dismissed Mursi, Khalifa's son turned up: a good-sized strong boy, whom I was glad to take on for basket-carrying. I am in need of boys and girls at present. (27.3.1884)

According to the 27.5.1884 Journal, Petrie finds Khalifa taking money from workers, and discovers that a brother of reis Muhammed is 'a regular dealer': 'This looks a very bad case, one for ordering him off under threat of police'. He closes the Journal, at the end of the first season at Tanis, on a negative note: 'I have dismissed old reis Muhammed and Khalifa, without any bakhshish, beyond a couple of days to the end of a week.'

In the second and third Delta seasons, Petrie refers by name only to the supervisors in his workforce, and his cook, on-site competitors and a dealer. Recruiting supervisors for Delta sites was less difficult second time round, perhaps partly from the closer location, as Petrie moved between northeast and southwest Delta. However, now past 50, Ali Jabri evidently had better things to do:

> He suggests that I could have two elder brothers of Muhammed; and as he did not wish to leave home at present, Abu Saud his son would go also. This is just the sowing time when the land has to be attended to, and so he wishes to stop and look after his crops now; but probably he will go later on with me when I go to the San district. Next day Ali came in to Cairo, and said that I could have Abu Saud, and Muhammed and his brothers; so I offered 4 piastres a day (10d) as before to Muhammed and the others, and double that to Abu Saud, considering that he can read and write Arabic. Of course I should not give the same as to Ali (21 piastres a day) as he has not any experience, and knows nothing of English or <u>antikas</u>. Two days later Muhammed came in to Cairo, saying that they were all coming on those terms. He seemed delighted to come again with me. My staff will now be Abu Saud, Muhammed abu Daud, Said abu Daud, and Abd es Salam Abdullah. None of them know more than a stray word or two of English so if any insurmountable difficulties should turn up I shall march all parties to Tel Barud station and get the station master to settle them, as he speaks very good English. ... If I want another element in the business I shall get Ibrahim, the donkey man that I took on the boat last year. (24.11.1884)

The reader of this Journal learns that archaeology is an optional side-line for Ali Jabri, who has fields and herds (a preceding sentence reports a theft of seven of his goats). The other Giza men provide all necessary skills for an expedition, including literacy in the case of Abu Saud. Petrie is not the only one to appreciate his reading and writing, for the Antiquities Service acknowledges the Giza writer with a formal position on the expedition: 'The letter from the Museum that I shew as credentials has Abu Saud's name in it, as the man appointed by Maspero to represent him' (24.11.1884). When he met them again, Petrie recalled all during the Giza survey: 'Ali came up to Cairo with the party. Said abu Daud is a man I knew well and liked at Gizeh, and Abd es Salam I also remember there. Abu Saud and Muhammed abu Daud are of course old friends' (4.12.1884). The few other references to them demonstrate knowledge of sites and ties of kinship to the Giza antiquities trade:

> Said abu Daud tells me that he has seen in the village a stone inscribed on three sides. (4.12.1884)

Abd es Salam capped it all by saying that a headless statue which I bought of (his cousin) Suleiman at Cairo came from there. This greatly increases its value to me, and above all, this figure has three long inscriptions upon it, mentioning that the man, Psamtik-seneb, had built the temple of Neit which had fallen into disrepair [referring to site Tell Afrin]. (31.1.1885)

I have had a talk with Abd es Salam, and find he knows all the unknown land south of Mareotis. I should much like if possible to go over it with him, & see a dozen unknown Kums. (3.3.1885)

For the third season, Ali Jabri again declined to join the expedition, and Abu Saud and Abd es Salam disappear from the record, to be replaced by two new assistants:

Out to Pyramids. Met Ali, riding in to Cairo, and he turned and went back with us. I engaged Said and Muhammed, at rather higher wages than before; I was quite intending to raise them, in one way or another, and as they both asked for it, I gave it at once, 1½ francs a day. Also Tulba, a younger brother of Muhammed, a nice boy, who will I think come up well; and Mahajub, an elder brother of Said's, if he will come. (8.12.1885)

A month later, on the way to a new site back in the northeastern Delta, a new supervisor appears, on an occasion when Petrie left Giza men entirely in charge:

I sighted Tell Nebesheh, about 3 miles in from the canal; so went back to the boat, took out my things, left the new man, Midani, and Tulbeh in charge of them, (£100 of cash in my bag no one knew of) by the side of this canal in the wildnerness, and went off with Muhammed to the Tell, to get camels. (16.1.1886)

Another name slips in a day later: 'Mursi goes on very well, and is a good hand I think' (17.1.1886). This seems to be someone new, not the Mursi dismissed in 1885.

Despite continued reliance on Giza supervisors, the second and third seasons saw one innovation that transformed the internal relations of the expedition, and the possibilities for the future. In 1884-1885, Petrie was joined by another foreigner, Francis Llewellyn Griffith, an Oxford student teaching himself Egyptian language and hieroglyphs in the absence of anyone to teach him (Drower 1985: 85). One of the most brilliant philologists in English-language Egyptology, Griffith later became Professor at Oxford. When this young Welshman was starting his career, England and Wales offered no more formal opportunity for learning than Egypt, where a short-lived government school for training Egyptian students in ancient Egyptian language had closed even before the occupation (Reid 2002: 116-18). However, certain structures to the advantage of the European university student were already in place. Histories and grammars of ancient Egypt had been written in English, French, German and Italian, published in Europe though circulating to libraries in Egypt. Moreover, by the end of 1884 the now entrenched military occupation itself assigned dominance in the production of knowledge to the occupier, by the psychological, material and financial terms of colonialism. The paths of Abu Saud and Francis Llewellyn Griffith cross briefly with no evident reflection in 1885. Within a year, Griffith and Petrie have a third European as helper, another Oxford student of classical archaeology, Ernest Gardner. In the publications after 1886, the named Petrie co-workers are to be these foreigners in training.

During phase II, the Giza supervisors are still more valuable than the English student, as Petrie implies when he moved to a new excavation, with Griffith ill, leaving the Giza men in charge: 'I was loth to leave him, and go to Defenneh; however he had Mursi and Midani, and promised if he was any worse, to go up to Cairo; and as a number of men had dropped work, and were waiting to start with me, I went off' (22.3.1886).

Once, Petrie names the sheikh of the village nearest to the site, on a visit to establish good relations at the start of the excavating season: 'We went to market, and called on the shekh, Muhammed Jabri, in the afternoon' (14.12.1885). Similarly, the year before, he named a local notable Agub Pasha, though not in the text, but beside a sketch-plan of his house (11.12.1884).

A cook would be one key figure for the expedition, over the years more or less outside the digging work. In the second season, Petrie identifies a new cook by ethnicity as well as name: 'Engaged a cook, name <u>Auad Umad</u>, a Berber; he proves to be a clean and tidy man, does whatever he could be expected to do in our quarters, and never needs to be told anything about his work. I think he is a success' (7.12.1885). Ill within a fortnight, he provided his own replacement: 'Auad soon brought his substitute, – Mukhtar Ali – a Berber like himself' (23.12.1885).

Muhammad Baraysh and a horde of bronzes

Another three names crop up in the March 1885 Journals in connection with removal of finds on the site being excavated by the Petrie workforce. This episode shows loyalty to Petrie from his younger, closest supervisor, finally eclipsed in practice by networks involving clan loyalty and a longer history of living and trading together. In his version of events, Petrie first notes the arrival of unwanted competition: 'The Giza dealers have turned up, and my own Gizeh men are indignant, particularly little Muhammed … the people now know and trust me (so far so that all our accounts for small things are booked by me, and paid up, in lumps, as change is scarce) and they do not like the Gizeh dealers, in so much that one boy entreated me to bring out my scales and money to buy some silver "and come now, before the Gizehwiyeh come here" ' (2.3.1885). Here again is a rare instance of reported speech giving the words of a worker, albeit unnamed. Almost immediately, there is trouble:

> Now for a row. Market day there is no work as most of the people want to go to market; so some men who were about, and had been in my work, got into the pit where we had found some bronzes. There unluckily they hit on a large find and one of the Gizeh men Muhd Berish got wind of it, and taking all the best things escaped clear of the place. I only got to the spot just as they had all left. My Muhammed came just after me, and a man who had seen them gave me the names of several. Then we at once began chase. Going to the village we tackled man after man and insisted on having the things they had found. Two of the men who had been in our work brought out what they had at once, and a third when called for also came out to meet us with the spoil in his hands. At another house, the father of the boy in fault had already sold to me an hour before a lot for 5 francs near my house, and the elder brother rather insolently said he did not know where his brother was, he was not there; so as we stood rather foiled, and the crowd increasing, I suddenly caught the fellow by the shoulder shoved him inside the gate of the enclosure of his group of huts, and told him to go with me straight to the house and give me whatever he had. This surprised him, and he did as he was bid.

Once Petrie had recovered as much as he could, he called in local authorities: 'Then I sent word to the shekh that if Muhd Bareysh was still in the village he was to be arrested at once.' He finds that a companion of Muhammad Baraysh is Suleiman Khatab, and reports that 'old Italian or Albanian' in charge of local government property has caught another accomplice: 'The man gave his name as Abdullah Saidi from Saft nr. Gizeh' (9.3.1885). Moving up the scale, Petrie writes to Cairo, to the Antiquities Service authorities based at the Egyptian Museum, but there the *mudir* (in this context presumably the governor of Giza) opens another side of the story: 'I am very sorry to hear from Said, who returned from Gizeh, that the Mudir set Muhd Bareysh at large again, to <u>come and settle the matter</u> with me!' In 1885, despite official permit to work, the Museum seems to have seen less practical difference between two supplier of finds from a site, Muhammad Baraysh of Giza and Flinders Petrie of London. Petrie can now invoke colonial authority: 'I go to Cairo tomorrow to hunt out the case; happily we have English heads of police now, so it will be the worse for those who let him off'. When the Museum continues to obstruct a settlement in his favour, Petrie invokes the spectre of the feudal past under Mariette, and blames a personality, Emile Brugsch, deputy of Maspero:

> The general result of my Cairo business is very unsatisfactory. It seems that all the stringent measures of the Bulak Museum rest on private decrees and regulations of Mariette or others which cannot be enforced in law, and that consequently all the beatings, imprisonment, etc, were illegal and only to be covered by the despotic authority of the Khedive or his agents. Hence since

we have legalized the country to some extent, there is no power really left. Such at least is Brugsch's statement when pressed; he evidently wishes to avoid my taking active steps. (17.3.1885)

Petrie continues to trust in the power of the new order, although he begins to display some doubt, and transfer responsibility to others: 'I expect all the men will cave in when they really find themselves on the way to prison! (Mem. I do not quite know how I could <u>prove</u> that they should be imprisoned, only that a little detail which nobody seems to mind, and it is an affair of police and govt now, not of mine).' Then the final blow comes, a letter from Sheikh Omar at Giza, resolving the matter by the compromise of bringing the accused men to Giza. The exact manner of resolution is not recorded. Significantly, the medium for this local settlement is writing.

Petrie must have felt his prejudices about local justice confirmed, considering this a case of daylight robbery. For those in antiquities-selling networks, he had simply intruded into active landscapes of exploitation, and obligingly provided much of the labour for removing the earth in the way. Assessment from a twenty-first-century perspective is complicated by the stark difference in standards of recording, raised over the decades after the 1880s by people like Petrie himself. At the start of his career, exact find-place is recorded for a tiny minority of finds in any excavation, including those of Petrie; for him, as for few others at the time, the important innovation was more basically to note that items had been found together, establishing that they had entered the ground at one time and therefore probably together used, and often also made at the same date in ancient times. Only later did it become regular practice to mark findspots on a map, and, with growing precision in response to doubts over accuracy and new questions concerning excavated material, to draw positions of finds in relation to one another, horizontally and vertically, exactly as found. In general, in 1883-1886, and still on city sites to the end of Petrie's time in Egypt, there would have been no more exact museum information for a Petrie find than for a Muhammad Baraysh find. The great difference between them was the drawing of a plan, and the publication of plans and finds. This history places in rather different practical light the response of Emile Brugsch at the Museum, regardless of personality clashes.

Phase III. Between Egypt Exploration Fund and professorship, 1886-1892

Summary of names
Names in publications: Muhammed, overseer of fishermen M'haisin, Mekowi, Handawi.
Additional names in Journals 1886-1893 (in order of appearance): Said, Tulbeh, Mustafa Agha, Abd el Wahid, Omar, Murad Pasha, Ferhat Effendi, Hassan Effendi, Shaban, Farag, Latief Pasha, Abd er Rahim,

Ahmed, Ahmed Ali, Sidahmed, Ali (Gabri), Muhammed Mansur, Misid, Ali Suefi, Abdallah, Hussein, Girghis.

In 1886 Petrie broke with the Egypt Exploration Fund, but not with the men of Giza. The London committee exasperated him with delays in publication and lack of interest in small or mundane finds. He returned to Giza to recruit companions for a journey upriver, recording monuments in Upper Egypt as a private tourist. On the boat, with Griffith also accompanying him, Petrie may have shared more time with the men, and at all events seems to have found out more than he had in the divided dighouses:

> I have been much surprised to find how old our men are. Muhd whom I have always looked on as a boy is 24, and Tulbeh who seems far from full grown is 17; I should rather have put them down as 12 and 8 by comparison with English. Said is 30 and perhaps looks it. On the whole it seems as if they aged very slowly till about 25 or 30 to 35 or 40 and then look old quickly. A short mid-life, with long youth and old age seems the rule. Muhd is married this summer, about three months ago. (24.12.1886)

At Luxor he met Mustafa Agha, linked in with the supply of antiquities to foreigners. The only other Egyptian name recorded in the journal is Abd el-Wahid, mentioned with Muhammad and Tulbah on return to the north. At the Dahshur pyramids, south of Saqqara, Petrie obtained from Grébaut, Maspero's successor as director of the Antiquities Service, permission for small-scale excavation in the name of the service; Muhammad was named as the supervisor (rais) by the official order, but this came just as harvest was starting, and it proved impossible to recruit workers. Muhammad seemed nervous of Dahshur, but was prominent in discovery, finding the stone markers of an ancient road across the desert from the main Nile Valley to the Fayum towns.

By autumn 1887 Amelia Edwards and Petrie had found sponsors, enabling Petrie to resume larger-scale excavations (Drower 1985: 127-8). In his writings he presents these as his own work, but officially he was an agent of the Antiquities Service appointed by Grébaut and assigned Fayum governorate:

> He then gave me the reasons why he wished that I should take the Fayum; that he had no agency for working there, only an inspector of the district, the Arabs continually found things, and he wished to have someone to track up finds, and in short to organise and work matters out. Further he dangled the Labyrinth before me as a prize to work at, agreeing with my disbelief in Lepsius having found it. So he makes no reservations but hands over the whole district to me with good will. He then had two letters written and despatched to the Mudir and his inspector, in which he nominated me to work on his behalf as a direct agent of the museum, legally speaking, without needing any permission from the Ministry. This is no worse a position for me

than working under an agreement; and it has two advantages, not requiring any delay to pass the ministers, – and giving me the full legal powers of the department officially. (31.12.1887)

The arrangement would see some of the most spectacular and successful excavations in his career, uncovering the Roman Period panel portraits at Hawara cemetery, the Middle Kingdom town at al-Lahun, and the New Kingdom palace site at Ghurab. Relations with the Antiquities Service were never particularly smooth; Petrie names the dealer Farag on two occasions in order to attack Grébaut for allowing a dealer to clear sites in the Fayum area (24.10.1888; 2.11.1891). In 1891, Petrie accepts the not-too-immediate presence of an official from the Antiquities Service, as government inspector on his work, contrasting a previous inspector:

> Being now under a regular government agreement (instead of the mere verbal permissions of Grebaut) I am bound to have a 'surveillant' here. He came today, a quiet sort of old man, who will not give me much trouble I think. He was a guard at Sakkara: and he will stay at the hamlet about ¾ mile from here, and stroll up daily. So he will not be always on my back like the Turkish effendi. (17.1.1891)

This extract reveals that no written contract existed for his earlier work under Grébaut.

For supervisors in 1887, Petrie turned again to Giza, and found one person at least free to join: 'Muhammed came in on Monday, and as he has no other business, he will come with me again this year' (26.12.1887). He brought just one helper: 'Muhammed and his little cousin Omar (Tulbeh's younger brother) joined at the next station and we reached the Fayum at noon. Then leaving little Omar in charge of baggage, we went off to look over the Kom Faras and find a tenting place' (31.12.1887). Petrie himself had no other European co-worker this year. Muhammad is mentioned more often than any other person throughout 1888 and into the January of 1889, hard at work and at discovery to the end. For the initial work at Madinat al-Fayum and Biahmu they share the supervision of digging: 'As work goes Muhd. does all the main lot at the pylon, and I circulate and watch the outliers, and keep the pot boiling all round' (7.1.1888, Drower 2004: 67); 'We had settled that as the work at Biahmu would probably take not more than 6 or 8 days, it would be best for Muhd to go and live in the village, while I walked to and fro each day from my tent at Kom Fares to the work, about 4 miles. This would save the trouble of shifting tents and baggage, and yet M could see that the men kept full time when I was not there' (21.1.1888). At Hawara his close involvement in supervising and finding continued: 'Then just before sunset a boy came up announcing another mummy. Muhd went over, as I was busy, and in the dusk there came up a third portrait mummy to my quarters' (17.2.1888); 'But, beside this, I found Muhammed getting out a mummy with a stucco and gilt head and chest-piece' (3.3.1888; burial of Ammonaris). When Petrie doubts the antiquity of especially well-preserved tools, Muhammad confirms their authenticity: 'I could not believe them to be ancient until I considered the string and leather which certainly belonged to them, and Muhd assured me that the forms were not quite like the modern tools' (17.2.1888). At the end of the first Fayum season, when Petrie falls ill, Muhammad takes charge: 'I had to hand out £14 to Muhd to distribute judiciously on account, as it was pay day' (15.4.1888).

Most startling of all, Petrie lets slip that Muhammad can provide plans: 'Next day we got down into the chamber of a great tomb well. I did not go down as there were no foot holes and I rather distrusted being lowered by ropes; as it was only Ptolemaic and all under water I did not think it worth while. Muhd raked over the place, and gave me a plan of it all when he came up' (3.3.1888). As Petrie himself emphasised, planning finds can be considered the dividing line between plunder and science. If not only Mahmoud Issa and the engineering expert at Alexandria customs in 1880-1, but also Muhammad abu Daud at Giza can give a plan, even in words, the monopoly of the foreigner on archaeology fails.

For part of the second Fayum season, Petrie had the company of a resident foreigner, Maurice Amos, and during this stay Petrie finds out from a finder of burials with a large group of amulets that Muhammad has been taking a share of the wages from the workers:

And now for an unpleasant surprise. The lucky finder of all the things, asked in a timid way if it was the rule that Muhammed must have ¼ of his baksheesh. Then it came out that M. has been always compelling these poor fellows to hand to him ¼ of all the baksheesh they have received from me for things last year and this. They thought it such a natural sort of proceeding that they never thought he could be dismissed for it, so they had always given it for fear of his threat of having them turned out. It is very abominable of him, especially after his continual pious comments and moral reflections that he used to indulge in. At the same time one must not view it like a theft or such offence; it is no crime in Arab morality, and I must not forget the really good service that he has done. I held an enquiry, as soon as Maurice returned, summoning up, one-by-one, half a dozen of the best men, and questioning them in detail. They all agree that M. never tried to get the antiquities, but only to take a share of the money. This was inexcusable as I gave him a large baksheesh in a lump for himself beside good pay. I am perfectly certain that this is not a conspiracy to oust him, as I have overheard the men talking in the pyramid, when they could not possibly know that I was there, and expressing surprise at my first statement that M. would have to go. Further I find that he has been over-charging for everything he bought; a clear fact, as an honest fellow here told me he would bring things much cheaper, and he has done so. My decision was to send over all the money due to Mohammed, with a message of dismissal, by Maurice, as that avoided the need of blowing M. up as I must have done if I saw him. He is about as honest as, and far more clever and capable than, anyone else in the business. So I may need to make use of him on some future occasion. I also sent over with

Maurice three men who had given up their money to Muhammed, and a list of all claims we could make out; and told them to go at Muhammed on their own account, and try to badger their money out of him as I was paying him up his legal dues and money he had deposited with me. The result was that he went off quietly, and cashed up 30 s., which unluckily he gave to Maurice as a sort of composition. I have divided it among 8 men who had given him most. Exit Muhammed. I do not care so much about it personally, as I had been cool toward him this year, being disgusted with the grasping way in which he always bothered for advance of wages. But it is a nuisance to be without him just now. (2.2.1889)

Drower has published a letter from Petrie to Francis Griffith, indicating in less personalised terms that Petrie had been ready to supervise on his own:

I am now without any reis, Muhammad being over at Illahun always, and I get on quite well without him. I shall not engage any fresh reis if I should give him up, but be my own reis in future. (22.12.1888, Drower 2004: 68)

Petrie did employ probably this Muhammad again on his 1890 foray into Palestine for the Palestine Exploration Fund (Drower 2004: 78-9), but the Hawara revelation removed Muhammad from the developing precision in documenting excavations in Egypt. In the end, as Petrie considered, a different attitude to work-pay brought to an end the period of eight years during which Petrie had depended on the Giza bedouin; when Ali Jabri visits Maydum as a tour-guide, he is mentioned, but briefly: 'Old Ali from Gizeh came over today as guide to the party' (7.3.1891). A door closed on the acknowledgement of Egyptian co-directors within the workforce, and on the participation of named Egyptians in the Petrie story of archaeology.

In 1889-90, Petrie had the help of a European, Hughes-Hughes, but in 1891-1892 for excavation in Middle Egypt, at Amarna, he filled the gap with recruits from his 1888-1890 Fayum workforce:

I have one fellow of about 25, tall, one-eyed and split-nosed, a worthy fellow who has distinguished himself by never once grumbling at his work, though it was some of the hardest at Medum. I value Muhd Mansur in spite of appearances. Then there is Misid a cheerful affectionate lad about 17, who has I think been drilled out of a little laziness he had. Ali Suefi is one of the meekest, most conscientiously obliging, lads I ever knew; he was not thought smart enough by Hewat, to whom I recommended him; but he kept him as long as there was work for him. I was very glad to get him again as he is a most devoted fellow. A strapping lad of about 20 is Abdallah, who has the advantage of reading and writing (as Misid also a little); and he has a good sturdy way of doing his business. With him is Hussein, his brother about 15, a most winning, lively little fellow, full of jokes and fun, whose laugh alone is worth his 7½ d. a day. Such are my special five, whom I thought worth bringing all the way with me, more willing or kindly fellows no one could find. No doubt they might be spoilt by a few months carelessness; and in such a case I consider 'Woe to the man by whom offences come.' (21.11.1891, Drower 2004: 81, except final sentence)

71

Of five Lahuni workers, then, two can read and write.

Workers

During this phase, Petrie mentions few workers by name. Two letters in a handwriting identifiably not his, but perhaps copying letters from him, name the boy looking after the house as Ahmed Ali, with the European nickname for him, Cherub (27.2.1889; 11.5.1889). By nickname he reappears two years later, at Maydum, together with an evidently important figure never otherwise mentioned: 'Cherub, alias Cupid, is here with me again; but to work, and not as guardian; as my best man – Sidahmed – has gone home this week, Cherry is sleeping in my day tent along with his work-mate' (12.1.1891). Petrie also names two of the three boys joining in the first entry into the burial chamber within the pyramid at Hawara (6.1.1889): 'Then the slender lad, Abdir Rahim, and his brother, and another lad Ahmed, all went on clearing out the hole leading N filled with rubbish'; and, following a fall of blocks, 'When they [the falling blocks] had settled I crawled over them and looking up saw the chamber open above; so I at once went up into it with Abder Rahim and Ahmed following'.

Governors and inspectors

Before starting the dig in 1887, Petrie went to meet the governor, a Turco-Circassian aristocrat praised by the colonial administrator Colin Scott-Moncrieff. In this meeting, the family connections of the Giza family come into focus:

> Muhd also had something to say as his grandfather was well known to this mudir. Murad Pasha – for such is this governor's name – is a fine-looking, elderly, man; by birth a Circassian, Sir Colin told me. He impressed me with his particular considerateness, absence of all ostentation, and quiet politeness. From the people through Muhd., – from Corbett who educated his son, – and from Sir Colin officially, – I hear the same tale. His rule is so just, and kindly, that everyone loves him; several times he has intended retiring, but is always stopped by a deputation of the inhabitants going to the Home Office and begging and praying that Murad and no other man shall govern them. Such is the happiness of this province at present. (31.12.1887)

Soon after, though, Murad managed to retire; Petrie does not mention the name of the new governor. Another local notable came to see Petrie the same day, displaying a knowledge of, and interest in, the past that Europeans assume is not present outside European learning:

> In the afternoon a great effendi called; he is one of the two great landowners of the Fayum next in importance to Murad himself. His name is Ferhat Effendi, and he owns all the cultivated land about the Kom, and lives in Medinet. He offered to show me all he knew of here, and trudged about, over the mounds, pointing out the various stones that were uncovered, and having some turned to show the inscriptions. He is an intelligent and good sort of

man; and it is well that I shall have him to deal with, if I want to cut into cultivated land, rather than a lot of little pig-headed cultivators. Both he and Murad are fine specimens of un-Europeanised men, neither of them speaking any European language.

Petrie is less certain of the modernising second successor to Murad:

There is a new mudir come to Medinet. The last successor of good Murad was quite incompetent; but they have got King Stork now in place of King Log. He is too grand for the common herd to see him; sits up in his private rooms, and only sees those who send in their names ... This stir-about's name is Latief Pasha, and very _latif_ he is (polite); he looks an intelligent man, speaks very good French Hewat says (though I talked to him in Arabic when I saw him), and takes some interest in things. He looked minutely over some of the chipped flints we had found, and enquired about them; and talked intelligently enough. He knew something about pyramid theories, and had evidently read some French works on various subjects. Altogether he seems a promising man, though I hardly think that anyone will like him much. New brooms scrub horribly. (18.11.1888)

During the 1887-1888 season, Petrie mentions two officials of the Antiquities Service to illustrate the bad and good extremes of the system still dominant. At first, though unnamed, the local inspector creates a favourable impression: 'The museum inspector here is a very civil lad, who does not look over 16 or 17, but may be 22 or 23 perhaps. He has been about two or three times, and really does not get in the way or make himself troublesome' (7.1.1888, Drower 2004: 67). However, at lunch with the irrigation official Hewat and the new governor, Petrie mentions his departure under enquiry: 'Nor had he, or Mr H, heard the report that Hassan Effendi the museum youth here has beaten a man to death over some antiquity business. Certainly Hassan has been summoned to Bulak and has not returned and a new man has come in his place' (29.1.1888). The new inspector turns out to be from the same village as Muhammad:

The museum inspector turned up today. The fellow I saw before is deposed, and a new one is come in his place, called Shaban. He belongs to the pyramid village, and Muhd knows him well and speaks very highly of him. He is a meek, honest-looking young fellow, and I liked him: so I shewed him everything freely, telling him that I did not want the Medineh folks to talk about it to the dealers. While he was here there came up the shekh of Tutun, some 10 miles off, with a letter from Sir Colin Moncrieff. The business was that the shekh had been carrying stone for a mosque; was stopped by the police; went and saw Sir C.M., who then wrote to ask if I knew aught of the stones, or if they need be preserved or were worthless. After a vast quantity of talk I escaped from having to spend a day going to see them (which I could not do with my work here) and fixed Shaban to go and inspect. It is his strict duty to do so; and I was only appealed to in case I happened to know the place already. (10.3.1888)

A week later, Petrie shows his trust in the new Antiquities Service official:

> Shaban Effendi the museum inspector came over from Medineh and spent some time. He is a very nice young fellow, and I make no secrets from him either as to finds or future work. He tells me that Illahun and Tell Gurob are both legally in the Fayum, and within any present order, so I shall only need to have a renewal next season for those. The Greeks in Medineh are mightily sore at hearing reports of my finds: to think that they have had such a site close to them so many years, and have not poached in it. Shaban will take good care so soon as I go to inspect here and Tell Gurob constantly, so as to prevent any surreptitious work. I am working out all I touch here so that whatever I leave behind will be undisturbed plain, and will shew any attempt at further work. (7.4.1888)

Phase IV. Egyptian Research Account and Egypt Exploration Fund, 1893-1905

Summary of names

Names in publications of work to 1904: Ali (Suefi), Muhammed Mohassib, Abd er-Rasul, Girgis, Umran Khallil.

Additional names in Journals 1893-1904 (in order of appearance): Hussein, Mahmud, Yusuf (brother of Ali Suefi), Fatima, Abul 'elah, Aweys, Mekowi, Mohammed cook, Yusuf (Qufti?), Hassan Osman, Hussein Osman, Hassan Sudani, Mohammed Sherqawi, Mohammed Derwish.

Names in Sinai publication Petrie 1906a: Salah Abu Risq, Khallyl Itkheyh, M'teyr, Abu Qudeyl, Selameh, sheikh Abu Ghaneym, Yusuf son of a sheikh.

Additional names in Petrie letters to Hilda 1904-5: Musy Nasir, Aly abd er Rahim, Ibrahim.

Marriage and changes in journal-writing

During this phase of his career, Petrie hands over journal-writing in part to his wife, and the system of circulating letters falls out of use, later Journals being more often personal letters, often from Petrie to Hilda. This accounts for major changes in tone, visually clearer in the manuscript original, where the neat, not always joined letters of Hilda offer a strong contrast to Petrie's often barely legible scrawl. In the remainder of this chapter, letters by Hilda are distinguished as such. Hilda was of the next generation, 26 years old at marriage in November 1897 to Professor Petrie, then 44. Some of her letters might be to her own circle, and constructed in different terms; Drower mentions her writing her account of arrival in Egypt 'to Beatrice Orme and others of her friends' (Drower 1985: 239). Later letters may have been more to Petrie's circle, as he refers to her writing (weeks starting 22.12.1897, Drower 2004: 127). Sometimes Hilda emphasises the picturesque, including in references to Egyptians: 'I wish I could paint Ali now while he works. His slim little figure is so active, and he looks so picturesque' (9.12.1900, Drower 2004: 163). However, she was more than an ornament on the excavation. A letter to Margaret Murray from Dandara in March 1898 ends with a sketch and the caption 'Ali and ½ doz. men are crossing the desert from the Black Mastaba, Beb's mastaba BB, or rather Merra's mastaba MRRA, to our huts, across the great IVth dyn. part of the cemetery', mixing the picturesque with exact historical data on ancient *mastaba* (block-platform) tomb-chapels and names of their ancient owners Beb and Mereri. Margaret Murray, teaching for Petrie in London, and Hilda Petrie were both formidable workers in the field.

Ali Suefi of al-Lahun

From the number of references in this and the next phase of the Petrie career, it is clear that Ali Suefi of the al-Lahun *fallahin* 'farmers' takes the place that had been held by Muhammad abu Daud of the Giza bedouin, as the Egyptian at the forefront of Petrie expeditions. The 1890s seasons regularly start with news of his recruitment or arrival (8.12.1893; 26.11.1895; 1.12.1896; 21.12.1897; 29.1.1898). Petrie praises him in a particularly emphatic character sketch:

> A telegram from Quibell at Luxor said that Ali was coming down by the Sunday train to Beni Mazar; so my plan of going up on Monday morn will do well. It will be a great pleasure to have him about me again; for I feel as if all must go well with such a faithful, quiet, unselfish right-hand to help. As far as character goes he is really more to me than almost any of my own race. Few men, I believe, have worked harder for me or trusted me more. Perhaps none are sorrier at parting, or gladder when we meet again. A curious link in life but a very real one, as character is at the bottom of it. Kipling's 'East and West' is the only expression of such a link that I know in black & white. (1.12.1896, Drower 2004: 95)

However, this same passage reveals the regularity also of using European deputies, and this, rather than 'quiet' character, seems to keep Ali farther from power than Muhammad abu Daud had been.

Ali is credited with more discoveries than other senior workers in the Journals for these years. He figured as the principal excavator at Naqada in the publication for the work in 1894-1895 (Petrie 1896b, see above, p. 43). In a Journal for 1894-1895, Ali, called 'my best lad' by Petrie, retrieves Foundation Deposits of the temple of Min and Isis at Qift/Koptos (12.1.1894). At Bahnasa, where Petrie did not develop the potential for archaeology of Islamic Period monuments, 'In the town Ali found out an old public bath of fine building, probably XVIth cent, much of it filled up with rubbish, but still having a brilliant inlaid pavement of coloured marbles in the hall' (16.12.1896). Later the same season, Petrie goes prospecting for sites with Ali in Middle Egypt (27.12.1896, Drower 2004: 104). There, Petrie does not mention the precise role of Ali on the expedition, but his prospecting talents were acknowledged up to thirty years later: Reginald Engelbach records that Ali Suefi identified the cemetery sites near al-Riqqa in 1912 (Engelbach 1915: 1), and Guy Brunton credited him with discovering sites in the Qau-Badari area where the oldest settlements in the Egyptian Nile Valley were found (Brunton 1927: 1). In a reconnaissance for the season at Hu and Abadiya, Ali made a surface find of marked pottery, which Petrie acknowledged in his way: 'Ali picked them up and I copied 55 of them, such as [sketch]' (27.2.1898).

Closeness to Petrie caused jealousy, as Petrie records at Abadiya near Hu in 1898:

> It so happened that there was a little breeze among them, for which this stoppage was opportune. They were on day work – not piece – and got rather lazy when the cemetery was nearly done. I stayed in one morning as I had re-sprained my ankle; Ali tried to stir them up as they were slack, and they resented it. One of the oldest who was rather at feud with Ali organised them, and ¾ of them all stopped work and marched up to the house to demand whether Ali was their master or me. I know he is too fervent, and likes spurring up folks, but yet they needed it. So I said they were under me, and he had nothing to do their work, and enquired why they had left it. Whereat they all trooped back again. The net result was that Ali was at once moved on, with those who remained at work, and put on to the one fat place I had waiting; the other men were put on to some stiff piece work without any bakhshish, the boys were split from them, and next day half the party were dismissed for a fortnight to await our moving to wider ground at Hou. I do not think they will fuss again. Luckily the circumstances all enabled me to make these changes with good reason, and it was only a matter of selection to show them what I thought of it. (23.12.1898)

In the version recorded by Hilda, the name of the rival leading workman is given, Hassan Osman (18.12.1898, Drower 2004: 149).

During the work at Araba, Ali left under circumstances at which Hilda only hints in a letter from their next site, Ihnasya, not far from al-Lahun: 'Aly Suefy came over the other day with Currelly: it was quite nice to see him again. He did not leave us in disgrace, three years ago, only from momentary foolishness and impracticable behaviour, so we have no reason against taking him on again' (15.1.1904, Drower 204: 167).

The problem might have been at home, as Petrie spends consciously longer on the family affairs of Ali Suefi than on many more archaeological matters. His father seems to have been one problem:

> At Beni Mazar I found Ali waiting and all our baggage ready, from Luxor, Alex. and Cairo. So we got camels for it, and then I went on quickly on donkey to see over Behnesa before the luggage should come; I took with me Mahmud, Ali's younger brother, whom I had as a small boy years ago. He is a good, observant, sweet-mannered lad, much like what Ali used to be; rather more lively, and with less of that strength of righteousness about him of his elder brother. I am very sorry to find that though Ali is so saving he has not the power of keeping money. Out of the fortune that he got last year from the

work, about £25, but little is left. His family sponged on him for pound after pound, not for necessity, but simply to get it out of him into stuff they could keep. After three months he went away south with what he had left; but even then he took not only his wife and baby, but a destitute little girl – a cousin – and his younger brother. I fear that he is too kind-hearted to hold his own. As he has an elder brother in good business there is no reason for him to be sponged on thus. (1.12.1896)

The problems continue to concern Petrie as well as Ali the next month:

Ali was much cast down at finding that his unscrupulous father had not only swallowed so much of his money, but had sold his donkey, and called in his loans, and refused to pay a piastre. The old man must be a miser, and not a spendthrift, as it was only three weeks ago he had thus raised £3, and his wife urged him he had to pay Ali. Finding that nothing could be done, I told him he had better take it out in boys, whose services from eight or ten years old are worth more than their keep. So Ali is to confiscate the share of Mahmud's earning which would have gone to the father; and he carried off with him little Yusuf, his youngest brother, a sweet slip of a boy, who had much better be with Ali than with the father, and who can earn 12s. or 15s. a month beyond his keep. I give these affairs of Ali's because it is hardly ever that the real working of a fellah's life comes before one of us so fully.

There then arose a dispute with his wife, as she left to stay with her brother. Presumably this is the same wife as mentioned in a Journal from the season at Luxor in 1895, in a description of the vaulted store-chambers of the Ramesseum in which the expedition camped: 'the third which is for our men from Koft; and the fourth, much broken, in which Ali wants to settle in his wife and baby from their village near Negadeh' (26.11.1895). This wording indicates that his wife is from Naqada, and so presumably met Ali at the season of work there the year before that.

In the Journal for 10.1.1897, following the departure of the still un-named wife, Petrie continues on Ali: 'The morning after this he was greatly cast down about the maintenance orders he might have made against him by the Qadi; and so after much dole he went off to Illahun to get first word, pay whatever was needful to square that judicial authority, and be quit of future claims … I beg my friends' pardon if I give too large a dose of Arab affairs, but it is very seldom that one can see so far into their minds; and nothing is more fascinating to me than getting inside the thoughts of another race of men.' The following week, the next turn in the story reveals her name, as Ali is reported to return with 'the penitent Fatima' (11.1.1897). Two months later, the issue re-opens with the return of Fatima's brother:

So I ordered A. and my soldier Mekowi to arrest him, but they were very half-hearted. A. in fact had slunk into the dining-room, and had left him in possession of the field. So I seized his <u>defieh</u> wrap and stick, worth a pound or two; and told them to take him to the Shekh. But they began more bland expostulations on the way. (9.3.1897)

Despite his best efforts, Petrie has to watch Fatima returning with the baby girl to her brother:

So it is evident that she prefers the rascally half-brother, who has just been two years in prison, to the virtuous and laborious – though somewhat faddy and exacting – youth, who should be her all.

Petrie advises Ali to be stronger, and he does decide to send her away. Mekowi offers to take Fatima back for Ali, and Ali tries to keep the child:

This is all dreadfully unarchaeological. But there is nothing going on but copying and packing; and as some folks seem to be interested in this study of human nature I give this continuation of it. It is scarcely ever that a fellah's mind can be known so intimately, so it is well to understand it, and see the total absence of motives which are the strongest in other races.

Concluding in a racist turn, Petrie reports: 'I must do Ali the justice to say that he was wheedled into having Fatima by his mother, contrary to all his inclinations, as he declared he would sooner have the blackest negress.' In consolation, 'We had Ali in to dinner, as all the other men were away, and he enjoyed himself.' Eventually the problems seem to have been resolved, as a letter from Hilda in November 1900 refers to an unnamed wife of Ali baking the bread in the second season at Araba. From the same season, a Margaret Murray photograph album shows both 'Um Mohammed' (Fatima presumably) and Sara 'Ali's 2nd wife' making bread (below, Chapter 9).

Despite all the distractions, Ali was hard at work through these seasons. From the first year, Petrie wrote:

Close by our temple enclosure Ali worked at a tomb of XVIII dyn, whence we got several slabs of inscriptions of a man Siast, chief priest here. Part had been carried off by Daressy, so doubtless the rest will be kept in Cairo. Next I put him on a large building not touched in modern times. It proves to be waste place filled with all kinds of mummies and scraps, and dead dogs, and beads, etc, etc, the clearing of the cemetery in Greek times. But probably of the original tomb there remained a fine group in granite of two high priests of Osiris, Mery and Unnefer, seated side by side. (18.1.1900)

Part of his work involved training, as Hilda reports from the second year at Araba, November 1900:

Ali is delightful as ever ... He is now in a full place in cemetery E where plenty of good XII-XVIII things are turning up, and is very useful in working with 4 gangs of men at once, and training new recruits from Quft. When the holiday was over, and our 130 men returned from Quft, we had 60 new workmen on, mostly brothers and friends of the old ones, as Mr Garstang is digging some good ground for the Egyptian Research Account, and needed plenty of men for XIIth dynasty pits. (Drower 2004: 160)

With skills in finding objects and sites, and in training workforce, Ali Suefi might also have made a foreign archaeologist begin to feel dispensable. However, by this stage, the excavation-director had established a new pattern of recruiting supervisors from England for training, and Ali Suefi did not meet the fate of Muhammad abu Daud.

Others in the workforce, placed and unplaced

Among the other Egyptians named in the Journals of this period, place of origin is clear only in one or two cases. One, the Mekowi who helped Ali Suefi in his domestic troubles, is also known from his earlier work in the Fayum seasons (Petrie 1891: v), and his home village at Madinat al-Fayum is named in the Notebooks (below, p. 135). In a rare intrusion of political history into these sources, Petrie notes that Mekowi had in the interim served in the Anglo-Egyptian campaign to colonise Sudan:

My old worker Mekowi, who is back from his soldiering, has just lost his son, a boy of four or five, and is evidently cut up by that. Having heard from England a report that Kitchener was disliked for his severity, I asked Mekowi about it; but he says that 'Kittin', as he is abbreviated, is all right with the good soldiers, but very hard with the careless or dirty. Certainly his service has done Mekowi good, and he would do well as a chief workman in any place; he is orderly, respectful and clear-headed, and knows how to give directions and manage other men. I have left him in charge of my room at night while away, and fully trust him. (2.3.1897, Drower 2004: 112)

This report disrupts the smooth regularity of the Journals, with its two details of violence in life, the one on infant mortality hitting the home of the worker, the other on the colonial need to reassure conservative opinion against liberal criticism in England (Porter 2008).

Another Egyptian, Hussein Osman, is identified explicitly as from Qift, and said to be second only to Ali Suefi, in a story of conflict with local justice: 'We have been amused by the farce of the Kadi and the Turkey. A man of Kuft named Hussein Osman is our best and most trusty workman next to Ali: and he was sent to market one day at the village of Wakf nearby' (23.12.1898). Hussein bought five turkeys, and the qadi (local judge) claimed two were his: 'They disputed, and then went with the village guards to the Omdah, or chief shekh. The Omdah told the Kadi he could not claim to know his turkeys from all others.'

Against this, the *qadi* said that his wife would recognise them, had them taken to his house, and then kept one of the five. Petrie continues the tale:

> That evening the Kadi feasted on the turkey – the dearest dinner probably that he ever ate. In two days I sent to Dechna, and wrote to the chief of police complaining of the theft. The next evening the chief of police called here. He is a very intelligent and polite man; heard all our story, from me and afterwards from Hussein Osman, whom he carefully cross questioned. He desired to know whether I wanted to press the matter legally, or only to be compensated. I knew that the police being in the matter would make plenty of trouble for the peccant party, so I only desired my 14 piastres for the turkey. The next morning arrives a fine fat turkey from the Kadi, with a request for a receipt for it to prove its delivery. Next time that Kadi sees a strange man with five turkeys in the market he will look another way, and remember a certain dinner that cost him a police visit and sundry recriminations from his Omdah.

Tone depends so entirely on enunciation, context and local knowledge, that it is hard to know whether to feel alarmed at the immediate impact of a foreign expedition and the involvement of police, or to join a lighter laughter. The complicating factor that makes it so hard to be fair to Petrie is the historical environment, that is colonialism. This would be a good story to hear from Wakf villagers. As it is, we have in addition so far only the version from Hilda, ending 'F. is going to inform one of the judges in Cairo of the conduct of the Qadi of Semaineh' (Drower 2004: 151). Cairo records would reveal more on the case, if it did go to court.

Beside her references to Ali Suefi, Hilda refers in her letters most often to Muhammad the cook: 'Mohamed is a sweet youth, with wondrous manners, all salaams and salutations, and is becoming a good servant, quick and bright. All Arabs do unconscionably stupid things however, and are very childish in their incapacities' (6.2.1898). She is writing here to close friends, and, her saving grace, she describes herself doing unconscionably stupid things in other letters, as when, the following month, she takes the midday meal of rice for washing-water, to be rescued by Muhammad (20.3.1898, Drower 2004: 145). In later years he does not seem to have held against her even one rather cruel prank (November 1900): 'We had great fun with Mohammed the first day they were up: we shut the door, and he could not think of any knack for opening it, for some time, not knowing that handles should be turned.' In the first reference to him, a man or boy called Yusuf is helping him separate squabbling turkeys (6.2.1898). Hilda names two other men, as sole companions on return from one market trip: 'Ali himself went on to Dichna, so returning we had only the black groom, Hassan Sudani, with us, and one arab, Mohammed Shergawi, and the horse, but going to

Waqf we were a merry party of 16' (23.12.1898). She also preserves one of the rare instances of reported speech from a workman, in a near accident at Araba:

> Today the wall of the hut of Mohammed Derwish, one of our workmen, fell down: he only remarked to us, when he heard it – Rabbina kerim, izakan fil lel, ana tahtu 'Our Lord is bountiful: had it been in the night, I should have been under it.' (17.1.1899)

Petrie himself mentions two more workers, almost as illustration to fill in the detail on another episode of local injustice that he is describing, at Dishasha in 1897:

> I heard that the tomb-guard had been levying on the boys' wages from the work. So I made enquiries quietly of the boys, and found that two had had a piastre each (half a day's wages) screwed out of them on the pretext that they came from the next village. So I payed this pillage back, and when pay day came round I gave the guard 12 instead of 14 piastres, and remarked that as he had 1 piastre from Abul 'elah and one from Aweys that made up his money. Of course he shouted 'no, no' but I walked away and hear no more of it. He explained affairs to my men by saying that the boys had been repaying a loan that he had made to them long before!! This guard is a typical Bedawi. (2.3.1897, Drower 2004: 112)

The disparaging remarks on bedouin that follow seem far removed from the sympathy Petrie had shown the Giza bedouin, as when fallahin were blamed for the theft of seven goats from the herds of Ali Jabri (15.10.1881).

Otherwise, Petrie refers twice to his prized cook Hussein in his 1895-1896 season at Luxor (26.11.1895; 2.1.1896), and then, in his Sinai report, to Musy Nasir the 'old head sheykh of all the country'. His letters to Hilda also include two names in the context of some remarkable information on the literacy of the workforce:

> Our men have not had a single letter from Quft. Aly abd er Rahim desires you to tell Ib. that they are all well here, and wishes him to write this to Quft. They have sent several letters to Quft themselves. (9.1.1905)

A minimum of three literate people had to be involved in this communication network: Aly abd er Rahim might be the only literate Qiftawi with Petrie in Sinai, and Ibrahim the only literate man with Hilda at Saqqara, and then there would need to be one person in Qift to read the letters sent home there. This short note exposes the minimal literacy needed to give a considerable number of people access to networks of written communication, and raises the question whether any of the correspondence might survive locally anywhere. Workforces were linked to, and participated in, literacy. This overturns any assumption that these men could not write

81

and therefore could not participate at any 'higher' level in the production of knowledge – in archaeology.

Phase V. British School of Archaeology in Egypt, 1905-1930

Summary of names

Names in publications: Ali (Suefi), Sheykh Muhammed Abeyd of Mitrahina.

Additional names in Journals and letters 1905-1920 (in order of appearance): Aly Firnisi, Aly abd er Rahim, Huseyn Osman, Hasan Osman, Shehad Ahmed, Muhammed Osman, Khalifa, Aly Omar, Muhammed cook, Selim, Ahmed Muhammed, Ma'awad Taha, Abdullah Awadullah, Abd el Latif Abd el Aziz, Amina Nakhla, her late husband Makha'in (Michael), her daughter Shafya, Qattas Bibawy, his grandson Murgos Ibrahim.

Coda – Qift workforce in Palestine 1926: Hasan Osman, Umbarak and Sultan Bakhit, Ahmed Aly, Muhammed Sayed, Hofny Ibrahim, and the son of Nasr el-Din (= Sadiq?); 1930 Muhammad Osman the cook.

In the final phase of Petrie's career, the files of Journals contain more private correspondence, including, within the family, from Petrie to Hilda after the births of John and Ann in 1907-1908, and, after 1919, from Hilda to their children.

Hilda retained her feel for the picturesque: 'Here is Yusuf coming up: he still wears the little blue jacket, of a Well Road blue, and has the short indigo kilt, and thin spare legs beneath, and a great twisted turban' (17.1.1906, Drower 2004: 179); and, writing to John and Ann from Sidmant in 1921, 'The old sheykh Abdullah and his chief man called the same morning; they were on their way to look after their buffaloes in the Fayyum' (Drower 2004: 202). Her letters to her children in 1921 also reveal something of the life of a woman on the work:

> One of the 'men' is a quick lively woman named Amina Nakhla which means Amen Palmtree and she is a good worker, and shouts at her boy if he doesn't bustle back. (Drower 2004: 199)

> She is a poor widow Amina, with 6 childrn, and her husband was a Copt named Makha'in (Michael). I wouldn't have the little boy in the work, he was too small and weakly, but a sturdy little girl Shafya comes with her, and does her basketing, she herself wielding a hoe like all our men. There is another little Copt in the work, Sab-ha Girgis, by her name. (Drower 2004: 201)

A 1922 letter from Hilda to John and Ann introduces a Copt (Egyptian Christian) at the other end of the social scale, a local magnate at Bani

Mazar, Qattas Bibawy, whose grandson Murgos Ibrahim was going to London to study medicine.

The same season, Hilda included a reference to Ali Suefi that seems to reveal what all the earlier material had omitted, his main livelihood:

> Aly Swefy is here, one of our best old hands. Being a fisherman, he has a little rough boat below here, and rushes off sometimes to catch a fish. (17.2.1922, Drower 2004: 209)

> Aly has a small boat here, and one market-day, I hope to take an hour off work, and go out fishing with him. He catches the nar-fish, after whose name a king of the time of Mena was named. (25.2.1922, Drower 2004: 213)

Some letters from Petrie to Hilda also refer to local life or excavation logistics, mainly in connection with Ali Suefi:

> Aly Suefy is with them [Schuler and Ward, working with Petrie], chafering in his old way and glorying in running things. (15.1.1908, Drower 2004: 184)

> Now I have Aly and all the men wrangling outside and must take charge of the building [of the expedition house]. (30.1.1908, Drower 2004: 185)

> Aly has got his wives here. I found him bent zealously on it, so let him build a hut apart and they appeared. M. [= Muhammad Osman the cook] had been to Quft to see his son (just born) and when he came here, I said that the hut was Aly's 'Lakin fi niswan hinak' [But there are women there] said he. 'Eywa, beta'u' [Yes, his (women)]. 'U entah khallitum gai' [And you let them come], said M. disgusted. 'Eywa, izakan humma mush heneh yumkin gaad fil beled' [Yes, if they were not here, he would probably live in the village]. 'Ah, entaref esh shoghul' [Ah, you know the work] with a sort of siding up air, satisfied that I did not invite them. M. is very good this year, efficient and thoughtful. We have a tidy hut for him, about 7x4 ft next to the cooking hut out at the foot of the steps. The men say our house is 'Zay wahed locanda' [Like a hotel] and are impressed with its dignity. (7.3.1908, Drower 2004: 186)

> On the 4th I went off to Fayum. At station I found Md Osman, Hasan, and Aly a.r.Rahim whom I had telegraphed to come before the rest. Gave M. my order for letters to collect policy (? or packing?) and bring stores on, and went by light rail to Hawara station, and thence walked over 2 miles to the pyramid. Aly a-R following with my Memphis canteen and blankets. (8.12.1910)

> Old Khalifa has turned up after all, though not sent for. He seems more active this year. All the men are satisfactory and working well in spite of not being able to get enough boys here; some have no boy at all and carry all their own earth. (26.12.1910)

At Maydum, Petrie became briefly involved again in workforce organisation when one of his European expeditionaries fell sick, and, as a result, he names the supervisors appointed, with details of their area of excavation:

> As Mackay was unwell I went out and started all the men on the work. There are six main divisions, each put under one principal man.
> 1) On east face of the pyramid cleared down to ground in order to tunnel to the central mastaba. Huseyn Osman.
> 2) the temple site (?) at the foot of the causeway. Hasan Osman.
> 3) the big mastaba, of which no entrance can be found, and in which I got the lining (?) wall of the central pit of the chamber, 15 ft below the ground outside. Aly a.r.Rahim. The above are Wainwright's lot, with two fellows tomb hunting.
> 4) the deep ruins south of the pyramid, probably catacombs of royal family, with rock cutting and tunnel found before. Shehad Ahd.
> 5) the tombs near the pyramid on W. Aly Firnisi.
> 6) the tombs far out, south and west of the pyramid. Aly Suwefy.
> We have on about 100 men and boys, after two or three days work, about 40 being locals. (4.12.1909, Drower 2004: 191)

In four instances he provides names of finders:

> We have just got a marvellous flint from Covington's tomb [oval sketch] 15 long x 2 1/3 polished all over; not a knife as it has a flat edge 1/6 wide all round. It looks like a ceremonial substitute for a knife; I gave Aly Firnisi & Aly a.r.Rahim £3 on it. (Giza, 5.1.1907)

> Hasan Osman, digging over kiln rubbish for glazes found a jar neck against a house wall with four gold earrings, weight just over £2. (Memphis, 19.2.1910)

> We have been doing well. Aly er Rahim got three portrait mummies, 1 very good, yesterday. Hasan got 2 portraits, today ... An exquisite hard marble shabti figure of XII dynasty or so from Aly Omar. (Hawara, 28.12.1910)

> Aly has been getting some silver and stone beads, gold earrings, etc, deep down in the ruins. (Memphis, 14.3.1911)

Once, the finder is identified by role rather than name, in a letter from Hilda:

> Within a few yards of our tents, the cook-boy found a grave of late date, Ptolemaic, but containing some rather well-worked heavy gold beads, and a massive gold ring; the bezil shows a woman offering at an altar. The white stone bead or ornament has a silver hooping. 3 or 4 'alabastra' were stored alongside. (Kafr Ammar, 23.2.1912)

He is named in a letter dated ten days earlier: 'Lastly we stopped at Kafr Ammar, and were met by cook-boy Muhammed and 2 other men to carry baggage' (13.1.1912). In her letters from Palestine, Hilda refers to Muhammad Osman the cook more often than anyone else, indicating the colonial dependence on house staff (Drower 2004: 228-9, 235, 244-5). Perhaps as cook, he is not in the list of names of the eight work supervisors arriving in Gaza from Qift for the first Palestine dig in 1926:

> Down they came, in their Upper Egyptian dress so different from anything here – Hasan Osman, Umbarak and Sultan Bakhit, Ahmed Aly, Muhammed Sayd, Hofny Ibrahim, and one boy, (the son of Nasr-el-Din). (26.11.1926, Drower 2004: 216)

Of these, Hofny is mentioned collecting post the next month (Drower 2004: 229), but otherwise the record of names is centred on Muhammad:

> Muhammed sends you his best sala'ams. Today he was cleaning and making reminiscences as to my best old milk-can of afore-time, and reminded me it belonged to 'Dendera-time' that is 1897 (when he came into my service at the age of 14). His son is now table-servant in the American work. (12.12.1926, Drower 2004: 224)

At Tell Fara in December 1930, amid heightened security over the troubles from uncontrolled Jewish immigration into Palestine under British rule, Muhammad is the only one allowed inside the enclosure for the foreign archaeologists (Drower 2004: 244). In 1931, according to Drower, he is still travelling from Qift to work with the Petries at Gaza in Palestine (Drower 2004: 248). After this, the Petrie record of the men from Qift falls silent.

4

Acts of excision: anonymity in the
Petrie Journals

1. Meeting non-Europeans in travel
and recruitment

Local encounters with global horizons

Petrie's very first letters home in 1880 reveal in passing the integration of
North Africa – Morocco as well as Egypt – into the cotton trade of the
British Empire: on board the boat to Alexandria was 'an Arabic gentleman
for Gibraltar' (1.12.1880), of whom Petrie writes 'Our old Arabic trader,
who is a native of Fez, here left us; he deals in shirtings, and had been to
Manchester to make his purchases' (6.12.1880). By this date, Morocco had
been forced to allow English traders to use Essaouira as a free port; the
trading community there had strong ties with Manchester (Ben-Srhir
2005: 135-8 on the volume of Manchester imports). On arrival at Alexandria, Petrie found himself a victim of this trade: 'the end of the ladder
box had been smashed up by a huge bale of cotton goods, of which the
cargo mainly consists' (14.12.1880). Later, he would benefit from these
links, as the mill-towns of Lancashire, already linked to Egyptian
cotton farms, signed up to subscribe to funds for London-based excavations by the Nile.

In 1880, Ali Jabri was not the first Egyptian to surprise Petrie with
knowledge. In the initial encounter with Egyptian officialdom, with customs on disembarking at Alexandria, his low expectations had to be
rethought: 'The only decent official was one who spoke English very well,
had been in the engineers, and rather astonished me by volubly asking if
the theodolite was 6 or 8 inch, and who was the maker' (16.12.1880).

Rarely, Petrie refers to the many other non-European nationalities
present in Egypt for commercial or political reasons. In December 1884,
on his way across the Delta from Nabira to San al-Hagar, Petrie was
invited to stay at the house of a sheikh in two villages. The first he names
as 'Godabeh', and his host 'Yusuf Bey Hetateh who was in Cairo but his
son Khalifeh Hetateh was there and was giving judgement in the gate as
we came in'. The second, on the way to Tell Barud, is identified as Bittukh;
'Here we found another grand shekh's house, belonging to Hadji Mabruk
Bey ed-Dib'. In the second, the English were one of several nations:

There were several of the Harry the 8th type of Egyptian, beside various

86

strange characters: – a little, subtile-looking Indian lad, who told me that he was from Hind, that he had his papers with him, and with sundry pointing and mysterious sign-language to help his lame Arabic told me that he did not care for the shekh, that the shekh could beat the fellah & get money from him, but that he could not touch <u>him</u> because he had his papers (i.e. as a British subject) and did not care a snap of the fingers for the shekh. He was servant of the Syrian travelling dealer, whom Said dubbed a <u>Yehudi</u> to the Indian's disgust. Then there were sundry negro servants who accepted my general offer of a taste of quinine, as I was taking a dose. (11.12.1884)

Quinine is the medicine against fever that has been credited with facilitating European colonial control beyond temperate and coastal zones (critically Eternad 2000: 51-60). It recurs several times among the Notebooks (below, Chapter 5, iv), and its effects might explain why Maspero would call Petrie dozy, against his self-image: 'Petrie est venu me voir avec un second Petrie encore plus endormi que lui' ('Petrie came to see me with a second Petrie even sleepier than him', letter 10.12.1885, published David 2003: 87; on the heavily medicated colonial explorer, see Fabian 2000: 58-71). The presence of an Indian in the house recalls, even if only incidentally, that Indian regiments played a key role in the 1882 British invasion, occupying the east Delta town of Zagazig (Barthorp 1984: 65, 71, 73). Ties with India extended to much of the English administration, as senior to junior colonial officials, from the governor down, were relocated to Egypt from service in Indian military and irrigation positions in the decades of occupation (Owen 1965; Gasper 2009: 52-3). In 1921, Hilda Petrie wrote of the expertise she valued in a European supervisor on the Sedment dig, Major Hynes, 'the man who has been in the Indian army all his time' (10.1.1921, in Drower 2004: 199). An Indian presence was nothing new in the Nile Delta: in the sixth century BC, the Achaemenid Empire of Iran brought both the Indus Valley and Egypt under its rule, and trading traces survive in documents and other material from the period of Roman rule as well as in medieval times (Tomber 2008; Gosh 1994). The Indian encountered by Petrie in 1884 may have been one of the many Muslim Indian agents in Ottoman trade networks; this might explain his disgust when Said identified his Syrian master as Jewish, in the rivalries between religions of the Book. The list of nationalities hosted by Hadji Mabruk captures in microcosm a cosmopolitan identity more frequently associated with the capital.

In 1898 Hilda Petrie recorded that the Antiquities Service inspector on the excavation showed little interest in their excavations at Dandara that year, but had spent a year in London, and had enjoyed Mile End, Poplar station and the music-hall entertainment (Drower 2004: 146). Later, in the first excavation for their new British School of Archaeology in Egypt, she mentioned a startling instance of greater local appreciation of foreign archaeology, a man with a modern electrotype copy of a Mycenaean gold cup (17.12.1905, Drower 2004: 177). The original was one of a pair found

at Vapheio, near Sparta in Greece, in excavations by the Greek archaeologist Christos Tsountas in 1889 (Tsountas 1889; on his archaeological
fieldwork, see Fitton 1995: 105-8). It remains to be discovered where the
electrotype was made, and how and when it reached a villager in Wadi
Tumilat, rural but near the Suez Canal and so on international trade
routes, with a prominent Greek population (Piquet 2008: 250-1). Although
the cup was perhaps just an interesting and attractive object, Hilda
recorded in the same journal, after talking to some Egyptians at the
station, 'Two of them came over for a lesson in archaeology next day, and
they write us English letters in answer to my Arabic ones, and are very
obliging in procuring bread for us.'

Petrie as local in Egypt
In his second survey season at Giza, Petrie was assigned a museum
representative, who expected Petrie to behave like other foreigners:

> The museum official tried to frighten me about sleeping in a tomb apart from
> the village, and recommended a house he knew in the village, as I suppose
> wishing to get me quite under the eye of a man who would report my doings;
> as we walked to the village he again expressed his hope that I would go to
> this house, as there was a bed with a fine canopy, and a beautiful mirror etc.;
> I replied I only wanted bread, and dates, and water, and the rest was of no
> consequence; a speech which went down with the Arabs, who said I was an
> 'ibn el beled' (son of the country). (19.10.1881, Drower 2004: 35)

As 'Arab' in this context would mean the bedouin at Giza, they may not be
quite claiming Petrie as one of their own; in late nineteenth-century usage,
'ibn el beled' would have designated not any Egyptian 'man of the people',
but more specifically the inhabitants of popular quarters of urban Cairo at
this date (Messiri 1978: 30-5; Armbrust 1996: 25-7; Abu-Lughod 2001:
138-9). Nevertheless, here, before the 1882 occupation, Petrie seems to
achieve a degree of identification with modern Egyptians in terms that,
despite his consistent thrift, he would not use of himself again.

In one phase when he despaired of support from English officials for his
work, his own nationality became negotiable, at least in the rhetoric of the
Journals with their particular readership:

> If the British influence of the public at home is insufficient for this, I shall
> offer to work for Berlin if the Germans will screw proper terms out of the
> Egyptians, i.e. French. (29.11.1891)

> I should be sorry to become a German or American subject, but as matters
> now stand that is the only way to do work in Egypt. (21.1.1892)

In Sinai Petrie found himself claimed almost as kin by a Sudanese or
Nubian police officer, in opposition to the 'Arab', i.e. bedouin:

a Sudani policeman appeared with the old head sheykh of all the country, Musy Nasir, a splendid old man ... He was a fine fellow, capable of anything, and talked over things here. He rather chummed with me (black as a coal) as both representing civilisation in contrast to the Arab; came into my tent to do his report – writing in peace, and left me the best of friends. (18.12.1904)

Ethnicity-ethnography

Early in his career, in the second season at Giza, Petrie gave an extended character sketch without naming the subject:

I wanted eggs, so a basket was brought up with 56!. I remonstrated with Ali on the possibility of my getting through them all while good, and concluded by taking only 32, which will last me a week probably. The old man who brought them struck me much; he was very fine looking, with a more frank and cheerful face than the pyramid Arabs, who look as if their ceaseless quarrels over the cash had sharpened them ever since their birth. He belonged to the Delta, was of a Bedawi family, and had had a good education at the university-mosque of Azhar at Cairo; he had travelled much as a merchant in Lower Egypt, and now was settled in this village having married there. I told Ali I should like to have a photo of him, which he repeated; and the old fellow imediately assented, and offered to take me out to Bedawi Encampments for photos; but I declined from want of time. I intend when I get my stock of plates (for which please rub up Houghton quickly, if he has not sent them) to go down to the village and get a lot of the best examples I can find of the inhabitants. (10.11.1881)

A man elderly in 1881 would have undergone his Azhari education in the mid-nineteenth century (for schooling at al-Azhar, see Mitchell 1988: 82-5). His travels within Egypt are a reminder of the mobility of people at that time, even if we assume that bedouin travelled more. Marriage had caused him to settle at Giza, but this does not mean necessarily that he had been entirely nomadic beforehand, in the sense of living in bedouin tent encampments. In these seasons, Petrie built up albums of photo-graphs on Ancient and Modern Egypt (below, Chapter 9); Houghton is evidently his English supplier. The extract points to the involvement of Petrie in ethnographic photography, a practice widespread in colonialism, and subject of east-west joint projects in the Ottoman capital Istanbul, where photography had been encouraged from the decade of its invention (Erdogdu 2002; Vernoit 2006: 25-6, citing one 1873 collaboration).

During his first season, Petrie had noted among visitors to the Giza pyramids 'Egyptians': 'Several parties of travellers came; some Egyptian, two of whom brought a wife each' (13.1.1881, Drower 2004: 17). Not all tourists were foreigners. Nationalist interest in antiquities can also be felt in the speculation noted by Petrie (in the Anglophone community?) after the death of Auguste Mariette later that year: 'I heard that Mariette is dead, and that the Museum is by terms of his founding to be divided between French and Egyptian; everyone thought it to be all Egyptn. Govt., and certainly any such arrangement has been kept very quiet' (21.1.1881). Anti-European tension may explain in part an alarming incident later in 1881, when two soldiers robbed Petrie in Cairo at the start of his second season, as he reported in detail to the British Vice-Consul and police adviser Raphael Borg (letter 16.10.1881, reproduced Drower 2004: 33-5). He objected to local justice, and sought to use London newspapers. He commented on his police interview: 'I stopped it as soon as I could by remonstrating on questioning me only through a Turk speaking French, and demanded that I should not be examined unless with an English interpreter. ... The reason I make a row about this robbery, is that the more is known, the more likely the Govt. are to refund, in order to avoid scaring travellers away, just as the season is beginning' (17.10.1881). However his Scottish mentor Dr Grant advised that Egyptian witnesses, Copt or Muslim, 'would swear anything to support the Government', indicating the popularity of nationalism against European presence.

Confronted with destruction of sites, like Amelia before him in 1873, and so many since, Petrie declared his mission what we now call Rescue Archaeology: 'the savage indifference of the Arabs ... is only superseded by a most barbaric sort of regard for the monuments by those in power' (10.1.1881, Drower 2004: 16). In the context of his 1880-1882 writing, and at the Giza pyramid village, the word Arab carries its localised Egyptian sense, meaning the bedouin living at the site (cf. Schölch 1976-1977). Petrie suggested a system of 'concession' of sites to foreign expeditions for excavating and recording, as 'Anything would be better than leaving things to be destroyed wholesale' (Drower 2004: 17). Over the course of the 1880s-1900s, under English occupation, the Antiquities Service did gradually give up nationalised control and implement the concession system, by which foreign expeditions are still the main publishers in Egyptian archaeology today (cf. contributors even in a more balanced recent publication, Hawass 2003). The comments from 1881 express the view most often taken by archaeologists towards non-European governments as well as local inhabitants on archaeological sites, into recent times (cf. Mapunda and Lane 2004; Hollowell 2006). In 1899, the UCL eugenicist Francis Galton was to visit the excavation at Araba; on hearing that a guide from Luxor was to accompany the visitors, Petrie wrote to prevent this, because he did not want the entrenched network of Luxor dealers to gain entry to the excavations. In explaining the need to keep the workforce separate from locals, Petrie commented 'This system which we have had to make is, of course, so unusual that you could not anticipate it, or see beforehand what antipathy we have here to the sophisticated native' (Drower 2004: 158-9). However, Petrie is also a defender of Egyptians, even in the climate of looming confrontation during 1882. He takes issue with a letter 'by a German apparently' in the *Globe* newspaper, calling it 'bad in many points', and distinguishes between the good people of the country and the army (10.2.1882). In changed circumstances five years later, he contested a colonialist opinion repeated by Wallis Budge that Egyptians were unclean, as they struggled to find seats to travel back from Aswan:

> I replied, then we must go 3rd class with the Arabs. Budge said he could never stand that, they were the filthiest people he had ever seen, etc. I replied they had their own notions of cleanliness (in some ways better than our own), but he said that was a very kind way to put it. (23.2.1887)

The equation Arab = bedouin is confirmed in a Delta excavation report (5.4.1886):

> There are twenty Bedawin, mainly old women, who hunt all the neighbour-hood, and bring up stones daily ... At first, the Arabs used to rub the weights, to see if they were silver or no, but I have quite stopped that destructive practice by only giving ½ price for any weight that has been rubbed ... I have got hold of these Bedawin enough for them to be quite satisfied at my booking a debt, if I have not got change about me; they press me to do so, in fact, rather than take the things back until I can pay. I hear them now about ½ mile off, making a grand <u>fantasia</u>, clapping and singing, delighted with their gains.

However, three years later, Arab seems to denote workers from Madinat al-Fayum, who had not otherwise been noted as bedouin and may have been Egyptian fallahin: 'No wonder the Arabs yelled after all they had done, week after week, to get at it' (15.4.1889). Arab also seems a general-ised term for local inhabitants at Amarna, in a comment on constructing a viewing platform for the great painted pavement he tried to preserve on-site in 1892 (vandalised twenty years later, in a local dispute over pay or tourist access, and the remains moved to Cairo, see Weatherhead 1992: 180): 'The work cannot possibly be trusted to Arab carpenters, so I have to do it all myself' (26.3.1892, Drower 2004: 86). Despite this occasional apparently broader use, in general the Journals seem to keep to the expected practice in Egypt at the time, using Arab to denote bedouin in opposition to fallahin, as at Dishasha in 1897:

> So tomorrow I must go recruiting for good fellows in the villages, as I do not want to have too many Arabs of our hamlet, for they will not be tough like the fellah. I noted a good strain of lads in the next village. The real name of this hamlet is Er-Righa [Arabic] as I now hear it in other mouths. (11.1.1897, Drower 2004: 108 except last phrase)

Towards the end of the Petrie career in Egypt, Hilda explained in a letter to their young son John that they used the word Arab to mean bedouin, 'either wandering or settled into a village', and fallahin for the main population of Egyptian farmers, noting 'Our own men are upper class fellahin, cultivators of the soil' (20.1.1921, Drower 2004: 202).

For his Sinai season, Petrie found that fewer men at Qift were willing to join him in the desert: 'Many of the fellahun would not come out here, so about a third are new Ababdehs' (18.12.1904). The Ababda bedouin are a tribe of the eastern deserts across southern Egypt and northern Sudan; in the 1882 census they feature as one of the most prominent bedouin tribes, listed that year as under sheikh Mechattah Karrar of Isna province, southern Upper Egypt (Boinet 1884: section 6, viii-ix).

Within Egypt, real or perceived internal demographic divisions are commented on at greatest length by Petrie in a discussion of supervisors with Reverend Greville Chester, who had wintered in Egypt for many years, and purchased and sold antiquities to help pay the travel costs (24.11.1884; on Chester see Bierbrier 1995: 96-7):

I had a long talk with Chester over the various possibilities of getting trustworthy reises. He thought the Copts were so essentially town people that they would be rather scared and helpless when out in desert places where they would need to do their own catering and cooking, and take care of themselves: in short that they would be more plague than profit. The Berberi idea he thought better of, but if I had such they would inevitably fall under the jurisdiction of my Arab reises, and so be really only one party; in which case I had better have all Arabs and avoid the risk of squabbling which the difference of race would perhaps excite. On the whole I thought it best to put the whole matter in Ali's hands as then he is interested in making things go smoothly and has some sort of responsibility for the men; the risk of their combining and screening each other not being too serious, as I should know them to be probably honest and fair men.

In his first season at Tanis, Petrie commented on his enjoyment of local relations, not least from his system of paying for finds, often of base metal: 'The people can't believe in all they see and get; now they say my gold is <u>copper</u>. They are quiet simple fisher folks, with whom I get on very well. Now I have about 120 at work. I take every one by their <u>looks</u>, not by recommendation, and I know all my men now by sight' (8.3.1884).

2. Working life

Ideal working life
As at Nabasha in his earlier Delta work, in the first Fayum season Petrie found his ideal working conditions through local displacements of labour:

This plan of beginning a short work before going to Hawara has answered just as I hoped; I have got such a staff together now that I can camp out at the work instead of going to and from the village. If I <u>began</u> there, I should have had only villagers who went home each night, instead of a party to camp out with ... The tents are now pitched just between the pyramid and the canal close to it, and the men are all settled against the canal bank, with screens of bricks from the pyramid to keep the wind off, and some bushes cut from the canal to lay over them. They seem to like it very well, as there is a constant tootling of pipes, singing, clapping, shouting, and general jollity going on. (29.1.1888)

The next season, now without Muhammad abu Daud, Petrie retained these workers from Madinat al-Fayum for his continuing work at Hawara, but planned already to add men from al-Lahun when he went to the sites there, dividing between Lahun pyramid and town-site:

I have now 10 men and 20 boys on, and shall not probably take many more before I go to Illahun. There I intend to work the town with these men, and the pyramid with the Illahunites, putting one of my old men over them. (18.11.1888)

In 1891, there were three components to the workforce at Maydum:

I got over 8 men, with boys, from old Fayum men; and shall have 13 Lahun men; also 9 men are on, or engaged, from Medum. So I start next week with 60 men or boys. I have far more applications than I can need. (12.1.1891)

This employment of people from outside the immediate locality seems the cause of conflict during the Lahun-Ghurab work, although Petrie considered himself unconnected:

There has been a bother here with some of a shekh's family attacking some of my workers, and making a row; probably not intended for anything serious, but what could not be passed over. The shekh came round to try and talk off the matter; but I said unless he satisfied them, they would do as they chose about referring to the police. He did not take the hint to make peace, but tried talk and bluster, so the men asked for the police. Now the shekh and his folks are gone to the magistrate and my men are to appear there tomorrow. I think they were foolish to press the matter, after the shekh tried to talk it over, but it is no affair of mine particularly. It will do good in letting folks see that there is trouble for them if they misbehave. (11.5.1889)

The trouble may have arisen in part from the strict separation enforced, as later recorded for Qurna work: 'Of course our Koft outsiders are kept entirely to themselves, and have work apart from all the locals' (26.11.1895).

External threats to excavator space
Petrie was conscious of the fragility of his working world, and the power of the media to disrupt and construct a different public sphere. During his efforts to remove Grébaut from the position of Antiquities Service director, Petrie noted the power of newspapers in England against decisions by the relevant Committee in Cairo: 'All this has been much influenced by the recent outcry in England; and has been done without the slightest per-

sonal disagreement with any of the English officials. The whole discredit rests on the Committee who raised the difficulties' (11.1.1891). Journalism in other centres might work against him. On the value of one find of silver on his second Delta season, he commented 'This may be known in England, but not noticed in print on any account; the <u>Arab</u> papers even copy what appears in English papers about antiquities' (3.3.1885). Arabic-language newspapers had multiplied before the occupation, and print media could redefine channels of communication in a manner beyond the control of the archaeologist (on the expansion of the Arabic press at this time, see Gonzalez-Quijano 1998: 121-2, summarising 1980s research by Aida Nusayr). The history of newspapers in Egypt offers particular ground for research, into their growing impact through increased presence of journalists and newspaper offices at local level across the country. From the Petrie warning, after the 1882 occupation antiquities evidently continued to concern the new media in Egypt as much as in England, contrary to the still prevalent western belief that occupied nations are not interested in their past.

Another external force was health, on which Petrie prized his role as doctor. Of the famines and epidemics to strike Egypt during the half-century, the Journals refer to the heavy cholera epidemic in Upper Egypt at the end of 1902; later Cairo medical students such as Naguib Mahfouz joined the battle against the disease (Chiffoleau 1997: 141). At the same time, another excavation in the region was being directed by the American Egyptologist George Reisner, as Petrie records (14.12.1902):

> We have about 170 men and boys from Quft, and about 70 local boys, the largest number that we have ever had going, and I expect to have 50 or 100 more locals before long … There has been scarcely any cholera here, only about 70 in all. At Quft it was bad 250 dying; but not one of our men or of Reisner's was attacked; reason why – they are intelligent and have been trained to be careful. Evidently the least care about water and food is enough. Wherever the water supply was good, there has been no cholera.

Another reason would have been that excavators enlisted the healthier younger men.

3. Labour in practice

Skill

Local knowledge regularly introduces Petrie to a terrain, as in an extract just before his first large-scale excavation, where 'here' presumably denotes Cairo, from the reference to a foreign diplomat: 'I have met here (by means of the French Consul and an Arab doctor) with an excellent Bedawi who knows all the country well, and walks splendidly. I did 17 miles with him over the desert, going over 4 miles an hour on the good ground, but much of it was heavy sand' (11.12.1883). Again in 1886, local bedouin reveal an archaeological site: 'A fresh party of Bedawin have found out that I will buy, and they come from a district between here and San. There is a tell there, El Bahain, (or the place of cattle, called so from pasturage there) which seems to abound in the small brass weights' (15.5.1886).

Another local skill is a keen eye for finds, noted by Petrie as a relatively rare individual talent, in one case among bedouin ('Arab') children:

> A few more handles; but the Arabs have many of them moved away, including the family to which my regular handle-hunter belonged. None of the other children are sharp enough to take to the trade with success. (19.1.1885)

Occasionally Petrie notes that this local awareness of finds in the ground extends to a knowledge of ancient burial customs, and can be connected with contemporary practice by local residents as well as foreign archaeologists:

> A most interesting remark was made to me by an upperclass Copt here. I explained to him about the dishes of funeral offerings being buried, and he at once said that was what they still did, when a big man was buried they put dishes and wash-pots and traps with him in the grave. So long do the old customs last here. (Maydum, 21.2.1891)

> The most interesting matter is finding a new mode of burial. New that is to me, and to any record; though I find that the men employed to plunder by the Museum know all about it. (Dishasha, 11.1.1897)

> After going for a little – about 5 miles – we found two Arabs following, who had been sent out to protect us. They shewed us cemeteries, and I found out at last where those painted plaster heads come from, which have been sold during the last 2 or 3 years as being from the Oasis or from Meir. The pieces were lying about, and the guards told me that they had found them coloured, as those we know. (south of Mahdiya near Minya, 27.12.1896, Drower 2004: 105)

At Bahnasa (Oxyrhynchus), a resident without speech was able to guide Petrie with striking accuracy through the chronology and archaeological potential of the ruins:

> On returning after my morning's surveying I found my dumb friend here, and after lunch he went round the ruins to shew me what he knew ... Then he told me that quantities of papyri were found there, and began grubbing; in a couple of minutes he turned up a piece of Greek accounts 2nd cent. AD. But so soon as we got on the Arab part of the mounds – though I had not yet noticed the difference – he observed that there were not any papyri there, that was all no good, all of Muslim age. But the whole of the Roman part not capped with Arab contained writings. He is also very anxious that I should beware of untrustworthy men about the place. Altogether we get on as well with signs as with speech. (9.12.1896, Drower 2004: 99)

At Araba (Abydos), in excavation of tombs of the First and Second Dynasty kings, one of the most famous achievements in his career, Petrie noted his debt to the Antiquities Service inspector (November 1899):

> I have identified the royal tombs, partly by finds, partly by what the Effendi here tells me. He is a capital man and seems to be quite our friend. I knew him 15 years ago, as Maspero's servant.

The term servant is ambiguous, but might imply a career for an Egyptian along lines that the American, English and German Egyptologists never offered. In the Antiquities Service, French nationals held the position of Director, from the time that Khedive Said introduced the post in 1858 (Reid 1985). The chauvinist and racist obstacles to promotion of Egyptians to the highest positions are well documented, but there is less comment on the way that the French Directors employed Egyptians at intermediate as well as lower ranks, creating a largely Egyptian Antiquities Service. Contemporary foreign expeditions could have encouraged the formation of this Egyptian archaeology, by adopting a more positive attitude to inspectors. Instead, the new fieldwork was characterised by division into hostile forces in four camps: foreign Service directorate; foreign expedition directors and supervisors; Egyptian Service inspectorate (replaced under English pressure at higher grades by English nationals); and the Egyptian excavating workforces. The internal conflicts include not only those between the different foreign nationalities, notably English and French, but also between Egyptian middle and working classes, in the formation of nationalist professional strata (cf. Gasper 2009).

For the skill of literacy, Petrie provides occasional anonymous local instances. At Tanis, one of the village boys turns out to be literate: 'Next morning one of the boys here who can read and write (what a treasure a scribe on the premises is I cannot tell) told out in a long singsong drawl the contents of Ali's letter' (8.3.1884)

On her first season with the core trained workforce in 1898, Hilda Petrie recorded the impression at length:

> The workmen are an intelligent set of fellows whom F has trained in work at various places in various years, so most of them work well, and understand how to look for their walls and pits. They work in couples – man and boy – or in groups of 4. At present they are all engaged on mastabas, as the tunnels were worked out months ago. They sleep in the tunnels, so they are all within ¾ mile of their work, and are close to the huts. They all begin to sally forth about 8 am, in their long brown over-alls, like bees from a hive, from the great tunnel-mound, every morning, and get down to their respective pits with their green rush baskets like carpenters' baskets, and their short handled hoes; one works at the bottom of the hole, shovelling sand and stones into the basket with the broad edge of the tool, and the other, the boy, carries the basket to and fro, on his shoulder, and throws the stuff down in heaps outside, on the nearest spot where they will not want to dig. In deep

excavations, 10 or 20 or 30 ft, two boys haul the basket up by ropes. They sing weird monotonous tunes, somewhat like Gregorians, very frequently, but oftener quite unlike anything I ever heard. They are dressed in picturesque garments of white or blue or brown – which I now notice come in that sequence, and the variations mean varying degrees of dress and undress. The white shirt is loose-sleeved, and shaped round the shoulders and arms by means of a white or red string crossed over the back; on this is hung little square red leather packets or books, sentences of Koran therein, and considered as a sort of talisman, with a sundry bead or two sometimes added. The blue garment is likewise flowing and picturesque – sometimes a bright blue – the brown outer one is of very coarse canvas. The red slippers are taken off and laid aside for work. (6.2.1898)

The next year, Hilda reported home that 'our men held a derwish meeting by moonlight in the wady', with a full description (17.1.1899, in Drower 2004: 153-4), and the next month she recorded in Arabic and English the chant at a funeral (25.1.1899, in Drower 2004: 154). Thirty years later, moving to sites in Palestine, Hilda remarked again on the skill of this workforce:

At first we had but few men, beside the 7 Egyptians whom we brought as skilled excavators. After a month our gang of men, boys, and a few girls came to about 20, and our current expenses to over £50 a week for labour. We shall need even more workers, if we are to clear the most important end of the city by May.

The local workers here were settled bedouin, of whom she comments: 'I am surprised to see how well they work, though not equal to Egyptians; also how amenable they are, and ready to be friendly' (16.1.1927).

'Skilled excavators' is a clear assessment, but not followed to its logical conclusion, local empowerment and control. For an archaeologist in Egypt, Hilda shows a keen ethnographic eye and ear, but within the same horizon of colonialist ethnography that Fabian attacks for being constructed against sharing (Fabian 1983).

Pay

In the first season of his Giza pyramids survey, Petrie paid Ali £1 a week, and Muhammad four shillings (27.12.1880). In his second season, Petrie mentions the amount he paid to the six local men for unblocking one passage, and to the Antiquities Service representative ('museum man'): 'The actual amount of earth cleared out today is about eight feet length of passage, or about one cubic foot in five minutes; the baskets weighing about fifty pounds, and passing in about one and a half minutes each. Wages four shillings or five shillings, beside the two shillings per day to the museum man' (20.10.1881). Periodically, if rarely, he would raise rates, as for Fayum men taken some distance, to Amarna in Middle Egypt:

Having at last settled my men I told them that I should give 1 piastre a day more to each than before, raising 3 p. to 4 for men, and 2 p. to 3 for boy, in consideration of their having to buy all their food instead of fetching it from home; for I thought this only fair to them; the whole extra is only 1s a day. (21.11.1891)

On later excavations, Petrie considered his rates fair to both employer and worker, increasing pay by productivity through the system of rewards for finds:

It is satisfactory to find that I am paying less than any one else for labour. The Fund payed to Jaillon 60 cent = 95 paras per metre; government contracts used to be 60. Now they are from 50 to 40. And I pay from 30 to 20, according to the hardness, or 1½ to 1d per cubic yard. Col. Ross who was over here yesterday was astonished at the amount done _per_ man, and chuckled over cutting down the government terms. As 1 para on the metre means £10,000 a year to government, a minute change of rate is very important. Notwithstanding the low rate, my men are many of them earning double the ordinary day wages, they work so hard. (7.2.1891)

Petrie is sometimes forced to pay higher rates. Twice skilled stone-masons from Cairo dictated their own terms on pay and decent food, for cutting to the Hawara pyramid burial-chamber:

By Thursday comes a letter from the head man saying that the Cairo men want 4s. a day, and £3 each down to begin. This is heavy, but as it seems the only likely way to get the work done, of course I sent the money. (15.12.1888)

They will not stay here at night, because they want to get good feeding at Medinet; but as they come over reasonably early – an hour after sunrise – and do not stop work for dinner, in order to leave before sunset, they really get a fair amount of time here. I go and listen at the mouth of the tunnel, to hear the click-click of the hammer and chisel clearly going on all the time. (22.12.1888)

At Tanis he specifies his rates of pay for finds:

I have lots of little scraps and chips, handed over to me every day by the men, for which I give bakshish. Scale is thus: perfect pottery, saucers and small things 1/10 d. to 1/5 d.; pieces of small images 1/10 d.; small coins 1/10 d.; large 1/5 d.; green eyes 1/10 d to 1/5 d; larger pots 1 d. and so on. This scale is just enough to make them attempt 'plants' now and then: but I think I have rejected all such impositions. There are so many little points that they cannot imitate; the absence of rubbing; the character of the dust in the hollows, and its texture, hard or loose; the slight dampness of larger things; and the incongruities of period; all these points serve to check the genuineness of finds. (11.2.1884)

On the clearance of the tomb of Horwedja at Hawara in 1889, Petrie reminded his journal-readers, at a time when his funding depended on a particularly small number of supporters, of the relative values in play:

> I gave that most lucky party of four in that tomb the glorious baksheesh of £10; and though that may sound absurd to some folks, it must be remembered that I should say that they are worth in London 10 times as much, or more even. (19.1.1889)

In one incident at Dafanna, during his Delta work for the Egypt Exploration Fund, Petrie managed to save money for his sponsors by concealing the full value of a find from its finder, only to be caught out in turn by the basket-boy working on that section. From the detailed description he gives, pay and work are clearly matters for negotiation in which no one can be sure of winning or staying ahead:

> A good example of the chancey nature of work occurred this evening. Just before sunset, I went over to a man, at a little distance, who was put to clear along the side of an enclosure where iron and copper workers remains are; he had wandered away from the wall, and I took up his hoe to cut down some earth to retake the wall; I hacked down some, never thinking of finding anything when I saw I had broken a green bowl (pieces will fit clean and indistinguishable). I picked it out, and thought it was very thin, and then saw a little chunk of metal in the earth I had cut down, which I saw to be silver by the way it was cut, and picking it up, I saw a gleam of white where I had hit it. So I calmly put on a side and grabbed for more; soon I had 6¾ lbs of crucible lots of silver, much of it sufficiently alloyed with copper happily to be fairly green outside, and thus I saw my bowl was silver – the greenness made the man suppose it copper, so I just picked it all up, for fear he should look too closely at it, and as it was just sunset, whistled the men off. As my rule of giving metal value for every object of gold or silver – known to be such – cannot safely be infringed, I shall keep this quiet here. Happily I have saved £15 or 20 thus. If the man had followed the wall he would have found it all before I got there. I must set a big batch of new work elsewhere tomorrow, and draw him off on it, and then quietly clear the rest of the ground around this myself. ... Next day I went to the silver-site, and scraped all around, and turned over all the earth which had come from that part; but all to no result. At noon, however, the boy who had been at the place the day before, brought in to me the bowl of the dipper, of which I had found the handle, and gave it in to be weighed as silver. Of course I knew at once whence he had it, but if I asked any questions it would raise the subject of all the rest of the find, and <u>he</u> wished to say no more, because evidently he had bagged it, and kept it until he could hand it to me, clear of the man he was with, for fear the man should claim it, or a share of it. So I took it, weighed it without further remarks, and put down 7/s to his credit in the wages book, and he went off satisfied. (1.5.1886)

Workers may have been more often involved in playing with the archaeology than Petrie hoped (cf. Kemp 2007: 134). This feature of his work caused talk against which he had to defend himself in one journal at some length, noting: 'It is constantly asserted by D'Hulst that I am cheated of all the best things by my workmen, in spite of paying for things' (15.11.1890).

Resistance

Sometimes recruitment met resistance or indifference, as in Wadi Tumilat in 1905-1906, where Hilda recorded: 'The local people are polite, and curious; they seem interested in us, and well-meaning. It is however impossible to get boys to work here. Workers are scarce, some of the lads seem to be earning far higher wages than we should care to give for unskilled carrying, and many of the people have the Bedawy distaste for work' (17.1.1906). On occasion in the eastern Delta work, Petrie encountered an objection to his methods. The third season started with objections to payment by the piece-rate system, for quantity of work done rather than for time: 'Out, and found 100 or 150 people awaiting us for work; an awful Babel. I split them up according to villages so as to get a manageable number to deal with at once. Then offered work by the cubic metre, and <u>no one would take it</u>. They know that they <u>have</u> to work by that way, and cannot shirk it. At last I got four on to it. I took on a few of our best old hands, as I intended by the day, to clear in the Dioscuri temenos' (11.12.1885). However, resistance was brief, as he could report the next day: 'Got on six parties of <u>metre</u> men to day; so the refusal is breaking down as I knew it would.'

At Madinat al-Ghurab, unusually in the records, finders resisted parting with finds on aesthetic grounds:

> Beside the regular work the villagers have found that there is a large amount of beads to be picked up in the surface dust of the town. There are as many as fifty, mostly girls, to be seen crawling about picking up beads and scraps. These are offered to me, and most of them I buy; but they have a great fancy for them themselves and often they will not not take my price though I give 1d. and 2d. each for little glass beads of this size [sketch]. (16.3.1889)

Sometimes resistance was more individual:

> One afternoon a man came up asking for work; I refused him, as I have as many as I can attend to at present; but he took my answer so quietly, and looked such a capable man, that I strolled past him again, and ended by taking him. It seems that he was at Tell el Maskhuta last year, and he presses for work by the metre instead of by the day, saying that the wages are low. This shows that he made more by the metre; but it is impossible to work by quantity at present, as all is uncertain, and I can never tell 10 feet ahead what I shall want. (11.2.1884)

Twice in these records, bad weather caused workers to refuse work:

> 15 poor miserables came up for their pay, saying that they would rather go

home; but they will probably turn up again so soon as it is settled fine. (3.4.1884)

Last Sunday and Monday were like this: so bad that some men would not work at all. (22.12.1888)

One of the common epithets applied by richer to poorer (Scott 1985: 5), 'lazy', is often used by the work-driven Petrie:

In a few days I shall find out who are the lazy ones and be able to weed out. (Tanis, 27.3.1884).

It is no good scolding or urging them to work, as that only stimulates them while one is there, which is not necessary; by letting them take their own way, and watching who works and who lazes, one can dismiss the inefficients, and so keep the better ones up to the mark. This is the great convenience of having plenty of applicants. (Tanis, 2.4.1884)

I am now discharging for laziness freely, there are so many applicants for work ... I have got the people into tolerable order during this week; they all agree to take wages once a week now; and I have scared them by sundry sharp dismissals for laziness, so that they work fairly well when they do not know that they are watched. The place is so covered with house ruins that one can get up under cover pretty close to any part of the work, so as to see what is going on. (Madinat al-Fayum, 7.1.1888)

Direct confrontation is rare in these records. Petrie used the language of the factory in pursuing his ends by denying work, and so pay, to all his workers at times of dispute with one party. He cancelled one day of work at Amarna, when local guard-dogs kept him awake: 'The lock-out game answers excellently to enlist a strong anti-dog party' (13.12.1891). Near the end of the season, he resorted to the same tactic again, when two hammers disappeared: 'There is little to describe this week, for we have had a "lock-out" ... Evidently none of my workmen were implicated, as I kept them out of work for three days (beside a Sunday between) without their being able to find the hammers. However the loss of work will make them all careful about things disappearing' (12.3.1892).

At Tanis in 1884, Petrie resorted to more physical tactics when some workmen disagreed with him over rights to a find they made out of work hours but on the site being excavated:

We had a find today: the men who were grubbing on their own account turned up a little chapel or shrine of Ptolemy II ... At last one man, who was always too free and easy, went up to the house, persuading another to go also, opened the door and began to take the tablets out of the courtyard. Of course this could not be tolerated a moment. I ran up to the house, and ordered them to put them back; they hesitated; I punched at them with my fist, and they obeyed. I then ordered the man who opened the door to leave the place, and never to work here again; but bye and bye I found him down in the hole again at work. I made him clear out in spite of the voluble remonstrances of his companions and his poor wife patting me on the back, and assuring me it was 'ma alesh' (no matter). I had to give him some more fist very emphatically, before he cleared away down to the village. When a man passively defies one's order, and is so flagrantly in the wrong, it is necessary to be '<u>decissive</u>'. The improvement in the readiness of all the others around was remarkable ... I settled the whole matter alone, and was thus able to stick to my rule of never retracting what I have said, or <u>rather</u> never saying what I should have to retract. (27.3.1884)

A broader and more political resistance may be implied by the continual recourse to authority and, probably often obligatory, the cementing of relations with the necessary officials. In his writings Petrie was hostile to bureaucracy, but nationality and personal relations evidently diluted his aversion. After 1882, English officials of public works were the final judges on budgets affecting archaeology, and the head of this section, Scott-Moncrieff, was on particularly good terms with Petrie: 'Then I went to Sir Colin Moncrieff; he was as friendly – I may almost say as affectionate – as ever' (31.12.1887). Local European irrigation officals of this powerful department could intervene with force, as when the Lahun officer, Hewat, a strong supporter of Petrie, requests demolition of water-mills at Lahun apparently in connection with theft of wood from a bridge constructed by Petrie for his work (29.2.1888). However, the connections were not confined to the department concerned with antiquities. Petrie also made himself known to the London-appointed governor: 'I went to Baring, by request, and had a long talk about the museum business, and I wrote to him strongly about Grébaut not coming and had a very polite and friendly answer, so I have improved my position in that quarter' (24.11.1889). Petrie also knew English judiciary in Egypt, and found this to his benefit on encountering local opposition to his excavations at Amarna:

> The shekh here is troublesome. He told his people to secrete anything valuable and bring it to him, and he would pay them better than I do. This was so outrageous that as soon as I heard it I wrote a letter to Corbett on the matter, and sent it by a man who went for some bread next morning. The shekh, suspecting it concerned him, followed and took my letter and destroyed it; and the messenger returned, saying he lost the letter in the river. In the middle of all this, the shekh comes in his pushing way and demands why I am so annoyed with him! So I told him plainly. And when he heard that I knew the end of the letter and would write again, he came very differently begging interminably that I would not write (assuming all the time that the said letter was about him, and not to his credit at all, which proved the case completely); but I told him that I had many friends and should write to whoever I chose. Next morning I sent by one of my own men another letter to Corbett, adding the fate of the last; and asking him to get some official to write a little note of instructions to the Shekh for his soul's health. He is a fellow of unlimited effrontery, and requires to be firmly taken

down. I have told them that if I have anything going wrong in the work here I shall dismiss everyone, and go and live at the other village and employ their rivals.

Luckily I can always have the best advice legally, as it so happens that I knew the Chief Justice, and all the four English Judges of Appeal of the Native Courts, before they were any of them in their present positions. It is a curious coincidence, as I do not know very many officials in Cairo. (13.12.1891)

In regarding these friendships as coincidental, Petrie seems to hide from himself that he too is a member of a ruling establishment in a period when Egypt was under English occupation.

Before the 1882 invasion, Petrie mentions meeting Borg, head of police in Cairo, and the same official is still there after the occupation: 'Met Borg and had a talk' (11.1.1886). With English control installed, he writes in his first season of 'the police protection Col. Baker kindly ordered for me' (8.3.1884), and, two seasons later, 'The mamur – inspector of police – called just to see that I was all right, and there was no trouble' (14.12.1885).

At Nabira, on the Naukratis excavation, Petrie devised an informal policing arrangement to prevent antiquities being taken from the site by the Giza bedouin who had been exploiting it before he arrived, and had shown him where it was:

> I found one of the Pyramid Arabs here who first told me of the place, so I had a talk to him, and agreed that if he stayed away and kept away the other Arab dealers who come from the Pyramids so long as I was here, I would give him good bakshish when I left, more or less according to whether I bought more or less. In fact I have bought him out and made him act police for me to keep the others away. If we did not do so, I might lose most of the things; and his getting anything from me depends on his efficiency in the agreement. So he asked to have it in writing, that I should have any dealers that came there imprisoned, etc, etc, and with that wherewith to terrify his acquaintances, and a couple of francs in his pocket I dismissed him. I am glad to have settled this before the digging season begins. (4.12.1884)

As elsewhere, Petrie evokes explicitly fear and imprisonment. Resident foreigners tended to fare better in the judicial system of the day, as Petrie noted in 1888 over a case of theft from the collections accumulating at the house of his early mentor Dr Grant in Cairo: 'Of course the servant is in prison, and he will get far more sentence for arson than for theft', while the Greek accomplice was returned to Greece (3.11.1888). This made threats of police heavy deterrents against possible thieves, as in one episode at Hawara:

> When I came back to my breakfast, about 12½, I found two men dangling about – spies as I believe. One of them was here yesterday asking for work, and could hardly be driven off. Today he came again and went into the pyramid, while his companion dangled outside. I sent them both off sharp,

with a threat of police, if they came again. I have given orders to my men if these are seen here again to come up and seize them, and march them off to whatever their village may be, hand them over to their shekh, enquire all about them, and tell him to keep them to himself. They probably come from some Greek dealer; but possibly they are thieves come to spy the arrangements for a night raid. (12.1.1889)

That same season, over at Lahun, when a discharged worker arranged the removal of one inscribed block, Petrie secured its return in triumph merely by mentioning police and writing a note in English to Hewat:

We have had a row that has ended well. I had left a big stone of 4 or 5 cwt. at the bottom of a tomb well, until I should get new ropes to hank it out. Also another stone I had left until I should get any pick from Hawara work to cut it. Working at night it seems a rascal (whom I had discharged for stealing from other men's work) succeeded in getting the big stone and the face of the other up to the village, and was going to sell them to a Greek in Medinet. But to get them into a boat they needed to bribe my guards of the house here to silence. This the guards refused and blew up the whole affair. The big stone had been buried, and the men refused to give it up, asking for a price for carrying it over here. I replied that they were thieves and not one piastre should they have. Unless I had the stone I would hand them over to the police. When they saw me scribble a note to send to Hewat they caved in at once, and led me to the stone. I then said the matter was not finished until they delivered it here into the house. After some screwing they did it, and thus I have three tough jobs done for nothing: (1) getting the stone out of the well, (2) carrying it over here (which took 7 men) and (3) cutting the face off the other stone, by all of which the rogues are well punished. All's well that ends well. (23.3.1889)

In his publication of the season, Petrie reported this episode with more detail on the way in which the affair 'blew up': 'the reis of the fishings at the bridge – a very fine fellow, named M'haisin – heard about it, and called the irrigation guards of the bridge' (Petrie 1890: 11). In this instance the publication gives a name omitted in the Journal, a reminder that alternative strategies of naming/anonymity do not follow a simple line from unpublished manuscripts with names to publications without names. The 'big stone' of the episode originally formed part of the tomb-chapel for a chief lector Senusret Ankhtyfy of the nineteenth century BC, duly published in the second site report (Petrie 1891: 13, pl. XI), and preserved in the Egyptian Museum, Cairo.

In his second Araba season, Petrie found his local reception much improved with a new police chief, presumably after a less successful first season:

The people here are much better behaved this year; a new omdeh, a new shekh of the guards, and a new and excellent mamur of police at Baliana, have made some impression. The policeman is ordered to live in our camp as

104

a guard, and we use him when sending for money. So affairs are altogether in much better tune. (November 1900)

Work conditions: accidents

Petrie worked within a legal framework with local enforcement before and after the 1882 occupation, as one polite objection to his second Delta season illustrates:

> Then the shekhs came down, to whom I shewed Maspero's letter. But a flaw appeared; the letter is for the mudiriyeh of Sherkiyeh and Gharbiyeh; but it turns out that this is in Behereh. I also shewed them Naville's old letter from the Mudir of Zagazig, which impressed them more. But they said they wished to have some authorisation from the Mudir of Behereh or the police. Quite reasonable on their part, though rather particular. (4.12.1884)

Despite the formal legal framework, archaeological employers had, and have, fewer legislative constraints than their contemporaries in industry, most clearly in inspection of health and safety conditions. The safety of the workforce was a recurrent concern for Petrie, though not among the practical or ethical issues in the chapter titles of *Methods and Aims*. Sometimes he met resistance in relation to safety:

> Today I refused to find work for a man who objected to go on where he had been working, on the ground of its being troublesome and dangerous. As it was tunnelling at 15 ft depth in good firm ground, I might allow that his feeling, though not reason, was justified. (24.3.1884)

Within weeks of this, a fatal accident did happen, according to Drower the only fatality in his fifty years of excavating. Petrie wrote not in the circulars, but in a private letter to the main authority within the Egypt Exploration Fund, Reginald Poole, Keeper of Coins and Medals at the British Museum:

> The side of a cutting which was supposed to be quite sound, suddenly gave way; the slip buried two boys, of whom one was recovered uninjured, but the other one was found to be dead. I cannot tell you the misery this has been to me, it has undone me altogether. I have not the heart to do anything, and only the necessity of seeing that the work suffered as little as possible has kept me going on. I cannot write about it. I have not mentioned the whole affair in the journal, as so many persons see that and I thought that you might not wish it talked about at present. (April 1884 letter to Poole, cited in Drower 1985: 79)

Drower records that soldiers and a doctor came to the site, and that compensation was paid. I have not found whether news of the fatality ever reached Egyptian or English newspapers.

Three years later, the pyramid at Lahun proved a dangerous work-site, but Petrie here ascribed the risk to the carelessness of the worker:

> One of the two men there nearly did for himself; he carelessly cut under a block until it fell and pinned him, jamming him tight and scraping his back and leg. He lay helpless; and the other man, instead of loosening the stuff under him, and getting him out, ran off to the village (1½ hr. off) for men. About 30 men came, and then fearing he must be killed many ran away again, for fear they should be called as witnesses. Some wanted to break the stone up on the top of the man! At last, after two hours, the poor wretch was released. He looked rather shaky, and had his leg tied up, when I saw him two days later, but was beginning work again. I gave him a compassionate allowance of a shilling, for which I was heartily blessed; but protested that it was no affair of mine if he chose to squash himself. (8.12.1888)

Skilled stone-masons assessed work inside the pyramid as too dangerous:

> to my surprise by 3½ the masons said they were going back to sleep at Medinet; I remonstrated in vain at the absurd shortness of their day's work, but off they went with their baggage, and next day never appeared at all. A messenger came over from the arab head man, saying that these men would not go on with the work for fear the pyramid should fall on them! (15.12.1888)

At another pyramid site, Maydum, two seasons later, Petrie acknowledged the dangers of the excavation:

> I am very glad to have got this part pretty well done without any accidents, for tilting about and lifting such masses by men not trained to it is risky, and legs and arms would have gone like matchwood if there had been false moves. We have all got off with plenty of scratches and a few bruises and aches, of which I have a full share as I have of the work. (28.2.1891)

Fear

A recurrent motif in accounts of rural life is fear, in the face of the extreme violence of modern states, local, regional and external (Mitchell 2002: 153-78). In 1883, on the way to his first large-scale excavation at San al-Hagar, Petrie went over the battle-ground at Tell el-Kebir where, just over a year earlier, on 9 September 1882, the English and their Indian army contingents had outgunned the defending nationalist forces:

> The outworks of Arabi's camp extend far into the desert ... Most of the traces of the action have disappeared, and it was only on an outlying part, which had not been much visited, that I found the strew of empty cartridges where each man had lain behind the bank. The quantity of stores left lying about partly buried is astonishing. (11.12.1883, written at Kassassin, published Drower 2004: 45-6)

4. Acts of excision: anonymity in the Petrie Journals

In this season of work, local suspicion repeatedly links Petrie to impending military attack:

> the people here are such quiet folk, and so much afraid of soldiers coming down upon them, that there is no question about safety at all. I hear that the people who have not actually had to do the work and had the pay, are not yet satisfied but think the work is only a blind to some official matter. (15.2.1884)

> Ali tells me that the people about here cannot believe that I have come for antikas only; they say that some of the 10,000 soldiers (who have been telegraphed as coming out time after time) will be stationed here; and that I have come to begin quarters for them. Some outlying villagers said that I had 22 khawagas here, and they thought of fleeing the neighbourhood, so much was their fear of the coming garrison. Mariette's way of working was to get a requisition for so many men from a village, and then send over a reis for them; the reis levied the richest men he could venture on, they bribed him to get off, then he tried the next, and so on until he had fleeced all but the poorest, and they were marched off to work. No wonder that dealing by free contract, without any reis or shekh, is not identified as the museum style of dealing by these poor people. I have the satisfaction of knowing that no man or boy comes who does not wish for exactly what he will receive, and that none of it sticks in any man's hand between theirs and mine. They are not angels by any means, but they are not at all bad according to their light and way of life, and they do deserve honest treatment. I put down every worker's name, and against it the day of the month when I go over them in the morning, and then mark it through when paid in the evening. (11.2.1884)

In 1899 Petrie attacked French directors of Antiquities Service excavations along the same lines:

> It is important not to talk about these results for the next few months, as Amélineau's permit does not expire till 1 June, and if he knew how much he had left behind he might claim to go on again there. He merely worked by an ignorant gang, driven on by the lash, and not paying anything for results. He got hardly any of the minute results, and was grossly robbed of what was found. With trained men, well paid for every inscribed chip, the case is altogether different. (25.12.1899)

Anglophone Egyptology has retained this harsh verdict (e.g. Wilkinson 1999: 4-5), although Amélineau, partly spurred on by Petrie comments in print, provides in fact more detail on groups of finds by location in his excavation reports (Amélineau 1899-1905). Taken together, the French publication find-lists and English publication plans add up to a reasonable record of the site, and both, even separately, are advanced for their time. Comparison of the published plates and text pages offer the only fair comparison of their results. New excavation at the site over the last twenty years by the German Archaeological Institute has revealed how much Petrie too left behind, nuancing the original impression given by the

French and English publications. Other documentary sources might shed light on their relative working practices. In sum, more research is needed to establish a less biased account of Antiquities Service methods and local reception of expeditions from different countries.

The accounts by Petrie as the good employer include no mention of the English military presence in the country. The evils of feudal methods in oriental style (no reis or sheikh) are contrasted with the fair play in the system of the occupying land (free contract). The conscience of the wealthy party can be left in peace, confident in honest treatment meted out to the poor. One diagnosis might be that this unselfconscious self-justification is necessary to the continued existence of the colonial Ego, and tied to the system of pay by labour-purchaser to individual labour-seller.

Whereas Petrie expresses his dislike of the recruitment system in Egyptian tradition, he does not comment on military conscription, recording only its local impact during work at Maydum:

> A lot of my men are all called off to go home to be inspected for the register of future recruits; from boyhood, about 10 years old, every boy and lad is periodically inspected, and a register of all sound ones kept, from which recruits are to be drawn in future. (14.2.1891)

The consequences of collective resistance to conscription were visible to Petrie and his wife on their journey prospecting for prehistoric cemeteries in 1898 near Hu:

> We left the tents there next morning and went on to Kelfatieh, a village built over a prehistoric cemetery, where the Arabs used to dig out tombs under their houses and fill them up again. The villagers had been very unruly and defied the conscription, so last year the Government cleared them all out and ruined the village. Hundreds of houses stood with walls battered down to two or three feet from the ground, and the great bins and cupboards and fowl-houses of mud lying broken in and tipped over at all angles amid the confusion. (Petrie, 27.2.1898)

> The sight of Kelfatieh, a large village or rather a small town, levelled ruthlessly to within a yard of the ground, was very strange. (Hilda Petrie, 26.2.1898)

Despite this physical evidence, Hilda seems not to have taken local fear seriously the next month, when the European supervisors on the dig threatened the local sense of security: 'On the weekly holiday the men (M, MacI and D) generally go off to the river in the afternoon and get a bathe.' The villagers asked them to stop, because, if they drowned, 'they would all get hanged for it. They had threatened and expostulated with the bathers themselves, and dragged them out of the water apparently! It was rather an amusing incident' (13.3.1898).

Eight years later, villagers of Dinshawai in the Nile Delta rounded on a hunting-party of English and Irish soldiers killing their pigeons; when one of the hunters died, apparently of a stroke, four villagers were arrested and did get hanged for it – Hassan Mahfouz in front of his house for his family to see (for English reaction, Shaw 1984 [1907]: 39-52; Berque 1967: 241-2; Owen 2004: 335-1). Uproar over the incident led to the departure of Baring as governor (Owen 2004: 350-1, citing the 'Farewell to Cromer' by Ahmad Shawqi), and marked a turning-point in the nationalist movement to remove the British army from Egypt.

The Petrie Notebooks: individual issues

The Petrie Museum archives include 194 pocket-notebooks from Petrie's work in Egypt and, in a few cases, Palestine. Most are in the distinctive cursive handwriting of Petrie himself, but many have the neatly separated lettering of his wife Hilda, and others again are by English or other site-supervisors. Archaeologists have been their main readers, extracting precise data from the observations in survey and excavation. However, social and economic historians would also find compact masses of information on Egypt from the 1880s to 1920s. The contents range from routine travel expenditure to notes on photography settings, and include names of Egyptians individually, in small groups, and, above all, in the extensive name-lists of excavation workers, recording their enrolment, their work-attendance, and, often, their daily and weekly pay. In the stratum of recording represented by these Notebooks, the presence of Egyptians by name finally overwhelms the number of foreigners. The combination of personal names and places of work and origin brings into individual focus a great collective, the excluded majority in the labour of archaeology.

In many instances, the Notebooks preserve the first and immediate record of a point that would be presented later that week or month in the Journals, or later that year or after in the excavation reports and other publications. In a few lines that would make no sense without the Journal for 11.12.1884 (above, p. 86), Petrie recorded his hosts at Bittukh in the Delta (Notebook 44, scan 22):

[sketch of 'New Year flask']
father is Yusuf Bey Hetateh in Cairo
son Khalifeh Hetateh Bey – of El Godabeh
Hadji Mabrug Bey ed-Dib at Bittukh
½ m N of Dayr et Timsah

Similarly, the encounter with the learned local Umran Khallil is captured in a laconic entry by Petrie 'Umran Khallil of El Mesid' (Notebook 18, Dishasha 1896-1897: scan 4). Sometimes comparison of records allows us to identify the register at which the finder disappears from the scientific record: where a Journal mentions that Ali Suefi finds sherds with pot-marks near Hu (above, p. 76), Petrie recorded the find in a Notebook as 'marks on tops of stands', and sketched all the marks, but left no reference to the finder (Notebook 17c, Dandara, 1897-1898: scans 3-5). In other instances, the miscellaneous entries in the Notebooks lead deeper into the details of arrangements or points which the Journals and publications record more generically or re-present in narrative form. Deferring references to finds to Chapters 6 and 7, and photographs or other images to Chapter 9, here I consider the scattered, usually terse entries from across the five decades of Petrie excavation in Egypt under the following headings:

(i) Security, politics, law
(ii) Local networks and sellers, buyers
(iii) Recording individuals: assessment, history, place
(iv) Work conditions: health, pay, space of separation
(v) Notes in Arabic script or transliteration

(i) Security, politics, law

Security authorities

In his first full excavating season at San, early in 1884, Petrie recorded two important local officials of the local regional centre Fakus: 'D. Alexandre Habra medecin de l'hopital, Ibrahim Kamil Effendi sub inspector district Arin. Fakus' (Notebook 98c, scan 42). These names recur in the photographic lists (below, Chapter 9), and the appearance of the two men may relate to the fatal accident recorded in letters to the Egypt Exploration Fund office (above, p. 105). Twice in the 1885-1886 Delta excavations, Petrie recorded by name the regional official of the Antiquities Service, 'Ahmed Negib Inspecteur des Antiquités Mansura' (Notebook 74, scan 31; Notebook 74b, scan 3). These Francophone references set the excavator within a governmental framework of institutions. Even after 1882, this formal structure positions Egyptian officials above the outsider in facilitating and overseeing excavations, a relation continually resisted by Petrie as by other excavation directors.

At the start of his second Delta season 1884-1885, Petrie recorded several police authorities, perhaps where newcomers such as excavators were expected to register presence (Notebook 44, scan 22):

Suleiman Effendi Bahagat
Ma'aun Police Markaz Shifra Keit
Silim wihby
Ma'un = Sub inspector of Police
Baker, Gibbons, Cole, and Johnson
Deputy Inspector General of Police

These lines are written under and opposite notes on where to find particular individuals, perhaps in connection with the antiquities trade (see below), but the two sets of jottings may be unconnected. Later in the same Notebook, Petrie records his arrangements for site security, with a local

111

sheikh perhaps related to Ali Jabri of Giza (Notebook 44, scan 38): 'Shekh Muhd Jabr, Nebireh, gives guards on and off most nights'. Above are written two names: 'Abd er Rahim Musi black, Mirgam Neklawi with donkey', perhaps the names of the guards assigned to the excavation. Back at Giza, site security evidently concerned the immediately local authorities, perhaps in the tradition whereby the central government entrusted security at the pyramids to the bedouin. Notebook 44 from the Nabira 1884-1885 season contains a deleted copy of a message, recorded in English though possibly a personal literal translation from Arabic, and possibly a message delivered orally rather than in writing (scan 42):

> Shekh Abu Talib wants Mr Head to know that he has guarded the house at the pyramids all the time that Mr Head was away, keeping three or four men there every night; and he wishes to know now as Mr Head has returned and brought other people with him, whether Shekh Abu Talib is to attend to it still, or whether he is to leave it between Mr Head and Shekh Ali Mensi of Kafr Batran to Mr Head's men altogether.

Sheikh Abu Talib had been mentioned in the Giza Journals as one of the leading figures in the 'pyramid village' Kafr al Haram. However, the name of the second sheikh leads us into another level of the network of authority, overlapping with official domains and so visible in the print world of the 1882 census. The census identifies Sheikh Ali Mansi as one of six Najama bedouin leaders settled at Nazlat al-Batran, below the Giza pyramids, for which 176 individuals are counted under him, as compared with 235, 231, 222, 218 and 160 individuals for the other five; although his contingent is second smallest, Ali Mansi is the only sheikh there to be listed for Najama living elsewhere in the same Badrashayn district of the Giza governorate – all 315 inhabitants of Kom al-Aswad, and all 392 at Nazlat al-Ashtar, northwest of the Giza pyramids (Boinet 1884: 718). Farther north, and significantly for understanding social networks around the excavations, his authority extended to the small numbers of Najama bedouin registered as still nomadic in 1882: 109 in Sharqiya province, and 77 in Buhayra province, where Nabira (Naukratis) is located (Boinet 1884: 688-9, 692).

A Notebook from 1887 contains a short list of individuals providing logistical or political backing for the excavation, a list echoed in a Notebook from the following year. In the two lists, providers of transport-animals and postal service join English military officials in the colonial administration.

Notebook 32b, scan 2:
Colonel Scott-Moncrieff C.S.I.
Major Bagnold RE
Ali Ahmed donkey man Wasta
Selim Effendi post Luxor

Notebook 36 (spring 1888) scan 2:
[deleted line]
Bond E of Bank of Egt opp Milit Teleg
[deleted line]
Sir Colin Moncrieff K.C.S.I.
Selim Effendi post Luxor
Ali Ahmed donkey man Wasta

The two officials recur in other Petrie papers. Major Bagnold is cited by Petrie in a letter to Amelia Edwards as the official who had by his own account helped Wallis Budge smuggle seventeen crates of antiquities out of Egypt for the British Museum in 1887; that letter was written in self-defence after Edwards had heard from Budge a Cairene rumour of Petrie smuggling seventy-five crates of antiquities out of Egypt from his 1886 Delta excavations (Drower 1985: 124-5). From the occupation in 1882 until 1892, Colin Scott-Moncrieff served as the English, so controlling, Under-Secretary in the Ministry of Public Works, the department most involved in the conflict between demands of modernisation and preservation of sites. In 1889 Petrie appealed to him to override a move by local police (Notebook 48, Lahun 1889, scan 40: 'Sir Colin Moncrieff. Work at Illahun stopped by police of Beni Suef. Please telegraph them. Petrie'. This minor incident returns the colonial official in the background to centre-stage in executive matters.

Excluding local Egyptian officials, another list gives recipients of the Petrie book *Hawara, Biahmu, Arsinoe*, publishing his results from 1887 to 1888 (Notebook 35, 1888-9, scan 10):

Recd Hawara
Ross
Moncrieff
Grenfell
Griffith
Home
Haworths
Grant
Hewat
~~Mudir~~
Miss Marston
Artin

This list combines family (Home, Miss Marston), colleagues (Griffith), and sponsors (Haworths), but is again led by military and other colonial administrators, including Scott-Moncrieff. Lieutenant-Colonel Ross, Inspector General of Irrigation, sat on the Committee controlling the Antiquities Service (Drower 1985:170). Major-General Grenfell held the position of Sirdar 'Commander-in-chief' over the Egyptian army; in 1887, in charge of the Egyptian garrison at Aswan, he had overseen excavation of an ancient cemetery there (Drower 1985: 115-16). Major Hewat was the Fayum inspector of irrigation, and supported Petrie in practical matters such as finds-storage throughout the Fayum excavations (Drower 1985: 131). The interest of the colonial administrators in excavation underscores the importance of the new knowledge from archaeology, as part of their claim to be the only competent and informed authorities to rule the country (Said 1978; Colla 2007). Petrie had evidently considered sending a copy of his book to the Fayum governor (Mudir), but this is the only entry in the list deleted, and so it seems that he changed his mind, perhaps with the turnover of holders of the position. That left only one non-European on the list, Yaqub Artin, the Armenian official who served as Minister for Education (Drower 1985: 177; on Artin in his role as Francophone historian, see Crabbs 1984: 186-7). At the start of the 1890-1891 season, Petrie mentioned Ross again, beside another key figure in the security apparatus, citing their colonial awards and addresses in Cairo (Notebook 59, scan 3): 'General Chris Baker Pasha VC, Chief of Public Security Division, extreme SW corner of Sharia Medabesh. Lt Col Ross Cmg R E, No 9 Sharia Medabesh' (for Colonel Ross see also below, Terms of work).

At Hawara 1910-1911, for unknown reasons Petrie noted an address 'Major L.D. Rhodes, Kabushiya, Sudan' (Notebook 37, scan 1).

In the final decade of their work in Egypt, Hilda drew up a list of addresses, recalling the sets of names that Petrie grouped at the start of his time in Egypt, again with a strong colonial military and police presence, with Egyptian as well as English (Notebook 45, from Lahun season of 1914 or 1920, scan 32):

Rev. John P. Wright, W. Mid. Sum. Sch., Oldbury Rectory, Bridgworth, Shropsh.
M. Gustave Lefebure Inspecteur en chef du Service des Antiquites, Assiut
Abd el Hakim Ghalib: Ma'oun of Police, Madinet
Mohd Ahmed el Kholi (in Latin) al-Lahun al-Fayum (in Arabic)
Amin Mikhail and I. Bakanuny
Miss L.F.L. Sullivan S.W.Cor. 21st ... hunt sta
Steindorff Leipzig/ Gohlis Fritzschestr. 10
R.M.Graves Head of police (Minia and Medinet) Ministr. Inter, Cairo,
or Gezireh Ho. Cairo

At al-Araba al-Madfuna in 1921-1922, while London moved towards unilateral declaration of Egyptian autonomy as a kingdom, Petrie named together an English and an Egyptian local official he would need to know for excavation security (Notebook 5a, scan 1):

Col.Gent (?), Bashmufattish D ... Asyut
J. Sadik, Commandant of Police, Sohag

Another Notebook from that season appears to record other local authorities, not so exclusively involved in security (Notebook 76, scan 9):

Ahmed abd el Wahed
Hasan Mahmud
Arabeh

Abd el Azyz Yahya
Mudir Sohag

The most unusual Petrie note on authority appears to have a rather unexpected source in a commission from overseas. During his first season at Mit Rahina/Memphis, he jotted down notes on the topic of constraint (Notebook 68, scan 28). Apparently these were for a pamphlet published in 1908 in New York by the United States Brewers' Association in favour of freedom of choice during the debate over legal prohibition of sale of alcohol, *The Right of Constraint, essay. Fallacy of the prohibition theory* (copy not seen, information from web-page consulted 19.4.2009 at http://www.worldcat.org/oclc/84327184/editions?editionsView=true& referer=di):

Right of constraint
Right of constraint in interest of others
   a universal ground of government, v. selfishness
R of C in interest of actor, rejected by English law
   tacitly assumed (danger of assumption inquisition)
   1) when demonstrably best
   2) when perhaps best on a short view
      ignoring weeding (?) etc
   3) when intended to force conformity.
      supposed beneficial
1) factory act? Sultan, Benin and Mexican massacre
   Inquisition
2) parliament, repression of drink, harrying of
   disreputables, rule of India, Ireland, Egypt
      drop opium billing
3) local option, education, dear to puritans, past and present
   (are they more altruistic or more conscientious,
   or less tolerant, or less imaginative?
   or do all these make a puritan?)
   missionary work if bound to forms and our conventions
   (one convention is that we are not what we do
   not profess to be; other people are what they profess.)
   Conformity a curse when in diff. conditions
   as clothes in tropics

By whom.

status [?] of race not those of indiv

indiv needs self sacrifice for race
and needs to <u>be</u> sacrificed.

RC granted in aberration
are all cases we dislike to
be treated as aberration?
not if they are a class

Assumption that anything shocking
to moral reason is wrong,
but we shock decency of Asiatics
sense of decency a moral sense

Drinking bout in mts no woman or children
What is the offence? Constraint?

[with arrow to 'By whom':]
Trying to get over the fall by removing free will
(But where a man suffers the results of his
own actions he needs them for training.

A free will which only worked one way, and
never let a man down would be only
a supreme prize giving with no blanks

compulsory virtue is no virtue

In this draft, as in his book *Janus in Modern Life*, Petrie introduces politics into his writing. Historians of the period could comment on whether the range of his references reflects topical news in London circles that year. The 'Factory Act' that he had in mind might be 1891 and 1895 amendments to the 1883 Factory and Workshop Act, on health and safety issues including work accidents, industrial toxins, and child labour. 'Mexican massacre' might refer specifically to the suppression of the strike at the Cananea mine in Sonora under the increasingly harsh US-dominated Presidency of Porfirio Díaz (1906). Perhaps most revealing of the age is the link declared between Egypt, India and Ireland, united in resistance to the British Empire, where the right to use force aroused continuing debate and action in London as in the countries under occupation.

Judicial cases

Case 1. In spring 1885, the bedouin leaders would play the deciding role in the dispute over a horde of bronzes removed from Nabira during excavation (above, pp. 66-7, on the letter from Sheikh Omar settling the case). In Notebook 6 Petrie captured the details of the dispute as it appeared to him at the time ('Naps' denotes gold Napoleon coins, dominant in nineteenth-century Mediterranean currency):

116

5. The Petrie Notebooks: individual issues

Scan 25 left:
Suleiman Ruhumah) Not here before April 17
Ibrm Berech   )
Sadawi Khatab here before but I did not get him down
~~Hassan Goheda and Saada Gurob had ant=7 naps~~
(Saada Gurob, Aisa Makra, Yunis Juedeh
(Abd er-Rahman el-Hat-hody, Hassan el-Godi
(from Ezbet Tehowy Matkur, had 7 Naps taken
by Abd el-Gowi, Abd Jowad Beresh (bro M Berh)
Abdel Aziz Khatab, Ibm Beresh, Suleiman Ruhmah,
Sadawi Khatab, Mahd Shehad, all of Gizeh
5 pieces sold for 7 Naps and 13 to be sold for £30
(Omar Baradani's lot)
are in house of Hassan es Sahadi

Scan 25 right:
Achmed Ibrahim [in Arabic script beside] has bronzes from the find, burnt
ones and eel case, nephew of Farag.
Farag has some
Suleiman has some
A German bought a large cat
Was also a seated Bast large
a serpent on column large
same small
Isis and Horus ~~etc~~
long snake case

Scan 26:
[deleted name]
Ali Shafei Matawi bro Shekh Omar Khatab
Muhd Bereysh and others bought 20 March
figure with 2 snakes on head for 9 dollars
from Udain
All people here from Gizeh are under Shekh Omar
[deleted note below and, on right page, unrelated namelist and sketch of
face]

Scan 27 left:
Code
9 Public domain sect 10 monuments and all objects of art and history
belonging to the state.
8 Lands are (A) private or (B) govt or (C) unoccupied which can only be
occupied in accordance with the regulations
58 Buried treasure of wh former owner is not found belongs to master of soil.
If no master belongs to finder 'sauf l'impot, dans tous les cas, au profit de
l'état, d'après les règlements.'

Scan 27 right:
Muhd Bereysh
Find on Mon 2
M B left for Kom Hisn 3
– receipt dated at Bulak from Muhd Bereysh on 5th at 11 am
left Kom Hisn 5
At Bulak Fri 6
Cairo Sat 7

117

Gizeh Sun 8
Kafr Hasan Mon 9
police took him Mudir of Gizeh liberated him
and he left on Wed 11 to go to Nebireh
… 18th 5.30pm

Scan 28 left:

Abd es Salam says he is a boy, then says he does not know him in Kafr H'
[unrelated namelist inverse below]

Scan 28 right:

Muhd Shehad here 18 March
Abd el Gowi Abdullah (bro Abd es Salam)
Abd el ain Khatab
Abd el Gowad Bereysh = Abdullah Saidi
Took ant. 11th Wedn. went Thurs 12th
From Omar Baradani for 7£ from Great Find
Bought chalcedony seal. Hierg and phoenic
Shaieyb and Omar Baradani together.
Smain at Benha bought above of Omar Baradani for £7; sold to Gizeh men
for £20.

Scan 29 left:

All at Nebireh
Muhammed Berisht
Saadawi abu Khatab
Abdullah?
Suleiman Khatab

Cook Cairo
Please inform ~~chief~~ police!
Charge M B and S K of Kafr el Haram Gizeh with stealing bronzes from my
work ~~if they are~~ when arrested I will bring the witnesses Seize all ~~the~~ their
bronzes ~~they have~~ They ~~went~~ reached Cairo last night.

Suleiman Khatab here and says Muhd Berisht took 100 pieces
Caught Abdullah Saidi of Saft nr Gizeh on 8 March. had Arab ring bought
on Kom
really Abd el Gowad Bereysh

Scan 29 right:

[list recording more names and items]

Scan 30:

[inventory of finds in two columns, 'whole' and 'broken']

Case 2. A Nabira Notebook from the next season, 1885-1886, contains a curious report on donkey theft, involving guards, beside a name and address 'Midani Hamed Kafr et Asisi (?)' (Notebook 74, scans 28-29):

Scan 28 right, top

2 donkeys Muhd ~~Jabri~~ El Guni Shekh of Nebireh
~~who gave orders to Muhd Jabri Shekh of guards~~
Stolen by unknown thief

5. The Petrie Notebooks: individual issues

Continues scan 28 left:

Muhd Jabri guard and Muhd Ramadan guard went off to search for donkeys with written orders frm Shekh Muhd at Guni and reward of £6 offered, and a black joined them and asked for bakhshish if he gave up donkeys. Went to a village to see all donkeys at the market, and police caught the black.

Continues scan 28 right:

Police took Khairullah, black from Ezbet Hasan Bey Nesem as a general thief, no proof about donkeys; known at Mudiriyeh; gave false name Masaud. Police took him as being Khairulla and took guards up together, all to Mudiriyeh [governorate], on Khairullah accusation. And at Mudiriyeh Khairullah (having bakhshish from guards)

Scan 29:

(6 Naps [Napoleon coins]) said he did not know them. But guards were kept under confinement at Mudiriyeh, (and Shekh Muhd Guni sent for) on ground of guards having been with thief.

Petrie does not report why the incident was relevant; perhaps it interrupted the local provision of security for his site. Cf. case 6 below.

Case 3. At Dahshur early in 1887, Petrie recorded a local incident (Notebook 32b, scan 15):

Muhd abu Sumra blind   ) had 22 wts
Suleiman al Kis) boys   )
Iman az Zayat   )
Tabit az Zayat
The Mansur of Sakkara took the wts from them, reported 7 to Grebaut, and lodged the wts with the gaffir of Sakkara.
[3 lines deleted]
G. came down on Tues ... came to Sakkara Mon 18

These notes on ancient weights are difficult to explain without further documentation, but might amount to a case against Grébaut, then Director of the Antiquities Service, on grounds of inadequate supervision and local injustice. Cf. case 7 below.

Case 4. During his limited clearance work at the Dahshur pyramid field in 1887, Petrie recorded an incident involving the police, apparently in relation to unauthorised excavation work in the 'gebel' low or high desert (Notebook 32a, scan 29; not the incidents noted in Drower 1985: 122-3):

One (false) told
Policeman Bazaz of Maun that 12 men worked with Mansi in gebel. Bazaz and shekh gafurs (?) of beled (?) Sakkara took the 12, and went to Ayat rd, to work ... and at ... said give money, and took 12 riyal from them. Soldier Ali Auad stopping at Sakkara took money with Bazaz, and let people go, and tore up accusation

119

Twelve names follow, presumably the men alleged to have gone to the gebel:

Musi   Hawehi (?)
Sidahmed "
Suleiman el Kis
Abdel Falahi Dafani
Badawi   Burri
Mutwali
Saleh   "
Burri   "
Iman ez Zayat
Tubit   "
Omar   "
Abder Rahman Seif

To the right of the first three names is a note 'Maun not in fault on this business'. The name Musi Hawehi (?) recurs in the next list, recording the men working on the Petrie project to clear part of the Dahshur pyramid field (below, Chapter 8). As in the case of the Nabira bronzes, the issue of legitimacy lies at the core of this incident. In legal terms, through its claim to 'exclusive right to antikas', archaeological work is creating a new kind of land, in which a new kind of landowner asserts rights against previous users. In the early days of the formation of this claim, it would have been difficult to determine which digging is official and which illicit. In his *Methods and Aims* (1904, see above, Chapter 2), Petrie distinguished scientific excavation from plundering by the double criterion of careful recording and swift publication, rarely achieved by official expeditions today. Colonial authority broadly supported the territorial claims of science, and, in turn, that historical source of authority today complicates the legitimacy of the scientific work.

Case 5. A Hawara Notebook from early 1889 contains the direct evidence tabulated by Petrie from his extra-judicial investigation into the levying of worker wages by Muhammad abu Daud, leading to the dismissal recorded in the Journals, covered above in Chapter 3 (Notebook 39d, scan 21).

   This record (see top of facing page) reveals the names of the six men otherwise anonymous in the version that Petrie wrote home. Mekowi is the best documented in these English archives, as someone known from Manshiat Abdullah in Madinat al-Fayum (below, p. 135). Sen presumably denotes Senusi, a name found in other Petrie notes. The entry Ged, with no evidence recorded in the column below, might be Godi, prominent several years later on the Naqada excavations.

Case 6. At Dishasha in 1896-1897, Petrie recorded in a mixture of English and transliterated Arabic a second incident concerning a donkey (cf. Case 2 above), again without specifying here whether it affected his excavation logistics directly, or was an episode of external interest (Notebook 21, scan 8):

Evidence against Muhammed	Hassan	Mekowi	Hamda	Rasek	Sen(?)	Said	Ged Hab
Has he had money?	Yes	Yes wanted	Yes	Yes	Yes	Yes	
Day?	No	No	No	No	No	No	
or Bakhshish?	Yes	Yes	Yes	Yes	Yes	Yes	
Why gave it?		Threat of discharge	Threat	Threat			
How much?	1/4	1/4	1/4	1/4	1/4	1/5	
Total?	27	55 ½) 60½ 5)	16) 14) 32 2)	29	22) 12)	28	
From first?	Yes	Yes	Yes	Yes	Yes	-	
On all?	all	all	large	all	all	-	
or large?		large					
Wanted antikas?	No	No	No	No	No	No	
Had it before?	Before	Took before				Took before	

15 May Maktab [?] Giza al Fayum Told at Gizeh no need to look for donk before Fayum Carried donkey on at Wasta. Wakil Wasta telegr to Beni Suef told to wait till even. waited till even, donkey not returned. Told to go to Fayum and wait for donkey. Waited 2 days, Wakil Fayum telegr to Bel- lianeh. Reply from Bellianeh Donkey returned. Waited 5 days. Mafish donkey. abt 30 May Afterwards Mufattish from Embabeh told Fayum lazim homar ayn. Ali M. wrote reply yet examining the case – wrote for 440 PT, asked for donkey or money.
Bolica still with [breaks off]

Case 7. In 1899-1900, his first year at al-Araba al-Madfuna (Abydos), Petrie recorded a short set of accusations concerning circulation of positions and antiquities among local officials (omdeh), Antiquities Service inspectorate (mufattish), overseer (reis) and guard (Notebook 4, scan 7):

If anyone has 100 PT he gives it to the mufattish and is made guard.
At Kuft a mock reis with mock permit working for Gurnawis.
At Abydos mufattish, omdeh and reis get all small antiq. Girghis, Basta, etc, all busy.

As with the notes from early 1887 at Dahshur, these lines read as the assembling of an extra-judicial case, here against either Amélineau, still holding the concession to excavate at the site, or the Director of the Antiquities Service, Victor Loret. Later the same season, Petrie recorded how loosely Amélineau had supervised his excavations at one of the great monuments of Araba, the underground chambers of the tomb of king Khasekhemwy from the end of the Second Dynasty (Notebook 2, scan 8):

121

Khasekhemui. Baskets of stuff left by workmen in ... [deleted].
3 big knives found, one stolen by reis sold for £4 1.2
Big bowl stolen and sold for 10/s

Petrie had himself been on the receiving end of similar accusations of lax control (as he noted in his Journal 15.11.1890, above pp. 99-100), but he had survived; the campaigns against Amélineau and Loret succeeded in removing them. Amélineau first found out about the transfer of concession to Petrie in the newspapers (so Kemp 2007: 140). Loret was forced to resign on 1 November 1899 over his refusal to leave mummified bodies in the Valley of the Kings. To replace him, the Anglophile Gaston Maspero returned to service. Under Maspero the same mummified bodies had to be removed to the Egyptian Museum, Cairo, following an attack by anti-quities-thieves rifling them for amulets to sell on the local or foreign branches of the international antiquities market (Piacentini 2005: lii-lvi).

Case 8. At Memphis in 1907-8, Petrie recorded the negotiations over the intrusion of archaeology into the famous palm groves of the site (Notebook 68, scan 21): 'Decided by omdeh and ma'un that 5 metres must be left round each palm'.

Case 9. In the 1909-1910 season at Maydum, a European assistant of Petrie, either Mackay or Wainwright, recorded one specific instance of action against deception by a man on the workforce (Notebook 64, scan 5):

Haggar. Thief and liar: – stole my wedge, said he had not got it and produced it from his cloak. Took my wedge again, pretended he had not got it but produced one next day and delivered it up. was to bring the value of an a/c and brought it 1 PT short, with a yarn it wasn't owing. Finally said one week he had worked 7 days and took the money for 7 days from me, ~~which~~ I found out later he had only worked 6.
See Shahada

Terms of work
Sometimes the vocabulary of privacy and secrecy might be within the personal sphere, as in this entry from November 1883 (Notebook 98e, scan 7):

exclusive claim to antikas
entire disposal of time
unconventl
Sayce after 10 Dec
keep private
cabins which? large stern

The first three lines relate to the proposal by Petrie to the EEF officers Reginald Poole and Archibald Sayce, that he might acquire antiquities at sites outside his official concession, offer them to the Egyptian Museum, and add any not required there to the division of finds for the EEF (Drower 1985: 71). The note 'keep private' probably refers to the sensitivity of this 'unconventional' proposal, but the following reference to cabins and stern returns the notes abruptly to the private matter of finding a boat for a December 1883 Delta journey.

At Lahun in 1889 (Notebook 49, scan 30), Petrie drafted letters to Grébaut and Grenfell on the division of finds with a request to pass papyri without examination for reading in England, on the grounds that any selected by the Antiquities Service from a future catalogue could then be returned.

Dear M Grebaut,

~~As it is impossible for me~~ since I wrote to you last I have found in the Δ of Hawara a splendid table of offerings in alabaster with figures of 110 offerings nearly all named: this and a series of alabaster duck-bowls were for Ptahneferu, a daughter of Amenemhet III. These are the only important ~~monuments~~ inscriptions found this year and will of course remain in Egypt. As it is impossible for me to finish my work here this season I wish to know whether you can protect the place till next year, or whether I shall continue here through the summer until the work is done. If owing to the corruption [?] of the inspectorate, you should find it needful (as last year) to license a dealer to work in my absence, I should certainly not leave the country. [paragraph added in middle of facing page:] But if you would protect the place for ~~the months~~ a part of the time, my friend Mr Frazer of Minieh would come and hold it during the rest of the time I am absent, as he could work some of the less important parts here. [resuming first page] No very valuable objects have been found here, but the sites have proved of much scientific interest; I hope that you have already at Bulak the ~~finds~~ things that were found here by Farag while ~~working~~ excavating last summer, as he cleared out all that he thought worth working in the two cemeteries of the place during my absence. This is the more to be regretted for science as those sites ~~had not been touched so far~~ were yet intact, and the other things that I have found shew that great historical results may have thus been lost. Still I hope that you may have in the Museum at least the objects that he found here though their positions are not recorded.

Dear Sir Francis Grenfell, Thanks for your kind letter. I have accordingly written to M. Grebaut but do not know when he will get the letter. ~~The copy~~ I enclose the copy as you suggest. As you are a safe friend in the matter I may as well tell you <u>privately</u> why I am anxious about this place. I have found a town of the XII and XIII dynasties, and obtained ~~many~~ some dozens of papyri of that age, which may be of great historic value. These I wish to pass through to England without examination here, as my last years papyri were passed, subject to Grebaut's selection from the catalogue when prepared. After we have read them he is welcome to them for Bulak; I do not wish to evade the law, but only to secure the reading. I have found the <u>alphabet</u> and <u>Greek</u> pottery in use in a town of the XIXth dynasty here, a fact of the greatest importance, as Sayce agrees. But it is the cemetery of this place, where invaluable evidence may have existed, which has been ravaged by old

Farag under licence during my absence. I have also found the alphabetic signs developing as early as the XII-XIII dyn. I do not wish to talk about this publicly until I reach England. Of course it would be utter destruction to the subject for an Arab to plunder the place.

The Notebooks also include Petrie drafts of a letter to be sent in 1890 to the artist Edward Poynter, as secretary for a Committee for the Preservation of the Monuments of Ancient Egypt (Notebook 34, Ghurab 1889-1890, scans 17-19 and 20). This Committee had been set up following the enthusiastic reception of Roman Period panel portraits in Greek style, found by Petrie at Hawara in 1887-1888. Its first meeting, in the Poynter studio on 3 August 1888, was attended by the Director of the National Gallery Frederick Burton, the artists Alma Tadema, Frank Dillon, Henry Wallis, besides Poynter himself, and the Egyptologists Flinders Petrie and Wallis Budge (Drower 1985: 168-9). In his 1890 letter drafts, Petrie reacts to news of destruction in decorated rock-cut tombs at Beni Hasan and Bersha, major sites in Middle Egypt; the vandalised scenes included one famous in Egyptology, a rare depiction of a colossus being transported (Drower 1985: 170 for a February 1890 report from Greville Chester). The vandalism seems likely to have been aimed at cutting out slabs to sell on the art market, a common fate of painted plaster walls of rock-cut tomb-chapels in Qurna at Luxor, in a trade feeding private and public collections outside Egypt (Mekhitarian 1985). In his response to the crisis of security, Petrie here proposes a new English-controlled inspectorate parallel to Antiquities Service:

Scan 20, perhaps the initial draft:
My dear Sir,
The enclosed resolution, which I only intended at first to send ... in my own name, has been so far acceptable to other members of the Committee here (?) as to gather considerably more weight.
The recent deplorable [breaks off]

Scans 17-19:
[added at side at top: Poynter]
My dear Sir,
~~Although absent from England I hope you will allow me to move the following resolution at the next meeting of the Committee through yourself as secretary.~~
The recent deplorable injuries to the monuments at Beni Hasan, Bershah and ... shew that some active steps must be taken for their further protection. The action of the Egyptian Government and its English advisers appears to be hindered by French influence, the paralyzing effect of which in other questions (such as the conversion of the debt) is so well known that it need not be enlarged on here.
It seems therefore incumbent on a Committee which has been formed expressly for the protection of the monuments of Egypt to come forward with independent action.
I move therefore that steps be taken to secure the services of some English-

man, with a sufficient knowledge of direction [?] of antiquities and of engineering ~~construction~~; that his instructions should be (1) to travel over the country for the greater part of the year, (2) to note the condition of all monuments, especially those most liable to injury, in a regular series of Notebooks geographically arranged. (3) To copy all inscriptions not yet recorded. (4) To report in English and other newspapers ~~public newspapers in England~~ all wilful damages done by natives or tourists, that may come under his notice, and to frustrate all attempted injuries where possible. (5) While maintaining as cordial relations as possible with the official Committee on Antiquities in Cairo to be under no control except that of the English Committee in London by whom his salary is paid; and not to be influenced in his report by any consideration except the above instructions ~~not to preserve? anything which should be ..., out of consideration for any Egyptian official~~.

I would suggest that an attempt bemade to obtain such services as these here moved for at about ... in 400 per ann. including expenses. I will gladly guarantee £10 of this annually myself; and if such members of the Committee will do similarly in proportion to his position, the funds will be raised at once. The Egypt Exploration Fund might also be willing to join in the expenses, as instructions 2 and 3 carry out its purpose.

If no other suitable person can be found to take up this work, it might be well to offer it to Mr G W Fraser, son of Col. Fraser late adjutant to the Egyptian army. He is a civil engineer, young and active, knows Arabic, and has done all he can to preserve and copy the monuments in his own neighbourhood at Minieh. ~~He is professionally a civil engineer, and therefore he is qualified to b ... in that respect alone.~~

He may have other engagements: but if at liberty I know of no one more suitable for the purpose.

Hoping that the enclosed resolution may be favourably received by the Committee, and that it may be practicable to improve on the suggestions,

Believe me,

yours sincerely,

W.M.F.P [with note to right 'Add bit']

That year the Egypt Exploration Fund in London responded by launching an epigraphic recording project named the Archaeological Survey of Egypt (Drower 1985: 171), a now rather misleading label as the project was exclusively philological and art historical, and excluded technical surveys. Inked-in drawings of the scenes at Bersha and Beni Hasan were published over the following decade (Naunton 2007). Already in 1890 the Fund sent out Percy Newberry to direct the work, with the surveyor George Fraser and Marcus Blackden as draughtsman; the next year the expanded team included a seventeen-year old Howard Carter. Contrary to the recommendation from Petrie, the Egyptological careers of Fraser and Blackden ended in academic disgrace, when they copied important inscriptions at the nearby calcite quarries of Hatnub, and published them in advance of the actual discoverers Newberry and Carter, to claim the discovery for themselves (James 1991; Naunton 2007: 75).

In another 1890 letter copy or draft, Petrie writes in rough but clear

French to the Fayum governor, to announce the end of the excavation and to warn him, as responsible authority, of the dangers posed to the sites by 'the people here' (Notebook 34, scan 16):

> Votre Excellence   20 Feb
> J'ai l'honneur d informer vous que mes fouilles pour les antiquités ont finie aujourdhui. Et apres le 22me de cette mois, la place resterai en votre garde. Les gens ici sont tres mechant dans leurs fouilles subreptices pour les antiquites; tant à Illahun et à Medinet Gurob: et je prie vous a garder les droits du gouvernement par des visites frequent des police, en jour et en nuit. Votre, avec toutes respects,
> W.M.F.P.
> M. Sabri Bey   Mudir de Fayoum

Later that year, on the more local matter of his permit to work at pyramid sites, Petrie recorded a letter to Colonel Ross as member of the Antiquities Service commission (Notebook 59, scan 29):

> Dear Col. Ross   28 Nov.
> I have today had an interview with M. Grebaut on the subject of my application for permission to excavate, which I made last June. He expresses his accord with my desire to excavate in the district of Medum and Lisht, reserving the interior of the two pyramids of Lisht as future work for the museum. I hereby agree not to interfere with the interior of these two pyramids of Lisht under the permission which I now seek.
> I shall be extremely obliged to you to lay this request to excavate for 6 months from the 1st Decr. before the Commission, as soon as may be convenient. The terms as to the ~~share~~ decision of the antiquities I leave to the choice of the Commission. My address will be Rekkah.
> Lt Col Ross AE Cmg
> Under Secry of State for Public Works. p. i.

Perhaps a year later, at Amarna, Petrie copied or drafted another letter reflecting his resistance to attempts by the French directors of the Antiquities Service to tighten regulations on the official division of finds after excavations (Notebook 16, scan 10):

> Dear Sir E Palmer,
> As I have no expectation of continuing my work in Egypt under the present regulations, I should be glad to know if the bond for £100 deposited by me may be restored on the arrival of my antiquities at the museum. This bond having been drawn lately and being required to be presented, and the probability of ...ting to Egypt for some time to receive it, will I trust be sufficient reason for its return to me as early as may be. I may be leaving Cairo early on Saturday and if so Thursday is the last day I could call at the Office.

Elwin Palmer was Finance Secretary in the colonial administration at Cairo (Drower 1985: 188).

From the end of his first season at al-Araba al-Madfuna, another Notebook preserves a draft letter from Petrie to the Egypt Exploration Fund Committee, on the division of papyri found from 1896-1897 at Bahnasa, ancient Permedjed/Oxyrhynchus (Notebook 2, February to March 1900, scans 29-30). The finds quickly became famous in the English-reading world, because they included otherwise unknown Greek literary and Biblical compositions; a July 1897 pamphlet publishing one of the first finds, Sayings of Jesus, led to establishment of a separate Graeco-Roman Branch for the Egypt Exploration Fund (Rathbone 2007: 200, 226-7). The 1900 Notebook shows Petrie, perhaps unexpectedly, to be not an English nationalist, but defender of interests of the stakeholders in an enterprise, the north American museums sponsoring excavation here taking the role of shareholders in a commercial company:

> I hardly suppose that English members would like such a valuable collection to be allotted by an American curator to an American museum without any English representation being present. We might not so readily believe in the generous impartiality of others, as in our own (scan 29)

This principle of interest would apply equally to Egyptian nationals or Europeans in the Egyptian Antiquities Service, but such logical implications seem structurally invisible to Petrie as to other foreign excavators.

In the 1905-1906 season of work at sites along Wadi Tumilat, Petrie met technical local official objections to his work. In response he wrote to a French- and Arabic-reading, probably Egyptian, official in the Antiquities Service, M. Basil. The message, cordially expressed in French and Arabic, explains his need for a new permit that would cover all the area he hoped to excavate (Notebook 106, scans 10-11):

Scan 10:
    Bazil, Musée Caire
    Permission necessaire pour Zawia ~~pres a Saft~~ non
    inclus avec Saft Petrie
    [sketch 2 pots] M̶
    Lazim waraq tani min shan beled Zowyeh alashan laah mush Sawa wa (?)
    Saft
    [Arabic of same]
Scan 11:
    Cher M. Basil
    Il y'a lieu d'un petit desagrément que l'omdeh à Saft qui a fait protestation que les terrains à Saft sont seule son proprieté privée: et aussi qu'une gezireh pres de Saft est le terrain du village de Zowyeh, et que notre permis est seulement pour Saft.
    Par consequence j'ai adressé a vous une telegramme priant que vous donniez extension pour notre fouilles à Zowyeh. J'espère que cette formalité ~~n'est pas facheux~~ ne vous donne pas de peine.

(ii) Local networks and sellers, buyers

One obstacle to understanding the past was the modern production of antiquities. On his first journey into Upper Egypt in 1881, Petrie noted beside a sketch of Menkheperra between sa-bird hieroglyphs, 'Drawn by an Arab at Medinet Habu, who offered false images' (Notebook 33, scan 37). Another obstacle came in the form of competition for antiquities on an excavation site. During his third Delta season in 1886, after a February excursion Petrie drafted a letter to a sheikh on this subject (Notebook 74d, scan 34):

> Greek Girga, Zagazig Standela [?] Agostanti of Bulus
> Muhd abu Helawi guard
> Ali Abdullah went into hole
> Abd el Hag es Sad Shekh
> To Abd el Hag
> There are people of yours here on the Tell Bedawi who are good and whom I employ; but there are bad ones ~~also~~ of yours. Today 2, Muhd Helawi and Ali Abdullah went into my work, and while Muhd H went to talk to my people that they should not see the other, Ali Abdullah went into my work with fas and safih to dig ~~where I had work go~~ in my work for antiquities. This is not all, it is because of a Greek who stays here with Muhd Helawi, in fact a town man and he will not give his name, to buy antiquities from my people. First I want you to tell your people that they must not come into my work to dig. Second I want the name place and business of the Greek which is your business to know. If the bad people come to my dig again, and if the Greek stops there, there is no more work for any of these people with me.

He followed this with a draft letter to the Greek consul (Notebook 74d, scans 36-37):

> To Greek consul Zagazig
> Sir,
> I wish to call your attention to the illegal action of a Grk dealer in antiquities [deleted phrase]. I am here making excavations for antiquities on behalf of the Egypt Exploration Fund; everything found being by agreement the property of the Egyptian government; the British Museum having the choice of objects not required at Bulak ~~by M. Maspero~~. A Greek dealer has come here and gives his name as Agostanti, of Bulus or of Zagazig (the Arabs say his Christian name is Girghis); I cannot give the particulars as fully as I should as he refused to give me his name altogether, and only gave it at the Shekh's demand as indistinctly as he could. This man of course has a legal right to come here, but it is a distinctly illegal action to incite persons to theft. This is what he has done, visiting the place five times; and though I warned him the first time that everything was government property, he has come again and again, going into the houses of my workmen, and trying to persuade them to steal antiquities from my work to sell to him. I must therefore ask you to inform this Hellenic subject that his action is illegal, and to order him to abstain from such action in future. In case you are not able

to communicate with him immediately, I should be much obliged to you to give me an order in Greek to this effect, in case he comes here again.

According to the message to the Greek consul, Sheikh Abd al Haj must have complied with the request for information about the Greek national. No note on the outcome of the case has been found in the archive materials at the Petrie Museum.

Despite the problems caused by antiquities traders, Petrie remained an enthusiastic purchaser. Notebook 44, from the start of the second Delta season, 1884-1885, includes instructions, perhaps from the traveller Greville Chester (Bierbrier 1995: 96-7), on how to find antiquities shops (scan 40):

Wassili's room opposite Gibari's room (plate on door), first turn to left at top of 1st stair, in at pipe stick seller. Fort Caffarelli's opposite on E, shop antikat just beyond, next to gold bazaar, gt harbour rd and turn at Sarazo pal. in road to harbour, turn at a [sketch] column in corner of wall down toward harbour; antika shops some way down; hence get through to gold bazaar

When Petrie became Professor in 1893, he felt able to form a larger-scale purchasing strategy for building up typological teaching collections. In 1893-1894 at Qift he recorded names of four antiquities-sellers at the regional tourist centre, Luxor: Abd el Megid, Mohasib, Mohamd Todros and, below the outline of seated figure at a table (?) with measurements, Mahmud abu Hasan (Notebook 93, scan 14). On another page, more details follow, with strokes across the start of first, second, fourth and sixth entries (scan 17):

Abd el Mejid
Edrisi opposite A.M.
opposite Mohamed is a deaf youth wth stela
American Consul
Yusef Ahmed (?) opposite the English Consul
on the other side the Cope American Mission Schoolmaster's father
Ermaneos el Gournos [?]
Village of Kanae

A few years later, in his 1897-1898 season, Petrie recorded his exchange with a local government worker (Notebook17a, scan 22):

First day talked to chief worker. Proposed to stay in Dendera and not to trouble us by coming round. Said it was hard not to get bakshish on the finds as govt gave _him_ nothing for them, no doubt I would give him £1 or 2 when anything good came in.

Finally, during his 1910-1911 season at Hawara, Petrie displayed his continuing interest in traders or local residents with special knowledge of local antiquities in two entries (Notebook 37). The name N. Phraphes in

Greek letters is accompanied by a comment 'Fayum, knows important papyrus sites in Fayum' (scan 6), and a later entry (scan 32) reads:

Muhd Said, main dealer
Hasani Atiyeh
Muhd Omar
at Rubey, over the bridge W end Medineh

Names of sellers of antiquities in lists of objects in expenditure
Sometimes Petrie noted items shown to him by named individuals, without specifying whether he acquired the material or not; the present whereabouts of items can clarify their acquisition history. In a Notebook from 1884-1885 Petrie wrote the initials of Greville Chester, GJC, beside a copy of the hieroglyphic inscription 'son of Ra Sobekhotep beloved of Sobek lord of Nubyt' on a cylinder seal-amulet (Notebook 44, scan 28); from Chester this object went to the British Museum, where it is now numbered as EA 15701 (Ryholt 1997: 402). Later (scan 33), another entry records a purchase of '3 figs Suleiman £15', with hieroglyphic inscriptions identifying the item as a triple statuette now in the Petrie Museum, UC16650; the price seems high for such a small figure, and may have covered a group or 'lot', including the following inscribed items recorded scans 33-35. On his Upper Egyptian journey 1886-1887 (Notebook 46, scan 4), he drew late Middle Kingdom scarab inscriptions with title and name, beside their then owners Todros, G.J.C. (Greville Chester) and Murch (Chauncey Murch, American Protestant missionary and purveyor of antiquities at Luxor, see Bierbrier 1995: 302). During his brief season at Dahshur in spring 1887, he sketched two forms of weights, over the entry 'from Ibrahim' (Notebook 32b, scan 6), and on the next page he recorded a Late Period hieroglyphic inscription 'with Abd es Salam bro Omar' (scan 7). At Hawara the following year, Petrie noted the name 'Muhd Dakhakhni' under a deleted line about weights, but this may be a local supplier of other goods, as Dakhakhni meant tobacconist (Notebook 36, scan 7). At the start of his 1893-1894 Qift season, Petrie listed several antiquities with numerals, presumably prices asked or paid, including three beside the name Basta abd el Melek (Notebook 93, scan 18).

A Notebook from 1896-1897 lists items known to have been acquired by Petrie for his own collection or for others. One page records under 'fine Arab pieces many inscribed Pantazzi' the dimensions of steelyards now in the Petrie Museum, followed by 'Abd es Salam Khatat for the cats', almost certainly a reference to a group of marble and limestone cats in ancient Egyptian and ancient Greek tradition, now in the Department of Greek and Roman Antiquities at the British Museum (Notebook 21, scan 4). The same page has the entry 'jars and cones at Mus.', perhaps a reference to purchases of material at the Egyptian Museum for the Petrie typological collections, and beside a hieroglyphic inscription Sobek lord of land of

Anpet 'Mahmud son of Shekh'. The next two pages give lists of object names with numbers and totals, being the cost, ending with 'all Abdullah Smain abt 200 bits' (scan 5), and the following miscellaneous entries include the name 'Farag' beside a statue base 'no name Sakkara' (scan 7).

In general, the record of acquisitions was more standardised. Many Petrie Notebooks end with lists of expenditure which include general accounts of objects acquired, with a number specifying the amount paid, though generally not the currency (Drower 1985: 330). These object+number lists may include finds on site by the workforce, with the amount paid to the finder, along with antiquities acquired from sellers in Cairo and elsewhere. A few of the lists give the names of the antiquities traders:

Abd en Nur: Notebook 75 (1894-1895) scan 35 (marginal note, perhaps to correct previous 'Abu Nur'); Notebook 124 (1905) scan 27; Notebook 7a (1900-1902) scan 53

Abd es Salam: Notebook 19 (1896-1897) scan 26

Abu Nur: Notebook 75 (1894-1895) scans 33 ('Abu Nur on boat'), 35; Notebook 107 (1894-1895) scan 20

Abu Saud: Notebook 124 (1905) scan 26

Basta: Notebook 75 (1894-1895) scans 32, 35; Notebook 107 (1894-1895) scan 20 (cf. Quibell notes from the same season, Notebook 84, scan 37 'Anticas from Basta')

Egyptian Museum Notebook 75 (1894-1895) scan 33 (Ghizeh Museum)

Girghis: Notebook 75 (1894-1895) scans 34, 35 (address 'Girghis Uburiah, Tagarah antika, Keneh' beside Arabic 'abd); Notebook 7a (1900-1902) scan 51

Ibrahim: Notebook 75 (1894-1895) scan 32

Kyticas: Notebook 75 (1894-1895) scan 32

Muhammad Mohassib: Notebook 75 (1894-1895) scan 33

'Passing dealers': Notebook 75 (1894-1895) scan 34

Suleiman: Notebook 75 (1894-1895) scan 32

Todros: Notebook 32b (1887) p. 76 (not visible on published scan 6); Notebook 93 (1893-1894) scan 35 (offer of Wadjkheperra and amethyst Sobekwer scarabs)

'Travelling Qurnehis': Notebook 75 (1894-1895) scan 34

Two other names may also relate to sellers, in a record from the journey into Upper Egypt in 1886-1887 (Notebook 122, scan 38):

Ibshara el Khayat	) names
Mseah-ha brothers	) at Siut

On the following line, the words 'for Muhd' may belong with budget table below rather than with names above.

One curious addition in a Notebook from 1907-1908 is a loose receipt on official government paper mentioning the Antiquities Service, with the signature Tano for stones received on 27.5.1908 (Notebook 7b, scan 50). Nicholas Tano is otherwise known as a Cairo dealer (Drower 1985: 330); the receipt may be the form taken by export permits.

(iii) Recording individuals: assessment, history, place

(a) Najama bedouin men and boys from Giza

During his journey by boat through Upper Egypt in 1886-1887, Petrie wrote in his Journal of his surprise at the age of his companions from the family of Ali Jabri in the Najama bedouin settlement at Giza (above, p. 68). In one Notebook, the moment of revelation is captured in the form of a genealogy through the male line, back to a point where the ancestor of Ali Jabri had left Tunis. The home-town for the family is given as Jalu, in the Libyan desert, at a crossroads of Mediterranean to central African and Maghreb to Nile Valley routes (Notebook 46, scan 11):

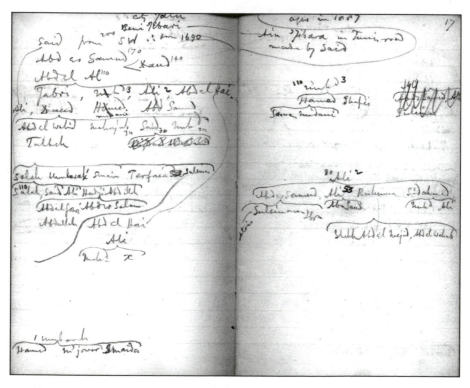

5.1. Family tree of Ali Jabri and Muhammad abu Daud, as recorded by Petrie in 1887, Petrie Notebook 46.

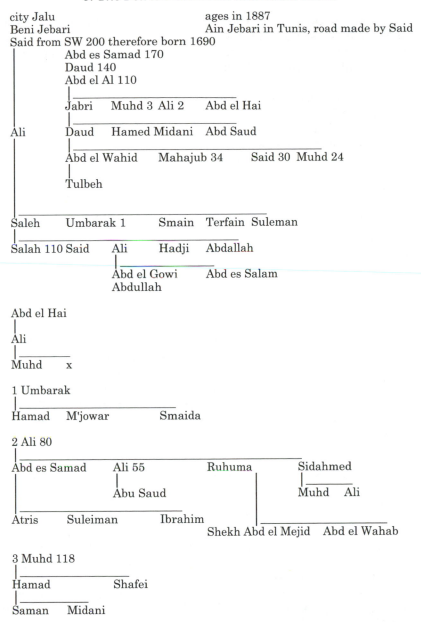

city Jalu   ages in 1887
Beni Jebari   Ain Jebari in Tunis, road made by Said
Said from SW 200 therefore born 1690

```
            Abd es Samad 170
            Daud 140
            Abd el Al 110

            |_____
            Jabri   Muhd 3  Ali 2     Abd el Hai
            |_____
Ali         Daud    Hamed Midani   Abd Saud
            |_____
            Abd el Wahid      Mahajub 34      Said 30  Muhd 24
            |
            Tulbeh

|_____
Saleh      Umbarak 1      Smain   Terfain  Suleman
|_____
Salah 110 Said    Ali     Hadji   Abdallah
                  |_____
                  Abd el Gowi     Abd es Salam
                  Abdullah


Abd el Hai
|
Ali
|_____
Muhd     x

1 Umbarak
|_____
Hamad    M'jowar        Smaida

2 Ali 80
|_____
Abd es Samad      Ali 55          Ruhuma        Sidahmed
|                 |                |            |_____
|                 Abu Saud        |            Muhd    Ali
|_____ |
Atris     Suleiman      Ibrahim   |_____
                        Shekh Abd el Mejid    Abd el Wahab

3 Muhd 118
|_____
Hamad           Shafei
|_____
Saman    Midani
```

These family relationships represent the understanding that Petrie had at this point in 1887, somewhat different from other expressions of filiation or brotherhood elsewhere in his writings. Despite a Eurocentric scientistic impulse in compiling genealogy, and despite the room for misunderstanding or miscommunication, this family-tree remains one of the most powerful documents in the archive. The timing may be structurally significant: Petrie had left the service of the Egypt Exploration Fund, and this river journey set him free of tasks to supervise, beside giving him more opportunity to spend time with the Najama.

(b) Egyptians recorded by Petrie on Egypt Exploration Fund Delta work, 1883-1886

From the December 1883 boat journey just before his first Delta excavation, Petrie listed the crew, with some notes of features by which he could distinguish one from another (Notebook 98e, scan 12):

Reis Ismayn Hassanen
Donkey boy Ibrahim
Black good ugly Mahmud
one eye Hassanen
Bright black broad face Ahmed Ise
Baboon black Hassan
Young man Abd el Halim
Old boy Khallil
young boy Abd el Halim
agent of Yusuf Said

There follows a table with column-heading numbers signifying the first nine individuals listed; judging from notes beneath the table, it was apparently devised to keep track of payments. The practice of noting visible features anticipates his later assessment notes in recruitment. Here the main reference is to facial features, but another option was clothing. At the start of his second Delta season in late 1884, four names are marked by robe-colour, a fifth by age (Notebook 44, scan 24):

Said Selim   black
Mustafa Derwis brown
Ahmed Johar   blue
Said Ali   old
Gotb Faraj   all blue

The distinctive visual markers of face and robe would remain principal criteria for Petrie in remembering who was who in his workforces, as far as he recorded his impressions for himself in Notebooks. In his first long name-list, for the large excavation force at San al-Hagar in 1884, Petrie sporadically used the following (Notebook 98c, scans 2-6; for the full name-list, see below, Chapter 8):

character (affecting work): discordant (Muhd Ali), stupid (Hassan es Salihi)
colour (of clothing): black (Ali Sad), black rags (Said Hassan), blue (Ahmed El Faghi, Hassanen Ali), grey (Muhd Daud)

134

complexion: fresh (Hassan Ali), pink (or clothing?) (Khadijeh um Ibrahim)
family or profession: boatman's son (Said Bakhsheed [?]), guard (Hassan Abdullah)
language (or origin?): French (Said Ali)
physical features: beard (Salim Mansur), fat face (Mahmud Salameh), gold ring (Sabha Muhd), high (Said ...), nose (Rakha Salameh), one eye (Arab Ali), paint (?) (Ibrahim abu Yusuf), pitted (Smain Salim), pretty (Ibrahim Sidahmed), squint (Said Um es Said), tattoo (Aziz[a?] um Ibrahim), ugly (Sidahmed Abduh)
place: Sharqawi (Hassan Muhd)
quality (of work): bad, bright (Said Umgrawadi), good (Hassan Muhd), poor eyes (Ihfaim [?] Abdu), sharp (Abdu Riani), too quick (?) (Ali Muhd)
size: big (Hassan Ahmed), small (Abd es Satur Ali, Amneh Ali, Buhadadi Said, Muhd Abu Said), tall (Amneh Salim, Buhadadi Mursi)

Sometimes Petrie combines features: Ahmed Hainawi (good, tall), Farha (tall, bright), Salim Hassan (big, open), Smain Hassan (one eye, bright)

(c) Fayumi recruits: **Madinat al-Fayum and Lahun**

At Dishasha in 1896-7, Petrie recorded one name and address: Mekowi Said, Menshiet Abdallah, Medinet Fayum (Notebook 19, scan 14). The location of this settlement on the plan of the site at Madinat Fayum is marked at the top of the sketch plan of the site a decade earlier in the Hawara 1887-1888 season (Notebook 36, scan 29). Mekowi appears in the Journals as one Fayumi who worked for Petrie as a boy, when he led the clearance of the Horwedja burial group at Hawara, and later as a young man, serving with the Anglo-Egyptian army in the occupation of Sudan (above, p. 79); this entry offers one of the rare instances where it is possible to identify more specifically the home of a key member of the workforce (cf. below, Chapter 8, Petrie Work-Phase IV, for identification by Hilda Petrie of specific hamlet or village for several of the men and boys from Qift.

Earlier, in 1893, Petrie had jotted down a short list of men he hoped to recruit on his way south, to train the Upper Egyptian workforce (Notebook 93, scan 8):

men wanted
Abdallah
Hussein
Ali Suefi
Sidahmed

Suleiman Muhd
Rustem
Abd er Robu

? Abd el Bageh Mustafa
Abd el Hadi Said

The first three names coincide with three of the five men who accompanied Petrie to Middle Egypt in 1891 (above, p. 71).

A few years later, a Petrie note refers to a request from Bernard Grenfell for four Egyptian excavators (Notebook 18, scan 4):

G wants from Lahun
Mahmud Siq
Ali Ahmed
Muhd Mansur
Godi

With another colleague from England, Arthur Hunt, Grenfell was directing EEF work at Bahnasa (Oxyrhynchus), where Petrie had left them extracting from town rubbish heaps thousands of fragmentary manuscripts, mainly in Greek. Petrie himself had moved north to look for earlier sites, and settled on the Old Kingdom cemeteries near Dishasha. From the same season, the Petrie Museum archives include a letter sent by Hunt from Bani Mazar to Petrie, dated 14.2.1897, in which he specifies the exceptional skills required for retrieving papyri (in WMFP1/115/2/2.2):

> If you can really spare a couple of Illahunis I should be very glad of Said and Mahmoud, but don't denude yourself at present if you want them. All of them will I hope come over here when you have finished with them, and if some of the Deshasheh people are not only honest but intelligent and like to come in March, ma'alesh. Brains are the absolute essential for papyrus digging. A workman may be as honest as the sun, but if he can't see the papyrus at once (and it requires a very sharp eye to do so in the perpetual clouds of dust) he passes it over or else knocks it to bits, and is therefore as bad or worse than a thief.

The dust-storm of desert town-debris can be seen in a photograph by Hunt of the work in progress (Rathbone 2007: 218-19).

In 1910-1911, Petrie jotted down the name and place 'Mursi Redwan, Maket Hawara' followed by an Arabic phrase 'kubri ganb el haram' 'bridge beside the pyramid' (Notebook 37, scan 2). This man may be a supplier rather than member of the workforce, as the name seems not to recur in the admittedly limited name-lists for that season (below, Chapter 8).

(d) Qift recruits

The first Notebook from the 1893-1894 season at Qift contains a list of names with payments, presumably for finds, where Petrie again, as in his Delta work, notes to himself the most distinctive visual features of the men – garment colour and presence or absence of beard and moustache (Notebook 93, scan 37):

5. The Petrie Notebooks: individual issues

Antiq this page 196   Ant Koft

	pay
lt beard and str must Abd er Rahim Mahmud	10
Muhd Ibrahim beardless yellow thick face	10
Ali Omar dark blue shawl	1/2
Ali Aleyn must turned up	7
Ali hamed najar slight beard wt and bk	5
Hassanen Hamed wt and bk beard short	3
Said abd el Main square chin 2 spits bd	3, 3
Hasan Muhd [sketch] slight must. yell face	2, 1
Ali Muhd slight beard blue bead [?] shoulder	5
red cap wt turban hollow jaws small chin	
bk robe Said Fahm 2 blue buttons	3, 2
Mahmud Ahmed smart full bk bd short	7
Deryas full must	17 (6, 8, 3)
Camel man	5
Umbarak Ali must, jaw bd	1
Ahmed Muh boy yell face	4
Smain abdel Jawad smiling little bd + must brown	16
[to left:]	
Hasan abd el Main no bd, brown 5, 4 1/2, 3	
Said Galab slt yell bd 7	

Another Notebook from the Qift season contains an entry 'Abd el Ati Abd el Ali known to Md Derwish', perhaps a note for recruitment during the season (Notebook 54, scan 10). The Notebook closes with his concluding assessment of thirty-nine men and boys (scan 26):

Good	Medium	Bad
	Ad Sehab	
Terfik	Said abu Lela	Md Hamed Galus
Ad Sehab [deleted]	Ali Muhd	Abd Rm Ibrim beard
Senusi	Ahmed Muhd	Najmedin
Amr	Abd el Azim	Hadji Osman
Awadeh	Yadin Derwish	Suli Smain
M Derwish + Yunis [with line as if moving to Medium]		
	M Khalifa	M Suliman camel
Husein Ahd	Masluk	Ahd Sul Hamadi
Abadeh Musi	Abd R Must dark	Hussein Ali
Hassan Osman smiler	Mubark Must	M Yunis
Hussein Osman smiler	Abdll Sudani	Ahd Yusuf
Umbark Ali	M.Wanis	
Yusuf Ahd Ababdeh	Ahd Yadin	
Awad		
Ibrm Shehad boy		
Muhd Abd er Rahim boy		

smilers brothers

This 1893-1894 Qift list captures Petrie at the moment of selecting men who would provide the core workforce for the remainder of his career. These workers became celebrated in archaeological Egyptology as the

Quftis, and were imported into work by foreign archaeologists throughout the Egyptian Nile Valley. The undated list categorises the men, in a private assessment without explicit criteria. A decade later, Petrie recorded his character assessments for two workmen on the Ihnasya season, 1903-4, perhaps both new men from the Qift area (Notebook 23b, scan 19):

> Said Osman good
> Umbarak Bakhit objectionable. not bad.

The Qift workmen are often recorded in groups, but individual notes for their names with specification of their homes are rare, only the following two so far being noted by me:

Notebook 84 (Qurna 1895-1896) scan 29 Quibell (?) note 'Gaud Smain Kuft'
Notebook 106 (Saft, Wadi Tumilat) scan 28 Petrie note 'Khalifa Ahmed, Mahamied, Erment'

For a far fuller listing, almost a census, compiled in 1903 by Hilda Petrie during the season at Ihnasya, see Chapter 8.

(e) Other local workforces

Besides the Giza, Fayum and Qift recruits, the sporadic work at sites throughout the land involved a wide geographical catchment. Sometimes it is not clear whether a local resident noted in a book is involved in excavating or in some other relation such as supplies. During his 1894-1895 season on the Theban west bank, Petrie wrote the entry (Notebook 110, scan 26):

> Yusuf Ibrahim
> Shekh Girgis Abu Jedullah
> Luxor

In the context of the dig, this might be interpreted as an address, but another Notebook records the name Yusuf in connection with prices, perhaps calculating costs for a commission, and this makes a commercial relation perhaps more plausible (Notebook 109, scan 7).

However, on other occasions, the work context is clearer. From his first season at the pyramid of Maydum, 1890-1891, Petrie recorded a short name-list, presumably for future recruiting (Notebook 59, scan 14):

> good Medum men
> Khamis Mansur   tall
> w Shaban Ahmed
> x Hassan Ahmed   Saft
> Ali el Hag   Muhd Said
>
> odb Khafafi   small bk beard and whiskers
>   owes 4 ½ 3 ½ PT

138

The note in the last two lines may not refer to Maydum men. In the note at the right, it is not clear whether Saft refers to Hassan Ahmed in the same line, or Muhd Said below; Saft is presumably not the Saft in the eastern Delta, where Petrie later excavated, but either a village in the Maydum area, or a Saft near Giza, mentioned as origin of one of the Giza men in the 1885 Muhammad Baraysh incident.

At Araba in 1902-3, for four local men Hilda Petrie records the name of the village: Harageh for Ahmed Yusuf and Haridi Muhamed (presumably a Harageh local to Araba in Upper Egypt, not the site near Lahun excavated and published by the British School of Archaeology in Egypt in the following decade), Nazlet Aktyri for Muhamed Feshni, and Nazlet Khadra for Huseyn Ahmed (Notebook 1, scan 36). The same Notebook places the workforce under two headings, 'Egyptian Research Account' (scans 2-11), and 'Locals' (scans 28-29, 32-33, 36). The non-locals can be identified as the men from Qift; similarly, a decade later at Mit Rahina, the workforce assigned to South, East, West, Central site areas have a mixture of Q and M prefixes, for men from Qift and Mit Rahina (Notebook 68b, scans 2-4).

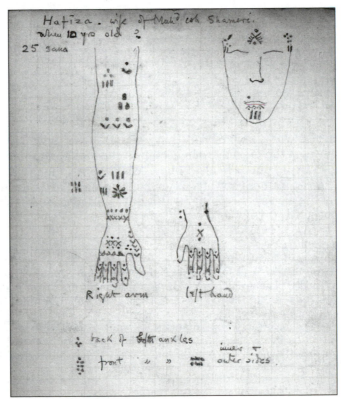

5.2 Hilda Petrie's notes on a woman at an excavation (1902?), Petrie Notebook 132.

Once in the Notebooks, Hilda Petrie recorded additional details on two women at the excavation, drawing their face and lower arm tattoo patterns, and noting alongside their names, ages, and age at which the tattooing was done, together with the family connection to the workforce (Notebook 132): 'Hafiza – wife of Mud esh Shameri when 10 yrs old? 25 sana' (scan 2), and 'Fatima 15 yrs (dr. Muhd Khallil)' (scan 3). The Notebook is not dated, but the main contents seem to relate to the journey of the Petries home to England through Italy in 1902 (Drower 1985: 267). The two young women would then be from the families of workmen in the 1901-1902 season at al-Araba al-Madfuna (Abdju/Abydos). According to Petrie (e.g. in *Methods and Aims*, see above, Chapter 2), Upper Egyptian excavation workforces did not include women, so these may be local residents of the Araba al-Madfuna region.

(iv) Work conditions: health, pay, separation of space

(a) Health
Amid the political upheavals of 1919-1920, Petrie listed in a budget column headed PT for piastres (Notebook 43, scan 10):

Medicines men	(335
	(75
Men doctor	150
Jeffris doctor	100

One G. Jefferies was a new recruit that year (Drower 1985: 349 with 459 n. 1), and perhaps the presence of a doctor on the team prompted Petrie to turn his ingenuity to public health policy. At all events, the same Notebook contains a Petrie draft or copy of a letter, containing a particularly explicit statement of his views concerning health at the excavation sites throughout the country (scan 19):

> Dr Dr Granville,
> during 40 years I have been giving remedies for obvious ailments to my workmen and others, and have wished that the people could obtain such cheaply at the PO. The dread of the extortions of the native doctor makes the fellah avoid him to the last. I have known men walk 12 miles from a mudiriyeh to buy a dose of quinine from me.
> If at every PO there were small quantities of some remedies in solid ready for use in bottle ~~colored~~ tinted according to the purposes, the people would soon learn to use such. They readily know what to ask me for in obvious cases. The most necessary, in order, I would suggest are
> Zinc sulphate solution, say 1 oz (in blue)
> Quinine sulphate solution, say 3 dozen 5 grs (in red)
> Carbolic in keroscene, say 2 oz (in yellow)
> Boric ointment, say 1 oz (in ...)

Aniseed oil, say 1/2 oz (in white)
The costs (from measuring) per <u>100</u> bottles (sold at 100 PT.) would be
Zinc   .4 mill
Quinine   75.PT now (normally only 30 PT)
Carbolic   .3 mill
Boric & Aniseed also very cheap.
Thus only the quinine would cost the actual price of 1 PT a bottle; the other things would pay for all the bottles and expenses. 10% on all sales should go to the post clerk, or he would deny medicine to save trouble.
I believe that this is a great improvisation; public health would be made to pay its own way, and the people taught to help themselves. None of the above quantities would be dangerous, or could be use for bad purposes.

At the start of his excavating career, in his Delta 1883-1886 seasons, Petrie had recorded his concern over misuse of material in an obscure note, possibly an indirect reference to political rather than medical matters (Notebook 74f, scan 37):

Fresh ... is best of all
but nasty medicine put in this
not so good
but most people to do somethin
wrong now

The list of proposed medicines also echoes past notes, recalling one from his Fayum work twenty-five years earlier as if his medicine chest for the season (Notebook 34, scan 19): Antipyrin, Opium, Calomel, Richter Hg, Arsenic, Strychnin, Belladonna, Carbolic*, Sulph zinc, ~~Peppermint~~, Quinine, Bromide Sodium, Peppermint. Given his concern over misuse of such substances, it is the more extraordinary that, in 1893-1894 at Qift, Petrie delegated control of stores to Ali Suefi and a Hussein (Notebook 54, scan 21):

Give
Ali.   Carbolic Acid and cotton wool
              Sulphate zinc   Quinine dawa el hama [Arabic 'fever medicine']
Hussein   Stores catalogue

The first of the two is presumably Ali Suefi, entrusted with the medical supplies, despite concerns expressed earlier and later about possible local 'misuse' of the material. It is less easy to identify the second, but he may be the Hussein among the names of the Fayumi men Petrie listed on his way to Upper Egypt in 1893 (above, pp. 71, 135-6). It is also possible that Hussein is from Qift; later, Hussein Osman of Qift would be called second only to Ali (above, p. 79). However, in 1904 Hilda gives his age as 25, so he would have joined the workforce at Qift at the age of just 14 or 15, see below, Chapter 8); this seems rather young to be assigned to looking after a stores catalogue in 1893.

In the first Delta season Notebook recording wages to April 1884, two names were recorded in two hands (Notebook 98c, scan 37): 'D. Alexandre Habra medecin de l'hopital' and 'Ibrahim Kamil Effendi sub inspector district Arin. Fakus' (Notebook 98c, scan 43). The facing page contains a note 'for the 8th April, paid to Muhd Salim on 3rd May'. This may relate to the early April 1884 accident in which a boy on the workforce died after being buried by earth-fall, after which 'soldiers and an officer had arrived with a doctor', and compensation was paid to the family (Drower 1985: 79). Both the doctor and Ibrahim Kamil are among those named in the photograph captions of Notebook 23, where the town name Zagazig is given for the doctor (see below, Chapter 9). Although it also housed a regiment of British occupation troops after 1882, Zagazig could well have been the nearest hospital in the series set up in the reign of Muhammad Ali by 1846. These offered free health care, reviving a tradition going back to the ninth-century AD maristan hospital at al-Maafir Fustat, and the Mamluk Bimaristan al-Mansuri, which was recorded by the Turkish traveller-author Evliya Celebi as the only medical centre operational in seventeenth-century Cairo (cited from Winter : 237-8). After 1884, there seems to be only one reference to the regional hospitals, from the last Petrie season in the Nile Valley, at Qau in 1923-1924. Petrie referred to hospital treatment in an entry in two budget tables: 'Man to hospital' (Notebook 79, scan 2), and 'Muhd abul Hasan hospital 42½' (Notebook 79, scan 4). Petrie does not specify which hospital, but the nearest to Qau would have been the one at Asyut.

Around 1902, despite the claims that colonial empires brought to subjects an increasing prosperity, the increasingly malnourished population succumbed to a severe epidemic of cholera. Excavating at al-Araba al-Madfuna (Abydos) in rural Upper Egypt, Petrie was already in touch with health authorities, perhaps for his supplies of medicine, as two Notebooks record the same name and address (from 1899-1900 Notebook 4, scan 17, Notebook 2, scan 27; from 1900-1901):

Director, Disinfecting Station, Sanitary Department, Abbasiyeh.
J.M. Akaoui, Pharmacie de la Bourse, Ezbekieh

A third offers the same name with a price, perhaps a payment (Notebook 7a, scan 14, in section from 1901):

Akaoui St Gabr. 95 PT + 3d (?), Pharmacie de la Bourse

These entries predate by at least a year the cholera outbreak noted by Petrie in his letters home (above, p. 94), but may relate to the same general problem.

(b) Pay-rates

Aside from the fuller data of the payroll lists, from which research by an economist could extract far more detailed information, the Notebooks contain only eight explicit references to pay-rates, all but one (Notebook 58) in Petrie's handwriting. The notes seem all to refer to local currency, by piastre and pound, but they span four decades, and differ according to region and type of work, complicating comparison. In phase II of his work, Petrie refers to payment for supervisors, in phase III to the rates offered by another foreign expedition, and only in the final phase V to terms agreed with, presumably, workforce supervisors. Provisionally, the figures seem to agree with information in Petrie publications and Journals; the rates given in 1906-1907 and 1910 are a little higher than those recorded in the 1904 publication *Methods and Aims* (above, p. 31).

Petrie phase II Delta excavations for the Egypt Exploration Fund, 1883-1886

1. Notebook 98d (San al-Hagar 1883-1884) scan 1, pay rates for supervisors, listed after heading 'Excavators Wages Book San 1884', before main name-list:

PT
£1.20 week Ali Jabri
4 a day Muhammed
4 a day Mursi
~~4 a day~~ 3 a day Abd er Rahim 14-20
3 a day Khalifa Ali (son of Reis) 15-20
4 Fakus [?]
4 a day Muhammed Hassanen (Reis) 21-

The reference to Faqus concerns connections between Petrie at the remote site and Faqus the local town, as outlined in the Petrie Journal for 22.2.1884 (above, p. 60).

2. Notebook 44 (Delta 1884-1885) scan 12:

	offered PT
– Abu Saud	8
– Muhd abu Daud	4
– Said abu Daud	4
– Abd es Salam Abdullah	4

This confirms the names and rates in the November 24 1884 Journal (above, p. 63).

3. Notebook 74 (Delta 1885-1886) scan 7:
Auad Umad from Cairo
70 francs for month;
Muhd, Said, and Mahajub   6PT

Tulbah   3 PT
                                  per day
Mukhtar Ali from Kafr Zayat at 40 frs per month

The two men whose salaries are calculated in francs are the Berber cooks employed by Petrie, according to the Journal for 7.12.1885 (above, p. 65). Between them are the four Najama supervisors from Kafr al-Haram, acknowledged in the publication of that season of work (Petrie 1888: 3, above, p. 38).

Petrie phase III excavations by direct Antiquities Service permit, 1887-1892
4. Notebook 39c (Lahun, Hawara 1888-1889) scan 30:
   Kruger contracts ½ to Bulak
   has 15 men, agreed to cut 150 metres a day
   pays 1½ PT a metre = 325 PT a day
   + real (?) wages are 45 PT. balance to
   Shekh

Petrie phase IV Egyptian Research Account/ Egypt Exploration Fund, 1893-1905
5. Notebook 109 (Six Temples Qurna 1894-1895) scan 7:
   PT   ins (?)
   5½   9½   Yusuf
   6½   11

These may be calculations for a particular commission to supply some material; the person named may be the Yusuf Ibrahim in a Luxor address in Notebook 110 scan 26.

Petrie phase V British School of Archaeology in Egypt, 1905-1930
6. Notebook 89a (Giza, Rifa 1906-1907) scan 5:
   Terms settled   42 PT to mid Dec, and after March
              52 from mid Dec to end March
   Germans paid 4-6 for men, 2½ for boys baskets
      and 5 for Quftis, 3-4 for tall boys

7. Notebook 58 (Maydum 1910) scan 2:
   Rate of pay Meydum 3½ PT for man
                       2½ PT for boy
   Agreement with men
   10 PT p wk for Quftis and local rate of pay.
   Locals and Quftis pd alike for work
   Shd average out to abt 7½ pd man and boy
   v. good man and boy might go up to abt 10 pd
   v bad   down   6 pd

Above is entered an exchange rate starting from 1 Sov(ereign) = 97½ PT,

2 = 195, and so on to 20 = 1950. The handwriting may be that of Mackay or Wainwright, both assisting Petrie on his fieldwork that season.

8. Notebook 68a (Maydum and Memphis 1910) scan 16:
    122 men average 9m day   54m week
    frontage 6m   )
    length abt 24m) 720 m3 each
    depth   5m)
    man + boy + carrier = 9PT 13 weeks work
                         to 3rd week May
    cost average 1P.T. £66 a week
        £860 in all
    paid 280
    bank 350
    coming 600
        1230£-200 = £1030
    to use land

(c) Separation of space: dig-house plans
Petrie phase II Delta excavations for the Egypt Exploration Fund, 1883-1886

The first dig-house constructed by Petrie, at San in the eastern Delta, is probably recorded in a Notebook from early 1884 (Notebook 98f). One house-plan is drawn over numerals and the name Muhamed Dafani early in the Notebook, and seems most likely to be the dig-house, built in January to February 1884 (scan 14); over the next page is an entry 'Muhd Ibrahim builder Samanieh', perhaps the builder employed for this construction (scan 15). Towards the end of the Notebook Petrie drew the plan of another construction, making it uncertain which is the dig-house; the facing page has a name and address 'Giovanni Stamatopoulo, Tel el Kebir, and Karaim', possibly the name of the owner of this second house (scan 42). In a letter home, Petrie gave a rough description of the dig-house (Drower 1985: 78-9); he took a photograph of the house itself, and the view of the temple from the door (reproduced in Spencer 2007: 40-1).

For his second season, 1884-1885 at Nabira, Petrie rented rooms in a large farmhouse (Drower 1985: 87): this may be the structure for which a rough ground-plan is given in Notebook 44 (scan 23).

Petrie phase IV Egyptian Research Account/Egypt Exploration Fund, 1894-1905

A Naqada 1894-1895 Notebook of multiple authorship, perhaps mainly Quibell and Duncan, contains two sketches of a house-plan with three rooms, perhaps the dig-house for the branch of the expedition excavating at the Ballas end of the series of cemeteries investigated that year (Notebook 55, scan 2). The front of a Ballas Notebook from the same season contains a similar sketch, with courtyard around two sides (Notebook 8, scan 1).

For the start of the season of 1896-1897, there is a plan by Petrie himself (Notebook 21, scan 10), with two side-rooms (stores?), a hall, and rooms marked as for 'men', Ali, Hunt, Gren<fell>, Geere and Cook. The named men are the members of the expedition who continued the clearance of Roman Period papyri from the town rubbish mounds of Bahnasa (Oxyrhynchus), after Petrie left with Ali Suefi to excavate and record the Old Kingdom cemeteries at Dishasha. The plan presumably designates the mud-brick huts constructed by Petrie and Geere out of bricks they made themselves, as none could be bought locally (Drower 1985: 225-6).

For the first season at Araba (Abdju/Abydos) in 1899-1900, the Egypt Exploration Fund had requested security from the English colonial governor Baring, following murder of an English couple at nearby Balyana; Arthur Mace had overseen construction of the house in advance of the arrival of Flinders and Hilda Petrie (Drower 1985: 256-7). For the second season, 1900-1901, a new house was built, with a room for the police guard, as Hilda had narrowly escaped being shot, and this may be the construction drawn by Petrie (Drower 1985: 264). In a Notebook from the second season, Petrie sketched the plan of a house with eight rooms marked with initials or words: F, H, S, M, D, store, in one room H and M, and in another Police (Notebook 3, scan 34). The first two initials are presumably Flinders, Hilda, and one M should be Mace, but other letters do not match the members of the European team: that season, Flinders and Hilda Petrie and Arthur Mace were joined at the work on the tombs of the First Dynasty kings by Amy Urlin, elder sister of Hilda, and a friend of Hilda, Beatrice Orme (Petrie 1901a: 1), while Anthony Wilkin and David Randall MacIver had a separate dig-house built for their work nine kilometres to the south at Amra (Drower 1985: 262; photographs of the house reproduced in Rowland 2007: 170-1). The plan in Notebook 3 may then record the Mace construction from the first season, with initials of occupants including the main Egyptians on the team, perhaps S for Ali Suefi, and in the shared room H and M for Hassan and Muhammad Osman the cook.

The royal tombs were a kilometre into the desert. For the third season at Araba, 1901-1902, the excavation moved to the town and temple remains by the edge of the fields, and Petrie had a new eleven-room house built; a quick drawing gives an impression of this larger construction as seen by Flinders or Hilda Petrie (Drower 1985: 264 and view reproduced on p. 347). A plan matching that view is preserved in a 1901-1902 Notebook (Notebook 7a, scan 16: the Notebook was reused for the 1907 season at Wannina, but the match between this plan and the Araba season drawing seems secure from the distinctive angled exterior wall of the courtyard). The Notebook 7a sketch-plan seems part of the planning for the construction, to judge from the calculations around it. Identifications for separate rooms again include F and H for the Petrie couple, Pol(ice), and a room shared by H and M for perhaps Hassan and Muhammad Osman. Other rooms have the letters GE, W, X, V and, in one room together, F and C; a small narrow space marked W and F adjoins a room with internal rectangle and circles denoting dining-table and chairs. Petrie listed the expected regular diners on the page facing the plan: H, F, Caulfield, ..., Weigall, Christy, and .... Of these inmates, Christy is presumably for Christie, an illustrator on the staff that year, and Weigall might be in room W; the previous staff-member Anthony Wilkin had died of dysentery in Cairo earlier that year after a journey to Kharga oasis (Drower 1985: 265).

Petrie was not always in brick housing. In a letter of April 1888 to Amelia Edwards, he included a sketch of his base at the Hawara pyramid, showing 'my tent' and 'Muhd tent' to one side of the brick store-rooms for their finds (page published Drower 1985: 139). Several decades later, at Sidmant, 1920-1921, he pitched tent in deep hollows, originally cut for tombs, to shelter his team (not necessarily including the Egyptian work-force) and his photography against the relentless wind (Serpico 2008: 103-4 with photograph).

(v) Arabic
1. Flinders Petrie
Petrie could understand and communicate in Arabic within his first two years in Egypt, when he is familiar enough with the script to be able to copy an inscription in the Great Pyramid. His own Arabic writing is identifiable in the Notebooks by certain peculiarities such as joining *dal* to following letters, and a tendency to separate the definite article *al-*. The longest passage in Arabic script is his copy of the contract with Sheikh Abu Ghanaym for supplies to the Sinai sites in 1904-1905. More often he transliterates into Latin script. All instances observed in the Notebooks are included here.

Petrie phase I Giza survey, 1880-1882
Among numerous copies of inscriptions left by early modern travellers in Latin script, Petrie copied one four-line Arabic inscription under a note about location in the inner Great Pyramid chamber known to early ex-ploreres as the 'Queen's Chamber': 'QC niche, no old graffiti till ~~two top niches~~ 2 top ... from top' (Notebook 26, scan 26).

Petrie phase II Delta excavations for the Egypt Exploration Fund, 1883-1886
At the start of work on his first season at San al-Hagar, early in 1884, Petrie wrote down eight Arabic words in transliteration, for which trans-lations are given below (Notebook 98f, Petrie scan 40):

heit	['wall']
beit	['house']
finn	['where']

hot   ['put']
hena   ['here']
shail   ['carrying']
bakar   ['come early morning/tomorrow morning']
badein   ['afterwards']

These seem to be a personal mini-vocabulary for directing the men who built a mud-brick house for Petrie as his excavation base (as recorded in his publication of the season, cited above, p. 44).

Between workforce name-lists for 7-19 April and 21 April-3 May 1884, at San al-Hagar, Petrie recorded a group of Arabic words and phrases in transliteration (Notebook 98c, scan 24):

khamista yom   ['Thursday'?]
arbata yom   ['Wednesday'?]
binit (bint)   ['girl']
etnean   ['two' or 'Monday']
ein eina
yoam   ['day']
kawisa   [for kwayissa 'good'?]
so-al (dol)   ['question']
a'ez (a[broken away]   ['I want']

Another three Arabic words are transliterated in a Notebook from the final Delta season in these years (Notebook 74b, scan 2).

In 1885, during the dispute over removal of bronze figures from Nabira during excavation, the name Hamed Ibrahim is written in Arabic over the slightly different transliterated form Ahmad Ibrahim (Notebook 6, scan 25 right). Petrie may be the writer of both transliteration and Arabic versions.

Petrie phase III excavations by direct Antiquities Service permit, 1887-1892
From the Fayum seasons, three Notebooks contain Arabic script or transliteration:

Notebook 35 (Hawara 1888-1889), scan 32 numerical calculation in Arabic.
Notebook 48 (Lahun 1889), scan 41 'Petrie' in Arabic.
Notebook 34 (Ghurab 1889-1890), scan 19 note beneath an entry (probably unrelated) 'Bus' Arabic phrase in transliteration 'Taaleh enteh min mashi, el harr gai'.

After his Fayum work, Petrie went to Palestine for one summer of work, to excavate at Tell Hesy for the Palestine Exploration Fund (Drower 1985: 156-67). The Arabic there was sufficiently different to cause Petrie to record vocabulary, sometimes with the corresponding Egyptian Arabic terms, on three occasions in the Notebooks:

Notebook 50, scan 28 transliteration of Arabic words in two columns (Egyptian and Palestinian Arabic?):

ragu	zelameh	['fellow'?]
dokhan	titin	['tobacco']
esh	khobs	['bread']
bikam	gud esh	['how much?']
khalli	desher	
kedeh	haak	
beta	taba	['belonging to']

ikra bet etn al netfit
16 hreb [?]

Notebook 50, scan 28 three tool names in transliteration with translation:
toothed reaping [sketch of sickle tool]   menjal
knife   "   karush
small, toothed   hashashi

Notebook 77, Petrie scan 23 six transliterated words in two columns:
chessar	hachj
chassajr	hach
chebir	kebir

Arabic writing practice, of *la* and *mim* combinations, is found in a Note-book perhaps from the 1891 return journey to England (Notebook 128, scan 3). From the 1890-1891 season at Maydum, a page of jottings includes a note on the local Saturday market with presumably its location in Latin script as 'matanieh' and in Arabic script, over initial *lam* (Notebook 59, scan 10).

Petrie phase IV Egyptian Research Account/ Egypt Exploration Fund, 1893-1905

At Qift, Petrie recorded two medical phrases, both in the same Notebook, and the first on the same page, where he entrusted Ali Suefi with stores (Notebook 54):

scan 21: 'dawa el hema' ['fever medicine'] beside Sulphate zinc and quinine
scan 24: 'duhr (?) nahl'

The next year, at Luxor, the name of a dealer Girghis 'Uburiah is accompanied by the transliteration 'Tagareh el antika Keneh' 'antiquities trader (at) Qena' and the Arabic writing of his second name, over 'Armen. Gabarian = Gabriel' with Gabriel also in Arabic script (Notebook 75, scan 35).

Another Notebook from the 1895-1896 season on the west bank at Luxor contains a longer passage in transliterated Arabic, recording a message sent to Ali Suefi (Notebook 109, scan 5):

Hat kullu el afsh sanduk moya u etnen Kufti wiak/al Nagada yom el talat neruk kibli sawa bil wab. Nimsek nas Ziaydah baaden. Darab gowab tele-graph al Petrie Hotel Nil Cairo
(Take all the things, a crate of water, and twenty Quftis with you to (?) Nagada on Tuesday; we will go south together in the ... Take Ziaydah people afterwards. Send message by telegraph to Petrie, Hotel Nil, Cairo)

There follows the word-count 36, and then, not recorded distinctly else-where, the address for Ali Suefi at the time of the Petrie arrival, with his fuller name:

Ali Muhammed Suefi, Nahiet Dum, Nagada

Followed by word-count 42, and then a note

Ali Suefi
and ~~wa~~ reis sandal Nagada
Imsek tezkireh sandalik Luxor ('Take the Luxor crates ticket')

Following Luxor are two deleted words, perhaps part of a name.

In autumn 1896 Petrie selected a region farther north, and recorded in Arabic script seven place-names from Bana to al-Minya, identifiable as Petrie handwriting by the gap after *al-* 'the' (Notebook 18, scan 33). A few pages later (scan 35) he wrote down in transliteration several Arabic words including special numerals used in bead-counting.

Three Notebooks from the seasons at al-Araba al-Madfuna (Abydos, 1899-1902) contain Arabic script:

Notebook 4 (1899-1900), scan 2: place-names of the area and several additional words irregularly spaced, followed by the names Regina Margarita, Genoa (hotel or ship?), Flinders Petrie, Hilda Petrie, and, of uncertain meaning, *mubarakah waram* (?).
Notebook 7a (1900-1902, reused 1907), scan 18: the place-name Helwan.
Notebook 3 (1900-1901), scan 45: separate Arabic signs, unidentified, with rougher copy in second hand beneath; scan 53: name of town Baliana in separate and joined Arabic over English capital letters in reverse, as if one European teaching another, and name of the English trainee 'John Garstang' in Arabic. Garstang had started excavating with Petrie in 1899 (Drower 1985: 255), and so possibly Flinders or Hilda Petrie is teaching Garstang.

The longest passage of Petrie Arabic handwriting is a rough copy of the contract for transport to supply the expedition in the difficult terrain of Sinai (Notebook 97a, scan 15, cf. Drower 1985: 288-9). The contract is drawn up between Sheikh Abu Ghanaym and Khawaga Bitry, with English notes summarising main points '20 PT', 'Suez 1 week', 'Bordis 1½ days', 'water 3 a day', '3 kanters', 'cash from Suez'. The initiator might be the individual whose name and scribal profession is recorded later in the same Notebook in transliteration (scan 43): 'Muhd Nasir <u>katib</u>'.

Petrie phase V British School of Archaeology in Egypt, 1905-1930
When Petrie encountered technical opposition to his fieldwork near Saft in 1905-1906, he wrote to an Antiquities Service official, recording his message first in French, then in transliteration and in Arabic script (Notebook 106, scan 10):

> Lazim waraq tani min shan beled Zowyeh alashan laah mush Sawa wa (?) Saft

Later in the same Notebook he recorded several more Arabic words:

scan 26: above, but not necessarily related to, crate-list, two words in Arabic script 'baray amalah' (baray separated signs); separately, deleted names M'ad Alyana, Mubarak Mustafa, Ibrahim Nur al Din, in Petrie Arabic (with *dal* joining)
scan 35: in Arabic 'Zagazig' with sign or motif following

Five years later, in a winter of work at Memphis and Tarkhan, he wrote down one more place-name in Arabic script, 'Dayr Mulyr', or possibly Mulyn (Notebook 101, scan 3).

2. Hilda Petrie
Hilda Petrie also wrote in transliteration, and once, for two place-names, in Arabic script. In her first season in Egypt, at Dandara 1897-1898, Hilda noted four phrases, translating three (Notebook 17c, scan 1):

abadan	never	maschi	bawa
temalli	always (deiwan)		
lall [?] in	bot		

Five years later at al-Araba al-Madfuna (Abydos), she was including transliterated words in her commodity account (Notebook 1, 1902-1903 season, scan 17), and on another page gives two transliterated words with English translation beside two transliterated phrases (scan 37):

fahm	charcoal	huna merdash
mab ret	sharpener, file.	Kam jarra

In the same Notebook, she showed her ethnographic and musical interests in her record of two lines of music with the start of a song 'yaa-mina' and the popular start to songs 'sall i sall', and then seven lines which may perhaps be read (scan 38):

Aly hahlak
hat melyan
ya shababi
daki aliya
ana harnistu
ya habibi
abu abu abuya

From the Lahun season before (1914) or just after (1919-1920) the First World War, another Hilda Notebook has the place-name 'al-Lahun al-Fayum' in Arabic script (Notebook 45, scan 1, again in notes of authorities on scan 32), and a series of transliterated and translated phrases (scan 7):

ana nezakha'nak I will shout to you
nessireh splinter, sa'altu p. t., tertib
masakr registered, sakru imper, sokartu p. t.
a'asal send, a'asalt p. t.
masarrif lessen? decrease

One more phrase is given later in the Notebook: 'insh'allah yizi kulli qwies' 'please God, if all is good' (scan 32). Finally, Hilda again noted in Arabic and transliteration local names for supplies in a market list for the early 1920 season at Lahun (Notebook 43, scan 27).

3. Other Europeans
The first English student for the Egyptian Research Account was James Quibell. In the first season, at Qift (1893-1894), it is probably Quibell who records in Notebook 55 a curious passage of Arabic in transliteration (scans 13-15). For the present book, Ibrahim Ibrahim has examined these pages, and identified the language as Fayumi dialect, indicating that the recorded speaker is one of the Fayumi supervisors enrolled by Petrie to train a new workforce at Qift. That person may be Ali Suefi, or perhaps a younger member of the excavation. The passage briefly outlines the process from ploughing land, to sowing, reaping, and winnowing, to grinding grain and making bread, as if he has been asked to explain the agricultural chain of production. There follows a shorter passage on 'M. u H.' growing corn, with the unidentified Arabic speaker as owner of sheep and goats. The pages end with a short vocabulary in transliteration and translation.

Quibell may again be the person writing down miscellaneous notes on a back-page, including the phrases 'letters, by Suleman' (possibly indicating the literacy of a worker or trader), 'nejungter er rahai' and, including the English translation, 'allah leh addar God forbid' (Notebook 113, Zowayda 1894-1895, scan 17). The next year, in work on the west Bank opposite Luxor, it may again be Quibell who records 'Ali's account' among budget notes, with entries in transliterated Arabic intermingled at some points with English e.g. 'merkeb from Ali' (Notebook 84, scan 13).

Two other instances by unidentified authors occur in records from the Memphis and Maydum season, 1909-1910:

> in Arabic script and in transliteration 'Hezbah' over transliterated 'Makafilah' (Notebook 68a, scan 43).
> in Arabic script 'Khallyl Muhammad Aly HaDl' below entry 'Khallyl Muhd Naj Handal Medum' (Notebook 64, scan 5)

4. Egyptian writers

Early in his second Delta season (1884-1885), Petrie jotted down a mixture of Arabic, Latin and hieroglyphic letters including name of Abu Saud (Notebook 44, scan 27). Beside the more hesitant two versions of Abu Saud, with English transliteration right to left to accompany each individual Arabic letter, a more confident ligatured writing of Muhammad Ali appears. Abu Saud is the name of Ali Jabri's son, to whom Petrie gave an Arabic-English alphabet at the end of his first winter in Egypt, 1880-1881 (above, p. 53). In this short practice sheet three years later, Petrie and Abu Saud may be teaching one another. Abu Saud is the higher paid of the four Najama joining Petrie on his western Delta season in November 1884, as listed in the same Notebook (scan 12, cf. Journal 24.11.1884, above p. 63).

A similar mixture of scripts occurs in a Notebook from the end of the 1885-1886 season (Notebook 74f, scan 24). The lower half of a page presents the name Mohamed Labib in florid Latin script, not by Petrie, over the name of a town in Sharqiya province, al-Salhieh, in Latin script, beside duck, lion, and owl hieroglyphs, perhaps for *S-l-m* (Salim?). Below the hieroglyphs the name Salhieh is written in two variants in a confident ligatured Arabic script, beside the joined Arabic letters *Ta-lam-ray*, and two cursive Arabic writings of *Misr*, 'Egypt'. Possibly here an Arabic-writer is showing Petrie the difference between the letters *Sad* and *Ta*, and *ray* and *ta marbuta*, in order to write Salhiya correctly. This may have been a practical measure, for accurate rendering of, for example, a post-office address near the excavation.

A different Arabic presence enters in the Fayum season 1888-1889, from which one Notebook preserves the imprints of the Arabic seals of the stone-masons Abdullah Ali and Ibrahim Zeid (Notebook 39b, scan 45). As formal signature these presumably confirm the legal agreement on cutting through the stones blocking access to the pyramid chambers (above, p. 98).

The most substantial sequence of Arabic is the name-list from a Delta season (Notebook 74e, scans 2-10). These may be in the hand of one of the Najama supervisors. Notebook 74e contains English entries relating to the excavation of Dafanna in spring 1886. In the Journal for 22.3.1886, on leaving for Dafanna, Petrie felt able to leave a sick Griffith at Nabasha because 'he had Mursi and Midani'; either might have been the writer of the Arabic notes. Arguably, the philological Griffith could have written the name-list to practise his Arabic, but there seems less reason for him to use Arabic for the sporadic notes of finds at the end of the Notebook (scans 33-34). However, the names in the Arabic name-list are closest to the Petrie name-lists for March-April 1884 (below, Chapter 8). According to the Journals, Ali Jabri was accompanied from Kafr al-Haram initially by Muhammad and perhaps a different Mursi, and Petrie had dismissed this Mursi by the end of March (above, p. 62). The name-lists by Petrie himself seem to run through the entire season from February to June without interruption, leaving no clear reason for the compilation of an additional list. April 1884 did see the single documented fatality on a Petrie dig (above, p. 105), and it might be thought that the doctor or military officer called to the scene compiled the Arabic name-list in relation to their official report. However, the inclusion of figures apparently relating to pay, and mention of pay-dates, as well as the notes of finds in Arabic at the end of the Notebook, all combine to give the impression of a record by someone on the excavation team, rather than by an external authority. This Arabic name-list adds precious evidence to other instances in the Notebooks and the Journals where Petrie took decisions against the normative colonial impulse of control. Ali Suefi may keep the medicine, and Hussein the stores, Mursi and Midani may direct the excavation of Nabasha while Griffith is sick, and here Arabic replaces English for the payment for labour and the crucial moment of recording finds as they occurred. This does not happen again within the Petrie archives.

6

Discovery names and object biographies:
individual features and finds

The Notebooks provide data for the critical point that has been absent in
the history of archaeology: on a large scale, the name of the discoverer of
single items or find-groups out of which archaeologists construct their
images of a past. This chapter covers the relatively rare instances in the
Notebooks in which European recorders refer by name to the individual
uncovering an isolated find or feature on an excavation site. The following
chapter turns to the discoverer-names recorded in long series of site
features, in nearly all cases burials in cemeteries, as documented in
Notebooks and, for select sites excavated 1909-1914 and 1920-1922,
printed index-cards, the 'tomb cards'. From these records, archaeology and
its museums have the potential to acknowledge, a century late, the named
principal finders of tens of thousands of artefacts deployed in their studies
and displays on predynastic and ancient Egypt.

The object biography in archaeology

Among the anthropological papers edited by Appadurai, *The Social Lives
of Things*, the contribution from Kopytoff had particular impact on archaeological theory, as noted by Gavin Lucas in his discussion of archaeological
conceptions of time (Lucas 2005: 56-7). Kopytoff outlined the changing
value as well as condition of any find as it moved through time, before
deposition, during its life in the ground, and after removal from the
ground. In archaeological and museum practice, conservators already
attended closely to these triple lives of the excavated object. Yet the
theoretical summary by Kopytoff brought a more explicit historical self-
consciousness into the specialised study of material beyond conservation.
Any object exists simultaneously in a variety of contexts, including the
aesthetic alongside the analytical, and various public as well as specialised
spheres of interest. Whether slowly developing or radically shifted, each
changing context must affect the meaning of a physically unchanged
object. For material items, the material context foregrounds itself, as a
socialisation – that is, the objects create a social group (cf. Bernback 1997:
76-81 on 'c[ultural]-transformations' in Schiffer 1987; Bernback notes the
critics of Schiffer who add the dimensions of repetition and complexity).

155

Each different material, form and use must imply different lengths of time in their social lives; as Bernback summarises from Schiffer, a basalt grindstone has a longer 'lifespan' than a thin-walled ceramic sherd (Bernback 1997: 77). Therefore each new grouping of objects creates a new and unique web of different lengths of time, each object bringing its own life history and associations of place, person and uses. From the moment when an object is deposited in the ground, its physical body does not remain static; in this phase of its existence, the separation of the 'natural' from the 'cultural' becomes more justifiable, because the material properties and effects become dominant factors in the life of the objects untouched by human bodies. In the ground the soil and other material around the object must determine its life, as conservators most closely observe in their struggle to maintain unearthed objects in existence. Damp soil may destroy organic components of the object, such as the wooden handle of a mirror, and immediately adjacent objects of different materials may leave their imprint more or less dramatically on one another, with staining or corrosion ('natural' processes of change, as the 'n-tranformations' of Schiffer, see Bernback 1997: 67). The construction of the primary physical context of a material object – what Colla (2007) designates artefaction in the case of any museum object – generates most of the potential for its dominant contemporary life. The stored, unpublished item has less chance of leading a prominent life in any context outside the collection audit. If that object is then highlighted in print- or online-publication or in gallery display, it may no longer be able to lead the same life, and its new life may affect the lives of other objects in its train. Whether isolated or grouped in the ground, 'finds' populate moving regimes of values.

Individual finds of specific finders

For a number of find records scattered throughout the Notebooks, the entries document the direct connection between a group foreman or individual finder and an excavation area or a particular object. In the following summary, by Petrie career phase, it might have been preferable to separate the evidence for the direct finders, the individuals whose manual labour uncovered objects from the ground, from instances where a name appears to relate more to a foreman. However, the foremen for each group of two to four workers were also themselves manual diggers, and the entries tend to mention only one name. The name-lists presented below in Chapter 8 confirm the system of pairing man and boy or girl in work as described by Petrie in print (Chapters 2 and 3). Evidently more research would be needed to differentiate within the hierarchy or spectrum from rank-and-file to 'subaltern'/supervisor in the excavation workforce (cf. the diagram of migrant labour hierarchy and roles, Toth 1999: 40, fig. 2.1). Provisionally, here, all Notebook entries are listed in chronological order, without attempting yet any further internal precision; the reader must keep in mind that a find 'by' or 'of' a named individual may be the result of work by more than that one person.

This chapter includes the examples of a single feature assigned one name. In such cases, it is particularly difficult to reconstruct the working practice, determining the number of people involved in any one act of discovery or clearance. A single man could remove all the earth and sand covering a large area, for example a house or a tomb-chapel, but further research may reveal the extent to which they carried out every aspect of the clearance, including the removal of earth. Work practices may be expected to have changed over time, as may be shown by comparing the 1889 work at Lahun and the 1909-1910 season at Maydum. In his publication of Lahun, Petrie stated that the earth was cleared from one room into the preceding, in order to preserve the site by back-filling; in such a routine, a digger might not need an assistant removing the earth. However, it is also possible that the Notebook record of names is incomplete, perhaps omitting, for example, any younger children assisting. The Notebooks may therefore not be easy to read literally as a full listing of the whole excavating force. For Maydum, the Notebooks reveal explicitly a detail missing in the Journals: the numbers of men working under each named supervisor. The relevant list from 1909-1910 is included in this section, as it illustrates the change in practice, and the range of work-crew sizes: four groups have twelve men under the foreman, whereas one team consists of only two men beside the man appointed as foreman. The spectrum of possibilities requires further research to identify the variable meanings of 'finder' in the collective excavation.

Petrie phase II Delta excavations for the Egypt Exploration Fund, 1883-1886

In his first large-scale excavation, at San al-Hagar early in 1884, Petrie made sporadic reference to finders in one list of finds (Notebook 98c, scans 38-41). Extracted from their context in the lists, the entries with names are summarised in the table overleaf.

Several other entries down to scan 45 have names deleted, either after payment, or from change in assessing identity of finder.

Among these entries, the only find number identifiable in the publications is 35. House 35 was the most important find group among the Roman houses uncovered by the Petrie team at San al-Hagar; the number of objects prompted an unusual and extended comment from Petrie on its monetary value in local and metropolitan scales (above, p. 60). Among its contents, the demotic inscription on a limestone statuette in Egyptian tradition gave a name read by Griffith as Bakakhuiu, from which Petrie called this the House of Bakakhuiu; the name has since been re-read Ashaikhet, and may refer to a deity rather than a private individual. In Egyptology, the most famous items from House 35 are the carbonised papyri of the first to second centuries AD, in Greek, demotic, hieratic and

Scan 38:

Nefertem	Muhd um Ibrahim		2
Alabaster cup etc, (Ali Baz house), No 35			3 ½

Scan 40:

Ptol 2nd B. Small head limestone		Ahmed Daud	37	2
Taur	37	Suleiman Amir		1
Shu	37	Khalil Omar		½
Bronze ring	37	Salahi (?)		¼
Eye, Ptah	37	Halimah		½
Weight ? pottery. eye	37	Ahmed Ahmed		½
Harpoc	36	Ibrahim Muhd		1
[no description]	36	Khal. Hass		2
Piece of mosaic	36	A S Pir..i (?)		3
Frog lamp + sculpture (well steps)		Elgrawi		3

Scan 41:

Pots		No 30	(Musi Shati)	3
Painted lamp etc	No 37	House	(Said Redani)	2
Bes, large terracotta		E of	(Ahmed Ahmed)	2
		my house		

hieroglyphic scripts; the only two published, both in hieroglyphic script, contain a sign-list and an encyclopaedic word-list since identified on numerous other manuscripts of the same period (Griffith and Petrie 1889; Osing 1998). The extraordinary range of finds brings to mind the fields of knowledge associated in earlier Egyptian writings with an institution known as the House of Life, linked to both Palace and Temple. However, any relation of San al-Hagar House 35 to the vast Amun temple complex there remains speculative. The reference on scan 38 identifies House 35 as the 'Ali Baz house', and therefore appears to ascribe the discovery of House 35 to Ali Baz (named also Ali Baz Pasha in the name-lists, see Chapter 8). However, other numbered finds on these pages clearly involved several people; six names appear with the number 37, and three with 36. Therefore, Ali Baz may be either the first finder, or the most important figure in a group of excavators on the site of a large house. The entry for House 35 does not name the finder, only the money given for 'alabaster cup, etc'; curiously, the publication does not identify any of the stone vessels from House 35 as a 'cup'.

On his second Delta season, a year later, Petrie wrote the name Fatimeh Barakat, with a number subsequently obscured by a stroke, on the same page as a draft label for a Naukratis weight to be 'Presented by the Committee of the Egypt Exploration Fund' (Notebook 74g, scan 20). It is possible that Fatimeh Barakat found that weight, in which case this page would preserve the chain that transmitted the object from local finder to excavation director to excavation society. However, the name and label may be two unrelated jottings.

From the third season, the exceptional series of Arabic entries in one Notebook includes records of finds at Nabasha, giving name and general location (Notebook 74e, scans 33-34). As suggested above, at the end of

Chapter 5, the writer may be one of the two supervisors left in charge while Griffith was ill and Petrie was at Dafanna: Mursi and Midani.

Petrie phase III excavations by direct Antiquities Service permit, 1887-1892
In spring 1889, Petrie directed one of his most important archaeological expeditions, to clear and collect the finds from what is still today the largest Middle Kingdom town-site, near al-Lahun at the entrance to the Fayum. In the first season recording the plan of the Middle Kingdom town, Petrie assigned a letter to each block of housing between parallel streets. At several points on his plan drafts in the Notebooks, he wrote the names of the men charged with clearing the rooms for him to measure. In Notebook 39b, names appear either side of the top of facing pages for the start of the clearance, along the block of housing numbered 'Rank A': Habbash and Sisi to left, and Ramadan with an unidentified name to right (scan 27). Later in the same Notebook, the name-list for calculating pay gives letters A to K, evidently the housing-blocks or 'Ranks' of the area cleared, in the separate western sector of the town site (scans 36-37). By letter, these are:

A Makluf
B Abd R Tant, Ahmed Siam
C Hassanen, Hassan Terfih
D Ibrm Hanafi, Ramadan
E Habbash, Ali Sis
F Sad
G Muhd Dahir, Hussen Oas
H Nasr Mabruk, Said M'haisin
J Farag Muhd, Abdl Hussain
K Muhd Osman, Shaban Muhd

In an earlier Journal, of 18.11.1888 (above, p. 93), Petrie noted that he would assign men from Madinat al-Fayum to the clearance of the town, and recruit men from al-Lahun for the work at the pyramid a kilometre to the west; the names above do recur in earlier name-lists, indicating that he carried out his plan. Comparing this list with the earlier page recording four names for Rank A, it seems that Petrie changed his method shortly after starting work on the town-site; he set four men on the western part of Rank A, and then, accelerating the pace of clearance, left one man to clear the rest of Rank A while each other Rank was cleared by a pair of workmen. This would help to explain why Rank A has the greatest concentration of precise findspots for specific objects or object groups. Here, according to the names in the Notebook, Ali Sisi discovered an exceptional deposit of objects related to birth rituals: a pair of ivory arm-shaped clappers and a figurine of a lion-headed or -masked naked female. In the chambers alongside, emerged the only mask to survive from ancient Egyptian daily life, now in the Manchester Museum. In Ranks B and C were found the oldest wills on papyrus, in the form of legal deeds of conveyance, among two exceptional deposits of papyri, now in the Petrie Museum. Notebook 49 contains further references to the excavators: one page (scan 2) has a note 'line of wall of Terfih's work', indicating the middle block of Rank N in the main town area, where Petrie recorded the find of another large group of papyri.

The following year, at Ghurab, Petrie sketched an oval enclosing hieroglyphs that give the name of king Thutmes III with epithet (Menkheperra-ms-Amun-Ra-s), alongside a note 'bronze ring fair found with 12 scarabs by Hasan Mabruk companion of Misid Hamada sold "A" ring' (Notebook 34, scan 11). The names Hasan Mabruk and Misid Hamada recur together beside a memo 'Write Fraser Hugh Main Prices Dealers at Illahun', apparently a reminder to himself (scan 14). The entries may or may not be related, leaving it uncertain whether the two persons named are digging for Petrie at Ghurab, or offering antiquities for sale at al-Lahun, or both.

In his recording at sites excavated in 1890-1892, Petrie entered the name of one person for a larger feature, where it seems unlikely, though not impossible, that a single individual could have cleared the area single-handedly. At Maydum in 1890-1891, Petrie labelled one large block-superstructure for an elite tomb as 'Mekowi mastaba ENE of [pyr]' (Notebook 59, scan 22). The year after, at Amarna, names appear beside some of the sketches of building-plans with measurements (Notebook 101); all but one of these were published, none with the names (Petrie 1894). In the recent survey by Sal Garfi and Barry Kemp, three of these structures could be identified, the rest presumably eroded beyond recognition or now beneath cultivation. The houses cleared by Abd er Rahim, Sulem (?) and Hamad (?) are unidentified, but the other structures appear on the later excavation surveys with alphanumeric grid-square references and structure number within grid-square (e.g. O47.21 is structure 21 within square O47):

Notebook 101	Notebook 101 caption	Petrie 1894 no.	current survey no.
scan 15	'Ali Suefi's house'	8	O47.21
scan 19	'Hamad's (?) house'	7	
scan 24	'Sulem's (?) house'	3	
scan 24	'Abd el Imam's (?)'	16	P43.3
scan 25	Suleiman	18	Q42.7
scan 25	Abd Rahim	unpublished?	
scan 28	Abd er Rahim	2	

The first of these Notebook captions, 'Ali Suefi's house', appears over the plan of the structure Petrie no. 8 = O47.21, and adjoins no. 9 = O47.19. The caption may mean that Ali Suefi directed or, perhaps less likely given the size, undertook alone the clearance of both parts. He may then be the discoverer of one of the most remarkable finds from the Petrie season at

Amarna, two fragments of a red jasper statue foot, of great anatomical precision, from the courtyard of no. 9 (Petrie 1894: 22, now UC150). The 'find', here, can be both a feature such as an architectural plan, and a portable object; it may be easier to appreciate the contribution of the manual digger or supervisor in bringing to light the singular object, but the plan may have brought greater impact in the construction of knowledge of the past.

Petrie phase IV Egyptian Research Account/Egypt Exploration Fund, 1894-1905
Qift, 1893-1894

In his work on the temple precinct at Qift, Petrie began to record depths and strata, in a rough application of what would become standard archaeological methods of stratigraphy. In Notebook 52, a heading 'survey in temple' introduces calculations with occasional names (scans 6-7):

'low wall S face' Mahmoud
'Outer N face low wall Misids'
'edge deep stone wall 93 S of wall face' zein (?) Ahmed
under bearings for 'SEΓ' 'Ali Smain'
'low wall S face' Hussein
'E face long low wall' Abd Rahim, Mustafa

At lower levels, the work exposed as the original soil 'a bed of tenacious yellow clay' (Petrie 1896: 3), and he refers to this as a stratigraphic marker in one instance with name: 'Farag deep wall yellow' (overleaf as 'Farag deep wall', Notebook 52, scans 12-13). This may be the feature marked as a thick 'low level early wall' on the published plan of the temple precinct (Petrie 1896: pl. I). It is less easy to identify two other named features recorded in the same Notebook, on a plan with line from 'Ali's well' to 'Mustafa's dept (?)' (scan 36).

Araba al-Madfuna (Abydos), 1899-1903

From the first season at Araba (1899-1900), an entry by Petrie records 'Muhd Ahmed overseer' at a distance above a sketch-plan identified in the handwriting of Hilda Petrie as 'Um el Qaab mound R' and 'ushabtis of Resh-uq' (Notebook 4, scan 26). R and 'Resh-uq' denotes the find of votive deposits including shabtis inscribed with the name now read Heqareshu, an official of the Eighteenth Dynasty (about 1550-1294 BC); Petrie observed, 'This ground was a favourite place for high people of that age to have their ushabtis buried in, so as to be near Osiris' (Petrie 1900b: 3). The entry with Muhammad Ahmad may be a stray jotting here, rather than giving the name of the overseer for the team excavating these important deposits.

From the second season (1900-1901), Petrie recorded a name over an object group (Notebook 3, scan 14):

Goergi M'awad
bronzes ... 1st lot all 1:3
2nd lot dipper (?) etc 1:5
pan & handle 2:7
.. 1:2
.. 1:5

This combination of name and find is, as in other instances, open to several interpretations. The entry might document a find with name of finder, either employed in the workforce or simply a local resident, or it could record a group of objects offered from a dealer. There is also the possibility that the numerals relate instead to scale for reproduction of images in a publication plate, in which case the name would be an unrelated jotting. In the excavations, the main finds of bronze vessels were in the tomb of king Khasekhemwy, re-cleared in 1901, but the descriptions and depictions in the publication do not match the list above (Petrie 1901a: 12, 27-8).

From the final season at Araba (1902-1903), during the clearance of the 'Osireion' (an Osiris-tomb for king Sety I behind the temple to his own cult), Hilda Petrie included in her calculations of pay a brief record of work progress, citing names for some dig areas (Notebook 1, scans 23-27). A summary diary covering the period from 6 February to 30 March includes several entries with names (scan 25):

Feb 13 New gang from Currelly. J.K, A.O. Hel.
Mar 4 Muhd Salim from Currelly A.O. E of lintel
Mar 15 A.O. moved down S to south of cross-hall
Mar 30 A.O. moved north

Overleaf she gives the names of the first team again, specifying the location of their work and implying that Ahmad Osman is the leader of the group (scan 26):

Ahd Osman E terrace Feb 13-23
Salim Khalil, Jad Kerim + boy. Helal

Below, the 4 March assignment of Ahmad Osman is repeated, followed by 'Th. March 12 Top terrace (AO 5d SK 4d)'. Some of the later work is recorded farther back in the Notebook, including A.O. 'Behind lintel' for 27 and 29 March, and 'A.H. gang' from 1 to 6 April, starting with the task of 'building retainer-wall' (scan 23). From the longer name-lists the named men seem all to be recruits from Qift (below, Chapter 8), among whom the initials A.H. might denote Ali Hassan, as a more prominent figure in the Notebook 1 name-lists.

Petrie phase V British School of Archaeology in Egypt, 1905-1930
Rifa and Giza, 1906-1907
Ernest Mackay recorded one name for an area of work during the re-clearance of a First Dynasty tomb south of the Giza pyramid field: 'East face of Mastaba cleared by Said Osman' (Notebook 88, scan 12). If Said Osman had any assistants, their presence is not recorded here. The tomb had been located by Barsanti and excavated by Daressy several years earlier for the Antiquities Service, but, by careful clearance of the surface, the new work revealed the traces of the superstructure. The western face retained much of the original niched brick facade, with smaller portions preserved on south and east (Petrie 1907: 3, pl. VI). Pottery and other finds indicate a date in the first half of the First Dynasty, making this one of the earliest extant examples of niched brick architecture in Egypt; since Jacques de Morgan discovered the earliest at Naqada (reign of Aha, second king of the First Dynasty), that architectural style has been at the centre of debate as one of a range of motifs apparently imported by unknown routes into Egypt from southern Iraq (for recent discussion, see Wengrow 206: 239-40).

At Rifa, one of the European assistants, perhaps Mackay again, recorded the names of finders in a list of the objects which Petrie called 'soul-houses' (Notebook 89, scans 17, 19-20). The term covers a range of pottery substitutes for stone offering-tables, ranging from plainer trays with sculpted depictions of meat-offerings over the surface, to structures evoking domestic architecture, with features such as columned portico, ventilation shaft cap (Arabic *mulqaf*), and steps to roof-level. A heading 'Soul House – Level Relation to Grave' (scan 20) indicates that the purpose of the list was to gather the evidence for the original position of the offering-trays; it is still not clear whether they were placed at surface level as focus for offerings to the dead after burial, or in the burial chamber or shaft, as part of the burial equipment to project an eternal supply of offerings, in case offerings above ground were interrupted or ceased.

In a third Notebook of the season, Mackay sketched a square, marked with cardinal points, containing a skeleton in a crouched position; above he wrote 'Tomb of Khalifa', and below are notes 'Head at N and facing east and at least 2 inches from body – the vertebrae were disturbed but otherwise the body was in good order' (Notebook 87, scan 11). There is no note of other finds, and the entry seems to relate to interest in customs of depositing the body with head separated.

Maydum, 1909-1910
A letter of 4.12.1909 relates how Petrie had to return to organising the workforce in six teams on his second dig at the pyramid of Maydum, when his European supervisor Mackay fell ill (above, pp. 83-4). A Notebook from the season adds the numbers of men and a seventh team (Notebook 68a, scan 3):

Big mastaba	Aly ar Rahim	12	(group 3 in letter 4.12.1909)
Lower temple	Hasan	4	(group 2)
Pyramid tunnel	Huseyn	12	(group 1)
Pit south	Shehad Ahmed	12	(group 4)
Western mastabas	Aly Firnisy	12	(group 5)
Outlying west tombs	Aly	6	(group 6)
E face N mastaba	Mhd Mensy	2	
		60	

In a separate 1909-1910 Notebook, either Mackay or Petrie's second assistant that season, Wainwright, referred to 'Arif's dromos' as a location of burials uncovered during the investigation of the pyramid complex (Notebook 62, scans 2-4). Two other Notebooks in the same hand preserve calculations on 'Arif's dromos' (Notebook 63, scans 18-20; Notebook 64, scans 12-13). The feature seems to be the approach to the pyramid, separate from the later causeway (Petrie *et al.* 1910: 2, 6-7); from its alignment and borders, it was identified as an initial phase of construction, at the earliest stage in the design of 'true pyramids', that is, pyramids with smooth sides, replacing the Step Pyramids of the preceding generation, at the start of the Fourth Dynasty (about 2650 BC). Like the other men named in these Maydum records, Arif is from Qift, according to the name-lists (below, Chapter 8); his contribution to Egyptian archaeology here relates not to the discovery of artefacts for display in a museum, but in the construction of scientific knowledge of the monumental architecture for which Egypt is famous. Here the product of the labour is an abstract and intangible object, rather than a displayable artefact, and in this area we have accumulated less expertise in calculating scope and price-tags for 'intellectual property rights'. As a result, the European recorder and consumer of the archaeological knowledge may find it easier to assign the finder an entirely passive role as the instrument of science, without reflecting on the way in which this migrant labour force collaborates with the recorder in the construction of knowledge. In the publication, Wainwright converts the team led by Arif into 'we', by which he probably intends, and the English reader probably accepts, the meaning 'the authors' whose names appear on the title-page – Petrie, Mackay and Wainwright.

Notebook 63 also contains entries for calculating pay apparently by quantity of sand removed, most ruled through, but legible enough to make out the names Arif, Huseyn, Hasan, Mahmud Hamid, Aly Rahim, Shehad Huseyn, Hamdan, H.O. (Notebook 63, scans 8, 10). Later calculations include one for 'Aly R's tunnel' (scan 13), and a day schedule for one Wednesday to Friday '8am Ahmed Osman, 1 local man to lift, 5 local baskets. 4pm Huseyn Osman, Mohd Sayd, 3 Qufti baskets' (scan 14). Here, similarly to the Petrie numbers, three to six unnamed workers stand behind the one or two named main workers from Qift.

6. Discovery names and object biographies: individual features and finds

Memphis, 1909-1910

In a letter dated 19.2.1910, Petrie wrote of the discovery by Hassan Osman of four gold ear-rings in a jar neck, beneath the debris of Roman Period faience manufacture at Memphis (above, p. 84). From the same season, he entered several further finds in a Notebook, in one instance giving the name and estimating date as Twenty-sixth Dynasty (664-525 BC): 'H Abul Hamad S of big wall XXVI [sketch] earrings etc' (Notebook 68a, scan 18). The name Abul Hamad recurs often among the recruits from Qift; the preceding H may denote a particular find, as the letters A, B and C are used to distinguish three houses on the same page. From the schematic drawing of one ear-ring, the group can be identified in the published excavation report, where the 'etc' has been revealed, perhaps after cleaning, as the more remarkable part of the find: '4 is a necklace of red coral and hollow gold beads with three hollow gold earrings. The thin gold is backed with plaster. It is seldom so much coral is found.' (Petrie *et al.* 1910: 44, with pl. 38.4).

Additional notes in another hand provide information on several of the inscribed stone blocks from dismantled temple buildings of kings Amenhotep III (about 1388-1350 BC) and Khnemibra Ahmes II (570-526 BC), unearthed in pits across the site (Notebook 68a, scans 42-43). Names are given for three of these sondages over sketches of the inscriptions, identifiable from the publication:

'Hole 58'	Aref	'Stone 16'	Amenhotep III, speech of Ptah
'Hole 59'	Umbarak Bahut	'Stone 15'	lower edge, Ptah and goddess
		'Stone 17'	Amenhotep III with epithets
		'Stone 18'	Amenhotep III offering vases
'Hole 62'	Must Mensy		Ahmes II pillar

Stone 17 is figured in the publication of the work that season (Petrie *et al.* 1910: pl. 29.2). Photographs of the work on an adjacent plate indicate how many people might be involved in clearing any one of these 'holes', even before the task of hauling out the block; in one example, seven individuals are visible at work (Petrie *et al.* 1910: pl. 30, no.7).

Hawara, 1910-1911

From the cemeteries of the early Roman Period (first-second centuries AD) behind the Middle Kingdom pyramid at Hawara, Petrie recorded three names for specific finds (Notebook 37). On one page he entered 'Rom sarc. Ali Omar' (scan 15), and on another two groups of panel portraits, his nos 33-35 with the name Khalifa, and nos 36-36A as found by Ali Hamad (scan 20). The Roman Period panel portraits from Hawara are famous for the realistic effect of the Greek encaustic technique (mixing pigment in wax). The largest excavated groups come from the fieldwork directed by Petrie, in 1887-1888, mainly supervised by Muhammad abu Daud, and 1910-1911. In 1911 the Egyptian Antiquities Service assigned the groups found

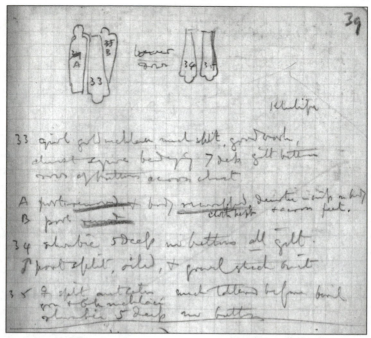

6.1. Names of finders in the record of excavation of Roman Period mummified bodies with panel portraits, 1911, Petrie Notebook 37.

6.2. Panel portrait of an adult woman, from a group burial excavated by Khalifa at Hawara, first century AD.

6.3. Panel portrait of a child, from a group burial excavated by Khalifa at Hawara, first century AD.

by Khalifa and Ali Hamad to Petrie for export; in the distribution of finds to museums contributing excavation funding, three of the five portraits were then assigned to three other museums, with Petrie retaining in his university museum the two more damaged examples. The current locations of these five portraits are (Roberts 2007: 70):

33	Petrie Museum UC36215
34	Brighton Museum R.137
35	Petrie Museum UC30088
36	British Museum AES 74715
36A	Manchester Museum 5380

These finds represent the opposite end of the valuation spectrum to the architectural features uncovered at other sites in earlier years, but, as evocations of the dead in burial, they also raise especially sharply the ethics of work in absence of consent. In contrast to the 'pure' scientific value of a site-plan or sequence of construction-phases, the portraits convey to European viewers in particular an immediate aesthetic and commercial value. The European establishment in both the art market and the scientific research community is united on the exceptionally high value of these portraits, as ancestors of a privileged branch of European artistic production, perspective portraiture since the Renaissance.

Their reception as classical European portraits has been encouraged by the standard practice of removing them from the wrappings and mummified bodies; removal was often necessary for the survival of such veneer-thin wood panels with wax-based pigment. On first encountering examples at Hawara early in 1888, Petrie agonised over how best to preserve them, and originally thought that he would not be able to transport any with the bodies to which they belonged (Journals 5.2.1888 and 12.2.1888, cited in Picton *et al.* 2007: 85-87). In both the 1888 and the 1910-1911 seasons, he also saw an unparalleled scientific opportunity in the survival of so many portraits together with the embalmed remains of the sitters, and endeavoured to preserve as many full bodies as possible, and, where not the whole body, the head, for future analytic comparison (Roberts 2007: 30-1). If the anatomical collecting seems ghoulishly close to head-hunting for the twenty-first-century western public, it may be set beside the decision by Petrie to bequeath his own head to a scientific teaching collection (Ucko 1998). The portraits and the physical remains of the elite Egyptians portrayed juxtapose what seem in the end irreconcilable regimes of value – monetary, aesthetic, sacred and scientific. The emphatically multiple faces of each reveal the complexity of what might otherwise seem a rather straightforward task of restoring to finder – whether restoring a unit of information, or an agreed price or value. In practice, such restitution cements a line of direction from the authorities that received the finds 'back down' to the finders. The more urgent and difficult task is a dialogue in which unconsidered regimes of value may intrude 'from below' and disrupt the diplomatic debates. Single features or finds may argue for this future less strongly than the greater masses of finds for which names can be found in other parts of these Notebooks, and in the index-cards of early twentieth-century excavation, presented in the following chapter.

Find-group records with finder names

The find-group as archaeological category

The find-group plays a central role in the development of archaeology as a discipline. A decisive turning-point was marked by isolating the group of finds as encountered in the ground at the moment of discovery. Within the emerging circles of those with exclusive focus on the material from the past, this emphasis on a find-group came to take precedence over the highlighted individual object. Already in art history and particularly in numismatics, individual objects were recognised as elements within another form of collective, the type-series. Encounters with natural sciences – first Linnaeus, then Lamarck, Darwin and Mendel – would help convert the type-series into the tables and trees of typology. With recording of spatial relationships, the find-group contributed a social dimension to that typological matrix of time. The institutional champion of the find-group was a nineteenth-century newcomer to the public sphere, the national collection, or Museum. Early in that century, just as a particular recreation of past time was becoming essential to the self-definition of the European middle classes, a Copenhagen museum curator Christian Thomsen reconstructed the sequence of Stone, Bronze and Iron Age, the Three Ages of Man, precisely from the delivery of objects to the museum in the groups as they had lain in the ground (Gräslund 1987). As a foundational category for archaeology, the find-group is too heavily collective to leave intact romantic assumptions of a directing Mind. In place of the singular genius of a great discoverer, collective uncoverers of find-groups appear as central agents of archaeology. The Petrie excavation archives preserve substantial numbers of the names in such collectives. This part of the record includes one of the most important advances in the uncovering of Nile Valley archaeology: the discovery of prehistoric Egypt at Naqada in 1894-1895, a discovery not recognised at the time by Petrie himself (on the recognition by Jacques de Morgan, see below).

Find-group finders in the Petrie Museum archives

In the excavation archives, the practice of naming finders derives from the need of the European dig supervisors to pay finders appropriately for finds. The entries tend to give a single name for each find-group, and in this way they may conceal the presence of a pair or trio of workers, as in the man-and-boy teams described by Petrie in his *Methods and Aims*

(1904). Despite this different original purpose, such accountancy devices hold the potential for a more specific history of archaeology in which more of the immediate workforce can regain name and role. The potential varies widely from one excavation season to another, with the different stage in development of recording methods and payment procedures, and the particular roles of each European recorder on site (not all were necessarily involved in payments). In the Petrie Notebooks, the main seasons with names of find-group finders are 1894-1895 for the cemeteries at Naqada and Ballas, 1905-1906 for the cemeteries at Saft, Suwa and Gheyta, and 1906-1907 for the cemetery at Zaraby and the monastery at Balayza. For later seasons, names appear on the new system of index cards for recording find-group, the 'tomb cards', used on British School of Archaeology in Egypt excavations at Haraga 1913-1914, Ghurob 1920, Sidmant 1920-1921, and Araba al-Madfuna (Abydos) 1921-1922. These two source-types are presented below, noting examples of groups that researchers have since particularly emphasised. In order to appreciate the significance of all groups, not only those already highlighted in research to date, it is important to consider the ways in which object biographies continue to develop beyond the moments of deposition and unearthing, in perpetual and unpredictable motion (cf. above, Chapter 6).

The find-groups covered in this chapter may be particularly susceptible to future re-evaluations. The potential derives from a pattern of object life repeated for most finds on cemetery excavations after 1893: the worldwide distribution of finds in combination with closer on-site documentation. After discovery and marking with a number to record their original context (see Chapter 3), the European excavation supervisors broke up the find-groups in order to pack all the material safely for transport off site; if they had not done this, heavier objects would crush any smaller, more delicate finds (for Petrie on packing procedures, see Chapter 2). Many items were left in situ, notably the undecorated pottery of forms already recorded from previous work. All finds removed from the site would be presented first at the Egyptian Museum Cairo, where mainly European senior officials on the Egyptian Antiquities Service would inspect, more or less carefully, the crates. After this official division, any finds not selected for the national collection would be allowed official export, and shipped abroad to London for exhibition to sponsors and the public. As Petrie lived in the days before British government funding of excavation in Egypt, he sent most finds on to public museums in return for, and in proportion to, their sponsorship of his excavating work (as already by agreement with the Antiquities Service for the Egypt Exploration Fund in 1882, see Drower 1985: 71). Although he himself underlined the importance of the find-group, and although many small and several of the more important larger find-groups were kept together, it would have been an immense clerical task to reunite hundreds of find-groups each year. In practice, then, it is not surprising that the majority of finds from one find-group were dispersed among two or more sponsoring museums.

As a result, few groups live in the public eye in a museum display, in the manner that so impressed Petrie in Bologna (Drower 1985: 185). From the plates of the excavation reports published at the time, many groups continue to exist in visual form as inked-in sketches, but most survive in a far less accessible format, the 'tomb registers' listing thousands of find-groups. Closer research often proves these lists to be incomplete or inaccurate, such that all need a monumental task of rechecking across the dozens of recipient museum collections, often themselves dispersed in the century since the journey from the Nile. In these conditions, find-groups add new dimensions to the usual opportunity for 'excavating the museum'. Group-oriented research might reveal any individual object as crucial evidence for old or new research agendas. This process of continual transformation should also keep the find-group finder at the centre of disciplinary self-awareness. Within this move, the very number of find-group finder names should also keep to the fore an awareness of the collectivity required for archaeological excavation.

1. Notebooks

Petrie phase IV Egyptian Research Account/Egypt Exploration Fund, 1894-1905
ERA Naqada and Ballas excavations, 1894-1895, sketches of burials as unearthed
The cemeteries at Naqada and Ballas were excavated in the same season, with Petrie as main supervisor at Naqada, and Quibell at Ballas. Both men were assisted by other Europeans for the recording – Hugh Price and Quibell's sister Annie, with shorter visits by a Reverend J. Garrow Duncan, for six weeks, and Bernard Grenfell, for a week (Drower 1985: 214). The documentation is incomplete with overlaps, but has been, and is still most easily, organised under the headings of Naqada and Ballas. Petrie already noted in Notebook 145 the problems of duplicate numbering that arose from employing multiple recorders (see below, Naqada or Ballas?); these problems make any indices provisional, pending publication of current detailed research by Ezzat Refaei into the record.

The burial assigned the identity 'Naqada 1863' by the 1894-1895 expedition illustrates the changing scientific value of an object group, since the moment when one or more Egyptians uncovered it to be recorded. In research into Naqada material distributed worldwide, for registering material in University College London, Elise Baumgartel identified a series of objects from the tomb, according to numbers pencilled and inked on the objects on site (Baumgartel 1970: LX): pottery vessels of polished red ware; sherds of cross-lined pottery; a pink limestone vessel; two siltstone palettes; carnelian and quartzite beads; an ivory comb; two ivory armlets; and a small limestone cylinder-seal. From the skeleton the body had been sexed female. In 1982, several Notebooks came to light in the then UCL Department of Egyptology (Crowfoot Payne 1987). One of these preserves the sketch by Quibell of the burial after careful removal of the soil (Notebook 140, scan 5). It shows the relative location of body, in crouched foetal position, and objects at the moment of recording soon after discovery, and gives no indication of any disturbance since burial. Quibell records the name Abd el Maksud as the single discoverer, without reference to any other person involved in removing enough earth to allow all the contents to be drawn without disturbing the remains.

Since Abd el Maksud received his payment for recovering these objects in 1895, all the Naqada finds have undergone substantial reinterpretation. Initially ascribed by Petrie to foreigners settling in Egypt after the Old Kingdom (Petrie 1896b), they were identified by Jacques de Morgan as native to the Nile Valley but pre-dating the unification of Egypt in the First Dynasty (de Morgan 1896-1897). The redating was confirmed from Petrie excavations of other cemeteries with similar material, from which, in combination with his careful records from Naqada, he deduced his Sequence Dating, a detailed chronological seriation (Petrie 1901b). Re-evaluating as prehistoric also implies revaluation in other terms; at the turn of the century, European and North American collectors and museums indulged a 'taste for the primitive', reflecting evolutionary thought at the height of direct colonialism. Another revaluation relates to all excavation: as forgery has shadowed art market taste, documented finds come to assume new value, because archaeological recording not only secures the date of a find, from association with other objects in find-groups, but it authenticates finds. By today, the Naqada 1863 burial goods have appreciated immeasurably in value, and, awkwardly for objective science, value here includes both scientific and monetary. One item in particular holds an exceptional position, as one of the 'Firsts' so treasured by museum journalism: the limestone cylinder seal, one of the smallest objects from the tomb. Parallels from the intervening century of excavation across Egypt and western Asia show that the seal was made in ancient Iraq. The Egyptian pottery from the tomb suggests that it reached Naqada not very long after it was made, perhaps within a century. Cylinder seals are among the small set of late fourth-millennium BC Sumerian materials and motifs that entered Egypt by unknown routes; they are closely associated in Sumer with the development of writing, itself one of that set of travellers. This fundamental and still enigmatic part of the history of Egypt is accessible to us thanks to the field-direction by Petrie, the recording by Quibell, and underlying them the dexterity, sharp eye, and manual labour of Abd el Maksud. His name recurs in other Quibell Notebooks, below; the long name-lists for work at al-Araba al-Madfuna give the forms Abd el Maksoud and Maksud during 1899-1902, perhaps a different man (Chapter 8). As a name at a task, he remains more elusive and less sought than the wearer of the cylinder seal who lived across the river from him five and a half thousand years earlier.

The group that entered archaeology as Naqada 1863 offers one of the more dramatic examples of changing scientific use-value, as a find is transformed from 1895 cylinder bead into 1995 primary evidence for inter-regional contacts underlying such central historical issues as the development of writing and state formation. In a more diffuse manner, every find-group in carefully documented excavations must be recognised as an essential element in the construction of our knowledge of the past. Some two hundred or more museums around the world still preserve the objects marked with find-group number, or linked by museum handwritten inventories to that number in a modern object biography from arrival in the museum to present location. In the decades following discovery, excavation numbers may disappear with erosion of the object surface, or be removed in the public interest of more aesthetic display, or lost in inventory changes and digitisation projects. Where the object has survived with its number, the museum staff and public have a chance to reach beyond the 1895 European recorder, through the hands and eyes of the Egyptian excavator, to ancient lives of use and deposition. The following lists offer the central figure in this connection between multiple past and present lives, for as many groups as could be found in the Petrie Museum archives.

Naqada tombs 1-573 and T57
Working from right end cover to left, Notebook 69 contains the sketches and notes by Petrie from the uncovering of the first fifty tombs in the Naqada cemeteries; he recorded nos.45-47 as 'Godi's $2^{nd}/3^{rd}/4^{th}$' (scans 11 and 10).

Notebook 70 contains the documentation by Hugh Price for miscellaneous Naqada tombs in the B cemetery, including nos 86-134, one of the large late predynastic T-tombs T57, and tombs in the sequence 501 to 573, with name of finder:

Godi	B89, 97-98, 100, 102, 104, 107-108, 110-112, 115-116, 118, 120-122, 124, 127-128, 130, 133;
	502, 504-505, 507, 509-511, 514, 518-519, 558, 560, 563, 568, 570
Mahmud	T57, B86, 92-93, 96, 99, 101, 103, 105-106, 109, 113-114, 117, 119, 123, 125-126, 128, 131-132, 134
	501, 503, 506, 508, 512-513, 515-517, 520, 526, 557, 561, 564-567, 572-573
Mohammed Khalifa	559, 562, 569, 571
Mohd Mansur (?)	T57

Further loose sheets from Price are collected as Notebook 135 (tombs 228-229, 232-234, 236, 239, 400-404, 600, 704-711, 717-719) but without names of finders.

Naqada tombs 1300-1918

1300-1329, 1345-1367	Notebook 136 Duncan
1450-1481	Notebook 136 Quibell
1490-1492, 1550-1559	Notebook 137 Quibell
1535-1585	Notebook 138 Price
1586-1661	Notebook 137 Quibell
1661-1699	Notebook 139 Quibell
1700-1729	Notebook 138 Price
1730-1759	Notebook 139 Quibell
1760-1779	Notebook 138 Price
1780-1787	Notebook 139 Quibell
1778-1854	Notebook 138 Price
1854-1916	Notebook 140 Quibell

Notebook 141 contains the Quibell record for tombs 1917 and 1918, without names.

Name of finder	*Naqada tomb number in Notebooks 137-140*
Abadeh Musi	1490, 1604, 1587, 1589, 1606-1607, 1612-1613, 1660, 1675
Abd el Maksud	1855, 1863
Abdulazim (?)	1824-1825
Abd. abd el Muli	1667-1668, 1877
Ahmed abd el Muli	1744, 1755
Ahmed Yadim	1560, 1687, 1819, 1845
Abul Hamd	1600-1601, 1816, 1829-1830
Abul Hassan	1705-1706, 1714-1715, 1717, 1722, 1727, 1768, 1787, 1808, 1812-1813, 1828, 1842, 1856, 1899, 1901
Ali Gedulla	1555, 1583-1584, 1590, 1609, 1615, 1618, 1630, 1633, 1643-1644, 1661-1662, 1708, 1716, 1730, 1766-1767, 1783 (Ali Ged), 1797, 1801 (Ali Gad)
Ali Redwan	1556-1567, 1597-1598, 1610, 1621, 1647, 1676, 1691, 1718, 1769, 1817, 1827, 1843, 1861
Amr	1758, 1771, 1773, 1831, 1835, 1849, 1874, 1898, 1907
Dahshur	1885
Khalifa	1596
Hamed Khalifa	1539-1541, 1573, 1577-1578, 1585, 1594, 1627-1628, 1634, 1672, 1700, 1702, 1707, 1709-1710, 1719, 1728, 1761, 1765, 1774, 1791, 1796, 1820, 1852, 1857
Hassan	1664, 1666, 1851, 1859, 1866, 1904
Hassan Osman	1535-1538, 1569-1571, 1639, 1721, 1725-1726, 1760, 1802-1803, 1814
Hussein	1891, 1897
Hussein Osman	1742
Iadem	1641
Ib	1875
Ib Amr	1602-1603, 1605, 1841
Ibrahim Moh	1801
Mba Must	1491-1492, 1542, 1545-1546, 1567-1568, 1574-1576, 1595, 1616-1617, 1629, 1631-1632, 1635, 1644, 1673-1674, 1690, 1695, 1704, 1723-1724, 1729, 1732, 1746, 1764, 1781, 1789, 1800, 1810-1811, 1818, 1836, 1840, 1853, 1870, 1876
Moh Abdurrahim	1763, 1798, 1803, 1821, 1860, 1872

7. Find-group records with finder names

Moh Hamed	1547-1549, 1579-1580, 1591, 1611, 1626, 1648-1649, 1671, 1734, 1752, 1762, 1848, 1850
Moh Mahmud	1826, 1832, 1873
M M	1833-1834, 1871, 1902
Senusi	1559, 1614, 1757, 1780, 1782, 1799, 1815
Smain	1550, 1558, 1561-1566, 1581-1582, 1654, 1685, 1689, 1701, 1711-1713, 1720, 1770, 1775-1778, 1790, 1805-1807, 1822-1823, 1858, 1867
Smain Abd Juad	1637
Tahir	1826, 1878
Yusuf	1586, 1588, 1599, 1608, 1619-1620, 1625, 1645, 1683, 1693, 1743, 1751, 1785, 1865, 1884
...alus (Galus?)	1879
... Shehad	1880

Ballas, 1894-1895

Authorship varies, though Notebooks 9 and 11 may be identified as by Duncan, from comparison with Notebooks from 1905-1906 when he returned to work with Petrie, and Notebook 146 is in the distinctive handwriting of Petrie himself. On the inside cover of Notebook 8 (scan 1) Petrie noted 'Did Senusi get payment for day we came?' alongside two other notes on payments for finders. Unless otherwise stated, all tombs here are prefixed Q (for Quibell). They are distributed in the Notebooks as follows:

1-36	Notebook 11, with a date Wed 2 Jan before Q5
51-71	Notebook 9, with a date Friday 11th January '95
72-103	Notebook 8
104-200	Notebook 142 (also contains Z21-28, see below under Zowayda)
201-352	Notebook 143 (also contains 183)
353-421	Notebook 144
423-519	Notebook 145
520-530	Notebook 146
531-688	Notebook 145
690-699	Notebook 147
700-710	Notebook 146
750-849	Notebook 147

Name of finder	*Ballas tomb number in Notebooks 8-9, 11, 142-147*
Ab	708
Abadeh Musi	109, 116, 121, 156, 161, 183, 275, 303, 340, 359, 363-364, 379, 404, 420-421, 429, 459-460, 464, 469, 476, 495, 548, 550, 556, 560, 621, 647, 662-663, 674-675, 682, 750, 760, 773, 792, 810, 855, 861-863
Abd el Aziz	175
Abd el Kerim Sebawi	131
Abd el Kerim Smain	139
Abd el Maksud	57, 151
Abd el Muli	260
Abderrahim	19-20, 23, 66, 77, 81, 162

175

7. Find-group records with finder names

	537, 541, 566, 570, 582, 610-611, 618, 679, 709, 767 (Hussy), 782, 798, 836, 845
Hussen Osman	12, 21-22, 52, 54, 123-124, 136, 161, 177, 185, 453, 510
Iadem	13-15, 'deep well' after 55, 62, 73 (no. uncertain, before 74), S4, 94, 96, 103, 107bis, 111-114, 118bis, 160, 171, 184, 190, 199, 206, 223, 236, 244, 258, 267-269, 277, 356, 395, 410-411, 432, 440-441, 443, 450-451, 462, 471, 480-487, 496, 505-506, 508-509, 514-516, 530-531, 540, 543-544, 558, 567, 572, 580, 602, 636-637, 639, 645-646, 671, 673, 688, 758, 777
Ib	55-56, 58-60, 69, 71, 149, 159, 173, 176, 192-193, 196, 205, 207, 215, 241, 246, 266, 354, 361, 394, 425-426, 430, 447, 461, 474, 704, 707
Ibrahim Amr	6, 16, 87, 91, 100 ('Ib Amr' + 'Amr'), 100, 195, 197, 497, 499, 504, 519, 551-552, 589-590, 598, 601, 615, 626, 667-668, 684 (?), 753-754, 761, 787-788, 790-791, 800, 822, 831, 838
Khalifa (Chalifa)	58 [bis?], 187, 375, 521, 524, 528, 586-587, 607, 625, 631-632, 648, 670, 696-698, 776, 778, 783
Khalifa Ahmed	9, 25
Mahmud Abdulla	36, 65, 74, 108, 151, 172, 186, 235, 237, 262, 276, 289, 292, 300, 351-352, 357, 365, 466, 527, 591-592, 605, 612-613, 630, 641, 655, 669, 677, 699, 770, 789, 796, 806, 814, 820-821, 829, 835, 837, 850
Mahmud Galab	115, 331, 342
Mahmud Mhmd	109, 116, 119 (girlish), 121, 156 (Mahmud the girl), 500, 507, 517-518, 535, 542, 568, 577
Mahmud Saal (Gaal?)	175
Mhmd Ahmed	140, 265
Mohammed Mahmd	144, 250, 490, 492-494, 538-539, 545, 559, 561, 581, 607, 629, 642, 649, 654, 665, 764, 781, 803, 839, 868
Mhmd Omran	127, 138, 147, 155, 184
Mhmd Salim	137
Mhmd Sherqawi	57
Mbarak	115, 182, 190, 206, 223, 236, 244, 285, 302, 856, 858, 864
Mbarak Ali	117, 122, 128, 130, 170, 181, 360, 530
Nur ed Din	140, 265, 314
Omar Mahrur	5, 166-167, 208, 211
Senusi	[1-4] (four burials sketched before no. 5), 11, 55-56, 58-60, 64, 71, 96, 103, 105, 143, 536, 564-565, 593-594, 606, 618, 659, 680, 703, 769, 834
Sharid	151
Sh Amr	132-133
Smain	442
Tahir	52, 54, 99, 107, 126, 134-135, 153, 815, 828
Yusuf	18, 51, 53, 63, 70, 95, 97, 104 (Yusuf Saleh), 106, 125, 129, 141, 142 (Yusuf Saleh), 148, 154, 157, 214, 218, 224, 230, 238, 242, 254, 257, 272-274, 284, 306, 376, 403, 448, 456-458, 470, 489, 491, 501, 511, 532, 546-547, 549, 569, 578, 588, 600, 624, 628, 643, 651, 656, 681 (?), 683, 751-752, 755-757, 775, 786, 802, 812, 816, 825, 847-848, 857

Naqada or Ballas? tombs from 1436 to 1496

In Notebook 136, one series of pages contains records by Duncan of tombs which he had numbered 436-449, 459-462 and 470-496; later most of these numbers were prefixed 1, to distinguish them from another set of tombs in the same number range (cf. Petrie note in Notebook 145, scan 2 '436-496 duplicate numbers'). Originally, the later organisers of the Notebooks identified the Notebook 136 tombs as Ballas, but later research suggested instead Naqada; in view of this uncertainty, they are presented separately here, in the form first recorded without the additional 1.

Name of finder	*Tomb no.*
A...hy... (?) Musy	436
Abadeh Mussy	445, 491-492
Abul Hamd	438
Abul Hassan	459, 462, 472, 495-496
Ahmid M	470, 475
Ali Redwan	437, 442, 481, 484
Ali Jadhullah	473-474
Amur (=Amr?)	443, 488-490
Firan	446, 485
Khalifa	449, 482 (Ahmid Chalifa)
Mahmud Abdulla	461, 471, 483, 494
Umbarak Ali	444, 476-477, 498
Umbarak Mustafa	439-440, 448
Yusuf	447, 478-480, 485-487

Zowayda, 1894-1895

For this separate small cemetery in the Naqada-Ballas region, the recorder named the finders for tombs 4-19A in Notebook 113, and for tombs 21-28 in Notebook 142 (where Z21-Z23 are written over <Ballas> 163-165):

Name of finder	*Tomb no.*
Abdulla	27
Abd Sudani	24
Abul Hamed	5, after 12, 28
Ahmet Musi	21-22, 26
Ali Redwan	14
Ali Smain	4
Amr	8a, 13
Bedr...?	25
Defalla	7, 9-10, 15-16
Hussein	27
Hussein Osman	19A, 23
Iadem	17-19, 25
Iadem <and?> Erfai	11
Khalifa	25
Mahmud Abdullah	6
Mhmd Ahmet	9a

| Senusi | 12, 26 |
| Yusuf | after 12, B2, B3 |

Dandara, 1897-1898

In the excavations at Dandara, Petrie was drawn by his interest in chronology to the large number of inscribed blocks from offering-chapels of the First Intermediate Period, one of the less well documented phases in Egyptian political history. Although a number of burials were also discovered, he devoted less space to these in his publication (Petrie 1900a). Names of excavator are recorded for only a few of these burials with their find-groups (Notebook 15):

Name of finder	Tomb no.
Abd er Rahman	tomb 25
Sudani	tombs nos 8-10, 19

Other tombs figure among the sketches of the larger offering-chapels, but the relation between name and find is not always as clear on these pages (Notebook 17b, scans 4-24).

Hu and Abadiya, 1898-1899

In one of his Notebooks from the series of cemetery excavations in this season, Petrie recorded (Notebook 40A):

Bricks big well IV by house Cem A Amr
13-14 x 5½ – 6½   A10

On the same page is 'A13 young body with pottery Ali's mastaba'.
For several tombs in cemetery W, Petrie records names of finders:

W70 M. Derwish soul house
over tomb W75 'Abul Hamd'
W78 Ahd Bakr well VI pots
W80-82 ... Ahd Osman beads mid pits
W83 Reshwan beads E ch<ambe>r

In this season, the new assistant Arthur Mace supervised part of the work, sketching many tomb plans, but only sporadically with name of excavator (Notebooks 40, 41):

Name of finder	Tomb no.
Ali Smain	W151
E (?) Mustafa	Y42, Y46
Fir... (?)	Y233
H Ahmed	Y45, Y184, Y187
H Mohamed	Y57
H Osman	G6, Y41, Y62, Y93, Y169 (=?176)

179

Khalifa	Y183
M Derwish	W157, Y150
M Smain	Y53
Mousa (?)	Y97
Reshwan	<W>154
Said J... (?)	Y170
Yusuf (?)	Y119, Y189

Al-Araba al-Madfuna (Abydos), 1899-1902

From the first season at Araba (1899-1900), a list of site features includes 'M1 Ali's first tomb', identifying Ali Suefi as the person uncovering some of the First Dynasty tombs in the Abydos temple enclosure (Notebook 4, scan 28).

Petrie phase V British School of Archaeology in Egypt, 1905-1930
Saft, Suwa, Gheyta, 1905-1906

One set of Notebooks lists burials and finds from the Wadi el-Tumilat season 1905-1906, in the large, cursive hand of an assistant of Petrie from his Naqada season, the Reverend J. Garrow Duncan. For most burials Duncan noted names of finders. Following corrections perhaps by Petrie himself, the idiosyncratic phonetic renderings by Duncan have been emended to the style of Petrie to ease comparison with other records (e.g. Ghalab for his Ralab/Rhalab; Ahmed for his Akhmed; Ibrahim Awad for his Ibm Mawet; Abu Zeyd Omar for his Ouezzid Omar).

Tomb nos	*Notebook no.*
Saft 1-344	90
Saft 345-531	91
Saft 532-846	92
Suwa 1-279	92
Gheyta 1-591	104

Saft

Abadeh	84, 134, 166, 181-182, 191, 204, 227-228, 258, 295-297, 330, 345, 356, 414-415, 433, 451, 470, 485, 502-505, 525, 544-547, 561, 572, 574, 589-590, 602, 657-658, 679, 684, 693
Abdel Aziz Hassein	141, 231, 234, 325, 375, 423, 461, 501, 549, 680
Abder Rahim Hussen	232, 240, 280-281 (Abder Rahim), 315-317, 366-368, 419-421, 430, 459-460, 515, 582, 591-592, 612-613, 650
Abdullah	46, 65-66, 126, 146, 188, 210, 233, 241, 277-278, 311, 313-314, 363-365, 388, 417, 429, 431, 464, 513-514, 516, 555, 593-594, 614-615, 627-628, 652, 654, 663
Abu Seyd Omar	78, 116-117 (Omar), 121-122, 134, 148-149, 166, 181-182, 186, 191, 204, 211, 227-228, 237-238, 258, 295-297, 309, 343-344, 432, 465, 557-558, 584-585, 656, 669
Ali Farnesy	61, 110, 167, 194, 213-214, 248-250, 265, 287, 303, 327-328, 336-337, 341, 349-352, 392-395, 424, 436-438, 498, 531-532, 548, 565, 573, 588, 695
Ali Suefi	802-803, 816-819

180

7. Find-group records with finder names

Arif Ahmed	73, 156-157, 169-170, 212, 246, 262, 306, 338, 346, 376-378, 471-472, 506, 533, 536-537, 797, 834-835
Farag Zweli	60, 106, 160, 174, 196, 202, 215-217, 252, 290, 292, 302, 354, 401, 439, 477, 497, 526, 538, 543, 563-564, 571, 619
Hussein Ahmed	64, 137-138, 158, 171-172, 183, 244-245, 268, 293, 332, 339, 353, 380, 396-399, 425, 434-435, 473-476, 507, 566-567, 576, 603, 647, 659
Ibrahim Awad	77, 123, 150, 164, 185, 261, 271, 308, 357, 357 ½, 358, 416, 466-467, 510-512, 596-597, 608, 625, 642, 653, 670 (Awat)
Ibrahim Shehat	51-52, 165, 320-323, 372-374, 386, 453-455, 462, 519-520, 522-523, 551-553, 598, 605, 618, 624, 630-631, 637-638, 661
	From 664 Shehat (some may be Mhd Shehat?): 664, 675, 704-707, 723-725, 730, 743-750, 768, 774, 779-780, 790-793, 798-801, 813-815, 825, 828-829, 832-833, 840, 845-846
Khalifa Gulali	75, 136, 152-153, 180, 184, 242, 260, 270, 307, 342, 433, 468-469, 488, 508-509, 560, 599, 607, 640-641, 649, 671, 676, 685, 696
Khalifa Sen... (?)	686, 702-703, 805-807, 821, 830-831, 843-844
Khallyl	24, 81, 187, 272-273, 279, 310, 359-361, 404-406, 478-479, 489-490, 527, 539-540, 629, 666, 775-778, 822
Maghrabi	3-6
Mahmud Ghalab	50, 139, 11-162, 178, 198-199, 206, 224-226, 256-257, 266, 298, 355, 369-371, 447, 482, 494, 496, 530, 542, 578, 632, 636, 651, 660, 665, 673, 678, 689-691, 698, 709, 728-729, 736-737, 764-767, 769-771, 788-789
Muhammad	595, 609-611, 616-617, 643, 655
Muhd Abd el Muly	626 (?), 668, 682
Mohammed Hammed	53
Muhammad Mensi	49, 193, 222-223, 255, 294, 329, 411, 440-445, 480-481, 528, 541, 577, 633-634, 683, 692
Mhd Shehat	142, 192, 195, 205, 239, 282-284, 318-319, 324, 384-385, 422, 456-458, 517-518, 521, 554, 580-581, 606, 621-623, 662, 672, 697, 820, 823-824
Mursy	69, 133, 143-145, 190, 203, 209
Reshwan Mensy	63, 159, 230, 243, 263, 267, 288-289, 304-305, 333-335, 340, 347-348, 387, 426, 452, 463, 487, 524, 550, 681, 694
Said Osman	1, 54, 103, 120, 175, 179, 200-201, 218-220, 229, 254, 259, 299-301, 389-390, 407, 446, 450, 484½, 491-493, 529, 562, 570, 579, 604, 635, 639
	From 664 Osman: 667, 674, 677, 688, 700-701
Serhan	74, 154, 163, 168, 208, 247, 269, 326, 331, 379, 486, 499-500
Yad	23, 82, 100, 135, 147, 189, 235-236, 274-276, 285-286, 312, 362, 381-383, 418, 428, 556, 583, 600-601, 629, 666, 687, 699, 708, 720-722, 726-727, 731-733, 739-742, 761-763, 772-773, 787, 794, 808-812, 826-827, 836-838, 841-842
Yusef El Abady	56-57, 119, 173, 176-177, 197, 207, 221, 251, 253, 291, 412-413, 427, 448-449, 483-484, 495, 534-535, 568-569, 575, 586-587, 620, 645-646, 648, 693

Suwa

Abadeh	23, 66-67, 76, 109, 159, 165, 188-189
Abder R. H.	22, 99, 112, 125, 152, 178, 228, 250, 264, 276
Abu Seyd Omar	3, 29, 34, 43, 94, 98, 110, 121, 135, 171, 173, 196, 204, 217, 230 (?), 266
Ali F.	26, 35, 40, 63, 122, 138, 152, 174, 197, 209, 234
Ali Suefi	220, 222, 261, 272
Arif Ahmed	5, 25, 42, 102, 118, 129, 167, 265, 172
Aziz	27, 61, 64, 111, 117, 177, 200, 210, 248
Farag	7, 12-14, 55-59, 79, 86, 89, 100, 142, 172, 183, 198, 212-213, 228, 233, 244, 253
Ghalab	185, 199, 211, 221, 237, 241, 252, 270, 274
Hussein Ahmed	251
Ibrahim Awad	21, 45, 47, 51, 81-82, 104-107, 124, 131-134, 179, 190-191, 202, 215, 232, 245, 269, 273
(Ibrahim?) Shehat	184, 218, 262-263, 275
Khal Qulali	4, 10-11, 28, 32-33, 41, 52-54, 71, 77, 90-91, 96, 114, 137, 145, 149, 161, 163, 175, 193, 201, 225, 238a, 256
Khal. Sen. . (?)	48-49, 72, 74, 78, 83, 88, 115, 147, 164, 246, 278-279
Khallyl	194, 203, 268
Muhd Mensi	19, 31, 37-38, 69, 87, 101, 119, 126, 136, 151, 157, 162, 176, 208, 237, 243, 267
Muhd Muly	18, 36, 80, 92, 103, 128, 144, 148, 157, 181, 214, 236, 254
Muhd Shehat	227
Nasr ed Din	223, 240, 260
Omar	46 (Ibr? Omar), 62, 73
Reshwa	15, 113, 120, 146, 180, 207, 217, 242, 271
(Said) Osman	27, 44, 65, 68, 93, 116, 141, 143, 158, 170, 195, 205, 219, 224, 249, 277
Serhan	70, 95, 166, 192, 238, 257
Yad	187, 235, 259
Yusef	1-2, 6, 9, 20, 30, 39, 50, 60, 75, 97, 108, 123, 127, 130, 150, 156, 168-169, 182, 206, 216, 255, 258

Gheyta

Abadeh	6(-9?), 21, 23-24, 32-33, 37, 41A, 54-57, 59-63, 72, 80-84, 90-91, 95, 100-102, 119-123, 135-136, 140, 164-165, 170-171, 174-178, 196, 209-212, 238-242, 253-258, 294-295, 322-327, 365-372, 385-386, 398-399, 411-416, 428, 459-460, 462, 464, 469-470, 487-493, 500-503, 514, 551-554, 580-589
Abder Rahim Hassan	1, 20, 24 (Hassan), 31, 34-35, 46, 64, 98, 103-104, 108, 131 (see Mursy 219)
Abdullah	2, 4, 11, 14, 18, 29-30, 40, 49-53, 68½, 69, 73-74, 93-94, 111, 113-116, 118, 125, 134, 138-139, 141-145, 158, 168, 172-173, 180-183, 202-208, 220-228, 279-281, 286-292, 328-337, 54-360, 387-388, 392-398, 421-422, 455-458, 465, 468, 479-483, 504, 504½, 505-507, 528-539, 556-560
Ahmed Jad	13, 15, 28, 41, 47, 77-79, 110, 112, 132-133, 137, 159-163, 190-192 (Yad), 200-201 (Yad), 249-251,

7. Find-group records with finder names

	282-285, 314-321, 373-374 (Yad), 389 (Yad), 408-410 (Yad), 431-432 (Yad), 442-443 (Yad), 461 (Yad), 471 (Yad), 483 ½ (Yad), 484-485 (Yad), 498 (Yad), 515-518 (Yad), 540-544, 568-570, 591
Ahmed Khallyl	5, 10, 12, 22, 25, 36, 96-97, 545-547, 561-567, 579
Bukadadi (deleted?) Khallyl	16
Khallyl	43, 48, 243-248, 383-384, 401-404, 429-430, 433, 444-449, 472, 476-478, 486, 508-513
Khallylen/ Khallyls	27, 38-39, 65-67, 72, 85-88, 99, 105-107, 126-129, 146-151, 166, 184-189, 197-199, 259-267, 296-307, 350-353, 361, 499
Muhammed	308-313, 362-364, 390, 417-420, 450-454, 466-467, 473-475, 519-522, 548, 550, 590
Muhammed Abd el Muly	268-269
Mursy	3, 19, 26, 42, 44-45, 58, 68, 70, 75-76, 89, 109, 117, 130, 152-157, 167, 169, 193-195, 213-219 (refers to Abd er Rahim at 219), 229-237, 252, 270-278, 293, 338-349, 375-382, 405-407, 423-427, 434-441, 463, 494-497, 523-527, 555, 571-578
Nasr ed Din etc	17

Zaraby and Balayza, 1906-1907

Supervising excavation of a small late Old Kingdom cemetery at Zaraby, south of Asyut, Ernest Mackay recorded the names of excavators of burials as part of his succinct descriptions, without sketches (Notebook 112):

Name of finder	Tomb no.
Abadeh Musy	71, 82, 95, 116
Abder Radi Hassan	93-94
Abder Raziq Huseyn	73
Abu Zaid Omar	25, 33, 36, 58
Ahmed Abady	27, 50, 97-98
Ahmed abder Rahim	100, 114
Ahmed Ibrahim	43-45
Ahd Jad	7, 14, 28-29, 39, 70, 72, 88, 99
Ahd Khallyl	22-23, 54, 67, 69, 74, 111
Ahd Masoud	119
Ahd Osman	20, 46, 55, 83, 117
Aly abder Rahim	32, 41, 60, 66, 85, 101, 107, 118
A. Firnisi	5, 15-16, 30, 40, 59, 76, 90, 104, 120
Ali Hassan	18
Badr Aly	8-9
Bakr Selameh	10, 49, 86-87, 102, 105
Bergi	112
Farag Swahli	75, 77
Gimini (?)	81
Hasaneyn Hamed	13, 57, 78
Huzeyn Achmet	12, 34, 89
Huseyn Muhd	53
Ibrahim Abady	19, 31, 79
Ibrahim Selameh	11, 21, 42, 52, 61, 84

Muhd abder Karim	56, 80A, 96
Muhd Mahd	37-38, 63-64
Muhd Mensy	62, 92, 103
Muhd Muhd	51, 68, 91
Muhd Musy	26, 35, 80
Nasr el Din	24, 108-109, 121
Smayn ab Gowad	6
Sudany	17, 48, 65
Yusuf	115

Another of the 1906-1907 assistants, perhaps the Edinburgh curator Edwin Ward, left the most extensive record of finds and their finders from a later settlement site, the Byzantine Period monastery at Balayza (Notebook 86, scans 11-12):

Antiqua Balaiza Camp
Farag Suweyleh Piece of metal (gold) and bead – 2 large jars – large piece of inscribed stone and 4(?) blue beads – large slab of carved stone and 4 smaller bits – piece of stone in Greek letters
Huzeyn Ahmet Fragments of pottery 3 carved stones w yellow paint – More fragments of yellow stone
Ibrahim Abady 2 inscribed stones, and (?) slab of alabaster. Scrap of (1 in) parchment. 3 pieces of inscribed stone. White stone capital Large slab of carved stone, and 3 smaller pieces.
Mah. Muhd – Thin iron spike. Triangular inscribed stone. Tiny scrap of parchment (tin). Large slab of lettered brown stone in 3 pieces – piece of alabaster, and 6 fragments.
Mah. Musy Inscribed stone, and piece of parchment. Long shoulder fluted jar, and square carved stone.
Seyn Mohd. Many fragments of red pottery – Clay sealings.
Antiqua – Balaiza Camp
Ahmet Khalyl. Pieces of pottery – ram's horn Large carved capital, and 2 fragments
Abd el Latif Mhd. Large block of inscribed stone. Inscribed slab, and 2 fragments pottery
Ahmet Hassan Inscribed Stone Wooden dish, and scrap of parchment. Inscribed stone and small jar Black stone Capital. Carved stone. Smooth surface stone, and small black jar.
Oward Ahmet
Aly ar Rahim. Fragments. 2 large stones with painted carving. 3 smaller stones. Large quantity of papyrus (in tin)
Badr Aly. Small jar and coin. Fragments. Small valve (?) pottery bowl, and small pointed hammer stone. Fragments of papyrus. Small spoon and bell. Clay bowl – dried seed pods.
Bukadady Khalyl – Iron spike Wooden peg. Fragments of wood. Several pieces of parchment (in tin). Parchment in bowl. Wooden stick and pad – red bowl.

Several finds from Balayza were published by Petrie, and others are identifiable now in the Petrie Museum either from marks on the objects or from labels with them. These indicate that the list above is far from comprehensive, excluding even favourite types for museum display such as writing pens and wooden keys. Two prominent types of object are manuscripts and 'inscribed stones', both traditionally privileged material categories. Correspondingly little research has been devoted to material other than the inscribed tomb-stones (Thomas 2000: figs 95-6) and the manuscripts later sent to the Bodleian Library, Oxford (Kahle 1954). Other finds, including manuscript fragments preserved in UCL, await fuller assessment, which would require careful re-excavation of this extensive monastery site.

Qurna, 1908-1909

From the Theban West Bank cemeteries that Petrie labelled A and B, his assistant Ernest Mackay recorded burials without sketches, without names of excavator except in two instances (Notebook 81). Abadeh Musy is given as finder of B25 (scan 17); this is recorded, without sketch, as having two chambers, one yielding five pottery vessels, a scarab and bronze earrings, perhaps late Middle Kingdom or Second Intermediate Period (eighteenth-sixteenth centuries BC) to judge from the material and object types and the apparent proximity to burial B23, source of a late Middle Kingdom incised pottery vessel in the form of a duck (UC13479, Bourriau 1981: 34). At the end of the Notebook, over a tomb-plan without cemetery letter or tomb number, is the name Ali Awadullah (scan 25).

Maydum, 1909-1910

The following names of finders are recorded for numbered Maydum tombs, prefixed MD (Notebook 67c):

Name of finder	Tomb no.
Abder Gaud	66
Abu Ahmed	75
Abul Hamed	50, 57
Ali Firnisi	62-63
A Sweifi	53, 56, 60
Ali Hamed	54
Hamed Aly	71
M... abder Rai	52
Mahmd Ghalab	79
Muh Musy	55, 59
?	61

To these, Notebook 67b gives 'Ali Firnisi' for a tomb 19 (scan 12), while Notebook 66 adds 'Ali Swefi' for MD101 (scan 6), and 'Ali Firnisi' for an unnumbered tomb (scan 11), as well as the 'Burial of Khalifa' by 'D N. XXVI' (scan 17).

Sidmant, 1920-1921

Notebooks 34a, 95a, 95b contain the detailed notes by an assistant of Petrie's, one Major Hynes, recording the names of principal workers for most burials (for Hynes, see Serpico 2008, 102). These pages overlap substantially with the 'tomb cards' presented below. The 'tomb cards' provide probably the first record for names of finders for the material secondarily (?) recorded in Notebook 34a (tombs 206 to 283), and Notebook 95b (tombs 260-274, 286-300, 500-600). Notebook 95a covers tombs 1501 to 1650 and 1700-1739, of which the cards record names as far as tomb 1605. For tombs without names on the cards, the following names of finders are recorded in Notebook 95a:

Name of finder	*Tomb no.*
Abd er Rahman	1608
Abu Hassan Osman	1612, 1628, 1636 (Abu Hassan), 1639, 1649 (Abu Hassan), 1713
Ahmed Ali Omar	1617-1618, 1620, 1626-1627, 1635, 1648, 1710, 1736
Ahmed Ghad	1614, 1634, 1644, 1702, 1708, 1718a, 1719, 1728
Ahmed Moh Mahish	1625, 1638, 1643, 1700, 1714, 1716
Ali Abd er Rahim	1609, 1624, 1631-1632, 1640, 1646, 1709, 1720-1721, 1729
Ali Abdul Zahi	1613, 1641, 1647, 1704
Ali Omar	1606, 1615, 1622-1623, 1645, 1701
Bergi	1732
Hassan Osman	1607, 1621, 1642, 1711, 1725, 1727, 1730, 1734
Hofni Ibrahim	1722
Mohmd Abdul Rahman	1619, 1633, 1703, 1705-1706, 1724
Mohd Gad al Karym	1718
Mohd Moussi	1610-1611, 1629-1630, 1637, 1650, 1712, 1717
Moh Osman	1731
Mohamed Said	1715, 1738
Nasradin	1707, 1723, 1737
Omar Swalym	1726, 1733, 1739

2. British School of Archaeology in Egypt 'tomb cards', 1909-1924

From 1908, English excavation directors introduced printed index cards to standardise the recording of cemetery finds; these 'tomb cards' may have been first used in 1908-1909 at Araba al-Madfuna (Abydos) by Eric Peet, working for the Egypt Exploration Fund (Serpico 2008: 5). Within three years, the system was adopted by the British School of Archaeology in Egypt. As with Petrie Notebook records of excavation, many of these cards preserve the name of the man or boy who uncovered the finds. Names are found in the dig documentation for the following sites: Haraga 1913-1914; Ghurab 1920; Sidmant 1920-1921, Araba al-Madfuna 1921-1922, Qau 1923-1924. However, no names were noted from initial checks of the earliest cards preserved from Petrie British School of Archaeology in Egypt excavations, directed by Petrie at Maydum and Tarkhan, and by

Wainwright at Gerza and Maydum. On the British School of Archaeology in Egypt cards, boxed fields are titled to prompt the recorder to identify the types of pottery, stone vessels, beads, metal and other finds, alongside tomb measurements, sex of human remains, comments on wrappings and body-casing, and whether the find was intact or not. Name of finder never became a formal field pre-printed on these cards; by contrast, the Egypt Exploration Fund 1908-1909 cards include 'Name of Finder' as one of the principal categories of information, though they offer only a simple listing space for an undifferentiated 'catalogue of objects' found.

The principal reason for documenting a name would probably be to ensure accuracy in the accounts. This becomes explicit where, for example, Sidmant and Araba al-Madfuna cards record the sum in piastres paid to the finder. Whatever their intended use, like the more detailed records of find groups from Naqada 1894-1895 and Saft/Wadi Tumilat 1905-1906, they bring specific modern names on a larger scale to the large object collections from that early funerary archaeology. In effect, the cards and Notebooks connect an ancient with a modern social history, outside the parameters of disciplinary archaeological discussion. Below, the names are indexed for each site, followed by individual examples of the connections between individual modern name and current distribution and appreciation of the ancient finds.

Haraga, 1913-1914 excavation directed by Reginald Engelbach
The cemeteries at Haraga yielded a high number of Middle Kingdom finds, among which burials 112 and 211 illustrate once again the difficulty in itemising value, as it changes over time or varies from monetary to scientific context. The publication gave relatively full accounts to both these finds:

(1) Tomb 211 (Engelbach 1923: 16, among 'special graves and tombs'):

Tomb 211 (Middle Kingdom). This large tomb stood by itself to the North of cemetery A and had been partially robbed. There were traces of a coffin and of a male skeleton, of which only the skull and the femora remained. In a corner of the chamber we found a very fine cylinder amulet, shewn full size on Pl. XIV, 5. The core is of copper, and the gold casing very thick. On this casing are soldered small globules of gold to form a series of inverted triangles (University College London). A similar example of work is to be seen in the Cairo Museum, from Dahshur. With this were found the gold cowries and the cylinder amulet shewn on Pl. XIV, to the left of the amulet described above. The cylinder consists of a copper wire threaded through green felspar and lapis-lazuli discs, with gold caps at either end. A considerable number of amulets of this type were found in the tombs at Harageh.

The dimensions of the tomb, together with the types of pottery and beads found in it, are given in the tomb-registers on Pl. LIX.

The tomb register records the tomb as a rectangular shaft 65x120 inches, 330 inches deep, leading to a 95x330 inch chamber on the south side, 60 inches high. The burial equipment is listed as pottery of type 2m (broad bowl with multiple cord marks), bead types 73j (small goldfoil barrel), 79jkm (spherical), and the jewellery described in the main text. The cowries are associated more with burials of women; the partly robbed tomb may originally have contained more than one body.

To this published record, the tomb card adds the information that the shaft was lined (with bricks), that the beads were amethyst and carnelian, and that the finder was, not 'we', but 'A.S.', Ali Suefi. Already prized at discovery, the gold cylinder amulet (now UC6482 in the Petrie Museum) is an outstanding item in the history of technology in Africa, as one of the earliest examples of granulation from Egypt, a technique known earlier in, and presumably imported from, western Asia (cf. Aldred 1971: 113, illustrated by late Twelfth Dynasty examples, now in the Egyptian Museum, Cairo, from tombs at Dahshur of women with the title king's daughter: pl. 29 in a set of foreign jewellery buried with Khnumet; pl. 46 for cylinder with granulation among Egyptian jewellery buried with Mereret).

(2) Tomb 112 (Engelbach 1923: 11-12, in the section on 'Middle Kingdom graves, sherd deposits and objets'):

> Pl. XIV, 1. Group of pottery, human figures, beads, double scarab, lion bead, cartonnage, limestone eye, flint flake and copper hook from grave 112.
> The use of these pottery figures is by no means clear ... The scarab shewn here is not very characteristic; it is double with a beetle on one side, and a double scroll on the other ... The centre figure is part of a group of a boy carrying a calf on his back, well known in this age (*Ramesseum*, II, 2); it has been attached to the boy by pegs. On the left is an alabaster model of a game board.

Behind this mixture of description and interpretation ('model of a game board' seems unlikely in the absence of parallels), the tomb register on pl. LIX records location as in cemetery A, human remains sexed as M(ale), tomb dimensions as shaft 40x110 inches, 280 in. deep, giving on south to 80x160 in. chamber, 80 in. high. The burial equipment is recorded in the tomb register as pottery vase types 41m (bright red), 67s, stone cosmetic vessel types 26 (calcite 'shoulder jar'), 76 (lower part of a granodiorite cylinder vase), and a slightly different contents list: fish hook, 2 flints, ivory pin, beside the 'glaze figures, double scarab, etc' on pl. XIV.1.

The tomb card adds a few more objects: there were two pottery vases of type 67s, rather than one, striped cylinder beads, and a granodiorite vase 'stand', and the list of small finds reads 'Fish hook, 2 flints, Ivory pin, animal, 2 rubbers, Eyes from cartonnage [so cartonnage is not a separate find, as the publication might be taken to imply], Shells – Piece of shell, Lion', and, more faintly written as if added later, 'Rough stone'. The name of the finder is given as M. Hamdan.

The 1923 publication already demonstrated, in the coded manner of specialists, the importance of the ivory figure as a parallel for a key 'type group' of the period, from a reused late Middle Kingdom tomb under the Ramesseum precinct at Thebes, published by Quibell. Engelbach also drew attention to the rarity of the double scarab, and speculated on the coarse faience figurines. Yet for those who do not specialise in the archaeology of the period, it may come as a surprise to find that remarkably few significant tomb-groups have been published. Even in fragmentary condition, the object types are evidence for ancient choices shared across the country, shown by the overlaps with the Ramesseum group and other Theban finds (double scarab from the tomb of Neferhotep). Together the different sets of elements make up a variable set of portable personal protection for the afterlife journey, on patterns we are still trying to discern. Tomb 112 marks a significant contribution to the 1850-1750 BC chapter in the history of burial customs on the Nile, and Muhammad Hamdan as much as the foreign recorder deserves acknowledgement for his role.

Name of finder	*Tomb no.*
Abul Hamd	102, 121, 123, 145, 209, 215, 234, 251 (?), 255, 274, 286, 299, 307, 395, 595, 603, 615, 618, 630, 641
A R	236, 369, 376, 387, 392, 394, 665, 668, 670, 674, 677-678, 804
Ah a. Hafid	103 (Ah a.Hamd Hafid), 147, 151 (with Ib M)
Ah Ali	243, 278-279, 295, 306, 317, 553, 604, 613, 620
Ah Awad (Ah Aw)	110, 117, 131, 161, 260-261, 264, 270, 277, 282, 291, 300, 308, 345, 377, 608, 649, 664, 675, 803
Ah A	207, 550, 560-562, 572, 627-628, 631
Ah Hd	365
Ah Jad (/Gad)	106, 111, 118, 132, 142, 205, 214 (Ah G), 253, 258, 322, 361, 378, 556, 575, 598, 633-634
Ah M Mahysh	95, 116, 130, 160
Ah M Musy	115
Ah S	152, 208, 213, 222
Ah Salam	325
Ah?	379
Ali A	338
Aly Omar (A O)	97, 109, 134, 136-137, 159, 241, 302, 318-319, 333-334, 343, 356, 360, 372, 381, 563, 629, 662
Aly Suefi (A S)	99-100, 138, 211, 228, 235, 250, 257, 265 (A Swefy), 268, 284, 296, 309, 311-313, 329, 337, 374, 450-451, 457-458, 460-461, 463-472, 474, 476-478, 586, 616, 619, 626, 625, 644-645, 652-653, 666, 676, 800
Amyn M	144
Bakrur (Baru'a)	154-155, 219, 266, 289, 301
Bedawy	93, 119
Bergy	105, 262-263, 273, 292-294, 310-311, 331, 344, 350-351, 359, 383-384, 386, 397, 554, 557, 564, 566, 574, 591, 593, 609, 632, 640, 669
Dabsha	101, 330

Emin Mohammed	223
Esa Salem	224 (<Ahmad Salem), 256, 269, 297, 565, 637, 639
Gaballa	267
Geballah Mansur	220, 227
Hamed Ah (H Ah)	98, 104, 124, 210, 226, 287, 323, 339, 353, 363, 399, 549, 551, 573, 611, 638, 642
Ibr Mansur	332, 346
Ibr Muh	151 (with Ah a Hafid), 221, 238, 242, 370-371, 388, 390, 605-606, 614
Ibr	228
Khalifa	88, 113, 321, 559, 567 (? Khlfalla?), 588-590, 635 (Khlfla), 648 (Khafalla), 650 (Khalfalla), 654 (Khalla), 667 (Khf), 673 (Kh)
Mah Ghallab	96, 114, 128, 135
Mansur Geb	127
Muh Hamdan	94, 112, 129, 240
M Musy	120, 122, 140
M Sayd	150
Moh Sh	107-108, 133 (with U Hamdallah), 162, 218, 280, 288, 298, 303 (M Sah?), 305, 348 (M She), 357-358, 368, 385, 398, 602, 624
M Shahat	206, 328, 341
Mustafa	92, 349
M A	558
M Derwish (?)	316, 646
Nasr ed Dyn	156-157
Qasim (Qasim M)	91, 143, 225, 231, 272, 335, 354, 366, 382, 396, 543-544, 555, 592, 599, 612
Sh Muh	355
Umb Bakhyt	125-126, 149
Umb Hamdallah	133 (with M Sh), 216, 254, 258, 275, 290, 304, 315, 342, 352, 362, 373, 548, 610

Ghurab, 1920 excavation directed by Reginald Engelbach and Guy Brunton

For Ghurab, another pair of finds can open up another dimension of our quest for a past, between richer and poorer in time. One great advantage of the Petrie approach to archaeology is inclusiveness: the monumental is not the exclusive focus, as in much traditional Egyptology, nor is it excluded, as in some attempts to find a perfectly egalitarian antiquity. There are limits to this inclusion, because the focus on typologies of objects tended to write out of the record any deposits without objects, including probably the majority of burials. In some periods, it was not the custom to place objects with the deceased, as in a high proportion of Late Period tombs with groups of mummified bodies (after 700 BC). In other instances, the custom of placing objects with burials may not have been affordable for the majority of the population. At Ghurab in 1920 Engelbach and Brunton recorded more such object-poor burials than perhaps any other expedition of the time, allowing an encounter with a socio-economic group

largely excluded from the account of the Egyptian past. Two groups of
different dates offer the illustration of different forms of ancient life
brought to the present by the excavation force.

(1) 'Tomb 356. Female on left side, hands over pelvis. Shell beads, on
each wrist; on the left also the amulet pl. XII, 70 of two standing lions, face
to face. This may be compared with the Twins amulet found at Qau, of
VIIIth dynasty. Undisturbed.' The tomb card adds only a single ovoid
pottery vessel with short neck and thick rim, and traces of wood indicating
the presence of a coffin (Brunton and Engelbach 1927: 8, pl. X tomb
register, pl. XI pot, pl. XII silver amulet on faience core). The tomb-card
adds the name of finder, 'Umb.', in the context of the series most likely
Umbarak Bakhit. Symmetrical twinned animals or deities are a recurrent
if relatively rare feature of precious metal amulets over paste cores, from
the Middle Kingdom (2025-1700 BC). In recent years, Austrian Institute
excavations at Tell el-Daba uncovered a gold example with pair of dogs on
boat; one parallel for its composition, material and technique is the
'Master of Animals' pendant in the most famous treasure of the Greek
Bronze Age, found on the island of Aigina. Intriguingly, the motif on the
Ghurab amulet recalls the more leonine images of the birth goddess Ipy,
adopted and transformed in second millennium BC Greek Bronze Age art
(Weingarten 1991). In combination with the Aegean connections of the Tell
el-Daba dogs pendant, the woman found by Umbarak Bakhit enters an
academic debate over elusive links between the worlds of ancient Egypt
and Minoan Crete. Yet her other burial equipment seems modest, and she
had been laid to rest in a pit only 35 inches deep, and, at just 23 by 85
inches, presumably cut to size to take just the coffin. Her status within her
society remains hard to gauge.

(2) Tomb 367, of the third millennium BC, was the burial of a child on a
mat in a thin, red polished pot, broken anciently and repaired (Brunton
and Engelbach 1927: 8, pl. V tomb register, pl. VII.15 pot, pl. VIII.4; pot
now in the Petrie Museum, UC17865). The tomb card mentions that the
'pot, tho' inverted over burial, was almost full of sand'; the age of the child
was estimated as one year. The burial was recorded as a round pit 30
inches deep. Although third-millennium tombs often contain no goods,
the burials in this Ghurab cemetery are mainly equally shallow and
give a general impression of poverty in comparison with other cemeteries of the period, for example the still not very rich graves excavated by
Petrie at Kafr Ammar, in the next province north. Indeed this seems to
be one of the only poor cemeteries excavated and published in Egyptian
archaeology. The card gives the name of the excavator as Sh. Ah,
identifiable from the series as Shahat Ahmed. Despite the four millennia between them, the excavator and the infant here may come from
similar relative social strata.

7.1. Pottery brewing-vessel re-used as coffin for a child, about 2500 BC, excavated by Shahat Ahmad in 1920 at Ghurab.

Name of finder	*Tomb no.*
Abul Hamd (Abul)	11, 16, 26, 74, 91, 105, 132-133, 223, 231 (with? Qass), 232-234
Ahd	62
Ahd Ali	84, 95, 271-272
Ah A O	225-226, 249, 260
Ahd Awad	77-78, 87, 141-142, 147, 201
Ah Kh	348, 369-370, 393, 414, 423, 504, 519-520, 529, 532, 539
Ah Os	394, 442, 454, 464, 475, 531, 548, 600, 604
Ahd Selam (?)	34, 92
Aly Omar (A O)	17-18, 24, 28-30, 42, 49, 53, 67, 79, 85, 96, 101-102, 106-108, 111-115, 125-131, 135, 200, 202-205, 218-221, 224, 242, 251, 267-268 (with Shahat Ahd), 279
Aly Suefi (A S)	8-10, 12, 14-15, 20, 32, 40, 44-45, 47, 68, 70-71, 81, 103-104, 109-110, 117-122, 206-208, 212A, 229 (with? El Aguz), 262, 265-266, 280-284
Bergy	56, 80, 134, 136-137, 146, 210, 246
El Aguz	229 (with? AS), 256, 285, 294-296, 404, 476, 478-479, 555, 601, 610
Ghulam Mohd	83, 89
Halym	261
Hamed Ahd	7, 13, 21-23, 33, 61, 76, 94, 209, 228 (?), 237-238
Hofni (Hof Ib)	19, 57, 88
Huzeyn Ahd	6, 35-36, 82, 90, 99, 162, 164-167, 170, 172, 174-182, 185-186, 192, 215, 222, 241, 257-259, 264, 269-270, 310, 311 (Huz), 321-324, 344-345, 360-361A, 362, 364, 383-386,

	388, 389-390, 396-397 (Hz), 421, 458 (Hos Ah), 469, 474, 501
H Os	273, 276A, 276C, 277-278, 346, 413, 420, 424, 438, 463, 473, 607
Has Os	456
Ib Abb	275, 318, 326, 336-337, 340, 349, 537
Ib Umb (Ab Umb)	75, 243
Maghr Has (M Has)	199, 302, 317, 328, 343, 352-353, 379-382, 425, 436-437, 439, 459, 507-508
M Gad (el Kerym)	59, 93, 124, 183-184, 189-191, 235-236, 312-315, 325, 357-359, 361B, 387, 398-399, 429-430, 433, 500, 521-522, 546
Mahd Ghall	300, 307, 422, 502, 506, 540
M Musa (M M)	194, 197-198, 305-306, 327, 332, 377, 455 (?)
M Said (M S)	51, 63, 86, 139, 144, 148, 153-159, 160-161, 168-169, 171, 211, 213-214, 227, 239, 247, 252-255, 263, 274
Maqsud (Maq)	41, 46, 58 (?), 72-73, 230, 244-245, 400-403, 405-406, 409-410, 412, 415, 417, 427-428, 445-450, 452, 465-468, 477, 480-486, 490, 495, 499, 549-550, 552, 556-557, 559, 605-606, 609, 611, 614
Mustafa	293 (?)
N e D (Nasr)	301, 316, 320, 333-334, 354-355, 376, 378, 419, 426, 435, 441, 443, 451, 509-513, 518, 544
Omar S	50, 60, 149-152
O Sw	173, 240, 248
Qasim	231 (with Abul H), 286-292, 297-299, 407, 488-489, 491-494, 496-498, 553-554, 558, 602, 612-613
Ram Has	43, 48, 52, 55, 64, 66
Shahat Ahd (Sh Ah)	250, 267-268 (with AO), 330-331, 335, 347, 367-368, 374, 391, 460-461, 505, 516-517, 530, 538, 542-543
Sh Hz	187-188, 363, 365, 545
Umb Bakh (Umb)	195, 309, 329, 338-339, 350, 356, 431-432, 440, 444, 457 (? EmB), 514-515, 533
Umb Os	462
Yusef	303-304, 341, 351, 392, 418, 453, 471-472, 476A, 503, 527-528, 608
Yusuf Ali	140, 145
Yusuf Abb (el ab)	196, 308, 319, 371-373, 375, 395, 523-526 (Yusef A)

Sidmant, 1920-1921 excavation directed by Petrie

Name of finder	*Tomb no.*
A e Rm	774, 779
Abu Hassan	229 (Abul Hassan), 231-233, 239, 1577, 2028 (Abul Hassan)
Abu Hassan Osman	259 (Abul Hassan Osman), 271, 1528, 1541, 1557, 1583, 1588, 1590, 1602, 2029 (?)
Abul Hamd	756
Ahmed Ahmed (?)	2010
Ahmed Ali	267, 533, 1504
Ahmed Ali Omar	201, 234, 245, 532, 549, 574, 1503, 1505, 1514, 1532, 1536, 1542, 1555, 1562, 1569, 1585-1586, 1596, 1605, 2022, 2025

Ahmed Alirahim (?)	208
Ahmed Gandir	238, 240
Ahmed Ghad	281, 284, 576, 581, 583, 587-588, 593, 595, 599, 750, 1513, 1524, 1531, 1547, 1552, 1566, 1573, 1587, 1589, 1601, 2022, 2025, 2030
Ahmed Hamdan	201, 252
Ahmed Moh Mahish	585, 592, 597, 1501, 1516-1517, 1540, 1548, 1561, 1572, 1584 (Moh Ahmed Mahish), 1591-1592, 1604, 2030
Ahmed Suliman	201, 243, 247, 254, 265, 268
Ali Abdul Zahi	1515, 1530, 1534, 1551, 1556, 1568, 1579, 1599-1600
Ali Abul Hassan (son)	275
Ali Omar	201, 227, 235, 240-242, 256, 261, 277-278, 282-283, 286-288, 295, 298, 503, 506-509, 516, 518, 521, 523, 525, 527, 529, 550, 559, 571, 575, 579, 582, 586, 590, 596, 598, 1502, 1523, 1525-1526, 1539, 1544-1545, 1565, 1574, 1582, 1595, 2030
Hamed Ahmed	275, 290, 293, 300, 510, 519, 543, 553, 562, 565, 577, 580, 2004-2005
Hassan ab Sehal (?)	2031
Hassan Osman	221, 237, 244, 250, 264, 266, 402-403 'Not yet worked. Discovered by Hassan Osman and reserved for him' (Petrie), 1506, 1520-1521, 1527, 1529, 1535, 1543, 1550, 1558, 1564, 1570, 1578, 1593-1594, 1603, 2033
Ibrahim Umbarak	201, 226, 240, 243, 2028
Mahmud Abderahman	1507, 1522, 1537-1538, 1546, 1554, 1563, 1567, 1571, 1580, 1581
Mohamed Abdul Hamid	201, 251
Mohd Abderrahim	206, 2010
Mohd Hamdan	221, 237
Mohd Moussi	246, 270, 272, 275, 289, 296-297, 502, 513, 522, 524, 528, 538-539, 544-545, 551, 555-557, 563, 584, 589, 591, 594, 600, 742, 754, 1508-1512, 1518-1519, 1533, 1549, 1553, 1559-1560, 1575-1576, 1597-1598, 2024, 2026, 2032
Mohamed Osman	212, 218, 225, 239
Mohd Said (MS)	291, 294, 299, 511, 514-515, 534, 537, 552, 554, 560, 569, 786
Nasradin	248, 252, 258, 263, 280, 738
Salym	754
Sh Ah	811
Sultan Bakhit	207, 209-211, 217, 219-220, 222, 227, 230, 253, 276A, 504-505, 512, 526 ('Bakhets'), 530-531, 540-541, 570, 2028
Umbarak Bakhit	207, 209-211, 214-215, 217, 248-249, 255, 262, 269, 273, 285, 292, 501, 517, 520, 526 ('Bakhets'), 535-536, 542, 546-548, 558, 564, 566-568, 747, 754A, 2023, 2027

Araba al-Madfuna (Abydos), 1921-1922 excavation directed by Petrie

Name of finder	*Tomb no.*
Ahmed Ghad	43, 52, 56, 57, 59, 62, 63+64, 65A+B, 71, 72A, 73, 75A+B, 78-79, 90, 901, 902A, 902B
Ahd Mohd (Mahish)	14, 27A, 29A, 29C, 34, 37, 39, 45A, 58, 69-70, 74A, 74B, 93, 97, 98, 904, (907)

7. Find-group records with finder names

Ahmed Mohamed	20A
Ali ar Rahim	3-6, 31, 50-51, 53B, 56B
Bergy	9, 14, 41A, 41E, 46A, 52, 54-55, 57, 59, 62, 63+64, 65A+B, *2nd* after 82, 90, (907), 951, 953-954, 956, 959
Hasan	7-8, 11, 25, 26B, 26C, 30A, 30B, 30C, 33, 94A, 94B, 99C
Hasan Osman	20A, 26A, 91B
Hofni	3-6, 14, 31-32, 38A, 40C, 48, 50-51, 53B, 56B, 67, 1st after 82, 92, 95, (907), 950, 952, 955, 958
Jaher Ahmed	27A, 29A, 29C, 34, 58, 93, 97, 98
Mhd Said	7-9, 11, 14, 20A, 25, 26B, 26C, 30A, 30B, 30C, 33, 42A, 47, 66, 76, 77, 80-83, 91B, 94A, 94B, 99C, 903, 905-906, 907, 908+909

Qau, 1923-1924 excavation directed by Petrie

Name of finder	Tomb no. (series 001-, later prefixed 7-, published as 7001-)
Abbady Mousa	292, 370, 389, 392, 513, 525, 558, 574, 665, 667, 669, 672, 714, 750, 767, 776, 787, 829, 852, 951
Ali Abul Hasan	552, 813, 823
Aly Omar	276, 304, 346, 351, 361, 364, 377, 379, 398, 503, 506, 522, 526, 530, 539, 550, 573, 642, 647, 650, 654, 657, 684, 705, 713, 725-726, 728, 730, 732, 741-742, 756, 761, 764, 771, 773, 785-786, 818, 828, 853, 861
Bergy	285, 327, 510, 515, 521, 531, 581, 652, 719, 733, 748, 809, 816, 863, 871, 878-879
Bughdady Khalil	323, 360, 367, 381, 395, 512, 546, 560, 577, 643, 689, 701, 722, 724, 729, 740, 751, 766, 772, 789-790, 796, 824, 884, 890, 894
Hamid Ahmad	322, 345, 368, 371, 386, 388, 502, 507, 509, 553, 567, 668, 671, 676, 679, 687, 693, 696, 700, 704, 712, 734, 736, 738, 758, 762, 777, 822, 873, 877, 881, 902
Hasan Osman	288, 298, 315, 320, 336, 355, 380, 385, 505, 549, 649, 690, 718, 723, 739, 765, 781, 794, 806, 817 (Hasan), 885
Hufny Ibrahim	287, 289, 302A, 306, 317, 330, 332-333, 338-339, 353, 532, 534, 565, 568, 571, 578, 658, 678, 682, 685, 694, 706, 708-709, 711, 754, 757, 768, 792, 797-798, 807-808, 833, 835, 839, 868, 876, 943-944
Mahmud Radwan	300, 316, 537, 675, 698, 707, 721, 749 (Radwan)
Moham Seyid	516-517, 520, 570, 580, 778, 801-802, 810, 812, 821, 830, 836, 860, 862, 874, 883, 887, 940, 950
Muham abul Hasan	278, 290, 307-308, 331, 348, 373, 376, 393, 508, 528, 688, 746, 762A
Nasr ed-Din	284, 293, 305, 314, 318, 325, 334, 343, 349A, 357, 372, 378, 382-383, 391, 394, 518, 523, 536, 541, 548, 566, 572, 579, 651, 674, 715, 743, 755, 764, 769, 774-775, 782, 788, 804-805, 811, 814, 825, 864, 882, 941 (?)
Selym Muhammad	301, 309-310, 313, 326, 342, 356, 375, 387, 399, 527, 543, 556, 564, 697, 717, 735, 737, 752, 791, 795, 800, 826-827, 832, 858, 926
Shahhat Ahmad	291-292, 296-297, 311, 319, 324, 328, 340, 350, 352, 362, 365, 369, 390, 396, 501, 511, 524, 544-545, 555, 563, 575-

195

	576, 680, 691-692, 710, 727, 745, 799, 820, 834, 865, 875, 897 (Shehad)
Sultan Bakhyt	277, 279, 286, 294, 329, 335, 337, 341, 344, 347, 354, 359, 363, 366, 374, 397, 514, 535, 540, 547, 663, 699, 753, 759, 779-780, 783-784, 815, 819, 831, 837, 855, 866, 870, 888, 908
Umbarak Bakhyt	274-275, 295, 299, 303A, 312, 321, 384, 504, 519, 529, 533, 538, 542, 551, 554, 557 (Barakat), 561-562, 569, 673, 681, 683, 695 (Warakat), 702-703, 716, 720, 731, 744, 747, 759, 763, 770, 793, 803 (Barakat), 838, 889 (Umbarakat Bakhit), 938, 942

On the reverse of the card for tomb Qau (7)913, in the handwriting of Petrie, is an annotation inverse to the rest of the record:

Aly abd el Meguid	O	)	Shehad
Muhd Ahmed	in place	)	
Mukheba Azyzy	O	)	M Sayd
Aly Saued	in place	)	
Aly Sultan	O	)	Buk
Muhd abu Zayd	in place	)	

These lines recall the support workforce behind the names of finders. The circles perhaps denote the basket carrier, and the phrase 'in place' (reading uncertain) perhaps the person collecting the earth to be removed by the basket carrier away from the burial place. In addition or alternatively, the circle might denote the siever checking for finds in the removed earth before disposal. Whatever the interpretation of the trios, the additional pairs of names are not found in the tomb cards among names of finders, and introduce the essential differentiation between intermediate and bulk workforce. Here the term 'subalterns' recovers an original narrower meaning as the troop stratum appointed by external organisers to mediate between forces posited as executive (officers/managers) and instrumental (soldiers/workers; on the range and development of meanings of 'subaltern' in the work of the modern writer who used the term most influentially, Antonio Gramsci, see Green 2002). In one theoretical and political tendency, the separately and additionally organised workers are considered to carry a dual potential: (1) they can continue to organise the accomplishment of the executive plan in daily details (channelling orders from the outside, and returning the gains of labour), and (2) they can continue to articulate the different interests of the workers, reformulated from within their mediating position in the structure of work. In the second trajectory, they operate in effect as ground-level vanguard of a resistance, at the day-to-day level of micropolitics, but without the more organised articulation of a more generalised movement. As dig manager, Petrie avoided resistance by his two strategic operations of recruitment:

first by dislocation of his workforce (recruitment at a distance from place of work); and secondly by maintaining strong internal division of the workforce by place of origin (recruitment of main workers at different place to rest of workforce). The relations between the core and the rest of the workforce – and between each and the external organisers – can then be recognised as a crucial factor in the development of archaeology as a managerial practice over the half-century from 1880 to 1924. The importance of internal workforce relations explains how satisfying it might seem and how false it would be to stop at the recognition of the core workforce, the men who were paid for clearing find-groups for recording. The full working structure can only be assessed from a fuller listing, and that appears in impressive form in one of the least studied features of the Petrie Notebooks – the great name-lists for pay and attendance, focus of the next chapter.

Notebook base: name-lists

From the dozen named individuals in publications (Chapter 2), and several dozen more in the Journals (Chapter 3e), the number grows in find-records (Chapters 6-7) to such an extent that it might appear, at first sight, to include the whole working population. Yet the picture remains selective, by its focus on one moment in the chain of operations, discovery, excluding the support force removing the earth to a distance, or supplying food to the excavators. The social economy of the excavation does surface sporadically in the Notebooks. Some entries may provide names of suppliers in local market towns, as in Notebook 86 (1906-1907), inside back cover: 'Ahmet Mesoude 31 not settled' and 'Hassan Dawdah? 10 settled'. A series of shorter name-lists, headed *suk*, 'market', repeats many of the names familiar from the find-records that foreground the trusted workforce core recruited from Qift. Market shopping must have been a feature of excavation logistics from the start, implied in entries such as 'suk Saturday Matanieh' (Notebook 59, scan 10, 1890-1891). Market name-lists appear after Hilda Petrie joined the excavation team. They make more explicit, and perhaps in practice made more systematic, the ways in which the European supervisors stratified the workforce. Five Notebooks introduce lists with a heading *suk* or 'market':

Notebook 1 (Araba 1902-1903, Hilda) scans 31, 35 'SUK'.
Notebook 5b (Araba Temple 1902-3, Petrie) 2 'Market Men', 11, 14 all with
    13 names.
Notebook 89a (Giza, 1906-1907, Petrie?) scan 37 'Suk' over eight groups of
    2-6 names with no.
Notebook 68a (Maydum, Memphis 1909-1910, Petrie) scan 22 lower 'Suk'
    over 5 names.
Notebook 68b 1913-1914 (Petrie) scan 23 names + no. headed 'Suks (?) 26
    March'.

By comparison with these, lists in another seven Notebooks may also relate to supplies:

Notebook 19 Dishasha 1896-1897 (Petrie) scans 20-21 small groups with
    numbers after name, heading Henassieh = Ihnasya
Notebook 15 (Dandara 1897-1898) 64 to inside back cover names without
    nos, and 6 names with single numbers
Notebook 3 (Araba 1900-1901) 106 ten short lists

8. Notebook base: name-lists

Notebook 5b (Araba Temple 1902-3, Petrie) scan 3 'Well' (11, 14, 13
    names)
Notebook 105 (Tell el Yahudiya, 1905-1906, Hilda) scan 40 insertion 8
    names with no.5
Notebook 65 Maydum 1909-1910 (Petrie) scan 11 23 names with no.
Notebook 5a (Araba 1922, Petrie) 1 with 8 names, 76 with 5 names = suq?
    or well?

For the 1904-1905 expedition in Sinai, where logistics presented particular difficulties, Petrie recorded names at three points in Notebook 97b, perhaps all related to stores purchases:

scan 29, names with nos
    Ali Firn
    Shehad
    Smayn + H O
    Ib + Md Sh
    Erfay

scan 30, list of expenditure
(a) ten names to right of entries 'Tobacco men' and 'Calico men':
    Said Abedi
    Said Osman
    Ahmed "
    Abadi Mursy
    Md Musi
    Md Shehad
    Sm Gowad
    Md "
    Ibrm Abadi
    Yusuf
(b) names among stores expenditure items, with number after each name:
    Smayn Gowad
    Said Abadi
    Aly Muhd Abd
    Aly a r Rahim
    Yusuf Abd
    (*two lines with stores expenditure items*)
    Yusuf Gedullah
    Yusuf Abd
    Yusuf
    good (?) Suez

Future research may develop means of identifying both the extent of support from the distant home villages of the workforce, and the social networks of supply in the market towns supplying the excavation force. For the present, we can widen the scope of visibility at least to include pay-place alongside find-place, by turning to another part of the archive: the extended name-lists.

199

The main workforce lists, by Petrie work-phase

A great number of the Petrie Notebooks contain long name-lists recorded for a variety of reasons, most often to keep track each week of payments to individuals on the workforce. These pay-lists and recruitment-lists are the main source for the men, boys and girls who worked on Petrie excavations in Egypt. The majority of these named individuals do not appear in any other source other than as anonymous figures in photographs, or as a collective anonymous presence in letters and publications. The lists are, like any written source, a strongly mediated record, product of an encounter of sometimes lighter, sometimes heavier tone, between a foreign middle-class man at different ages through his career, and old or new recruits of different backgrounds and different opinions on the foreign employer. They ought not be read too innocently as a direct account of local populations, for two reasons. First, the idea of giving a name to a foreigner might have been an occasion for confusion, or fun, or the kind of deliberate tricks of substitution cited by Petrie in his *Methods and Aims* (Petrie 1904, see above, p. 30). Secondly, the foreigner may misunderstand, simplify, or modify to the sounds familiar to him, not least because the purpose of the record is to ensure accurate payment, not to take a census. These are records for the writer, and not for any other reader. Petrie orthography of Arabic names varies over his five decades of work in Egypt, and may not always produce a form recognisable to the person named or other Arabic-speakers today. The safest guide to interpreting them may still be sought in studies of census-taking in rural areas, particularly under occupation (cf. Scott 1998), although it may have been safer most of the time to play games with the name-taker. Petrie seems more embroiled in local social life than most excavators, but he too devised strategies of dislocation to remove his workforce from their home settings where he could (above, pp. 41-2).

In many of the longer payrolls, Petrie Latinised the Arabic names in west European alphabetic sequence. Where he attempted a Latin alphabetic order, he would foreground one or other of two personal names for reasons not recorded and probably varying from one week or month to another. In the following collations, the dominant alphabetic sequences in the records have been adopted as closest to source, even though they may make it harder in specific instances to find a name. Sometimes different arrangements are given, a common type being the pairing of, presumably, older and younger worker, as described in his *Methods and Aims* (1904). In this chapter, collations of the main lists are presented in chronological order.

Phase II. Work for EEF, 1883-1886

For the first season at San al-Hagar (1884), much of the rhythm of enrolment can be reconstructed from Notebook 98f. The main sequence of work lists is preceded by this brief summary (scan 15):

Men	Boys
Hassanen	Smaine Salim
Muhammed Daud	Mustapha Ali
Muhammed Dafani	Muhammed Said
Said Ahmed	
Ali Muhammed	
Muhammed Abu Ali	
Ali Abu Basha old man	
Hassanen Abu Smaine	
Said Mutwali	

The same twelve names then duly open the following attendance list for 6, 8-9 February and, for Hassanen only, 10 February, with six more names for 8-9:

Said Abdullah
Medani (?) Sidahmed
Abu en Ain Abdullah
Muhamed Ibrahim
Muhd Tunras (?)
Ibrahim Sidahmed red cap

Overleaf (scan 16) the list continues with another sixteen names for 9 February only:

Muhd Musi
Mustph Abu Said
Muhd Hassan
Mutwali Mud
Muhd Salim
Ali Sidahmed big
Said Hassan
Ahmed Muhd
Muhd Hassan
Ali Salim
Ali Abu Hassanen
Muhd Basha
Muhd Abed
Daud Muhd
Muhd Abu Habib
Hassanen Abu Etnan

Underneath is the note 'for Abd er Rahman'.

These dates and names were then incorporated in the full 'Excavators

Wages Book San 1884', the title for Notebook 98d written just above the list of wages for supervisors (scan 1, see above, p. 143):

The 1884 San al-Hagar workforce: the first large-scale Petrie excavation

The following collation of the lists provides access to the workforce through their names as recorded by Petrie in English for the San al-Hagar excavations from February to June 1884. In April 1884 Petrie sent Reginald Poole news of the one fatality known from his archaeological work, but, owing in part to the relatively high turnover, the name of the victim has not yet been traced within the lists.

Key for the lists cited:

Notebook	*Date in 1884*	*No. in collation list below*
98d scans 2-7	February 6-20	1
98d scans 8-13	February 15-23	2
98d scans 14-16	February 25-27	3
98c scans 2-6	February 25-March 8	4 (see Quirke 2007b)
98c scans 7-11	March 10-24	5
98c scans 12-17	March 24-April 9	6
98c scans 18-23	April 7-19	7
98c scans 25-30	April 21-May 3	8
98c scans 31-36	May 5-21	9
98h scans 3-8	May 19-31	10
98h scans 9-14	June 1-14	11

Abd el Al Abdullah	7-11
Abdullah Ibrahim	11
Abd el Al Muhd	6
Abd er Rahim	2 (Gizeh)
Abd es Salam Hassanen	10-11
Muhd (abu) Abdeen	3-7
Muhd Abdeen	6 (...)
Sidahmed Abdeen	11
Abdu Ali	2
Abdul en ain Abdullah	1, 5-6
Abd el Al Ahmed	7-8
Abudain (?) Muhd	1
Abu Ali	1
Ahmed Adib	2-11
Aid Abdu	2-11
Fatimeh um Afi	4-6
Agad	10
Muhd Agab	11
Ahmed abu Ahmed	6-7
Ahmed Ali	8
Ahmed Ibrahim	6-8
Ahmed Muhd	1-11
Ahmed Muhd	1 (*2nd*, W)

8. Notebook base: name-lists

Ahmed Muhd	1 (*3rd*, W)
Ahmed (abu) Said *Salahieh*	1-2
Ahmed es Said	4-11
Ahmed Shehad	2
Ahmed Yunus	2
Said Ahmed	3
Aisha Muhd	10
Ali abd el Al	6
Ali Abdu	5-6
Ali (Ahmed) abu Afi	3-10
Ali abu Ahmed	2-3, 10-11
Ali Ahmed	2, 3 (grisly [*sic*]), 5, 6 (broad face), 7-11
Ali abu Amir	11
Ali Hassan	6
Ali Hassanen	1
Ali Kehabi (?)	2
Ali Muhd	1 (*1st*), 4 (too quick *or next?*)
Ali Muhd	1, 2 (*2nd* bro Musi), 3 (bro Musi), 5-8
Ali Muhd Yusuf	2, 5
Ali (abu) Salim	1-3, 4 (brick), 5-7, 11
Ali Sidahmed	1 (big)
Ali Suleiman	6
Muhd Alik (?)	4
Salam Alik	2, 3 (brown), 5-6
Ali Amar	7-10
Muhd Amar	8
Amar Salim	9-10
Amneh um Ahmed	11
Amneh (um) Ali	3, 4 (small), 6, 8-9
Amneh Ali	10 (big)
Amneh Hassan	10-11
Amneh Hassanen	11
Amneh um Muhd	5
Amneh Salameh	6
Amneh Salim	2 (grown), 3-4 (tall), 5-11
Salam Amtawa	3-4 (on stone), 5-6
Arab Ali	2-4 (one eye), 5-9, 11
Hajineh (?) Ata	5
Ibrahim Ata	2-11
Atieh Daud	6
Atiz Ali	8-11
Fatimeh Atullah	10-11
Mahd Atullah	9-11
Auad Muhd	3, 5
Auad + Ali Jafir Muhd	4
Auadullah	6-8
Auadulla Salim	10-11
Muhd el Azab	8
Aziz um Ibrahim	2, 3-4 (tattoo), 5-6
Hanen (?) Azizda (?)	6
Amr Bakhit	6 (black)

Abd er rasak Bakhshish	9-10
Said Bakhshish	4 (boatman's son), 5-11
Balassi Ahmed	9-11
Balassi (abd en) Nabi	9-11
Balassi Mustafa	3-8, 10-11
Fatimeh abd el Bar	2-3
Ali abu Basha	1-8
Muhd (abu) Basha	1-11
Ahmed (el) Baz	6-8
Ali Baz	2-8
Ali Bedawi	1-11
Ali Bedawi (old)	9-11
Hassanen Bedawi	9-11
Said Bedawi	1 (?), 2-11
Bedawi Muhd	2-5, 6 (Bedawieh)
Bedawieh	7-8 (um…lid)
Begarieh um Usufu	3
Ali Behereh	6-8
Abd el Bermidad (?)	3
Ali Budran	9-11
Muhd Budran	10
Bukadadi Musi	1-2, 3-4 (tall), 5-11
Bukadadi Said	1-3, 4 (small), 6-8, 10-11
Buharieh (um Usuga)	6-8
Ali Dafallah	2-8, 10-11
Ibrahim Dafallah	2-5
Fatimeh Dafani	7-11
Khadri Dafani	1-10
Muhd Dafani	1, 3-10
Muhd Hassan Dahabiyeh	1-6, 8-11
Yusuf Dahabiyeh	4, 5 (blue), 6-11
Ahmed Daud	1-8
Daud Muhd	1-4, 6-11
Daud Muhd	1 (*1st*, W)
Muhd Daud	1-2, 3-4 (grey), 5, 6 (abu Zergin), 11
Muhd Derwish	6-8
Muhd Dueb	7
Hassan Etman	6
Hassanen (abu) Etman	1, 3, 4 ('Donkey 5 days at $3\frac{1}{2}$'), 5 (once substitute Ali Muhd Yusuf, also listed separately)
Ibrahim el Faghi	3 ('black, good' – or note for next or both?), 4
Ahmed el Faghi	3, 4 (blue), 5-6
Farha	2, 3 (laughing), 4 (tall, bright), 5-6, 8, 11
Faraj Hassanen	4, 7
Faraj Salameh	6
Hassan abd el Fatah	2-6
Hassanen abd el Fatah	11
Ali abd el Fatah	2-5, 11
Fatimeh (um) Abdullah	6-11
Fatimeh um Ahmed	4-5, 6 (small neck), 7-11
Fatimeh Ali	9-11

Fatimeh um Basha	4
Fatimeh um Basha Ali	3
Fatimeh Ibrahim	10-11
Fatimeh Lamir	6
Fatimeh (um) Muhd	5-9, 11
Fatimeh um es Said	5
Fatimeh um Salah	9-10
Fatimeh Suleiman	11
Fatimeh Umbarak	1
Abd el Gadur	6-8
Abd el Gadur Ahmed (Mutwali)	1-5
Abd el Gafez Salim	6
Ali Gandil	6
Muhd Gandil	6, 8-11
Gandur	7
Abd el Al Gandur	1-4, 7-11
Hassanen Gandur	2-6, 8
Muhd Gandur	7-8
Gandur Abdullah	6
Gandurah	8
Ali Ganeb	2-4
Gazam Ali (Basha)	2-7, 9-11
Gemal um Ali	6-11
Gemal Hussein	6
Ibrahim Gemal	5-6
Gemeleh Salameh	11
Muhd Genedi	6
Said el Gezireh	6-8
Abd el Gofar	9-11
Abd el Gofar Salim	8
Hussein Gonem	11
El gouri ...	6
Muhd abu Hadji	9
Hadjizieh	7-9, 11
Hadjazieh Mahd	5-6 (close eyes)
Abd el Hafi	6
Abd el Al (abd el) Hafi	6-11
Abd el Khalij (abd el) Hafi	6-11
Ibrahim (abd el) Hafi	6-10
Abd el Hag	7
Ahmed Hafnawi	3-4 (good, tall), 5-6, 9-10
Halimeh	4 (or Ibrahim Ali), 5-7, 8 (um Ibrahim), 9-11
Abd el Al Halod (?)	5
Hamdeh El Awad	1
Ali ... Hamid	11
Muhd Hamid	11
Ibrahim Hamleit	5-11
Hanafieh	6 (um Ali), 8-11
Hassan Abdullah	1, 2-4 (guard), 5-6, 11
Hassan abu Hamed Ahmed	3

Hassan Ahmed	6
Hassan Ahmed Salameh	6
Hassan Ali	2, 3-4 (fresh), 5-6
Hassan Ahmed	4 (big), 5
Hassan Helwani (?)	6
Hassan Ibrahim	10
Ibrahim Hassan	8, 10-11
Hassan Muhd Sherqawi	1 (father Sherqawi), 2-4
Hassan Muhd	2, 3-4 (good), 5, 6 (good), 11
Hassan Muhd	6 (sharp)
Hassan Muhd	6 (*first of three in this list*)
Muhd Hassan	11
Hassan Nasr	1
Hassan Salim	6 (new), 7-11
Hassan Umb	5 (good)
Hassanen abu Smain	1
Hassanen Ali	1, 2-4 (blue), 5-11
Hassanen Muhd	3 (for Said Abdullah)
Ali abu Hassanen	1-6, 10 (su<bstitute> Said Ise), 11
Fatimeh Hassanen	9-11
Ibrahim Hassanen	7-11
Hana Helwan	5
Helwan	7-8
Ali Husein	5, 6 (Ali H'sein)
Hussein Ali	6, 11
H'sein Ali	6
Hussein Smain	7-8
Fatimeh Hussein	5, 6 (Fatimeh H'sein), 9-11
Hussein Suleiman	11 (father Ibr Hass)
Suleiman Hussein	11
Ibrahim abu Al (?)	6
Ahmed Ibrahim	10-11
Ibrahim abu Ahmed	11
Ibrahim Ali	1-2 (grown), 3 (tall), 4-5, 7-11
Ibrahim Ali Yusuf	2
Ibrahim abu Ali	2-5
Ali Ibrahim	6-11
Ali Ibrahim	6 (*second*)
Ibrahim Muhd	2-10
Ibrahim Salim	2-8
Ikfaim Abdu	2-4 (poor eyes), 5-6, 9-11
Hassan Imran	7-8
Muhd Imran	6-8
Ali Jafer	1-8
Muhd Jafer	3-10
Jafer Hassanen	4-6
Abd el Halim Jawa	8
Jawa Muhd	8
Hassan Kadr	6-9, 11
Ali Kamush	6-7
Khadidjdah (?)	5-6

8. Notebook base: name-lists

Khadijeh	7
Khadujeh (um) Ibrahim	1, 2-4 (pink), 8-10
Khadujeh Mahmud	5-10
Khadri Muhd	5-11
Khadri (um) Salim	6, 10-11
Khadri um Smain	10
Khalifa Farjani	2 ('Gizeh ... Mariette?')
Khalifa Muhd	11
Muhd Khalifa	6-10
Abd el Khalig	5
Khalil Hassanen	2-3 (Ro red), 5-7, 11
Khalil Hassein + substitute	4
Khalil Muh	5-6 (red cap), 7-8, 10-11
Khalil Omar	2-7
Ahmed Khawa	6
Hassanen Khawa	6, 10-11
Lamir Ahmed	3-8, 10-11
Ali abu Lel	6, 11
Suliman abu Lel	6
Mabruka um Ali	3-4
Mahabub (um) Ise	9-11
Mahajub Muhd	9, 11
Mahjab Imam	5
Mahmud Salam	11
Majahed Abdulla	6-10
Majahed Muhd	10
Mutwali Majahed	10-11
Said Majahed	5-6, 11
Yusuf (a<bu>) Majahed	7-11
Amir Maj'–l	5
Medallala	4 (um Hassan), 5-8
Abd el Ati Mansur	3-8
Abdullah Mansur	3, 4 (+ Mutwali), 5-6
Ali Mansur	3-5
Derwish Mansur	3-10
Khamis Mansur	3-9
Musi Mansur	3-6
Salim Mansur	3-6 (beard; 6 adds O stone ... basket)
Salimeh Um Maraka	1-5
Mattah Sad	4
Amneh Minajdi	6
Hussein Minajdi	6, 9
Sabha Minajdi	6
Sabha Minshawi	10-11
Um el Sha Minajdi	6
M'najdi Hassan	6
Abul Saif Muftah	4, 6
Amir Muftah	6
Muganem Ibrm	11
Muhamdiyeh (?) Ali	8
Muhamdiyeh (?) Salim	8

M...ieh um Ise	8 (maktub?)
Muhd abu Ahmed	6
Muhamed abu Ali	1, 6
Muhamed abu Habib	1
Muhamed abu Hassan	1
Muhamed Abder Rahman	1
Muhd Ali	2-3, 4 (disconsolate + Khallil), 5 (disconsolate), 6-10
Muhd Ali (small)	11
Ali Muhd	11
Muhd Hassan	2-5, 7, 10-11
Muhd Hassan	3-4 (*2nd*)
Muhd Hass Hanadir (?)	11
Muhamed Hassanen Hadak	1
Muhd Ibrahim	1-11
Muhd Ibrahim	1 (*2nd* from Samaneh), 10-11 (*2nd*)
Muhd um Ibrahim	2-9
Ibrm Muhd	11
Muhamed Naser	1
Muhd abu Said	1-2, 3-4 (small), 5-8, 9-11 (Muhd es Said)
Muhd Said Abdullah	1-4, 6
Muhd Salameh	7-8
Muhd Salim	1, 4, 5 (or Yusuf S), 6 (or Yusuf), 7-11
Muhamed Sherif	1-3
Mursi Muhd	2-11
Musi (abu) Ahmed	6-8
Ali Musi	7-8
Ibrahim Musi	4-11
Muhd Musi	1-4, 6-7
Said Musi	9-10
Saida Musi	11
Mustafa Ali	9-11
Muhd Mustafa	5-6, 11
Mustafa Muhd	9-11
Musi abu Shati	1-6
Mustafa abu Said	1-5, 7-9
Mustafa Said	6, 10
Mustafa (abu) Said *Salahieh*	1-2
Mustafa Ali	1, 5-6
Mustafa Khalifa	1
Mustafa Muhammed	1
Mutwali Muhd	2-6
Aisha Mutwali	10-11
Asharieh Mutwali	4-11
Ibrahim Mutwali	9-11
Muhd Nur	1-6
Said Nig'ni	5-11
Osmali	4, 10-11
Abd er Rahman Muhd	3-4
Muhd abder Rahman	2, 3-4 (on stone), 5-6
Fatimeh um Rakha	2-8, 11
Rakha Aki	2

Rakha Salameh	1-2, 3-4 (nose), 5-6, 8, 11
Salimeh um Rakha	6-8, 11
Sidahmed um Rakha	5
Ali abu Ramadan	10-11
Ramadan Ibrahim	8-10
Abdu Riani	2-4 (sharp), 5-6
Ali Salim Riani	1-7
Fatimeh Riani	1 (Fatimeh um Riani), 2-4, 6, 8-11
Ibrahim Riani	5-11
Shehad abd er Robu	5-6, 9-10
Sabha Abdullah	11
Sabha Ali	6 (+ Shalabi Ali), 7-11
Sabha Ali Salameh	6, 8-9
Sabha Muhd	4-6 (gold ring), 7-11
Sabha Mustafa	2-6, 10-11
Sabha Ali Salameh	3, 4 (+ Sidahmed), 5 (tall), 7
Sabha Salameh	10-11
Ali Sad	3-4 (black), 5-6
Said Abdullah	1-2, 3 (*substituted by* Hassanen Muhd), 4, 6-11
Said abu Ali	5-9
Said abu Ise	1-11
Said Ahmed	1, 11
Said Ali	2, 3-5 (French), 10-11
Said Ali	1-2, 4 (+ ~~Basha~~)
Said Ali	1 (builder)
Said Hassan	1-3, 4 (*1st* on pylon), 5-11
Said Hassan	2-3 (black rags), 4 (*2nd* black rags)
Said um Ibrahim	9-11
Said Muhd	2-3, 4 (+ Fathy), 5-6
Said Mutwali	1
Said ... [illegible]	4 (high)
Saida um Muhd	7
Salah (?) Abdullah	10
Ali Salahi	5-6
Salam Ali	1, 4
Seyid (?) Salameh	5
Salam Ahmed	6
Salam Muhd	6
Salameh Ahmed	6
Ahmed Salameh	10-11
Salameh Ali	1, 5, 7
Ali Salameh	9-10
Hassan Salameh	6
Mahmud Salameh	2-3, 4 (fat face), 5-6
Muhd Salameh	6, 11
Saidah Salameh	10-11
Salim Ali	11
Salim Hassan	2-3, 4 ('big (open)'), 5 (+ Dafallah), 6, 10-11
Salim abu Hassanen	10
Ibrahim Salim	8-11
Ibrahim Salim	9 (small)

Salim Ise	6 (+ Smain)
Salim Muhd	11
Salim Said	11
Salim Salameh	6
Salim Salim	11
Hassanen (es) Salahi	3, 4 (stupid), 7
Sarieh um Salim	7
(Abd es) Satar Ali	3 (bro Said Ali), 4 (small), 5-6, 9-11
Ibrahim Saud	7-8
Ahmed Shalabi	6
Muhd Shalabi	5 (…)
Shalabi Ali	1-4, 5 (…), 6 (+Sabha Ali)
Shalabish	9, 10 (red)
Shalabish Muhd	11 (red)
Shalabish Muhd	11-12 (blue)
Shalabish (um) Muhd	7-8
Shams um Muhd	5
Sabha Sharqawi	1-8, 11
Sharshir Ali	11
Salim Shati	6
Ibrahim Shawish	5-6, 9-11
Shehad	5 (marginal top note), 7-8, 11
Abd es Shehad	11
Muhd Shehad	9-11
Shehad Salim	10-11
(Abd es) Shehati	7-11
Abu Nigi Shehati	10-11
Smain Shehata	6
Shinawi	7
Said abu Shindi	4-6
Shirbina Hassan	1
Ahmed Shirbini	2-6, 9, 11
Muhd Shirbini	5-6, 9, 11
Said Shirbini	11
Showar	6
Shurbaji Hassanen	9, 11
Sidahmed Abdeen	1-3, 4 (ugly), 5-6
Elgrawi Sidahmed	1-5, 7-8
Hassan Sidahmed	11
Ibrahim Sidahmed	2-3 (red cap), 4 (pretty), 5-8, 11
Muhd Sidahmed	11
Said Sidahmed	2-5
Said Sidahmed	3 (*2nd*)
Sidahmed Salim	10-11
Smain Abdullah	7-11
Abdullah Smain	6
Ahmed Smain	4-5 (Maskhuta), 7, 11
Ali Smain	11
Smain Hassan	1-2, 3-4 (one eye, bright)
Hussein Smain	6
Smain Muhd	6

Smain Salim	1-2, 3-4 (pitted), 6-7, 9
Sobhi (?) Shalabi	6
Sobhi Muhd	10
Muhd Sugi (?)	10-11
Ibrahim abu Suggr	6-7
Ibrahim Usugger	8
Abd es Suleiman	6
Suleiman Ahmed	1-4, 8-10, 11 (?)
Ali Suleiman	4-5, 11 (+ Muhd Ali *or note for preceding?*)
Suleiman ali ed din	3-6
Suleiman (um) Amir	8, 10
Hassan Suleiman	5-6
Suleiman Hassan	10-11
Suleiman Hassanen	7, 9-11
Suleiman Hussein (?)	10
Suleiman Ibrahim	7-8
Muhd (es) Suleiman	3-4, 6-7
Suleiman Muhd	5-8
Suleiman Selajneh (?)	6
Suleiman u (?) Amin	7
Suleiman u Gamel (?)	6
Suleiman ...	9
Sultan Salim	10-11
Muhd Timras	1-11
Umalkher Hassanen	4-6, 9-11
Umalkher um Daud	1-8
Umbaraka um Ibrahim	1-4, 6, 11
Hamed Umgrawadi	9-11
Said Umgrawadi	1, 2-4 (bright), 5-9, 11
Said um es Said	4 (squint), 5-11
Ali abd el Wahab	6
Hassan Wahab	9-11
Salim (abd el) Wahab	5-6, 10-11
Sueilim (abd el) Wahab	5-6, 9-10
Suleiman (abd el) Wahab	5-11
Yusuf (abd el) Wahab	7-11
Ali Muhd Yusuf	3, 6
Ibrahim abu Yusuf	2, 3-4 ('pasty'?), 5-6
Yusuf Muhammed	2 (es Said), 3 (es Said), 6
Yusuf Muhd	4-5 (+ Riani), 6 (*2nd*)
Yusuf abu Said	2-3, 4 (+ Riani), 6
Yusuf es Said	7-11
Yusuf Salim	5 (bro Moh Os), 6
Yusuf (Wusif) Salim	5, 6 (Wasif Salim)
Zedan abu Hassan	6-7
Zenab Ali	10, 11 (Amneh)
Zenabeh Ali	9, 11
Abd el Gaui (?) Zenati	10-11
Ibrahim Zenati	11
Suleiman Zenati	10
Zenib	7

This collation removes data available in the layout, and in particular the arrangement of names in Notebook 98h from the later part of the season, in May-June 1884 (from the Petrie pagination at scan 19 right '6', scan 18 right '8', at this juncture he is evidently working back from the right-hand end of the Notebook). These pages give for the date 7 June a record of working groups with, mainly, six to nine, names, each name with a number, probably payments for unspecified finds, but possibly for metre-work as in the 1884-1885 season (see below). Sub-totals are given for most groups. The names recur in the main name-lists. The groups may reflect assignment in working groups to different parts of the site. On scan 19, in most groups the first or, more rarely, second name is underlined: Ibr Hass, Muhd …, Gonem (?), Ali Sad, Sul Hassan, Khalij, Ali Fatah, Ibrm Muhd. These underlined names do not appear with higher numbers. Petrie does not seem to refer to foremen of small work-groups, and the underlining might reflect a means of ordering the workforce at payment, rather than a system of sub-foremen in the process of the excavation itself (compare Hawara 1911 Notebook 38b scans 21, 22, 23).

East and West Delta workforces: San al-Hagar and Nabira, 1884-1885

For the second Petrie Delta season, at San al-Hagar and Nabira 1884-1885, Notebook 74g contains several name-lists with single numbers and letters. The first is headed '1885 Ap' (scan 11), and comes a few pages before a list of finds at San al-Hagar, 'House 35 additional objects', and contains the names below (reordered alphabetically). Several names are found in the 1883-1884 paylists, indicating that this list most probably relates to work at San al-Hagar in the east Delta, rather than Nabira in the west Delta:

Ali Jafer
Bakhshish Said
Daud Muhd
Fatimeh Dafani
Fatimeh Riani
Hassan Muhd
Hassanen Ali
Hejazieh Muhd
Ibrm Ali
Khadjujeh
Khadri Dafani
Khadri Muhd
Muhamd Jafer
Muhd Said
Muhd Timras
Muhd um Ibrm
Mustf Said
Said Ali

Said Mutwali
Said Umgrawadi
Sakha Sherqawi

Later in Notebook 74g (scan 21), two pages present another series, this time with names not found in the 1883-1884 San al-Hagar paylists. This second list incorporates three references to antiquities (sphinx scarab, Apollo bowl level, Serapis); all are types found at Nabira (Naukratis), and the list therefore most likely relates to work there, rather than at San al-Hagar:

Abd er Rahman Yusuf (on second page)
Abd er Robu 'to Ali Mattar Δ'
Abd Gowi Ibrm
Abd Hamid
Abd Majd Nagih (repeated on second page)
Abdul Bejni
Ahmed Negib
Aid Jab
Aisha
Ali Jabri
Emin Ali (repeated on second page)
Emin Sad
Ferjani (or Terjani)
Gazaleh Muhd
Hassan
Hejazi D (on second page)
Ibrm Derdiri (?)
Kallam M (on second page)
Khadra Zemain
Mansur Derawi (?) (repeated on second page as Mansur D)
Muhd Abd Jedid
Muhd Jabri
Muhd Jawdi
Muhd Musi
Muhd Osman
Mursy
Mustf Majur
Saada Ali
Said Khalil
Said Lelin (?)
Said Salim (on second page)
Saidi Zayati
Sal Shawi (?)
Smain Ali
Smain Jabri
Smain Mahagni
...bid

The identification of this list as part of the workforce at Nabira (Naukratis) can be confirmed from comparison with Notebook 73 name-lists which have letters written over the finished list, providing a series from B to E (scan 27 B, scan 28 C, scan 29 D, scan 31 E; the missing 'A' list might be one without a letter on scan 24, from its location in relation to the others). The series is continued in Notebook 74g, among records of Nabira work, with two further lettered lists (scan 44 F, scan 46 G). The lettered lists have single payments in c(ents?) or T(halers?); the timing of the payments is not recorded, but was perhaps weekly. Lists F and G are in a roughly alphabetical order. The following name-list summarises the lists lettered B to G as the clearest single guide to the excavators at Nabira.

Hassan Ab (?)	C
Abbas	C, D
Abd el Al	B (Abd el At?), G
Abd el Al Muzi	G
Abd el Hamid	C
Abdullah	G
Abdullah Gmhawi (?)	G
Abdullah Said	F
Abul Mejd Ibrm	F, G
Abul Mejd Shoh	B, D
Agub	D, F, G
Muhd Agub	B, D, F, G
Aid	B, F, G (Aïde)
Hassanen Aisa	B, D, F
Aisha	F
Said Alam	C, F, G
Hassan Alan	C (Hassan Alim), D (h over end Hassan for Hannah? Alim?), F
Ali Abdu	D
Fatimeh Ali	G
Mustafa Ali	D, E,F
Said Ali	B, E, F
Ali She:eyb (sic?)	F
Yusuf Ali	F
Muhd Amr	D, E, F
Mahmud Andereshehbin (?)	F
Ibrm Aram	D, F
Ali Aruji	C, D, F
Muhd Atah	F
Ibrm Atawi	F, G
Muhd Atawi	B, D, F, G
Azab	B (small)
Mabruk Bah	B, E, F, G
Smain Barakat	C, D
Said Bedr	D, F, G
Bedr Yus (?)	D
Ali Behereh	D, F, G
Salim Behereh	F
Muhd Beshbish	B, E (Muhd Beshbeshi), F, G (Muhd Beshbeshi)

8. Notebook base: name-lists

Muhd Beyumi	F, G
Dakroh	C ('to Said Alam')
Muhd Dakroh	B, C, F, G
Muhd Deraz	B, D, F
Hassan Derdash	F, G
Muhd Derdash	F
Sidahmed Derdash	F, G
Muhd Derwish	B, F (small)
Muhd Desuki	F
Shuf Edib	F
Edris	F
Emin Ali	G
Etman Muhd	D
Faraj Muhd	C, F
Muhd Fatah	F, G
Daud Fiqqi	B, C, D
Muhd Fiqqi	B, D, F, G
Hannah Gali	F
Salim Gandash (?)	F
Muhd Gandil	D
Sidahmed Ganefi	G
Hassan Ganem	B
Khallil Ganim	C, F, G
Abd Maksud Gani	C
Hassan abd el Gani	D
Abd el Hamid Gaui	C, D, F
Muhd abd Gedi	F
Abd el Gelil	G
Muhd Abd el Gelil	C, D
Gelowieh	G
Hassan Godda	D
Salim Godi	F, G
Hameda Guni	F
Hassan Guni	D
Muhd Guni	B, G
Shehat Guni	F
Ibrm Hadari	F
Hafafi (?)	D
Abd el Haï	F
Abd e Gowad Halabi	C
Ibrm Halim	B, D, F, G
Hamadi	B
Hameda Hassan	F
Ibrm Haweilin (?)	D
Ibrm Hawish (?)	G
Hamid Hedrazi	F, G
Akhnat Hejaz	C
Hussein Helali	C
Amr Hosubah	B (Said follows, next name?), F, G
Ibrm	C, F
Ibrm 'Aid	B

215

Ibrm Hashish	F
Ibrm Hawishi	E
Igdur Ali	F, G
Ali Jabullah	F
Gotb Jabri	F, G
Hameda Jabri	C, D, F, G
Hassan Jabri	F
Mabruk Jabri	B
Shenaf (?) Jabri	G
Ai Jabrim (?)	G
Muhd Jaj	G
Sahi Jazil	G
Ibrm Jewdi	E, G
Khallil Jewdi	F, G
Muhd Jewdi	B, C
Abd Jowad	C, G
Ali Khabiri	C
Gotb Khadr	B
Bedawi Khallil	D, F, G
Hussein Khallil	F, G
Khanis	F
Ko...	C, D
Abd el Latif Lanzari	G
Ali Lashir (?)	G
Muhd Lemmat	B, D, F
Mabruk	F
Mabruk Guni	F
Mabruk Sewi	C, F
Hassan Mahfud	E, F (or Madful?), G
Amr Mafud	C, D, F
Abd en Nebi Maiuf	B, D, F, G
Yusuf Makluf	G
Maluma smiler (?)	F
Mustafa Mansur	D
Maruf Megid (?)	F
Ali Matta	F, G
Membereh (?)	F, G
Ahd Mersum	E
Minaji	D, E, F, G
Muhd abdel Jedid	B
Abd e Azim Muhd	E
Muhd Abdu	B
Gazim Muhd	E
Muhd Hamad	E, F
Muhd Helali	E
Muhd Homms	D
Muhd Khadr	G
Muhd Khashab	D (?), F, G
Muhd Marut (?)	C
Muhd Merenna	D, F, G
Muhd Murshedi	E

216

Muhd Noweshi (?)	F
Muhd Razlan	F
Muhd Zaj (?)	F
Murai Faraj	B
Ahmed Murami (?)	G
Mursi el Abd	B (?), C, D, F
Murzi Abder Rahim	C (?), D, F, G
Mursi Lazal	F
Mursi Zayat	C, D
Abd Hamid Musi	F
Ahmed Ali Musi	C
Aisa Musi	G
Ali Musi	E, F
Hussein Musi	D
Khallil Musi	B
Muhd Musi	F, G
Shehat Musi	B, D, F, G (Shehati)
Smain Musi	E, F, G
Muhd Mutwali	G
Umbr Mutwali	F
Umbr Mutwali Jewdi	F
Muhd Najar	B, D
Sharaf Negib	B
Salah E Neim	F
Hassan Nejib	F
Abd Munim en Nejar	D
Abd el Musi en Nejar	C, F
Mabruk Nejar	D
Mursi Nejar	G
Smain Nejar	E, F
Ibrm Niel	B, C ('to Ibrm Sharaf'), F, G
Mabruk Niel	C, F
Omar Alam	F, G
Omar Ibrm	C, D, F, G
Ali Osman	F, G
Abd er Rahim	G ('shy'?)
Abd er Rahim Adib	D, G
Abd er Rahim Ahmed	C
Abd er Rahim Mursi	E
Abd er Rahman	C, D, F, G
Abd er Rahman Alam	F, G
Ali Ramadan	E
Hassan Risq	D, F
Ibrm Risq	F
Muhd abu Rizak	B
Abd er Robu	B, D, F
Abdullah Saad	G
Sidahmed Saad	D, F, G
Faraj Salah	B, D, F, G
Abd es Salam	G
Ramadan Salim	G

217

Abu Saud	F, G
Hameda Saud	F, G
Muhd abu Saud	G
Ali Seis	B, D, F, G (?)
Said Selim	B, D, F
Ibrm Seruzi	B, D, F, G
Abdek Sewi	F
Abdek Sewi Adib	F
Ahmed es Sewi	G
Ibrm abu Sewi (?)	G
Abd er Rahman es Sewi	C, D (?)
Mabruk Sewi	B, F, G
Said Shaban (?)	C
Ibrm Shafi	B
Hassan Shalabi	F
Ibrm Shalabi	C, F
Khallil Shalabi	C, F, G
Muhd Shalabi	B
Said Shalabi	E, F
Salim Shalabi	C, D, F (?)
Ahmed Shalil	F, G
Suleiman Shami	G
Ibrm Sharaf	B, C, D (?), F, G
Sharam	G
Heleh Shehi	F
Gazim abu Shelil	D, F, G
Shenafi	G
Abu Shenafy	D
Sheraf Jabri	F
Ikfai Shur	G
Muhd abu Shushi (?)	C
Muhd Sueil	B, D, G
Emin Sulemin	D, F
Ali Sulemin	E, F
Sultan Ali	E, F
Ibrm Usayami	C, D, F
Muhd Wakil	E (boy), F, G
Muhd Yunis	F, G
Yunis	D, F
Yunis Jajib	D, F
Yusuf Zaufil	C (or Taufil?)
Abdel Gelil Zeman	C, F
Muhd Zeman	F
Muhd Zedan	F
Abu Zey	F, G

From other records in Notebook 74, such single-payment lists can be seen to relate to 'metre-work', with payment by amount of earth removed, rather than by day of attendance (cf. Chapter 2). A metre-work name-list by site-sector is dispersed across scans 13-21, beginning at scan 13, right page, with the introductory heading 'Begin here all work'; each name is

218

recorded with a calculation including the letter M for metre-work, summarised in a numerical account on scan 26 headed 'All metre total before Tues'. At intervals Petrie specifies site-sector, e.g. scan 18 heading 'cross trenches by Gt Tem' (the Great Temenos, one of the major features of the city-plan as the Petrie season recovered it). These spatially arranged lists would provide the basis for a more detailed reconstruction of the Nabira excavation and the profile of individuals or groups of excavators in the retrieval of both the city-plan of Naukratis and the celebrated finds of Greek and Egyptian material from the site.

Shorter name-lists from Nabira work include c/T single payments to the following men, within but apparently unrelated to the record of the Muhammad Baraysh bronzes affair (Notebook 6, scan 26):

Muhd e Fiqqi
Ali Musi
Muhd Osman
Saada Hassan
Muhd Eyub
Mahmd Eyub
Ishatta Musi
Hassan Derdash

The distinctive Eyub names may be variants for Agub in the lettered list, a sign of the variability in transliteration, or may be transient workers, reflecting the sporadic pattern of recruitment and/or job-hunting at this locality.

Nabasha and Dafanna, January to May 1886

Notebook 74a contains the attendance lists for the work at Nabasha, the first dated 'Jan 7 1886 Nebesheh' (scan 3). The lists are cited in the index of names below as follows:

Scan 3	January 18-19	1
Scans 4-8	January 18-30	2
Scans 9-13	February 1-13	3
Scans 14-19	February 15-27	4 *in a different hand (Griffith?)*

Notebook 74e continues the fortnightly sequence for spring 1886. As the handwriting is that of Petrie, the March 26 to May 24 lists ought to refer to his work at Dafanna, as he records his move to the new site in his 22.3.1886 Journal:

Scans 12-13	March 26-April 5	74e2 5
Scans 14-15	April 5-17	74e3 6
Scans 16-17	April 19-May 1	74e4 7
Scans 18-19	May 3-15	74e5 8
Scans 20-21	May 17-24	74e6 9

219

The first part of Notebook 74e (scans 2-10) contains name-lists in Arabic; as discussed above, their contents are closest to lists from March and April 1884, and therefore they have been presented following those, above.

Abd ed Di Umbarak	1-2
Abd el Al Abd el Al	5
Abd el Al Ahmed	2-4
Abd el Al Abdullah	2 (San)
Abd el Muli Rahman	5-6
Abd el Qadi	4
Ali Abdullah	2 (San), 3-4
Mjahed Abdullah	2, 3 (brown), 4 (Imgahud), 5-6
Abll (?) Muhd	1
Said Abdullah	1-4, 5-9
Said Abdullah	2-3 (San)
Saida Abdullah	2, 4, 6-9
Smain Abdullah	2-9
Muhd el Adel	1-4
Muhd um Afi	5
Jemil um Afi	5
Ahmed Ahed	8-9
Fatimeh Ahed	6-8
Muhd Ahed	6-8
Abd el Qadi Ahmed	4
Ahmed Abdeen (*? or* Abdun)	5-7
Ali Ahmed	2-6
Ayesha (um) Ahmed	1 (yellow), 2-4, 6-8
Ibrm Ahmed	2-3, 5-9
Muhd Ahmed	1-2, 4-8
Aid Abdu	2-4
Alfi Muhd	2-4
Hassanen um Alfi	3
Hasuba um el Alfi	4
Hussein um Alfi	2
Ali Ali	4
Amneh Ali	2-4
Ibrm Ali	2-4
Ali Ibrm	3 (San), 4-8
Hassanen Ali	4-6
Istoba Ali	2 (Benaso), 3 (~~Benaso~~), 4
Mabruk Ali	1, 3, 4
Ali Muhd	1 (*1st*), 2
Ali Muhd B	1 (*2nd*), 2
Muhd Ali	2, 6-7, 9
Muhd abu Ali	1-2
Ali Mustafa	5-8
Ali Said	7-8
Ali Said (Maadi ?)	6
Ali Said Ali	5
Amir ~~Daud~~ abu Udeh	5
Amneh Ahmed	3-4

8. Notebook base: name-lists

Ahmed Amr	1-2
Ahmed abu Asi	2-4
Smain abu Asi	2-4
Um Smain abu Asi	2-4
Muhd Ata	8
Ati Ali	5-7
Fatimeh (um) Auad	1-4
Muhd Auad	2-4
Ayesha Helali	2-5
Ayesha Muhd	2-3, 7-8
Aziz Ibrahim	2-4
Mutwali Bahari	5-9
Balassi Muhd	5
Ahmed Baz	5-6
Ali Bedawi	2-3
Bestawisi Muhd	3-4
Said Bestawisi	3-4
Ali Binti	2-3, 5-6
Buhadadi (abd el) Muli	3, 4 (Bugadadi), 5-9
Derwish Muhd	1-4
Ibrm Derwish	1-4
Dish Muhd	1-2
Ahmed Embabi	6-7
Muhd Embabi	8 (~~Ahmed~~)
Said Etman	5-6
Faraj Ahmed	3-4
Farakha (?) Muhd	6
Muhd Farjani	2
Ali (abd el) Fatah	2-4
Fatimeh abd er Rahman	2-3, 5-6
Fatimeh Ahmed	2-4
Fatimeh Ali	1-4
Fatimeh Faraj	2, 4
Fatimeh Jibali	2-9
Fatimeh Muhd	1-9
Fatimeh Muhd	3 (*second* brown), 4
Fatimeh Sidahmed	1-3
Ferhan Ibrm	1-2
Muhd (el) Ferjani	3-4
Abd el Gadur Ahmed	2-3
Abd el Gadur Ibrm	1-3
Hassanen (abd el) Gandur	1-9
Said abd el Gadur	5 (Hadji), 6
Said um al Gandur	2, 3 (Said um Gandura), 4
Abd el Gelil Hassan	3-4
Ghazi Ali	5
Habib Hamed	1, 3-4
Hadi (um) Jabr	1-2, 4-6
Ali abd el Hadi	2-3
Ibrm abd el Hadi	2
Muhd abd el Hadi	1-3

221

Yusif abd el Hadi	4
Hafizeh	2 (um Auad), 3, 4 (Awad)
Abd el Hag Muhd	1-2
Halimeh Ali	1-4
Halimeh Mustafa	2-3
Suleiman Hamed	7-8
Hamza Ali	3-4
Hassabu abd el Al	1-4
Abd el Al Hassan	1-4
Hassan Abdullah	3
Ahmed Hassan	2-4, 8-9
Hassan Ahmed	8 (black beard), 9
Ali abu Hassan	1-2
Ferhani Hassan	4
Hassan abu Hassan	1 (tall)
Hussein Hassan	3-4, 6-9
Hassan Muhd	3
Muhd Hassan	2 (San), 3-9
Muhd Hassan	2-4, 6, 7 (one eye)
Said (abu) Hassan	2, 3 (bro Muhd tall), 4
Ahmed Hassanen	4, 8-9
Hamed Hassanen	3
Hassanen Hassan	2 (old), 3-4
Muhd Hassanen	8 (no entry), 9
Ali Hindawi	5-9
Abd el Al Hussein	1, 3-4
Ali Hussein	2 (old), 3 (grey), 5-8
Hussein Ali	3 (San)
Hussein Hassanen	1-4
Ibrm Hussein	5-6
Muhd Hussein	1-4
Said (abu) Hussein	5-6
Ahmed Ibrm	5-6
Ferhan Ibr	3, 4 (Ferhani)
Helayeh Ibrm	5, 6 (Helait ?)
Ibrm Muhd	1-3
Ibrm Said	2-6, 8-9
Ibrm Said	6 (*2nd*)
Said Ibrm	1, 3-4
Iman Umran	2-3, 4 (El Iman Umran), 5-9
Abd el Hadi Jabr	2
Agal Jabr	2-3, 4 ('Aqel Gabr), 5-9
Jebrin Sakran	1-6
Kammar Muhd	2-3, 4 (Qammar)
Abd el Karim	2-4
Khadra Ibrm	2-4
Ali abu Khallil	2-4
Ibrm Khallil	1-8
Khadjyeh Hassan	4-8
Khadra Khallil	1-2, 4-5
Khadra Muhd	5-6

Mabruka (?) Khalil	4
Muhd Khallil	2-9
Khallil Salameh	1-2
Khui	2
Khui (abd el) Muli	2-3, 4 (Khuje), 5-8
Sabtah Khueta	1-2
Lamir Ahmed	2-4
Said Lamir	2-4
Abul Ma'ati	2-3, 4 (Abul Ma'ati Salim), 5-6
Mahabub abd el Al	2-8
Hassan Mansur	6-9
Mariam Ahmed	2-4
Hassan Minajdi	2-3
Hussein Minajdi	2-3, 4 (En Nagdi)
En nagdi Hussein	4
Mnadi Muhd	5-6
Sabha (um) Minajdi	2-3, 4 (En Nagdi)
Um al Kher Minajdi	2-3, 4 (En Nagdi)
Misra (?) Muhd	1-2
M'jahad el Bab	1-2
Muhd Ahmed	2-3
Muhd Ali (Sabieh)	5-6
Ali Muhd	2-4
Muhd al Asfar	1-2
Ayesha Muhd	4 (Esha), 5-6, 9
Ferhan Muhd	4
Hadije (?) Muhd	4
Ibrm Muhd	1-2, 4
Muhd Ibrm	2
Muhd Maruf	7-8
Musi (abu) Ali	1-4
Ibrm Musi	1-2, 5-8
Ayesha Mutwali	2-4
Mutwali Muhd	2-3
Ali Osman	2
Daud Osman	5
Ali Radwan	5-6
Rehiem abd el Hi	2-3, 4 (abd el Hai)
Muhd Rise	5
Sabha Hassan	5-8
Sabha Minshawi	5-6
Sabha Sherqawi	3
Sabra (um el) Gandur	1 (red), 3-5, 7-9
Amir Sad	2-4
Ibrm Sad	2-4
Sad Smain	4
Ali Sagr	3-4
Abd er Rahman Said	5-6
Said abu Ali	3 (San)
Said Ahmed	3, 5-9
Said Ali	2 (Francais?), 3 (French), 4

8. Notebook base: name-lists

Sidahmed Khalil	5-6
Sidahmed (es) Said	7-8
Shehata Sidahmed	3-4, 7-9
Sikins Muhd	2
Amneh Smain	6
Khadra (um) Smain	1-3
Smain Said	2-9
Smain es Said	4
Muhd Sugar	5-6
Aish Suleiman	2-4
Ali Suleiman	3-5
Suleiman Ahmed	1-4
Suleiman Hassan	2-4
Salim Taha	1-2
Um Ali	1-4
Um es Sad	3 (*over* Khadra Smain), 4 (/Smain)
Umbaraka Muhd	6-8
Hassan Salim Wahab	5-6
Muhd Salim Wahab	5
Sueilim Wahab	5-7
Suleiman Wahab	5
Yusuf Wahab	5-9
Abd el Wahed Salim	6-8
Yusuf Ali	8
Ali abu Yusuf	1-3
Arifa Yusuf	1 (yell), 2-4
Atieh Yusuf	2
Yusuf Jabr	2, 4
Minadi Yusuf	2 (Musi *above*), 3, 4 (Nadji um Yusif)
Saida abu Yusif	4
Suleiman Yusuf	2-4
Zeinab Musi	1, 2-3 (um Ali), 4 (no entry)
Zeinab Mustafa	1-3
Zenab (um) Ali	1, 2 (deleted), 4

Two short name-lists in Notebook 74b may relate to start of work at Nabasha in 1885:

Scan 25
   Muhd Salim 4
   Abd el Hades to go
   Habib 4
   Ibrm Ahmed 2c
   Alfi 1A
   Said Ibr 2A
   Smain Abdullah 1A

Scan 27

Alfi 2c	Ibrm Ahmed 30A
Ali Salim 1	Alfi 6A
Yusuf (?) Jabr 1	Said Ali 1c
Nadi Jabr 5c	Abd el Karim (?) 1A

Agal Jabr 4c   Said Ibrm 1c, 7½ c
Faraj Ahmed squint (?) 2½ c Muhd Ali 8A
... 1c
Abdull Salim 2A

Notebook 74d includes another short name-list, for days 8-13 (scan 31), presumably for February 1886 (date on scan 5), with sigla for Arabic words, w for *walad* 'boy', b for *bint* 'girl', unmarked presumably adult men:

W Faraj Ahmed
B Halimeh Ali
B Hannah (?) Suleiman
W Muhd abd el Jowad
Shafei Hussein (?)
Alfi Muhd
~~Hassan ... 1A~~
Habib Hamid
B Salimeh Auad
B Salha Suleiman

Phase III. Privately-sponsored work in Fayum and Middle Egypt under the Antiquities Service, 1887-92

Dahshur, 1887
At the end of his journey into Upper Egypt, Petrie obtained permission for a brief project of clearance work at the Dahshur pyramid field, with the following names listed for work on April 30 to May 8 (Notebook 32a, scan 30, original not alphabetic, w denoting the Arabic word *walad* 'boy'):

Abd el Al Ali
Abd el Al Zekri
w Abd el Ba'ai
w Abd el Gowi ...d
w Abd el Towab
Abder Rahim Sho'al
w Abeys (?) el Faiumi
w Ali el Edi
w Ali Hamadi (?)
w Beyumi Auad
w Hassan el Edr
w Farag Mustafa
w Hassan el Kis
Hussein Muhd
Ibrm el Kis
Ibrm Gonem
Iman Omar beard
w Iman Hassanen Abiad
Kamis abu Zayan
Muhd abd el Al

Muhd abu Sumara
w Muhd Ali
Muhd Mahmud
w Muhd es Saidi
w Muhd es Sisi
Muhd Hassanen
Musi Hawehi (?)
Mustafa Dahshuri
w Said Ali
Said Muhd
w Said Smain
w Salam el Abiad
Tabit Jodi (?)

Main excavation seasons, 1887-1892

The following Notebook pages, cited by the numbers of the published scans, contain lists of workmen for the main 1887-1892 excavations at the Fayum sites of Hawara, Lahun, Madinat al-Ghurab, at nearby Maydum, and at Amarna in Middle Egypt:

Fayum, 1887-1888
Notebook 38, scans 27-34, 36-40, start of season
Notebook 39a, scans 32-40, end of season

Fayum, 1888-1889
Notebook 39c, scans 35-39, start of season (end of Hawara work)
Notebook 39d, scans 28-31 start of season (end of Hawara work)
Notebook 39b, scans 31-37, early 1889 (start of Lahun work)
Notebook 49, scans 22-23

Fayum, 1889-1890
Notebook 35, scans 10, 21
Notebook 48a, scans 3-9

Maydum, 1890-1891
Notebook 59, scan 11 pairs with days (start of work?)
Notebook 60, scans 3-17 pairs

Amarna, 1891-1892
Notebook 16, 8-11 pairs

All these lists record weeks of daily payments (Notebook 39b specifying for C, T, L, pyramid), except for Notebook 35 where scan 10 has 18 names with 2 incomplete columns, third column with C or T, and scan 21 has 19 names with numbers and days. In addition, Notebook 59 from the 1890-1891 season contains a list of names in pairs with days, perhaps from the organisation of the start of work (scan 11). The main lists in Notebooks 35, 38, 39a-d, 48a, 49 and 59-60 have been collated for the index of the core Fayumi workforce, presented below. Many names occur only in Notebooks 38 and 39a, from the 1887-1888 season; further research into the pace of recruitment and turnover might separate the Manshiat Abdullah workers from the al-Lahun recruits. Similarly, the Maydum Notebooks 59 and 60 contain many names not previously registered, and these may be more local, but the continual arrival and departure of excavators makes this uncertain pending further assessment of the lists. The one season where a separate geographical recruitment can be more safely identified is 1891-1892 at Amarna, more distant from the other sites, with precise archive information on the non-locals. The 1891 Journal records how Petrie recruited five Fayumi supervisors on his way to Amarna (above, p. 71). Notebook 16 confirms this, with four of those names at the head of a list of new names (scan 2), a table with all five (scan 14), and a separate entry of two of them beside the new Hassanen Hadieh (scan 16); accordingly, the five Fayumi names are included in the collation below, but new names are listed separately after the Fayumi workforce index.

Name	*Notebook*
Abbas	39b
Abd el Al	39c, 60
Abd el Aziz	49
Abd el Aziz Alam	38
Abd el Gani	39a
Abd el Gani Ali	38
Abd el Gofar Alam	38, 39a
Abd el Gofur Ham	39c
Abd el Gowad	39b (?), 59, 60
Abd Gowad? Khalil	48a
Abd el Gowad Khatib	38
Abd el Hafi	60
Abd el Harid Graib	39a
Abd el Kadir	60
Abd el M'tuleb Osman	38
Abd en Nebi M'kowi	38
Abd en Nebi M'wehab	38
Abd er Rahim	39c, 48a
Abd er Rahman Hassan	38, 39a
Abd er Rahman Tantawi	35, 38, 39b, 39d, 48a, 60
Abder Rasek	35, 39a, 39b, 39c, 39d, 48a, 59, 60
Abder Rasek Ali	38
Abd el Wahab	35, 39b, 39c
Abd el Wahab Alam	38
Abdel Wahab Muhd	59, 60
Abdullah	16 (in table with Ali Suefi, Misid), 35
Abdullah Hussein	39b
Abdullah Muhd	48a, 59, 60
Abu Khalifa	39b

8. Notebook base: name-lists

Abul Anim Muhd	38
Abd el Mejid Ibrm	38
Ahmed	59, 60
Ahmed abder Rahim	38
Ahmed abder Rahman	38, 39a
Ahmed ibn Ahmed	38
Ahmed Ali	38
Ahmed Hameda	38
Ahmed Hussein	48a, 59, 60
Ahmed Hussini	48a
Ahmed Muhd	48a
Ahmed Siam	35, 38, 39b, 39c, 39d, 48a, 49
Ahmed Sigr	38
Aid	39c
Aid Farag	39a
Aishawi Abdullah	48a
Ali Ahmed	38, 39c
Ali Barakat	38
Ali Guma	60
Ali Hassan	38, 39a
Ali Hussein	35, 39c, 39d
Ali Muhd	38, 39a, 39c, 60
Ali Omar	38
Ali Radi	60 (round face)
Ali Rizq	38
Ali Rubi	38
Ali Sad	35, 39b, 39c, 39d, 48a, 49, 59, 60
Ali Said	60
Ali Sisi	35, 38, 39a, 39b, 39c, 39d, 48a, 49 (Sisi), 59, 60
Ali Suefi	16 (Illahun, in table of foremen), 59, 60
Ali Umran	38
Ali ...	60
Anim	39a
'Aqub Mansur	39c, 39d
A Dahir (=Muhd Dahir?)	39b
Atweh Mabruk	60
Bakr Aid	60
Bayumi Muhd	39b
Bedr	39b
Agami Bedr	38
Bedr Ali	38
Beyumi	39b
Derwish Tulbeh	38
Auad Farag	38
Hanneh Farag	38, 39a (?)
M'awad Farag	38
Farag Muhd	39b, 49, 60
Farid Dafullah	35, 38, 39a, 39b, 39c, 39d, 48a, 49, 60
Gabr abu Shahr	38
Gedan	38, 39a, 39c, 48a
Gibeli Graib	38

Ibrahim Abdullah	38
Ibrm Ahmed	59, 60
Ibrm Hanafi	38, 39b
Ibrm Hussein	38, 39a
Ibrm Mesieh	38, 48a, 59
Ibrm Salim	38
Ibrm Suleiman	38, 39a
Ibrahim Terfih?	48a
Khalifa	39c, 39d, 59, 60
Khalifa Mensi?	48a
Hawafi Khallil	38
Gad Khatib	38
Mabruk Nasr (or v.v.)	35, 39b, 39c, 39d
Ma'auad Shaban	35, 39d, 48a
Mahmud	60
Mahmud Ali	38
Mahmud Si'a	48a, 59, 60
Makluf	35, 39a, 39b, 39c, 48a, 49, 59, 60
Makluf Ali	38
Mansur Ali	60 (tall black)
Ibrm Mansur	38
Mansur es Sheikh	38
Ali Mattar	38
Mekowi	35, 39a, 39b, 39c, 39d, 48a, 49, 59 ('+ bro'), 60
M'kowi Said	38
Mensi Muhd	60
Mergowi	39a
Mergowi abd er Rahman	38
Misid Hameda	16 (Misid, in table of foremen), 60
Abd el M'saud	38
Hamd M'sud	38
Muhd M'saud	38
M'shiet Abdullah	38
Said abd el M'sieh	38
Muhd brother of Bakr Aid	60
Muhd abd el Bai	60
Muhd abd er Rahman	38
Muhd Ali	60
Muhd Dahir	39b, 39c, 39d, 49
Muhd Genowi	35, 39b, 39c, 39d
Muhd Gobashi	38
Muhd Godi	38, 39a
Muhd Hassab	39b
Muhd Hussein	38, 39c
Muhd Khatib	38
Muhamed Maklous	48a
Muhd Mansur	16 (in table of foremen), 48a, 59, 60
Muhd Nasr	39a
Muhd Omar	38
Muhd Osman	35, 39b, 39c, 39d, 48a, 49, 59, 60
Muhd Said	60

Shaban Muhd	38 (*2nd* w)
Shilani (after Farid)	48a
Sidahmed	48a, 59, 60
Sidahmed Muhd	49
Smain	60
Smain Mabruk	48a
Smain Mergowi	39a
Smain Muhd	38
Smain Shahr	38, 39c
Smain Sisi	38
Suleiman Bares	60
Suleiman Ibrm	38
Tantawi	39a, 49
Tantawi bro	39a
Terfih	39b, 60
Tulbeh Nasr	38
Umbarak Muhd	38
... Hasan	60 scan 7
... Shafa	60 scan 7

1891-1892 Amarna workforce

Notebook 16 contains lists with names not found in other 1887-1892 examples, and so most probably local to et-Till and the other villages of the Amarna area where Petrie excavated in 1891-1892 (scans 2-5):

Abadeh Md
Abd el Al Iman
Abd el Gelal
Abd er Rahim
Abd Robu
Abdll Ali Smain
Abdll Haz
Abul Elab
Abu Zeid
Ahmed Rahman
Ali
Ali Mabruk
Ali Muhd
Farag
Hadieh (scan 16 Hassanen Hadieh)
Hassan Abdullah
Hassan Jedullah
Husein Ali
Husein Muhd
Hussn Khalifa
Muhd
Muhd Hamad
Md Shehad
Nafeh (?) Mahmud
Rustum
Serhan

Shehat
Siliem (?)
Suleiman
Suln Hassan
Suweilim (?) Ali
Tusun Hassan

Phase IV. Upper Egypt and Sinai, 1893-1905

At the start of this phase in his career, newly appointed as Professor at
UCL, Petrie recruited a core workforce at Qift for his season there in 1893.
Overshadowing the group of Fayumi men who trained them for Petrie, the
Qift excavation force has become the most famous, employed into later
generations by other foreign expeditions and in the work of the Antiquities

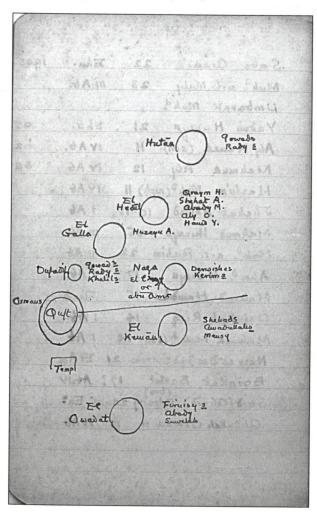

8.1. Hilda Petrie's
sketchmap of villages
in the Qift area with
names of workforce,
Petrie Notebook 134.

Service of Egypt. The most revealing source for this core Petrie workforce is preserved in a Notebook that was not included in the CD-ROM publication of the Petrie Museum archives (Notebook 134). Its contents include an exceptionally precise record by Hilda Petrie of the workforce names, ages, homes, and first year of work for Petrie. At the right end of the book or front, reading from right to left, Hilda drew a diagrammatic sketch-map of Qift and the adjacent hamlets and villages with the names of the workmen from each. From south to north, these are, in her spellings:

El Owadat	Firnisys, Abady, Suweleh
El Keman	Sheads, Awadullahs, Mensy
Quft	Osmans
Dufadif	Gowads, Radys, Khalils
Naga el ... or abu Amr	Derwishes, Kerims
El Galla	Huzeyn A.
El Hedil	Qraym H., Shehat A., Abady M., Aly O., Hamed Y.
Hutan	Gowads, Radys

Another page gives two family trees:

(1) brothers Huseyn Khalil, Hamed Kh., Abul Hasan Kh, with Aly Hamed as son of Hamed Kh.
(2) brothers Abul Hamed and Muhd Hantish, with Hashim Muhd and Um Muhd as son and daughter of Muhd Hantish, and Aly Suefy as husband of Um Muhd.

Taken in combination with the evidence for Aly Suefy at Naqada the following year, the second of these family-trees appears to record the Qift-area family into which Aly Suefy married.

A full list with ages and first year of work for Petrie occupies six full pages and three lines each on another two, with one added later. As the clearest and most detailed record of the men recruited from Qift, it is reproduced here in full, before the index for all the names recorded for the seasons 1893-1905:

Saba Aisa	22	Ehn.	1903
Muhd a.l.Muly	23	III Ab	
Umbarak Muhd			
Yadim Huseyn	21	Ehn.	03
Aly Hamed (son)	11	IV Ab	Dufadif
Mahmud Aly	12	IV Ab	02
Haslu'm Muhd (neph.)	11	IV Ab	
Shehat Ahmed	10-15	I Ab	
Mahmud Huzeyn	25	III Ab	
Muhd a.r.Rahim	22	II Ab	
Ahmd. Huzeyn	17?	I Ab	(? Dufadif)
Mahmud Hamdan	15	Dend	
Dafullah. Risq	14	I Ab	
Mahmud Muhd. (son)	14	I Ab	

Nasr ed Din Jad e Kerim	21	El Am	
Barakat Bakhit (bro)	17?	Ab.IV	
Said (Ahmed) Abady	20-25	Ehn	
Abdullah Osman III	13	IV Ab	Dufadif
(added) Ahmed Huzeyn	20		
Huseyn Khalil I	30	Dend.	Dufadif
Hasan Jody	22	El Am.	"
Abul Hasan Khalil	26	III Ab.	"
Hamed Suwelin	27	IV AB.	
Hamed Khalil III	30	Ehn.	Dufadif
Muhd. Aly	25?	I Ab	
Abul Hamed	40?	Naq.	
Aly Hamed	40	El Am	
Aly Edris	22-25	II Ab.	

8.2. Hilda Petrie's record of the Qift workforce, Petrie Notebook 134.

Muhd a.l.Megid	35	IV Ab.	
	30-40		
Abady Musy (Abady)	25?	Quft	Hedel
Bedawy Hamdan (Ahmed)	24?	Dend	
Abdullah a.l Muly I			"
Muhamed Menzy		Quft	Keman
Mursy a.l Muly II	24	El Am.	
Umbarak Bakhit	23	El Am.	
Muhamed a.l.Muly III	25	El Am.	
Said Osman I	28	Quft	Dufadif
Ahmed Osman II		Galla	
(added) Khalifa Ahmd	45?	Naqada (10)	Mahamid Erment
Muhamed Aly	12?	Ehn	
Shehat Muhamed says 18	14?	IV Ab.	
Ahmed Muhamed	20?	IV Ab	
(abd er Rahim with line to Ahmed in line above)			
Abd er Rahim Muhd	27	Ehn.	
Huseyn Mahmud	16	II Ab	
Mahmud Ahmed	16	IV Ab	
Badr Aly	17	II Ab	Galla
Ahd a r Rahman	15	I Ab	(? Hutan)
bro Atetu Suleyman (bro)	12	IV Ab	
Musy Ahmed	19	II Ab.	
Muhd. a.r. Rahman	12?	II Ab.	
	15		
Yusuf Hasan	15?	I Ab.	
	12		
Aly Smayn	13	I Ab	
Mahmud Ahmed	18?	IV Ab	
bro Muhamed Hamdan el Abady	15	IV Ab	
bro Bukadady Khalil	15	IV Ab	
Mahmud Ahmed	16	II Ab	
Abd er Rasiq Huseyn says 13	15?	IV Ab	Hutan?
Hamdan Yusuf	20?	Dend.	Hedil
Muhamed Sayd	20?	I Ab	
Sirhan	19	II Ab	
Aly Awadullah	20?	I Ab	Keman
Ahmed Awadullah (bro)	20?	III AB	Keman
Ahmed Jad	20?	I Ab	N.abu Omr
Hasan Dofedah	30	Hu	N.abu Omr
Huzeyn Ahmed	32	ii Quft	Galla
Muhd el Berqy	22	I Ab	Hedel
Umbarak Sulyman	25	II Ab	
Ibrahim M'Awad	19	I Ab	
Ibrahim Shehat	22?	Quft	Keman
Kheyr Muhamed	21?	I Ab.	
Muhamed Shehat	25	Dend.	Keman
Muhamed Hamed	41?	Quft	Hedel
	really 50?		

237

Qraim Hamdan	20	Dend.	Hedel
Ahmed Khalil	21	I Ab	
Maslub Smayn	16	Hu	
Abd el Latif Mahmud	23	III Ab	
Hasan Yusuf		15	Ehn.
Shehat Maghanam			
(bro) Abd el Latif Hasan			
Atieh Ibrahim			
Musey Jedullah			
Ahmed Da-udy	15?	Ehn.	
M'saud Sudany			
(bro) Yadim al Kerim	15?	IV Ab.	
Seman Ibrahim	11?	IV Ab.	
Umbarak Sayd	19	Ehn.	
Atetu abul Hasan	15?	Ehn.	
Ahmed Hamdan	18	Ehn.	
Ahmed Ibrahim	12?	I Ab	
Hasan Ahmed	20	Ehn.	
Mahmud Aly Ashery	15?	I Ab	
Smayn Umbarak	18	IV Ab	
Muhamed a.r.Rahim	18	Ehn.	
Smayn Hasan	20	Hu	Shekh Aly
Ahmed abu Bakr	19	Hu	"
Aly Hasan			
Muhamed Salim			
Aly Smayn			
Hasan Osman	29	Quft	
Huseyn Osman	25	"	
Muhamed Osman	22	"	
Muhd. a.l.Kerim	20	Hu	N abu Omr
Abu Zeyd Omr	19	I Ab	N abu Omr
Yadim Derwish	40	Quft	N abu Omr
Muhd. Derwish	34?	"	N abu Omr
Muhd. Musy	30	IV Ab	Dufadif
Aleyn Mustafa	25?	III Ab	
Nasr a.l.Naim	30	I Ab	
Hasan a l Naim	25	IV Ab	
Dakruny Smayn		I Ab	
Shehat Ahmed	26?	Qurn.	Hedel
Mahmud Aly	20	III Ab	Hutan
(son) Muhamed Salah	12	Ehn.	
Hasan Hagady	13	II Ab.	
Jodah Musy	22	II Ab.	
Salah Bakhit	35	IV Ab.	
Muhamed a.r.Rasaq	27	IV Ab.	
Helal Ahmed	24	Hu	
(added) Mahd. Muhd. Ghalab el Sherif			

8. Notebook base: name-lists

The Notebook 134 list names dominate the fuller list, below, of men and boys from various places, working for Petrie from 1893 to his final break with the Egypt Exploration Fund in 1905. Some of these add place-name, notably Notebook 69 (Naqada 1894-1895) where one pair of diggers is introduced as (from) 'Ali's village' (Smain Muhd, Muhd Awda), and another from Nahiet Dum (Hamed Shaban, Husein abd er Robu). This evidence reinforces the Notebook 109 copy of a message sent the following year by Petrie to Ali Muhammad Suefi at Nahiet Dum, Nagada (above, p. 150), to indicate that Ali Suefi had moved from Lahun in Fayum province to settle near Naqada, across the river from Qift, after 1893 when he joined Petrie to train Qift villagers to excavate there. Of these four fellow villagers, Smain Muhammad appears in later seasons (if the man with this name in the Araba name-lists is the same person). The Notebook 69 list also introduces pairs of diggers with the place-names Tukh, Kom Belal, and Neqada, but these might be excavation sites rather than home villages.

The collation below draws on the following Notebooks:

Qift/Koptos, 1893-1894
Notebook 54 (Petrie) scans 4-9, 17-19

Naqada, 1894-1895
Notebook 55 (Quibell?) scans 5-7, 11-12
Notebook 69 (Petrie) scans 3-8
Notebook 71 (Petrie) scans 2-4
(torn page at back of Notebook 72, scan 64, from these or similar week-pay-lists)

Qurna (Ramesseum and Six Temples), 1895-1896
Notebook 84 (Quibell?) scans 4-8
Notebook 107 (Petrie) scan 16

Dandara, 1897-1898
Notebook 15 (Petrie) scans 9-14
Notebook 17a (Petrie) scans 19-21, 23-25

Hu, 1898-1899
Notebook 40a (Petrie mainly) scans 7-12, 15, 17-21, and summaries scans 13-14, 16

Abydos, 1899-1903
Notebook 4 1899-1900, scans 22-23, 51-52
Notebook 2 1899-1900 (Petrie): scans 9-11, and summary scan 12
Notebook 3 1900-1901 (Petrie): scans 4-13, 15-18; 41 summary (?) by Hilda Petrie

Notebook 1 1902-1903 (Hilda Petrie): scans 2-11 pairs, weeks of daily payments; scans 19-20, 22 summary, initials

Ihnasya, 1903-1904
Notebook 134 (Hilda Petrie) not on the published CD-ROM: sketch-map of Qift villages and list of names with age and first year of work with Petrie

Name	*Notebook*
Abadeh Musi	2, 15, 40a, 54 (scan 26 'Good'), 107, 134 (25?, Quft, Hedel)
Ahmed Ababdeh	54 (scan 26 'Good')
Abd Awedeh	2
Abd l Ali	2
Abd el Azim	2 (Muhd), 15, 17a, 40a, 54 (scan 26 'Medium'), 55, 69, 71, 84
Abd el Beyum?	54
Abdel Ghany Huseyn	1 (scan 28 'Locals')
Abd el Hadi	15
Abd el Halim	69 ('Abd el Halim Ali lad'), 71
Abd Hamd	55
Abd el Kerim	69, 71
Abdel Kerim Ahmed	2
Abd el Kerim Muhd	69 ('Sakkieh')
Abd el Kerim Smain	107
Abd el Lahi	107 ('Ballas')
Abdel Latif Ahmed	1 (scan 28 'Locals')
Abdel Latif Hasan	1 (scan 28 'Locals'), 134
Abdel Latif Husayn	1 (scan 28 'Locals')
Abd el Latif Mahmud	134 (23, III Ab)
Abd el Lela (deleted)	3
Abd el Maksoud	2, 3
Abd el M'siah	2 (p. 14 from back 'of Abydos shewed place of Khasekhemui')
Abd er Radi	2, 54
ARRahim alHalim	1
Abd r Awad	2
Abd Rahim Ibrahim	54 (scan 26 'Bad')
Abd er Rahim Mhmud	55
Abder Rahim Muhamed	1 (scan 28 'Locals')
Abd er Rahim Muhd	134 (27, Ehn.)
Abd er Rahim Mustafa	54 (scan 26 'Medium'), 84
Abd er Rahim ...	1
Abd er Rahman	1, 2, 15, 17a, 84, 107
Abder Rahman Muhamed	1
Abd er Rahman Ellowi	1
Abd er Rasiq Huseyn	134 (says 13, 15?, IV Ab, Hutan?)
Abdullah	54
Abdullah a.l Muly	3, 134 (I)
Abll Ahd	3
Abdullah Ali	15, 17a

Husein Abdll	2
Abadullah Massad	54
Abdullah M'awad	3, 15, 17a, 55, 107
Abll Md	3
Abll Muhd	3
Abdullah Osman III	134 (13, IV Ab, Dufadif)
Abdullah Sudani	54 (scan 26 'Medium')
Abdll Suleiman	2
Abu Bakr	2, 3
Abu Hamad	3 (Abul Hamed), 17a (also as Ab-l Hamed), 134 (Abul Hamed, 40?, Naq.)
Abu Sitteh	2
Abu Zaid	3
Abu Zaid Omar	2, 134 (19, I Ab, N abu Omr)
el Abudi	3
Abul Hamed	2, 15, 40a, 55
Abul Hamed Ali	2
Abul Has	84
Abul Hassan Karar	2
Abul Hasan Khalil	134 (26, III Ab.)
Agar	2
Ahmet	84
Ahd abd el Ghofar	2
Ahd ar-Rahim	3
Ahmed abd er Rahman	3, 40a (following Muhd separate?), 54, 134 (15, I Ab, ? Hutan)
Ahd Abdullah	15, 17a
Ahd Abdll	15, 17a
Ahmed abu Badr	1, 17a
Ahmed abu Bakr	134 (19, Hu, Shekh Aly)
Ahmed ab Hassan	55
Ahmed Ali	1 (scan 28 'Locals'), 2, 15, 17a, 54
Ahmed Awedeh	2, 17a (scan 26 Awadeh 'Good'), 15, 55, 71, 84 (?)
Ahmed Awadullah	134 (bro Ali Awadullah, 20?, III AB, Keman)
Ahmed Bakr	1, 2, 3 (Ahd a Bakr)
Ahmed Da-udy	134 (15?, Ehn.)
Ahmed ed Dengi	2
Ahmed Firnisi	1, 2, 3, 17a, 40a
Ahd Ghalat	40a
Ahd Ghalib	2
Ahmed Hamdan	2, 3, 15, 17a, 134 (18, Ehn.) (and see Bedawy Hamdan)
Ahmed Hamdeh	54
A Helal	3
Ahmed Hussein	2, 3, 134 (17?, I Ab., ? Dufadif)
Ahmed Huzeyn	134 (20)
Ahmed Ibrahim	1 (scan 28 'Locals'), 2, 134 (12?, I Ab)
Ahd Jad	3, 134 (20?, I Ab, N.abu Omr)
Ahd Jedullah	69, 71
Ahmed Jellal	2 (last page)
Ahd Khalifa	2

241

Ahmed Khallil	2, 3, 134 (21, I Ab)
A Mahmoud	84
Ahmed Masoud	1 (scan 28 'Locals')
Ahmed Muhamed	15, 17a, 54 (scan 26 'Medium')
Ahmed Muhamed	1 (scan 28 'Locals')
Ahmed Muhamed	2, 134 (20?, IV Ab)
Ahmed Mursi	3, 17a, 107
Ahmed Musi	2, 107
Ahmed Mustafa	15, 17a, 40a, 84
Ahmed Osman	1, 2, 3, 15, 17a, 40a, 107, 134 (II, Galla)
Ahmed Ramadan?	1 (scan 28 'Locals')
Ahmed Said	2
Ahmed Salameh	2
Ahmed Sehab	54 (scan 26 moved from 'Good' to 'Medium')
Ahmed Shamrukh	1
Ahd Sharqawi	15, 17a
Ahmed sid Ahmed	1 (scan 28 'Locals')
Ahmed Smain	2, 3, 40a (brother Gowad Smain), 54
Ahmed Smayn Hamam	1
Ahmed Suleiman	55 (Der Bahri)
Ahmed Yadim	54 (scan 26 'Medium'), 55
Ahd Yusuf	54 (scan 26 'Bad')
Ahmed Yusuf Howi	2
Ahd Zeid	2
Ahd ... Hamadi	54 (scan 26 'Bad')
Ahmed al ...	1 (scan 28 'Locals')
Aisa Aid	2
Aisa Reshwan	1 (scan 28 'Locals')
Aisa a Sa'ud	3
akh.	2 (p. 15 from back, unidentified abbreviation)
Ali	17a
Ali Abid	84 (see Qurna lists below)
A Kerim	3
Aleyn Mustafa	134 (25?, III Ab)
Ali R.al el Kerim	3
Ali abder Rahim	1, 3
Ali Abdullah	2, 3
Ali Ahmed	1 (scan 28 'Locals'), 2
Ali Awad	15, 17a, 40a, 107
Ali Awadullah	1, 2, 3, 134 (20?, I Ab, Keman)
Ali Dagan	54
Ali Edris	3, 134 (22-25, II Ab.)
Ali Firnisi	1, 2, 3, 40a
Ali Hamdan	2
Ali Hamed	2 (Hamed Ali), 3, 134 (son, 11, IV Ab., Dufadif; and 40, El Am.)
Ali Hasan	1 (scan 28 'Locals'), 2, 3, 40a, 134
Ali Hasan	3 (second in scan 6)
Ali Jedullah	15, 17a, 40a, 69, 71
Ali Khallil	3
Ali M'awad	2

Ali Muhd	2, 40a (brother Ibrahim), 54 (scan 26 'Medium')
Ali Musi	107 (among Qift names)
Ali Omar	1, 2, 3
Ali Redwan	55
Ali Salim	84
Ali Sheti	84 (see Qurna lists below)
Ali Smain	54, 55 (different from next by age/date given in 134)
Ali Smain	2, 3, 134 (13, I Ab)
Ali Smain Ghat	3
Ali Suefi	2, 3, 15, 40a, 54, 69, 71, 84, 107
Ali Suleiman	55
Alieh Ibrahim	1
Amr	40a, 54 (scan 26 'Good'), 55 (Amr Abadeh), 84, 107
Arabi Mersah (?)	3
Aref	2, 3
Aref Ahmed	2, 40a
Aref Ali	2
Aref …	1 (scan 35)
A'Smain	2
Asrau Hasan	1 (scan 28 'Locals')
Atetu abul Hasan	134 (15?, Ehn.)
Atetu Suleyman	134 (bro, 12, IV Ab)
Atieh Ibrahim	134
Atullah Abdullah	69, 71
Auad Smain	54
Awad	54 (scan 26 'Good')
Awedeh Gibran	107
Awedeh Muhd	15, 17a, 40a
Azim Abdullah	69
Badr Aly	134 (17, II Ab, Galla)
Bairs (?)	107 (among Qift names)
Bakar Rahman	17a
Bakhit	15
Balash	2 (penultimate page)
Barakat Bakhit	134 (bro, 17?, Ab.IV)
Barsak Smayn	1
Bedawy Hamdan (Ahmed)	134 (24?, Dend) (and see Ahmed Hamdan)
Bedri Yadem	55
Bekheit el Sudani	2
Berberi	84
Bukadadi	2 (Bukd abd r Rahman), 15 (Buk a r Rahman), 40a
Bukadady Khalil	134 (bro, 15, IV Ab)
Burieh Ahmed	1 (scan 28 'Locals')
Dafullah. Risq	134 (14, I Ab)
Dahshur	2 (once +ahl), 17a, 40a (brother Hamdan Yusuf), 55
Dakruni Said	2, 3 (Dakrumi S.)
Dakruny Smayn	134 (I Ab)
Defulla Aid	55
Eisa M	55
Erfai	1, 2, 3, 55, 84
Etai Abll	3

243

Hasan Mahmud	1 (scan 28 'Locals')
Hassan Mahmud	84
Hasan Osman	2, 3, 15, 17a, 40a, 54 (scan 26 'Good'), 55, 84 (Hassan), 107 (H Osman, could be repeated Hussein Osman), 134 (29, Quft)
Hassan Osman	17a
Hasan Said	54
Hasan Sudani	2, 15, 17a, 40a (Hassan horse)
Hasan Terfih	15, 17a
Hasan Yusuf	2, 15
Hasan Yusuf	134 (15, Ehn.)
Hashim Gazim	107
Haslu'm Muhd	134 (neph., 11, IV Ab)
Hassanen Hamed	2
Helal	2
Helal Ahmed	1 (Helali Ahmed), 2 (Helali), 3, 134 (24, Hu)
Howas	17a
Hozny? Ahmed	1 (scan 28 'Locals')
Husain	2 (Husein), 17a
Hussein	54, 69, 71, 84 ('Cookie' [sic], Quibell writing)
Husn abder Robu	69 ('Nahiet Dum'), 71
Hussein Abdll	2, 15, 17a, 40a (Huzein Abdullah)
Husein Ahmed	1 (scan 28 'Locals'), 15, 40a, 54 (scan 26 'Good'), 134 (32, ii Quft, Galla)
Hussein Ali	54 (scan 26 'Bad')
Huzein Ali	3
Hussein Bedri	55
Husein Fatah	2
Husein Hamed	2
Husein Ibr	2
Husein Khalil	2 (also as Hussein Khallil), 3, 15, 17a, 134 (Huseyn Khalil I, 30, Dend., Dufadif)
Husein Muhd	2, 134 (16, II Ab)
Hussein M	84
Husein Osman	2, 3, 15, 17a, 54 (Hussein: scan 26 'Good'), 55, 84, 107, 134 (25)
Hussein Suleiman	54
Hutut	15, 17a, 40a
Ibaid Ahmed	2 (last page)
Ibrahim	40a (brother Ali Muhd)
Ibr Ahmed	15, 17a
Ibm Ali	2 (Ali Ibr), 3
Ibrahim abd el-Kerim	1, 2 (Ibrm al Kerim)
Ib Amr	84
Ibrahim Awad	1, 3
Ibrm Erfai?	2 (or two names on one line?)
Ibrahim Hamam	1 (Hammam), 2
Ibrm ~~Hasabullah~~	15
Ibrm Hasan	2
Ibrm Khallil	1 (Ibrahim? Khalil), 2
Ibrahim M'Awad	134 (19, I Ab)

Ibrm Muhd	2, 15, 17a, 55, 69
Ibrahim Shehat	2, 3, 15, 17a, 40a, 54 (scan 26 boy 'Good'), 69, 71, 84, 107, 134 (22?, Quft, Keman)
Ibrahim Smain	2 (Smain Ibrahim), 40a, 69, 71
Isa Abdullah	54
Jad el Kerim	1, 3, 69 ('Kom, Belal')
Jodah Mursi	3
Jodah Musy	134 (22, II Ab.)
Jodi Musi	2
Khaled Ahd	17a
Khalifa	2, 3, 84,107
Khalifa Ahmd	134 (45?, Naqada (10), Mahamid Erment)
Khalil Abdullah	1 (scan 28 'Locals')
Khallil abd el Qader	2
Khallil Ahd	2, 3, 15
Khallil al Qadi	2
Khallil Dafullah	69, 71, 84 (? Chalil)
Khallil Jad	2
Khallil Sad	2
Kheir	2
Kheyr Muhamed	134 (21?, I Ab.)
Kraim Hamdan	15
Lazim Hd	3
Lazim Muhd	2 (also without Muhd)
Mahmud	54, 69, 71
Mahmud Abdullah	55
Mahd abu Bakr	15
Mahmud Ahmed	54, 69
Mahmud Ahmed	134 (16, II Ab)
Mahmud Ahmed	134 (16, IV Ab)
Mahmud Ahmed	134 (18?, IV Ab)
Mahmud Ali	2, 134 (12, IV Ab 02)
Mahmud Aly	134 (20, III Ab, Hutan)
Mahd Dahshur	15
Mahmud Ghalab	3, 15, 17a, 40a, 55, 107
Mahd Hamad	2 (Mahumd Hamid), 3
Mahmud Hamdan	134 (15, Dend)
Mahmud Huzeyn	134 (25, III Ab)
Mahmud Ibrahim	1 (scan 28 'Locals'), 2
Mahmud Khalifa	54
Mahmud Mesoud	1
Mahmud Muhd	15, 84, 107 ('Old' i.e. from previous seasons)
Mahmud Muhamed	1 (scan 28 'Locals'), 2, 3, 134 (son, 14, I Ab)
Mahd. Muhd. Ghalab el Sherif	134
Mahmud Musi (?)	69 ('Tukh'), 71
Mahmud sid Ahmed	1 (scan 28 'Locals')
Mahmud Sulyman	1 (scan 28 'Locals')
Mahd Yusuf	15, 55
Maksud	2, 3
Mansur Saleh	54

8. Notebook base: name-lists

Maslub Smayn	3, 134 (16, Hu)
Masluk	54 (scan 26 'Medium')
Masri Ahmed	54
Mayit	84, 107 ('Old' i.e. from previous seasons)
Mhasib Mus	84
Mo Ali	17a
Moharrab	2
Moli	2
Misid	54, 69, 71
Ms'aud Farag	3
M'saud Sudany	134
M'saud Yusuf	15
Mubarak Agab	2
Mubarak Ali	54
Mubarak Mustafa	40a, 54 (scan 26 'Medium'), 84
Mubarak Smain	54
Mubarak Yusuf	54
Mufarag (?) Abdullah	69, 71
Mughraby	3
Muhammed	15, 17a, 40a
Muhd abd el Azim	2, 54
Muhamed abdel Iswad?	1
Muhd abd el Kerim	54
Muhd. a.l.Kerim	1, 3, 134 (20, Hu, N abu Omr)
Muhd a.l.Megid	134 (35/30-40, IV Ab.)
Muhamed a.l.Muly III	134 (25, El Am.)
Muhd Abd er Rahim	15, 54 (scan 26 boy 'Good'), 55, 71, 107
Muhd a.r.Rahim	2 (Muhd a Rah), 134 (22, II Ab)
Muhamed a.r.Rahim	13 (18, Ehn.)
Muhd ar Rahmn	17a, 84 (M Abdur)
Muhd. a.r. Rahman	134 (12?/15, II Ab)
Muhamed a.r.Rasaq	134 (27, IV Ab.)
M Abedulla	84
Md a Lela	3
Md abu Leleh F.S.	2
Muhd abu Ahmed	54
Muhamed Abu Reby	1 (scan 28 'Locals')
Md el Agur?	3
Muhamed Ahmed	1, 2, 3, 15, 54, 55, 71
Muhd Ahd esh Shomeri	2 (p. 14 from back 'of Abydos shewed place of Khasekhemui')
Muhamed Ahmed Huseyn	1
Muhd Aisa	3
Muhd el Berqy	134 (22, I Ab, Hedel)
Muhamed al Muly	1, 134 (23, III Ab.)
Muhd Ali	15, 17a, 40a
Muhd Ali	15 (second in list)
Muhd Ali	134 (25?, I Ab)
Muhamed Aly	134 (12?, Ehn)
Mahmud Aly Ashery	134 (15?, I Ab)
Muhamed Amid	1 (scan 28 'Locals'), 2 (Amid)

Muhd Awda (?)	69 ('Ali's village'), 84 (M. Aueda)
Muhd Azim	2
Muhd Bakr	2
Md Bereys	3
Mud ed Digag (?)	84
Md Derwish	2, 3, 15, 17a, 54 (scan 26 from 'Good' to 'Medium'), 134 (34?, Quft, N abu Omr)
Muhamed Farag	1 (scan 28 'Locals')
Md Firnisi	2 (also Zan Md Fir p. 8 from back?)
Muhd Galab	54
Mhmd Gasala	55
M Genawi?	2
Muhd Gowad	3
Muhamed Halabi	1 (Muhamed Hallaby), 54
Muhd Hamad	2, 3, 15, 17a, 54, 55, 69, 71 (or next?), 107 (or next?)
Muhd Hamed	54 (in same list as Muhd Hamad, scan 4), 69 ('father')
Muhamd (?) Hamed	69 (in same list as another Muhd Hamed and a Muhd Hamed father)
Muhd Hamdallah	2
Muhd Hamdan	2, 3
Muhamed Hamdan el Abady	134 (bro, 15, IV Ab)
Muhamed Hamdan al Bergy	1, 2 (also as El Bergi)
Muhd Hamed	2, 40a, 54, 134 (41?/really 50?, Quft, Hedel)
Md Hamed Gal…	54 (scan 26 'Bad')
Muhamed Hedawi	1 (scan 28 'Locals')
M Ibrm	15
Md Jedullah	15, 17a, 84 (M Gedullah)
Muhd Jelal	2
Muhamd Khalifa	54 (scan 26 M Khalifa 'Medium')
M Khallil	15
Muhd Kheir	2
Muhd Khudeir	2 (once as M Khodeir)
Muhd Mahd	15, 17a, 69 ('Tukh', 'brown'), 71, 107
Muhd Mahd	69 ('lad')
Muhd Mansur	69
Muhd Mensi	2, 3, 134 (Quft, Keman)
Muhd Mud	3, 17a
Muhd Mustafa	40a, 54, 55
Muhd. Musy	134 (30, IV Ab, Dufadif)
M M Abadeh	84
Muhd Osman	2 ('cook'), 15 ('cook'), 17a ('cook'),134 (22), 107
Muhd Osman el Jodi	2
Md Qenawi	2
Mhmd Rokham	55
Muhamed Said	1, 2, 134 (20?, I Ab)
Muhamed Salah	134 (son, 12, Ehn.)
Muhamed Salim	1, 3, 134
Muhamed Semau	1 (scan 28 'Locals')
Muhd Sharqawi	2, 40a, 55
Muhamed Shehat	2, 3, 15, 17a (Shahad), 40a, 134 (25, Dend., Keman)

8. Notebook base: name-lists

Muhd Smain	2, 15, 17a (also as M Smain), 54, 55, 84
M Suliman	54 (scan 26 'Bad')
Muhd Yunis	2
Muhamed Yusuf	1, 15
Muhd …	3
Muhamed … Hasan	1 (scan 28 'Locals')
Muhden Agar	2
Muhawi Muhamed?	1 (scan 32 or Muhamed Muhamed?)
Muhareb Abll	2 (p. 8 from back)
Muharib Awad	2
Muharram Abulelah	2
Md Mursi	3
Mursy a.l Muly II	134 (24, El Am.)
Mursi …	55
Mustafa Muhamed	1 (scan 28 'Locals')
Musy Ahmed	134 (19, II Ab.)
Musi Hasan	2
Musi Gedullah	1, 134 (Musey Jedullah)
Musi Zeydan	69, 71
Mustf Ali	3
Nagar Ali	2
Najnidin	54 (scan 26 'Bad')
Nasr abd el Nami	2, 134 (Nasr a.l.Naim, 30, I Ab)
Nasr ed Din Jad e Kerim	134 (21, El Am)
Nazim Muhd	15, 17a, 40a
Omar Ahd	15
Omar Ali	17a
Omar Mahrur	55
Osman	1, 3
Qraim Hamdan	3, 134 (20, Dend., Hedel)
Md ar-Rahim	3
Md a Rahman	3
M a Rah	2
Refai	2
Rehabu…	3
Reshwan	2 (once Muhd Reshwan), 55
Rashwan Mensi	1, 15, 17a, 54
Rashwan Sabr	3
Reshwan Mansur	40a
Saba Aisa	134 (22, Ehn.1903)
Sad Hasan	54
Sadik Hasan	2 (Sadik), 40a
Sadik Muhd	2
Safair (or Safein?) Hussein	69 ('old', 'Khatereh (?) Negadeh'), 71
Sagars Hasn	3
Es Sagaw	2
Sagaw a r Rahman	2
Sagawi Hasan	2
Said	15 (or note to Husein Khalli?), 84
Said (Ahmed) Abady	134 (20-25, Ehn), 55 (Said Ahmet)
Said abu Lela	2 (Said abu Lel), 15, 17a, 54 (scan 26 'Medium'), 84

Taman	3
Terfih abd er Radi	54 (scan 26 Terfih 'Good')
Tewfik	2
Tewfik Hassanen	2
Tewfik Husain	2
Tuni	54
Umb	107
Umbarak Ahd	2
Umbarak Ali	15, 17a, 54 (scan 26 'Good'), 55, 107
Umbarak Bakhit	3, 134 (23, El Am.)
Umbk Gemal	2
Umbk Hamdan	2
Umbarak Muhd	134
Umbarak Mustafa	2, 15, 17a
Umbk Sagowi	2
Umbarak Sayd	134 (19, Ehn.)
Umbk Smain	3
Umbh Suba	3
Umbarak Sulyman	1, 134 (25, II Ab)
Yadim	2
Yadim al-Kerim	1, 134 (15?, IV Ab.)
Yadim Derwish	2, 3, 54 (scan 26 'Medium'), 134 (40, Quft, N abu Omr)
Yadim Huseyn	134 (21, Ehn.03)
Yem (?) Ahmed	55
Yesin Ali	2
Yonis Yadi	1
Yunis	2, 15 (Wanis), 17a, 54 (scan 26 from 'Good' to 'Medium'), 69, 71, 84
Yunis Ali	69, 71
Yunis Hasan	2
Yunis el Jemal	2
Yunis M'ghanen	15
Omar Yunis	2 (and as Yunis Omar), 3 (Yunis Omar), 40a
Yunis Yadim	1, 3
Yusuf	2, 15, 17a, 54 (scan 26 'Good'), 55
Yusuf Abadeh	2, 3 (Abadi), 107
Yusuf Aisa	2
Yusuf Hasan	134 (15?/ 12, I Ab.)
Yusuf Husn	3
Yusuf Ibrm	2
Yusuf Naimeh	2
Nsaud Yusuf	17a
... Wanis (?)	54 (scan 26 'Medium')
Zeidan Mahmud	2
Zein	84
Zein Abdll	2, 3
Zein Ahmed	54
Zenn Daddy	107 (among Qift names)
... Mud	17a
... Ahd	3
... Hasan	54

Separate teams

1. Qurna, 1895-1896

The published excavation report records how Petrie protected the dig from infiltration by the long-established networks of local antiquities traders (Petrie 1897: 1-2). He combined his Qift team, in their third year working for him, first with local recruitment among people at Qurna, and then, dismissing the Qurnawi and instead 'drawing many from the villages around' (Petrie 1897: 2). The process is documented in the name-lists across Notebooks 109 and 107. Notebook 109 preserves Petrie lists for the first week of work, adding to many names any features that might help him distinguish individuals, as in his early lists at San al-Hagar (above, pp. 134-5). None of the distinctive names in Notebook 109 occur in other seasons, confirming the impression that these are first-time local recruits. Thirty names are annotated 'B', probably an abbreviation for a place-name; many of these recur in Notebook 107 from later in the season. Those absent from later 1895-1896 lists are presumably names of Qurnawi, dismissed after Petrie found it impossible to break ties of obligation to local antiquities-traders. Below the Notebook 109 names are indexed in a Latin alphabetic order, with note of any coincidences with names in the main list above:

Abd el Aziz Aribui 'bk beard'
Abd el Hamid Muhd 'serious'
Abd er Rahman Doba 'far' 'B'
Abdullah Hashash 'Neg. wt bd'
Abdullah Lazim 'Neg.'
Abdullah Mahdi 'x x bricks' 'B'
Abdullah Muhd 'B'
Abid Muhd '?old'
Abul Hajai abder Rahman 'bk must.'
Abu Roah Muh '.sm...l mouth ?'
Abu Zeit Abdullah (deleted)
Ahmed Abdullah 'B'
Ahmed abd el Gelil
Ahmed Abidullah
Ahmed Ali 'Newberry's' (cf. nb 1, 2, 15, 17a, 54)
Ahmed Awad 'Muharram'
Ahmed Ayat 'fas pleasant young x' 'B'
Ahmed Ibrm (not man of same name in nb 1, local to Araba, or of nb
     2, 134, with first year of work with Petrie 1899-1900 Araba)
Ahmed Lot 'pleasant'
Ahmed Muhd 'B' (cf. nb 15, 17a, 54)
Ahmed Muhd O (cross) br must
Ahmed Muhd Suleman
Ahmed Musi bl. (son Rasul) (cf. Ahmed Musi nb 2, 15)
Ahmed Uswali 'B'
Ahmed Yusuf 'bk short bd' (cf. nb 54)

Ali Abid
Ali Fuli
Ali Halebi 'x' 'B'
Ali Hamed 'B' (cf. nb 2, 3, 134 x2)
Ali Said 'like Gowdi (fas)' 'B'
Ali Shehdi 'small dark'
Ali Smain (cf. nb 54; another in 2, 3, 134 identified in latter as working first
    for Petrie in 1899-1900 at Araba)
Awad Mashabr 'mat [?] face x'
Awad Nabut 'left hd bad' 'B'
Dabrik Bakhit 'rt eye wt'
Dar Reshwan 'chin' 'B'
Deir [?] Darawalli 'deleted'
Deir din Abdullah 'far' 'B'
Dendari
Gazim Omar 'B'
Hafni Ibrahim 'B'
Hassan Darawalli
Hasan Mahmud
Hassan M Awad 'B'
Hasan Mustafa 'B'
Hassan Timsah. O
Hussan Said
Hussein Genawi
Hussein Musi 'young x'
Ibrm Mahmud 'B'
Ibrahim Muhd (Muhd circled) el Amir 'small' 'B'
Ibrm Muhd Kelb
Ibrm Muhd Raga 'small bd'
Jowdi Roba 'B'
Mahmud Abid '?' 'B'
Maktabuktar 'Copt' 'B'
Masud Mahmud 'x Luxor' (?)
M'babeh Hassan 'B'
Muhd Abdullah 'B'
Muhd Ahmed 'medium' 'B'
Muhd Awad 'small talker' 'B'
Muhd Hussein Nebut 'old wt bd'
Muhd Lazim 'tall gy bd x'
Muhd Said 'big ~~black~~ dark'
Muhd Yusuf (cf. 1, 15)
Radi Mansur 'small bk bd'
Said Ahmed 'lad x' 'B'
Said Mahmud 'thin' 'B' (cf. nb 2)
Salim 'B'
Tahir Ibrm Hussein 'B'

In the original order, the final entry is Ali Fuli with the numeral 60, perhaps for the number of recruits to this point. Following this, Petrie added twelve more names, four marked 'B', the rest familiar from the lists of Qift recruits:

Abadi Musi
Abd er Rahim Muhd 'B'
Abul Hassan Osman
Ali (last name, note '12 days pd'; the different treatment suggests this is Ali Suefi)
Ali Jedullah
Hassan Osman
Hussein Osman
Galus 'B'
Mahmud Muhd
Muhd Smain 'B'
Muhd Yunis 'B'
Umbarak Mustafa

In Notebook 107, place-name is given for a high proportion of the name-lists (not included in the published CD-ROM). A section on pp. 8-9 is headed Bishara, one on pp. 14-15 has Beirat at the top, and the name Beirat recurs beside several names on pp. 12-13; for the second name, on his first visit to Upper Egypt, in the winter of 1881-1882, Petrie recorded 'Kom el Beyrat village' east-south-east of Medinet Habu on a sketchmap of Thebes West (Notebook 33, scan 36). These groupings are reproduced below. On pp. 18-19, 'Kofti' heads a group mainly known from Notebooks for other seasons, and repeated for later work on pp. 20-1. The names of men from Qift and Naqada, including Ali Suefi, recur on a list, pp. 10-11, for January 18-26 [1896] under the heading 'Old', followed on pp. 12-13, without sub-heading, by a mixture of old and new names. Similarly, lists on p. 1 name Qift men, followed by lists on pp. 2-7 with new Qurna area recruits, many with home-place recorded. The references to Qift and Naqada men known from previous or later seasons of work are included in the main concordance list above. Two men are noted with the word Cofti (Mahmud Bakri and, deleted, Must Aisa, on pp. 12-13): this may be a way of noting that they are from Qift, but it seems more likely to refer to another place of origin, as the spelling has not been found in other Petrie records. All other Qurna area recruits who appear only in the 1895-1896 records are recorded in their separate groups below, noting if they also occur in Notebook 109.

Beirat (pp. 2-5, 12-15):
　　Abd el Hag Gurgar
　　Ahd Ayat
　　Ah Makkah
　　Ahd Mawad
　　Ah Md Gibran
　　Ah Md Hamed
　　Ali Arnut
　　Ali Hamad
　　Ali Muhd ed Dik
　　Arid (?) Akhat

El Emir Muhd
Hasan Abdullah
Hasan Mawad
Hassanen (?) Sultan
Hussein Ahmed
Husn Ali Ramadan
Husein Muhd
M'babeh Hasan
Merai Muhamadan
Muhd Lot
Muhd Nob
Muhd Yusuf Hamed
Rubi Sultan
Said Ahmed

Bishara (pp. 4-5, 8-9):
Ahd Amr
Ali Md Aweys
Bukadadi abd el Al
Ghotas Musi
Harb Musi
Husein Musi
Ibrm Amr (?)
Ibrm Md Hasan
Mahd Degageh
Mhd Amr
Smain Hakim

Meris (place name? pp. 16-17):
Ali ar Rahim
Mohamed Ahmed

Qurn/Gurn/Gur (pp. 2-5)
Abd el Galil
Abd Lazim
Ahd Muhd Suln
Hasan Ghotas
Saleh Ali Hamed
Smain Khallil

Notebook 107 names without place-name, not in Qift/Old sections,
noting if also found in Notebook 109:
Abd r Doba (109 B)
Abdll Daud
Abdll Hashash (109 B)
Abdullah Mahdi (109 B)
abu Gelil Ahd (cf. 109 Ahmed abd el Gelil?)
Ahmed Ali (109 Newberry's)
Ahd Lot (109 B)
Ahmed Muhd Ali (cf. 109 Ahmed Muhd B)

255

Ahd Muh Gibran
Ahd Md Hamed
Ahmed Umran
Ali Abid (109)
Ali Halabi (109 B)
Ali Said (109 B)
Ali Shehid (109)
Ali Smain (109)
Awad Md abu Zeit
Awad Nebut (109 B)
Farli (?) Musi
Godi Ayat
Hasan abd el Gelil
Hasan Abdullah
Hasan Ali Selim
Hasan Lot
Hasan Mahd (109)
Hasan Mustf (109 B)
Hofni
Jodi Roba (109 B)
Johar Sudani
Khalifa Gurgur
M'saud Mahd (cf. 109 Masud Mahmud Luxor)
Muhd abdr Rahim
Mhd Ali
Muhd Lazim (109)
Muhd Omar
Mohameden Abdll (cf. 109 Muhd Abdullah B)
Said Said
Tahir Ali
Umran
Yunis Said
Zahir abd el Hadi

2. Dishasha, 1896-1897

In 1896 Petrie resumed working with the Egypt Exploration Fund, ten years after he had resigned over the lack of attention in its Committee to small finds and to swift publication. The first new joint dig was the survey and excavation of the area from Bahnasa to Bani Suef, from which the papyrologists Grenfell and Hunt started their retrieval of mainly Greek papyri from Bahnasa (Oxyrhynchus), and Petrie conducted his excavations of the cemeteries at Dishasha. For the latter he evidently recruited a local force of excavators, as few of the names recur elsewhere in the records; this is in marked contrast to the mix of local and Qift excavators for the seasons at Dandara and al-Araba al-Madfuna (Abydos). Only the first eight names in the list on the pages numbered by Petrie pp. 37-41 seem to be recruits from previous years: Ali, Muhamed, Said, Ali Sad, Ibrahim, Yusuf, Ali Sisi and Mekowi (for the latter in this season, see above, p. 79). Accordingly, the rest of the Dishasha names are listed

8. Notebook base: name-lists

separately below from the record of the 1896-1897 season in Notebook 18, noting any possible identifications with names in the main list above:

Abd el Hati (cf. Nb 15)
Abd el Kerim Ali
Abd er Raza'
Abd es Salam
Abdullah Ahmed (cf. Nb 3)
Abdullah Hasan
Abdullah M'saud
Abu Ghanim
Abu Hamed (cf. Nb 3, 17a, 134 Qift worker since Naqada 1894-1895)
Abu Hamed Saleh
Abul ela Reshwan
Aisa Ahmed
Ali (abu) Ahmed (not same as in Nb 1, 2 as Nb 1 lists under 'Locals'
    of al-Araba)
Ali Bureyk
Ali Hasan M'zain 'Bahsamun' (home place?)
Ali Ibrahim
Ali Ma'aud
Ali Msa'ud
Ali Reshwan
Ali Shehad
Aweys Muhd 'good boy Er Riqa'
Aweys Suleman
'Ayd er Raga 'pointed chin'
'Ed es Suleiman
Ghanim Mirwan
Girghis Awad
Godi Msaud
Guma Derwish
Haj Ibrm Ibrm
Hameda abd el Gani
Hamed Bureyk
Hasan Aba'ti Atieh
Hassan B'uto
Hasan Muhd 'bk white'
Hasan es Said
Hussein Bedawi
Kraim Bedawi
Kraim Muhd
Mabruk 'Aid
Mahmud 'Fayum'
Mahmud Hamadi
M'tawi Muhd
Muhd abu Hussein
Muhd abu Telbub? ('?' is in Petrie original)
Muhd ahd Farag
Muhd Awad
Muhd F M'gahid

Muhd Merzu
Muhd M'saud
Muhd Musi (not same as in Nb 134 as first season there is 'IV Ab' i.e.
   1902-1903)
Muhd Sidahmed
Mutwali Msaud
Rizqallah Abd es Said
Sad Mah Mauad
Said Ahmed 'Fayum'
Said el Abd 'negr'
Said M'saud 'blue'
Shentur
Uburian Hamd
Yesin Ibrm
Yusuf (cf. nb 2, 17a, 54)

Phase V. BSAE, 1905-1924

For his new British School of Archaeology in Egypt, Petrie continued to
rely on recruits from Qift, supported by local recruits at each new worksite
to a greater or lesser extent, not always documented. For Memphis, the
proportion of local recruits is clearer, at least in Notebook 68b, where the
lists include small Q and M, presumably for Qift and Mit Rahina/Mem-
phis, before names usually following an unmarked name, as if for a
younger assigned to an older digger in a pair; below, the Qs and Ms are
added in parentheses after 68b. For other sites, more research into distinctive names and local memories is needed for assessment of the excavation-
force profile.

Tell el Yahudiya, 1905-1906

Notebook 105 Tell el Yahudiya (Petrie) scan 39-41 names with final (?)
payments
Notebook 106 Tell el Yahudiya (Petrie) scan 7 names (enrolment?); scans
8-9, 16 weeks of daily payments

Rifa, 1906-1907

Notebook 87 Dec 10-Jan 7 (Mackay) scans 3-6 pairs, weeks of daily
payments
Notebook 88 Dec 10-Jan 7 (Mackay) scans 3-8 pairs, weeks of daily
payments
Notebook 89 Jan-Feb (author?) scans 3-10 alphabetic name-list, weeks of
daily payments
Notebook 85 Jan 16-Feb 20 (Mackay) scans 2-14 pairs, weeks of daily
payments
Notebook 86 Jan-Feb Balaiza (Ward?) scans 3-4 12 names, weeks of daily
payments
Notebook 89a Giza (Petrie?) scan 36 alphabetic name-list, weeks of daily
payments

8. Notebook base: name-lists

Wannina/Athribis, 1908
Notebook 7b (Petrie+ neat) 2-48 pairs, weeks of daily payments

Maydum and Memphis, 1909-1910
Notebook 80 early 1909 (Petrie) scan 17 13 names (work group?); scan 26 maktubin 16 names in groups of four 'down by 7.30 am from Luxor', 27-28 'maktubin' longer name-list with +L, NW, S, SW
Notebook 58 scans 3-20 (author uncertain) weeks of daily payments
Notebook 68a 1909-1910 (Petrie) scan 21 22 names; scan 22 upper 23 names with days and totals

Hawara and Memphis, 1911
Notebook 38b (Petrie) first item, weeks of daily payments

Tarkhan and Memphis, 1911-1912
Notebook 99 (Petrie) scan 9 names, many with E (Engelbach)

Tarkhan and Memphis, 1912-1913
Notebook 100 Tarkhan 1912-1913 (Petrie) scan 2 pairs and small groups of names

Lahun and Memphis, 1913-1914
Notebook 68b (Petrie) scan 1 15 names; scans 2-4 small groups, pages by site area, week payments; scan 22 names grouped Maktub (14 names), Promised (11), Mitrehine (?) (3), Fayum (9)

Abady	86
Abady(/eh) A'ysa	7b, 68b, 88, 89, 100
Abady Awad	7b
Abady (/-eh) Musy	7b, 38b, 85, 86, 88
Abbas Musy	68b
Abd el Aziz	38b
Abd el Bary	68b
abd el Gayd Aly	38b
Abd el Gowad	100
Abd el Hafyz	68b (M)
Abd el Halym	38b, 68b (Fayum)
Abdel Haq Ahmed	7b
Abd el Hay	38b
Abd el Hufi Hofni	87, 88 (Abd el Hafy)
Abd el Iman Aleyn	85, 88
Abdel Latif	7b, 85 (Abdel Latif Mhd)
Abd el Maksud	68b (2 in one list: one Mitrehiny, one Fayum), 100
Abd el Munim? Sadyk	68b
Abd en Naby Muhd	38b (Abd en Naby), 68b (also as Abd en Neby, Fayum)
Abd el Qader Aly	38b (Abd el Qader), 68b (M)
Abd el Qadur Wuziya	68a
Abder Radi Hassan	85, 88, 105 (Abd er Radi)

259

Abd er Rahim Hasan	85, 87
Abder Rahman Ahmed	88
Abder Rahman Ay'sa	85, 88
Abd er Rasiq Huseyn	7b, 85, 87, 105 (HP)
Abd es Salam abd er Rady	38b
Abd el Tawby	68a
Abd el Wahid	100
Abd ez Zahir	68b (M)
Abdu Aysa	68b (M)
Abdul Arfud	89
Abdul Hallim	89
Abdullah?	89
Abll abd el Hay	38b
Abdll abd-el Muly	7b, 38b (Abdll Muly), 85, 88, 89 (Abdll Muly)
Abdullah Khatyb	68a
Abdll Osman	88
Abudy Muly	7b
Abuhrab (?) Selameh	85
Abul Hamed	7b, 68b, 85, 87, 89, 105
Abu Raziq	89
Abu Said Omar	7b, 38b, 85, 88
Abusalam	7b
Abu talib Katyb	68a
Abu Towab Ahmed	68b (M)
Ahmed	68b (M)
Ahmet Abadi	85
Ahmed abd el hafez	68b (Fayum)
Ahmed abder Rahman	7b, 89
Ahmed Ali	7b (2 in one list), 38b, 68b, 88
Ahmed el Khatyb	68a
Ahmed Awad	68a, 68b, 100
Ahmed Awadallah	7b, 85, 87, 89
Ahmed Awys	38b
Ahmed Firnisi	7b, 85, 88, 89
Ahmed Hamed	38b
Ahmd Hamdan	7b, 38b, 58, 68b, 85, 87, 89, 100
Ahd Hasan	85, 86 (note: 'change to Abadi'), 87
Ahmed Hassaneyn	68b (Fayum)
Ahmed Huseyn	85, 88, 105 (HP)
Ahd Huseyn Gowat	89
Ahmed Ibrahim	7b, 38b
Ahmed Jad	7b, 68a, 68b (Ahmed Gad), 85, 87, 88
Ahmed Jedullah	85, 88
Ahmd Khallyl	7b, 68a, 85, 86, 88
Ahmed Muhd	7b (2 in one list), 68b, 85, 88, 100
Ahmed Muhd	68b (M)
Ahmed Muhd Aly	38b
Ahmed Muhd M'saud	85 (Ah M'soud), 87, 88 (Ah M'soud)
Ahmed Muli	100
Ahmed Naql	38b
Ahmed Osman	7b, 58, 68b, 85, 87, 88, 100

8. Notebook base: name-lists

Ahmed Qadir	58
Ahmed Sad	100
Ahmed Salim	38b (weak), 58, 68b (M)
Aisaweyt	38b
Aleyn Ahmed	38b
Aly abdel 'Al	68a
Ali el Far	7b
Aly al Khatyb	68a
Aly ar Rahim	7b, 38b, 68a, 68b (*maktub* for 1913-1914), 85, 86, 87, 88, 100
Ali Awadallah	7b, 85, 87, 89
Aly Barakat	85, 88
Aly Bedaq	85, 88
Aly Bely	38b
Aly Firnisi	7b, 58, 68a, 85, 86, 88, 105
Aly Hamed	7b, 38b, 85, 88, 89
Aly Hasan	38b, 85, 88, 100
Ali Ibrahim	86
Aly Idris	7b, 85, 87, 89, 105 (HP)
Aly Jad	7b, 88
Ali Muhd	38b, 105
Ali Nasr	7b
Ali Nasarullah	7b (in *2nd* list = Ali Nasr in *1st* list?)
Ali Omar	7b, 38b, 68b, 85, 89, 100, 105
Aly Omar el Hawi	85, 88
Aly Smayn	85, 87
Aly Suwefy	7b, 38b, 68b (Fayum), 88, 105 (Ali S.)
Areby Hamdan	38b
Aref Ahmed	7b (Arif), 68a (Aref), 85 (Arif), 88 (Aref), 105 (FP, HP)
A.l.M	105
Ashur Hasan	68b
Ata Hasan	85, 88
Atullah Achmet	85
Atullah Gharbawi	85 (Atullah Gharbour), 87
Awad Ahmed	7b, 85, 86, 87
Awad Ibr.	89
Ayay?	7b
Aysa Huseyn	68b (M)
Aysa Salem	68b (Mitrehiny)
Badr Aly	68a, 85, 86, 88, 105 (Badr)
Bakr abd el Hay	38b
Bakr Awadallah	85, 87
Bakr Salameh	85, 87
Barur Aly	88, 89
Bedawy Yusuf	87
Bergi	85
Beshy Ali	7b, 85 (Ba'ashy Aly), 87 (Ba'ashy Aly), 89
Beyumi Ashir?	68b (M)
Bukadady Khallyl	7b, 85, 86, 87
Bukra Awadallah	89
Dakmuy? Smayn	105 (HP)

261

Eglan	38b
Erfay	7b, 85, 88, 89, 105 (FP, HP)
Farag	105
Farag Suweyleh	7b, 85 (Farraq Swahli), 86, 88 (once as Farrag Swahli)
Fayd (?) Ramadan	38b (local)
Gabr Mergan	38b
Gaud	68b (Q)
Gimmi Mahoud	85 (also as Gimmi, for Guma?)
Guma Sadyk	68b (M)
Guma Sayd	68b (Q)
Hafaz	85, 88
Haleby Haredy	88
Hamdullah Muhd	7b
Hamed Abd er Rahim Hassan	85, 87
Hamed Ahmed	7b, 38b, 68a, 68b
Hamed Ali	7b, 38b, 85, 88, 89
Hamed Muhd	38b (Hameda Muhd), 85, 88
Hamed Musy	85, 88, 89
Hamid Nasar	89
Hassan	85
Hasan abul 'Eneyn	68b
Hasan Aly	68b (M)
Hasan Dodafa	85, 88, 89 (Hassan Dofta)
H Gowad	89
Hassan Khallyl	68b
Hasan Osman	7b, 38b, 68a, 68b, 85, 88, 89, 100
Hassan Salaam	7b
Hasaneyn Hamed	85, 88
Helaly Ahmed	7b, 85 (? Helis (?) Achmet)
Helaly Musy	7b
Hashim	68a, 87, 88, 89, 105
Helaly Umbarak	85, 88
Heraji Ibrm	88
Hofny Abdll	68b, 100
Hofni Ib	100
Huseyn	105
Huzeyn Abdullah	85, 88
Huseyn Ahmed	7b, 58, 68b, 85, 86, 88
Huz Ali	68b, 100
Huzeyn Hasan	85
Huseyn Ibrahim	89
Huseyn Khalyl	68b, 100
Huseyn Muhd	85, 86, 88
Ibrahim Abady	7b, 58 (Ibrahim el Abadi), 68b, 85, 86, 87, 100
Ibrahim abder Kerim	7b, 68b, 85, 100
Ibrahim abder Radi	7b, 85, 87, 89, 105 (HP)
Ibrm Ahmed	68b (M replacing Yusuf)
Ibrm Aly	68b (M)
Ibrm Awad	7b, 68a, 88, 89, 105
Ibrahim Bedawy	38b
Ibrm Hasan	68a

Ibrahim Muhammad	87
Ibr Qasym	68b
Ibrahim Rib	38b
Ibrm Selameh	85, 88
Ibr Shehat	7b, 38b, 85, 87, 89, 105
Ibr Sulman	85, 88, 89 (Ibrm Selman)
Juma Mahd	85, 88
Juma Yunis	85, 87
Khalifa	7b, 38b, 68b, 87, 100, 105
Khalifa Ahmed	89
Khalifa Qulaly	85, 88
Khalla Smayn	7b
Khallyl Derwish	85, 88
Kheyr Muhd	7b, 58, 68a
Latif Mahmud	7b (2 in one list), 89
Maghreby	38b, 68a
Maghraby Hasan	7b, 38b
Mahfud Sayed	68b (M)
Mahd ar Rahim	85
Mahmud a.r.Rahman	68b
Mahmud abu Shuwaybeh	68b (M)
Mahd Ahmed	68b (M changed to Q), 85, 88
Mahmud Ali	7b, 38b
Mahmud Awad	7b, 68a (M'ahd M'awad)
Mahmud Bakhyt	68b (Q changed to M)
Mahmud Bakri	7b
Mahmud er Ray	68b (M)
Mahmud Ghalab	58, 68b, 88, 100, 105 (FP, HP)
Mahmoud Hamed	38b, 58, 68b, 85, 87, 88, 89
Mahmud Muhd	7b, 58, 68a, 85, 86, 88, 89, 105 (HP)
Mahd Muharib	85, 88
Mahd Osman	85, 87
Mahmud Say	38b
Mahmd Selameh	88
Mahmud Seray	68a
Mahmud Siq	38b
Mansur	7b, 68a, 68b, 85, 87, 89 (Mansur Ahmed)
Matif Ahmed	85
Mauad	38b
M'awad Eglam	38b
Mawy (?) Aly	68b (promised for 1913-1914)
Mofuu...(?) Abdallah	58
M'saud Sudany	85, 87
Mub Hamd	38b
Muhammed (cook)	68a, 89
Mohd Ab	58
Muhd abder Karim	7b, 68b, 85, 87 (Muhd a.l.Kerim), 88 (once Muhd Karim), 100
Muhd abder Rahman	7b, 68b, 85, 87, 88, 89
Mhmd Abdulay	89
Muhd *deleted* Abd el Gelub	68a

263

Qodb	38b
Radin Derwish	89
Rahman	85
Ramadan Hasan	68b (Fayum)
Reshwan	38b, 68b (Q)
Reshwan Mensy	7b, 88, 89
Risa Hasan	38b
Ryan Said	7b
Ryani Mahmud	38b
Sabra	100
Sadyk Muhd	100
Sayd Abdi	38b
Said abu Bakr	38b
Sayd abu Mersan	68b (M)
Sayd abu Omar	38b
Sayd Godb	38b
Said Hamed	38b
Sayd Musy	38b
Said Osman	88, 105
Sayd Sad	38b
Salam? Aly	68b (M)
Salym a.l. Gelyl	68b (Q)
Salim Aysa	68b
Seyd Goziyeh	68b
Salim abu/es Sayd	85, 88 (Salim abu Zeyd), 105
Seman Ibrm	68b, 85 (Selman Ibrm)
Seman Muhd	7b
Serhan	87, 105
Shayb Muhd	68a
Shehat Ahmed	7b, 38b, 68a, 68b, 85, 88, 89, 100, 105
Shehad Ali	100
Shehat Husain	85, 87, 89
Shahat Gharuam (Jehran)	89
Shehat Mughanem	85, 87, 89
Smayn Ali	7b
Smayn (abu) Gowad	7b, 85, 88 (Smayn abd l. Gowad), 105
Smayn Husan	85
Smayn Ibrahim	7b
Smayn Mahmud	7b
Smayn Nasar	7b, 38b, 88, 89, 105 (FP, HP)
Smayn Salim	68b (M)
Smayn Suweyleh	7b
Sudany	7b
Suleiman	68b (Q)
Suluman Ibrm	85, 88
Sultan	7b, 68b (Q)
Sureyr Abdll	68b (Q)
Suweyl	38b
Umbarik Aly	85, 87
Umbarak Bakhit	7b, 68a, 68b, 85, 88, 89, 100, 105
Umbarak Hamdan	38b

Umbarak Hamdullah	68a, 68b, 100
Wahbeh Aly	68b (M)
Yadim	105
Yadim abder Kerim	7b
Yadim Derwish	88, 89
Yunis	7b, 85, 87, 89 (Qina Yunis)
Yusuf	38b, 68b (M, deleted, replaced by Ibrm Ahmed), 85, 105
Yusuf Abady	68b, 100
Yusuf Ahmed	38b, 68b, 100
Yusuf a l Kerym	68b
Yusuf Hassan	7b (in same lists Yussef Hassan), 89
Yusuf Ib	68b
Zen (?) Abd Muly	38b
Zeyd	38b, 105
Zeyn Abdullah	85
...ad Firnesy	58
... Awad ...	58
...il u? Ibrahim	89

Shorter lists are recorded for the season at Saft 1905-1906, in the handwriting of Duncan (Notebook 90 scan 36 (repeated scan 37) 21 Feb: 23 names with nos., letters; Notebook 92 scan 34 names with nos. in five columns).

In the 1906-1907 season, Petrie noted names for five supervisors (Notebook 88, scan 11):

> Keep at Gizeh
> - Aly Firnisi and Co.
> Aly a.r.Rahim and Co.
> Abadeh Musy and Co.
> Muhd Musy and 3
> Serhan and Co.

In Notebook 47, containing the crate-lists for a season at Kafr Ammar (1911?), Petrie listed ten names, without numbers or dates (scan 18):

> Huseyn Ahmed
> Mahmud Ghalab
> M Muly
> Muh Hassan
> Muh abder ...
> M the Cook
> Yusuf
> Muh Bakr (?)
> Muh Mutwaly
> Ahmed Osman

Post-First World War BSAE work in Nile Valley, 1919-1924

From his last five years before transferring to the Gaza area of Palestine, fewer lists are recorded, presumably as Petrie transferred responsibility for pay-day to European co-workers whose pay records are not in this archive. The five short lists refer only to the Qiftawi core excavation force, using more abbrevation than in most earlier records.

1920 Lahun Notebook 43 (Petrie)

The Notebook from the end of the 1919-1920 season contains a name-list of recruitment for the following season, revealing the way in which the Qift workforce were enrolled ('muktubeen') according to their own wishes or expected availability, in combination with continuing assessment by Petrie, notably in line 29 for a 'boy', presumably that year on his first season, found to be 'bad' (scan 25). Column 1 is in a clearer hand, perhaps that of Hilda, except for the last line, which, like column 2, is in the more cursive handwriting of Petrie himself:

x fares Muktubeen	− not to be employed
x Hassan Osman	x Yusuf Abady
Huseyn ———"	Ibrm A..d
x Muhd "	Aly al Lahy
Aly Firnisi	x Sultan Bakhit
x Umbarak Bakut	Hamed Gholan
x Muhd Sayd	x Hamed Ahmed
x Aly abder Rahim	
x Nasr ed Din	Muhd Hamed
Aref Ahmed	x Hofny
Muhd Ghalab	?
x Muhd Bergi	Maghraby Hassan
Muhd Hamdan	?
Ahd "	?
x Huzeyn Ahmed	x Shehati Huseyn (fas)
Ahd Firnisi	
Muhd Shehat	Umbarak Hamdallah
x Shehat Ahmed	Mahd a r Rahman
x Muhd Musy	
Ahd Osman	?
x Aly Omar	x Ahd Aly Omar
Ahd Khallyl	
Ib Kerim	Ahd Muhd Mahysh
Ahd Jad	
Sulman Ibrahim	Ahd Qandil
...	x Bukadady
Aly Awadullah	Selim
Khalifa	
Abul Hamed	— boy bad
Muhd Musy	Ahd Suleyman
Ahmed Osman [in ink]	x Muhd Gad al Qerym
Ahd Awad	Ahd abdel Halym
Yusuf Aly	x Omar Suweylim
	Ibrm (Umbarak
	(Huseyn
Noted for 1921	

1920-1921 Sidmant Notebook 95c (Petrie)

On one page of a Notebook principally devoted to craniometric tables, Petrie jotted down a list of names, mainly highly abbreviated, of men from the core Qift workers, each with a single number between 4 and 22 (scan 23):

AO
Ib Ab
Huzeyn
Sh "
Hofny
A l Rahym
Bergi
Sultan
M G K
Sulym

1921-1922 Araba al-Madfuna (Abydos)

In Notebook 76, Petrie recorded a list of names with the letters of the cardinal points, a few pages before a brief record of Twelfth Dynasty tomb 199 among the First Dynasty 'Tombs of the Courtiers' at al-Araba al-Madfuna (scans 10-11). In the same season he worked at Bahnasa, but the proximity to the tomb 199 sketch suggests that this part of the Notebook relates to his al-Araba work:

Scan 6 left (no blue crayon page-number)

Aly Omar	E	(x Sat) mush wakt	
Muhd Mursy	N	x Hofny Ibrahym	W
Hamed Ahmed	N	Muhd jad el Kerym	N
x Ahmd Had	W ..	Sultan Bakhyt	N
x Aly a r Rahym apart	W	Ahd Muhd Mahaysh	W
Muhd el Bergy	E	Shehaty Huzeyn	E
Huzeyn Ahmed	E	Aly abd el Lahy Selym	N
Nasr ed Dyn	N	Ibrm Umbarak	E
Umbarak Bakhyt	N	Ahmed Suleyman	N
x Muhd Sayd	W	Muhd a r Rahym	N
Shehat Ahmed	W	Ahmed Aly OmarE	
Omar Suweylym	E		
x Muhd Osman	.		
H. O	W	boys	
		Hofny Ambarak	W
		/Ahmed Muhd	E
		Hafiz abu Lyf	W
		Aly abul Hasan (no letter after)	

268

8. Notebook base: name-lists

1923-1924 Qau

Notebook 79, scan 18

left (facing inside back cover):

Hamed Ahmed	1
Muhd Sayed	1
Aly Omar	1
Umbarak	2–57½
Yeivin [= foreign supervisor]	274
Wheeler	90
Greenlees	82
Dec 5	446
Bergy	27
Hofny	20½
Mhd (?) Bh	10
A Omar	25
Md Hasan	20
Aly e Ham (?)	12
H Osman	3
Md Seyd	5
Sulyman Md	16
Umb Bakh	10
Nasr Dyn	15
Sultan	8
Hamed Ahd	7

inside back cover:

Selym	½
Sultan	½

Taufik Hennah

Apart from these short end notes, this last Valley Notebook contains references to the workforce in two summary accounts. The first records the workforce only as a collective presence, distinguishing in blocks under wages 'Quftis' and 'Locals', and two laconic entries 'Man to hospital' and 'Muhd to 8 Jan'. The second gives the name of the patient, in the entry 'Muhd abul Hasan hospital', with 42½ in the wages column.

Total record?

In general the Notebook name-lists tend to shorten as the decades proceed, although the pattern is not even. For the 1880s, the lists give the appearance of a full census, even if mainly mediated in Latin transliteration, and allowing for repetitions and misreadings in the collation above. Several hundred names appear in the early Delta years, corresponding to the passing comments in the publications, and the Fayumi lists confirm the scale of the recruitment of the late 1880s, when Petrie wrote of 'over sixty' excavators taken on from Hawara to Lahun (above, p. 41). For later digs,

269

the coverage seems more variable, as the emphasis falls on the core force from Qift. Over a hundred Qiftawi are named, and several dozen 'locals' accompany them in the lists for 1896 at Qurna, 1899-1903 at al-Araba al-Madfuna, and 1908-1913 at Mit Rahina. Local inhabitants might reject the offer of work, as recorded by Hilda in 1906, in Wadi Tumilat (above, p. 100), and in such circumstances there might only have been excavators from Qift. However, the record becomes increasingly sparse even for this constant core. In 1906-1907, Petrie wrote only one of the six surviving Notebooks with paylists; for later seasons detailed lists seem not to have been kept, or at least are not preserved in the Petrie Museum archives. The decrease may be accidental and innocent, but it is not an entirely isolated phenomenon. The next chapter charts a similar decline in visibility for the names of Egyptians in excavation photography.

9

Faces and names: the photographs

Giza and Upper Egypt, winter 1881-1882

Ever energetic in technique and method, Petrie displayed great enthusiasm for photography, constructing his own camera already in the first
phase of his work (Laidlaw 2008: 11-12). Three albums with selections of
his earliest group of photographs, with captions in his handwriting, are
preserved at the Griffith Institute (Petrie Albums 5, 6 and 7). The full
sequence of 562 photographs is recorded in Petrie Notebook 33, with
shorter captions and details of settings. The albums bear the title 'Egyptian Miniatures' with sub-titles 'Part A Old Empire', 'Part B New Empire',
and 'Part C Modern'. The 'modern' category is the product of his ethnographic interests, as recorded in his Journal for 10.11.1881 (above, p. 89).
A front page of the first, Petrie Album 5, bears the date 1881-1882,
followed by these introductory observations:

> Those plates that have water in the foreground were taken from a Nile boat,
> mostly while going; hence they needed to be instantaneous, as well as those
> of Arabs. The plates were nearly all Edwards' dry plates, a few (of Medum)
> being the uranium dry plates which do not seem quite so good. The camera
> was made of sheet tin joined to a box which held 25 plates; the plates were
> taken out and put into the camera by hand, inside a dark bag joined to the
> box and camera; thus no plate holders were wanted, and I got rid of much
> needless weight. The stop generally used for still objects in the open air was
> 1/16 inch; and the definition in good plates is sharp to 1/1500 inch.

Another initial page gives the 'Index Map shewing volume and page of the
views at each place', and each photograph is accompanied by its original
sequence number.

The 1881-1882 landscape of the Giza pyramids appears in both Albums
5, by the date of the monuments, and 7, for focus on the modern setting.
Album 5, p. 23, no. 459 presents a view often since reproduced, of Petrie
at 'My dwelling tomb, Gizeh'; to the right the annotation 'Ali's tomb where
Muhammed slept' recalls the journal details of Giza survey accommodation. Out of context, the scene can be read more seriously than Petrie
seems to have intended with his exaggerated pose of relaxation. To Europeans, even after visiting Egypt, the idea of a tomb in the desert conveys
an impression of isolated and intrepid exploration. In its 1880-1882 context, the tomb lies immediately behind the village houses, offering a

9.1. Petrie 1881 photograph showing him at the rock-cut tomb where he lived, Petrie Museum archive.

9.2. Petrie 1881 photograph of the Great Pyramid from the East, showing the Old Kingdom rock-cut tombs where he lived, Petrie series no. 457, from Petrie Album 5 in the Griffith Institute.

458
Part of Kafr el Haram,
from the Pyramid hill.

9.3. Petrie 1881 photograph of Kafr al-Haram from the rock-cut tomb where he lived during his pyramid survey, Petrie series no. 458, from Petrie Album 7 in the Griffith Institute.

35
Kafr el Batran from my tomb.
High Nile.

9.4. Petrie 1881 photograph of Kafr al-Batran during the annual Nile flood, as seen from the rock-cut tomb where he lived during his pyramid survey, Petrie series no. 35, from Petrie Album 7 in the Griffith Institute.

9.5. Petrie 1881 photograph 'Sheikh Seidi and an ancient friend' at Giza, Petrie series no. 428, from Petrie Album 7 in the Griffith Institute.

9.6. Petrie 1881 photograph 'My friend Sheikh Omar holding a levee in a sunny corner. Gizeh', Petrie series no. 432, from Petrie Album 7 in the Griffith Institute.

274

9.7. Petrie 1881 photograph of Ali Jabri, Petrie series no. 386, from Petrie Album 7 in the Griffith Institute.

9.8. Petrie 1881 sketch of Kafr al-Haram from the rock-cut tomb where he lived, Petrie Notebook 25.

convenient backyard; this explains why Ali Jabri was using it as a place of safekeeping to store antiquities (journal 23.12.1880, above, p. 54). Readers of Album 5 would have seen on the same page the relation of rock-tombs to village, in view no. 457, of the Great Pyramid from the East with 'Arab village in foreground'. Album 7, p. 32 has further views of the Giza settlements Kafr el Haram (no. 458, see too p. 23, no. 1) and Kafr el Batran 'from my tomb' (p. 32, no. 35). As a collection, the views together convey a context embroiling past and present, in a combination that has been lost in later selections, and is already beginning to be lost from the moment when Petrie sought to divide his photographs between ancient and modern Egypt.

Several inhabitants of the village appear in Album 7: p. 23, no. 428 is captioned 'Shekh Seidi and ancient friend', and no. 432 alongside is listed as 'Shekh Omar and friend' in the index, but captioned more fully on the page itself 'My friend Shekh Omar holding a levee in a sunny corner. Gizeh'. The Journals refer to probably the same Sheikh Omar as an authority disputed by Ali Jabri and as antiquities trader (21.12.1880, above, p. 55); a few years later, his authority seems decisive enough, and did not work in favour of Petrie, in the written settlement of the incident of bronzes removed from the site at Nabira (Naukratis) during the excavation (above, p. 67). The most important individual in the Journals and publication of the Giza season is Ali Jabri, and accordingly he appears in several images, in Album 7, p. 25 no. 386 as 'The faithful Ali', and in an annotation to no. 424 on p. 40, a view of the 'Atl tree near Kerdaseh' in view of the pyramids, though here he is barely visible. Album 5, p. 4 no. 411, of Abu Roash, is annotated to left 'Ali standing', but his figure is again barely visible on the image. Not all subjects in the albums are captioned: on p. 34 in a view of Hawara, photograph no. 530, two men can be seen seated, but no mention is made of them. Similarly, Album 6, p. 18 no. 282, is labelled 'In the Ramesseum, Thebes' with the annotations 'Our tent', 'Mr. Ellis', 'Our kitchen', without mentioning the man at right; p. 1 no. 505 shows the 'Obelisk of Usertesen at Ebgig' lying on the ground, without reference to the man in the centre of the picture; and on p. 33 no. 84 the caption reads 'Late Roman brick tower. south of El Heibi' with no information on the man to the left. This lens of ancient landscapes somehow ellides their inhabitants.

The briefer Notebook 33 captions give slightly differing name forms and some information not recorded elsewhere (scans 24-25): nos 428-429 'Sheikh Seidri and old man', 431-432 'Omar and brother', 436 'snake killed by Abu Talib and 5ft rod', nos 451-452 'women and children, Kafr el Haram', no. 453 'gateway and women, Kafr el Batran', nos 454-456 'children, Kafr el Batran', no. 458 'Kafr al Haram', no. 459 'my tomb'. Notebook 25 contains perhaps the very first visual record of the impression of Egypt on Petrie, a set of sketches of the Najama settlements at Giza, with a view of Kafr al Haram just east of the Great Pyramid, and, probably, Nazlat Batran in the plain (scans 1, 9).

9. Faces and names: the photographs

Delta sites, 1883-1886

On return to Egypt to excavate in 1883 for the Egypt Exploration Fund, Petrie began a new series of photographs from no.1. For convenience these have been called the 'Tanis Series', after the site of his first large-scale excavation, although the sequence covers his work over three years and includes other Delta sites (Spencer 2007). Petrie Notebook 23 provides captions for these 1883-1886 photographs in a single sequence from 5 to 462, with details of time and stop. The Egypt Exploration Society preserves negatives and prints for the first and third seasons (1883-1884 and 1885-6), extending beyond no.462. Other or duplicate negatives survive in the photographic archives of the Petrie Museum, including a few from the second season 1884-1885. Among the Griffith Institute Petrie Albums 5-7 from 1881-1882, loose at the front of Album 7 are photographs labelled as no. 67 (?) 'In the market Nebireh' and no. 366 'Abd el Hamid abd el Gani and Smain Suleiman'; from the captions recorded for nos 359-366 of the 1883-1886 series in Petrie Notebook 23, both can be assigned to that series rather than the Giza and Thebes series of winter 1881-1882. In the

9.9. Boy and girl on the San al-Hagar excavation, 'Ahmed Hafnawi <and> Muhd Hassan (girl)' in Petrie photograph 'Tanis series' no. 105, from a copy in the Petrie Museum archives.

9.10. Three boys on the excavation workforce, 'Muhd es Said, Muhd Jafur, Muhd Timsas' in Petrie photograph 'Tanis series' no. 106, from a copy in the Petrie Museum archives.

9.11. Dr Alexandre Habra from Zagazig, in Petrie photograph 'Tanis series' no. 157, print in the Egypt Exploration Society Lucy Gura Archive.

9.12. Ibrahim Kamil from Fakus, in Petrie photograph 'Tanis series' no. 159, print in the Egypt Exploration Society Lucy Gura Archive.

9.13. Two boys on the excavation workforce, 'Abd el Hamed abd el Gani <and> Smein Suleiman' in Petrie photograph 'Tanis series' no. 366, from Petrie Album 7 in the Griffith Institute.

9.14. Muhammad abu Daud in 'Afrangi' pose, in Petrie photograph 'Tanis series' no. 373, Petrie Museum Archive.

9.15. Muhammad abu Daud in 'Beledi' pose, in Petrie photograph 'Tanis series' no. 374, Petrie Museum Archive.

9. Faces and names: the photographs

Notebook, eleven captions preserve names of individuals (in the CD-ROM publication of Notebook 23, nos 104-106 are on scan 5, nos 157-160 on scan 6, no. 319 on scan 9, and nos 364 and 373-374 on scan 10):

no. 104 Abd er Riani Sabha Sherqawi
no. 105 Ahmed Hafnawi Muhd Hassan (girl)
no. 106 Muhd es Said, Muhd Jafur, Muhd Timsas
nos 157, 158 Dr Alexandre Habra Zagazig
nos 159, 160 Ibrahim Kamil Fakus
no. 319 Saada Hassan's room in mound
no. 366 Abd el Hamed abd el Gani Smein Suleiman
no. 373 Muhammed (Afrangi)
no. 374 Muhammed (Beledi)

The names Alexandre Habra and Ibrahim Kamil recur in Notebook 98c, on the first season at San, on a page perhaps closely datable to April 1884. Captions to the prints preserved at the Egypt Exploration Society give instead of name the profession of nos 157-160 as doctor and police. The juxtaposition of the two professions implies that these are the officials inspecting the Petrie excavation in connection with the one lethal accident recorded from a Petrie dig (Drower 1985: 79, and see above, p. 105). The caption for no. 105 with the girl giving her name as Muhammad Hassan confirms this date in a general manner, as her claim had caught the attention of Petrie in his 22 February 1884 'Journal' (see above, p. 61). Entries nos 373-374 reveal an interest in the options for an Egyptian to change identity, with one depiction of Muhammad as Afrangi 'European' and one as Beledi 'rural'; the negatives with these numbers are preserved in the Petrie Museum, and reveal that the Petrie caption 'Afrangi' denotes the position of being seated upright, while 'Beledi' denotes the same person hunched forward. From the adjacent numbers, with views of Nabira/ Naukratis, the date of nos 373-374 may be identified as the second Delta season, 1884-1885. Prints and negatives preserved in the Egypt Exploration Society continue the sequence of numbers above 465, from the third Delta season, 1885-1886. These include another pair of photographs of perhaps, though not certainly, the same Muhammad, again in one upright and holding a stick, in another seated on the ground (the latter published Spencer 2007: 64-5). At this date the subject of the photograph is almost certainly Muhammed abu Daud. Evidently Petrie took photographs of him in two poses at the end of both the second and the third season. From the negatives preserved in the Petrie Museum, the terms 'Afrangi' and 'Beledi', foreign and local, are revealed to refer to upright and relaxed pose, rather than costume.

Caption changes reveal the same erosion of identity over time, as revealed in the publications (see Chapter 2). No. 106 changes over time into the three Muhammeds, and the subjects of both nos 105 and 106 have lost their names by the time of publication a decade and a half later (Petrie 1904, facing p. 20, 'workers at Tanis').

Upriver to Aswan, 1886-1887;
Fayum excavations, 1888-1890

The sequence started for excavation photography in 1883 is continued at the next round number and one, no. 601, as shown by intermittent lists in the Petrie Notebooks, by scattered negatives in the Petrie Museum photographic archives, and, crucially, by an album preserved in the Griffith Institute, Petrie Album 8, with captions in Petrie handwriting. These photographs were taken on the 1886-1887 journey upriver with Muhammad abu Daud and others (nos 601-760 and objects acquired on the journey, nos 802-814), and then on excavations at Hawara, Lahun and Ghurab in 1887-1888 (nos 820-868), and 1888-1890 (nos 917-962). In contrast to the earlier photographic sequences, and to continued themes in the Notebooks and Journals, the focus has moved from landscape and people to a focus exclusively on archaeological evidence – site, find, inscription – with a close link to the publication requirements of the archaeological excavation report.

In later Petrie photography, as UCL Professor and with a core workforce from Qift, groups of workers are often visible, but names seem never to be recorded. One undated photograph in the Petrie Museum may show Ali Suefi as a young man, in a studio pose, though it may have been taken in the expedition accommodation if not at home. Apart from that image, the record of Egyptian individuality seems to have been left to later first visitors to Egypt.

9.16. Undated photograph in the Petrie Museum Archive, possibly of Ali Suefi.

9. Faces and names: the photographs

Margaret Murray, 1899-1901

The Petrie Museum preserves one album of photographs by the woman who became his main assistant in teaching back in London, Margaret Murray. Her own precise annotations in the album identify the time and place as her two first winters of fieldwork in Egypt with Petrie, at al-Araba al-Madfuna (Abydos), 1899-1901 (Petrie Museum WFP/115/5/2). The album captions identify by name eight individuals: Ali Suefi, his sister Zeinab, and his two wives Um Muhammad and Sara; Muhammad [Osman, the cook], Muhammad Derwish, Smain Abjuad (perhaps Smain Abu al Gowad as in the namelists in Notebooks 2 and 54) and Hussein Osman, one of the first Qift recruits. The original captions are as follows, in the order in which they appear in the album, with the photograph numbers given beside the prints there:

> no. 12C 'Ali etc excavating in Khasekhemui' [= Abydos tomb of Khasekhemwy, Second Dynasty king]
> no. 1C 'Muhammed, drinking from water skin' [= Muhammed the cook]
> no. 10 'Ali's hut, sister Zeinab & child'
> sequence of four unnumbered fishing scenes, starting with 'Ali throwing fishing net', followed by a fifth, no.43, also showing Ali fishing,
> no. 55 'Ali buying trays from Soudanese'
> no. 57 'Ali helping build M's mud oven'
> no. 16 'Um el Mohammed bread making'
> no no. 'Sara breadmaking' and 'Keeping off the flies!'
> no. 9B 'old sheikh & Mohd. Derwish' Jan 8.01
> no. 11B 'Mohd Derwish' Jan 1st
> no. 10B 'Mohd Derwish, washing' Jan 8
> no. 1A 'Sheikh's tomb & Mohd'
> no. 19 'Smeine Abjuad etc digging XVIII pits'
> no. 13 'Hosein Osman XVIII graves'
> no. 36 'Sara Ali's 2nd wife'
> no. 51 'Hosein Osman with sugar cane'

The album provides a fuller visual dimension otherwise missing in the Petrie excavation archive, thanks to the names in these captions to the images. Two of the named men are familiar from the Petrie written archives: Ali Suefi and Hussein Osman (for the latter as 'our best and most trusty workman next to Ali' see above, p. 79). In addition, Mohammad Derwish appears in the name-lists from the Qift, Dandara, Araba and Ihnas, where his age in 1903-1904 is estimated at 34, and his village at Qift is named as Naga abu Omar. The letters of Hilda Petrie record his words, one of the very few quotations documented for any of the excavating workforce (above, p. 81). Smeine Abjuad is more elusive, possibly the man named in the Qift and Araba lists as Smain Abu al Gowad. The Petrie Journals mention the first wife of Ali Suefi in the account of family problems, and record the brief conversation between Petrie and Muham-

9.17. 'Ali excavating in Khasekhemui', Margaret Murray album 1899-1900.

9.18. 'Ali buying things from Soudanese', Margaret Murray album 1899-1900.

9.19 'Um el Mohammed bread making', Margaret Murray album 1899-1900.

9.20. 'Mohd Derwish',
Margaret Murray album
1899-1900.

9.21. 'Smeine Abjuad etc digging XVIII pits', Margaret Murray album 1899-1900.

9.22. 'Hosein Osman. XVIII graves', Margaret Murray album 1899-1900.

9.23. 'Sara. Ali's 2nd wife', Margaret Murray album 1899-1900.

9.24. 'Hosein Osman with sugar cane', Margaret Murray album 1899-1900.

mad Osman Kritliya over the presence of the wives of Ali Suefi at the Mit Rahina excavation. Here his wives and sister regain their presence, alongside such unexpected figures as the trading Sudanese women from whom Ali buys trays, or the children selling antiquities to the sister of Hilda Petrie, Amy Urlin. Named or anonymous, in the excavation album the local inhabitants of al-Araba al-Madfuna regain their living roles.

Henri Frankfort, 1922-1927

The Egypt Exploration Society archives in London include two albums, one looseleaf and one bound, from 1920s seasons of Henri Frankfort in Egypt (Naunton 2006). The looseleaf album dates to the mid- to late 1920s when Frankfort participated in or directed epigraphic work and excavation at Qurna, Armant and Amarna. Few of the leaves bear captions, none with names of individual Egyptians. Nevertheless, the range of views provides a useful guide to the operation and mentality of 1920s European Egyptology at work in Egypt. One set of views shows a ceremonial stick-fight performed in the centre of a group of Egyptians (reproduced Naunton 2006), while the European expedition members sit separated in the low-

9.25. 'The Quftis' band lined up for a welcome back – season beginning and employment', Henri Frankfort 1920s photograph, in the Egypt Exploration Society Lucy Gura Archive.

9.26. 'Ali Suefi and the village
guard', Henri Frankfort
1922-1923 album in the Egypt
Exploration Society Lucy Gura
Archive.

9.27. 'Mohammed Ismaïn',
Henri Frankfort 1922-1923
album in the Egypt
Exploration Society Lucy
Gura Archive.

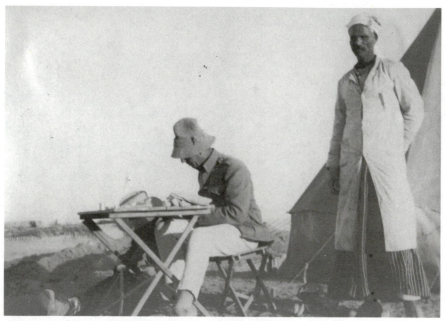

9.28. Ali Suefi and Guy Brunton, Henri Frankfort 1922-1923 album in the Egypt Exploration Society Lucy Gura Archive.

9.29. 'Mr Brunton and Ali Suefi decide which of the many villagers hoping for pay are to be enrolled', Henri Frankfort 1922-1923 album in the Egypt Exploration Society Lucy Gura Archive.

9. Faces and names: the photographs

9.30. 'Mahmud Osman, Starkey, Youssouf, Khallawi en Mohammed Hassan bij Tatters botten onder Sheikh Ibrahim's huis', Henri Frankfort 1922-1923 album in the Egypt Exploration Society Lucy Gura Archive.

9.31. 'Youssouf, bones, parafin', Henri Frankfort 1922-1923 album in the Egypt Exploration Society Lucy Gura Archive.

walled court in front of a small excavation house. In other images women walk with water jars and collect water from the river or a canal. Two of the most striking photographs show a musical performance, with a later biro caption 'The Quftis' band lined up for a welcome back – season beginning and employment'.

The bound Frankfort album bears captions in Dutch by Henri Frankfort himself, starting on the inside front cover with the general identification 'Qau el Kebir 1922/3'. That season Petrie remained in London, leaving Guy Brunton to begin the excavations at Qau (Drower 1985: 355, 357). Five captions in this album name Egyptians. One shows 'Ali Suefi and the village guard', another 'Mohammed Ismaïn'. A third captures the tension implicit in a critical but generally overlooked moment in the political economy of organised archaeological excavation: 'Mr Brunton and Ali Suefi decide which of the many villagers hoping for pay are to be enrolled'. Another captioned photograph brings into sight for the first time with full list of names the whole team at work where a Notebook or journal might record only one name. At the foot of the village houses, a group of Egyptians and one European can be seen completing the clearance of earth from a burial. The caption identifies them as: 'Mahmud Osman, Starkey, Youssouf, Khallawi and Mohammed Hassan bij Tatters botten onder Sheikh Ibrahim's huis'. In the Petrie system, Starkey would be 'recorder' and either Mahmud Osman or Mohammed Hassan might be 'finder', but the photograph reveals a team of five. The fifth captioned photograph continues the action with Yusuf about to apply paraffin wax to consolidate the fragile bones (Dutch *botten*), with the caption 'Youssouf, botten, parafin'. The child Yusuf as conservator presents a forgotten side to the distribution of skills in the archaeological division of labour, at odds with the Petrie criterion of discrimination to define the archaeologist (see Chapter 2).

Proportions in representation

As with the long name-lists, coverage varies for the named individuals in photographs as a proportion of the total workforce. In the 1883-1886 seasons, Petrie referred to nine supervisors from Kafr al-Haram, the Najama settlement at the Giza Pyramids: Ali Jabri, his son Abu Saud, Muhammad abu Daud, Said abu Daud, Mahajub abu Daud, Abd es Salam Abdullah, Mursi, Midani and Tulba. Of these nine, two appear by name in the photographs for 1881-1882 (Ali Jabri) and 1883-1886 (Muhammad abu Daud). Of the several hundred Delta excavators during 1883-1886, nine are named in captions to images from the seasons (Smein Suleiman is the name for one boy at Nabira, not identified in the Notebook name-lists for the site). Among the seventy-five or more Fayumi excavators of 1887-1892, only one is known from photographs, Ali Suefi. For excavations directed by Petrie as professor, the name-lists record over a hundred men and boys from Qift, but only four are known from photographs taken in Egypt. No photographs have been found with names for the hundreds of supporting excavators recruited more locally in the later seasons. Archival fieldwork could expand the number, but seems unlikely to negate the general 'economy of absence' (El-Desouky 2007: 174) in the photographic record.

Parallel lives in the archaeology of Egypt

To raise a group of independent intellectuals is no easy matter; it requires a long process, with action and reaction, fusion and dissolution, and new formations in great number and of great complexity.

Gramsci 1975 [1933-1934]: III, 1860

I. Egyptian lives in the autobiography of archaeology

The literary genre biography may contribute to historical understanding, or become a powerful historical source, but it seems to require its writer and reader to accept perspective as the frame and rule of vision. Perhaps biography operates to particular effect within societies using perspectival visual arts, as both give expression to an underlying ideology concerning social and economic relations between individuals. By contrast, the auto-biography, ego-history or self-depiction would seem more widely attested in world history, as expressions of the individual within his or her social frame. Egyptologists have found it strikingly difficult to categorise ancient Egyptian self-depictions – biography or autobiography? (cf. Lichtheim 1988: 1-2) – as if the biographical frame of mind itself stops us from understanding other ways of presenting life in the world. From such considerations on genre, any English-language biography of groups or individuals in Egypt becomes an inadequate substitute for autobiography. Representation is so powerfully normative in European and Euroameri-can politics and ideology that Europeans and Euroamericans tend to avoid the consequences of the message that representation replaces presence (cf. Fabian 1992 in response to Said 1989). The writer and the reader can escape this double-bind, that writing is a representation, not an encounter, by the strategy of pointing to autobiographies to be found or written. That is the intention in this conclusion, in drawing together the glimpses and absences of Egyptian excavators through the Petrie archive.

1. Leading Egyptian Egyptologists and archaeologists
1a. Philology: Ahmad Kamal, 29.7.1851-5.8.1923
Nationalist Egyptology celebrates Ahmad Kamal as the first and one of the greatest Egyptian Egyptologists, noting his multilingual talents (Attiatallah 1984b). He graduated from the Egyptology Institute founded in 1879 by Heinrich Brugsch, the leading German philologist of ancient Egyptian at the time. The titles to his Arabic and French publications

confirm the emphasis on language and inscription, in the philological mould of Egyptology as a modern speech community around an ancient language and its scripts. Although Kamal followed the European Egyptological model that privileged language study above fieldwork, he did encourage Egyptian-sponsored excavations at key sites in Middle Egypt, and, crucially, published summary records of the work in French in the journal of the Antiquities Service. Many finds were assigned to the private Egyptian sponsors, and sold to foreign museum agents; this is how the Metropolitan Museum of Art New York acquired one of the most famous of Egyptian antiquities, heavily commercialised today, the blue faience hippopotamus figure from Meir (MMA 17.9.1, Hayes 1953: 227 fig. 142). His foreign colleague Arthur Weigall wrote harshly, in English, on the standards of his archaeological work (cf. Hankey 2007), and it is true that the French-language publications make it difficult to identify exactly what was found where (cf. Willems 1988: 82). Yet the articles published by Kamal imply a higher standard of recording than by most excavators of his time, and even many today, and he published more of his digs than most of his foreign contemporaries. The gaps in information might have resulted from translation and editing; only Arabic-language archival research into his records can reveal his archaeological standards in detail. From the publicly accessible foreign-language information, it can only be concluded provisionally that he was more philologist than archaeologist, and that this imbalance in Egyptology already in his time skewed Egyptian as well as foreign study of the Egyptian past. During his life-time, foreigners controlled the top positions of the Antiquities Service, in the colonial power-struggle between England and France, Germany and the USA. Even after his retirement in 1914, Kamal suffered personal attack from the secretary-general of the Antiquities Service, Georges Daressy (Reid 2002: 211-12). Despite such overwhelming obstacles, Kamal contributed the essential element to the development of an Egyptian Egyptology by teaching ancient Egyptian language and history, first in the school of Egyptology opened at the Egyptian Museum in 1882, and later at the new University in Cairo, founded in 1908, and by re-establishing the Egyptology Institute in 1910 (Reid 2002: 186, 203).

In all the publications, unpublished archives and images amassed in the preceding chapters from the work of Petrie, Ahmad Kamal is absent. Two related structural causes might be investigated. First, Petrie expressed repeatedly his aversion to officialdom, including the foreign officials managing the Egyptian Museum at Cairo, and, later, the English administrators in 1930s Palestine (Drower 1985: 386). In a sense, he energised himself by creating a foil of inaction, on the same model as an ancient Egyptian genre known in Egyptology as 'the King's Novel' where the lone king delivers What is Right to the acclaim of, and often counter to the advice of, the court, an anonymous collective (Loprieno 1996). Kamal might have been for Petrie one more invisible member of collective Museum officialdom. Secondly, Petrie seems to have placed himself out of contact with the professional middle classes that were developing in Egypt during his five decades of archaeological work there, much as they were defining themselves against the rural working population (on which see Gasper 2009). There is at least one exception, an Egyptian medic called Dr Sobhy; he and his wife dined with the Petries on their first return to Cairo after the First World War, as 'old friends' (Drower 1985: 348). In the Petrie journal *Ancient Egypt* Sobhy wrote on parallels between ancient Egyptian and contemporary rural Egyptian medical practices and beliefs, a strong overlap of interest between foreign and richer Egyptian views (Sobhy 1923). In the 1910s-1930s, the Egyptian medical profession was developing its own strand of a then prevalent Egyptian interest in the Pharaonic past, as part of the movement for full independence (cf. Chiffoleau 1997: 131-5). However, not all Pharaonists were nationalists in the complex personal politics of the interwar period. The dinner with the Sobhys demonstrates at least that Petrie had middle- or upper-class Egyptian friends. More specific information is needed on the exact times and spaces of movement, for both Kamal and Petrie, before it will be possible to account for an extraordinary absence in the Petrie written and pictorial record.

1b. Archaeology: Selim Hassan, 1886-29.9.1961

Among the students taught by Ahmad Kamal, Selim Hassan left the most tangible contribution, above all in his appointment as first Egyptian professor of Egyptian archaeology at Cairo University, and in his monumental series of excavation reports for the cemeteries around the Giza Pyramids, the best publication record yet provided for this central site of Egyptian archaeology (Hassan 1932-1960, cf. Attiatallah 1984b: 78-80, Hawass 1999: 156-7). Indeed, considered alongside the five foreign dig-directors working in Giza in the early twentieth century, Hassan served science far the best in print (for a general review of work at the site, see Der Manuelian 1999; on the importance of swift publication as expressed by Petrie, see Drower 1985: 432): the work of Daressy and Petrie on a First Dynasty monumental tomb south of Giza was only briefly reported (cf. Petrie 1907); Schiaparelli barely published, and Reisner, despite impressive documentation, brought little to completion, both leaving more an archival and museological legacy than a basis for advance of knowledge in their own time; and Junker published a full series of volumes but, as a highly-trained philologist, devoted most space to learned commentaries that might have better been delivered elsewhere. The volumes by Selim Hassan concentrate instead on description of finds as found, including pottery, the most common and so most crucial archaeological evidence, but often merely mentioned in passing by Junker.

The new Egyptian excavations at Giza began after Petrie had already left the Nile Valley to work in Palestine, and the difference in generations might account for a lack of contact between the two. Unlike Ahmad Kamal, Selim Hassan is not entirely absent from the Petrie record; in 1930 he contributed a short note to the Petrie journal *Ancient Egypt* on the Egyptian University excavations, and in other issues Petrie included summaries of articles by him and other Egyptian colleagues in his digest of Egyptological literature (Hassan 1930). However, the geography of the career pursued by this outstanding Egyptian archaeologist reveals a structural faultline in the formation of the discipline. For Hassan went not to London or Liverpool for advanced Egyptological study, but to Paris, and then took his doctorate under another Giza excavator, Father Hermann Junker in 1930s Vienna. At the same time, on the Giza plateau, the American George Reisner was training in photography and documentation evidently literate Qiftawi workmen from the families introduced to archaeology by Petrie (Drower 1985: 431). The nations and nationalities involved in the choices of these Egyptian and foreign dig-directors remind us that some chose not to support or train Egyptians in university education. While allowing for the inclinations of individuals, the differences in Egyptian relations with the various foreign institutions indicate impersonal forces at work. Diplomatic histories lie behind the willingness of Egyptian governments and individuals to seek higher education in Paris, Berlin and Vienna, and behind the openness of those cities to graduates and postdoctoral researchers from Egypt. Under English occupation, the education budget for Egypt was kept appallingly low, as the governor Baring sought to avoid either public expense or the consequences of an informed population (1.12% is the budget percentage for health and education combined as late as 1902, as cited in Chiffoleau 1997: 44). Yet government policy alone does not account for the gap between Egyptian and London archaeologists in later decades. Liverpool welcomed graduates such as Mahmoud Hamza and Sami Gabra in the 1920s (Attiatallah 1984b: 81), and, if London remained closed in archaeology, it was open in other disciplines such as medicine (e.g. the research grant for Muhammad Khalil to visit England in 1919-1920, and the medical higher education of Ahmed Zaki Abu Shadi in London 1912-1920, see Chiffoleau 1997: 89-90 and 144). These varying careers chart an historical geography of disciplinary formation, in which the Petrie archive occupies a still uncertain place.

2. Other ranks of the Antiquities Service of Egypt

From the time of Mariette until the 1904 Entente Cordiale between England and France, the staff of the Antiquities Service included more Egyptians than foreigners. Under Maspero, the number of foreigners at senior inspector level increased, and positions previously reserved for French nationals began to be given to Englishmen such as Carter and Quibell (Drower 1985: 260-1, Reid 2002: 195-6; see Drower 1985: 351 on 1920s appointments of Engelbach and Wainwright). Only the Directorate of the Service remained a French preserve, as it would until after the 1952 Revolution (Attiatallah 1984a: 63-4, 70-71; list in Reid 2002: 305). Petrie doubtless welcomed the replacement of French with English employees of the Egyptian state, but the change did not benefit, and may have worked against, the promotion of Egyptians. More research is needed into all tiers of the inspectorate.

Here, a comment by Petrie may be cited as a reminder of this other series of biographies overlooked in histories of Egyptology. In an entry from the season of work at Lahun in 1920, Petrie recorded from a visit to the Egyptian Museum, Cairo 'Panelled sarcoph tomb N of [pyr] opened in 1898 by Shaban Effendi and Omdeh' (Notebook 43, scan 11). Shaban is the name of the Fayum antiquities inspector, whom Muhammad abu Daud recognised at Hawara in 1888 as Najama kin from Kafr al-Haram (above, p. 73, Journal 10.3.1888). If this is the same man, his career might illustrate the model for another career structure, outside the spheres considered legitimate by the European university and academy, though close enough to the path taken by the self-trained Petrie. Shaban introduces precisely the source of interest most unthinkable in standard European writing on Egypt: a Bedouin villager in the heart of the monuments and the accompanying tourism and trade in antiquities. His interest and schooling attest to choices and opportunities taken in the formation of Egyptian Egyptology at exactly the same time as foreigners were beginning to construct archaeology as a career inside Egypt and in Europe. Another literate Najama on 1880s excavations is Abu Saud, son of Ali Jabri, acknowledged as the Antiquities Service official on the Petrie Delta digs in 1884-1885 (above, pp. 63-4), but Petrie does not mention him after the 1880s, and his later career, not necessarily in archaeology, remains to be researched. Shaban seems more prominent, inasmuch as recent authors record a Muhammad Shaban as 'having played an active and notable role in the development of Egyptology as a discipline' (Attiatallah 1984b: 77), and as pupil of the 1881-1885 school of Ahmad Kamal, and assistant curator after Kamal retired in 1914 (Reid 2002: 189). Arabic documentation centres can populate these histories, whereas the foreign archive can only remind European-language readers, from the outside, that they exist.

Another leading early Egyptian official of the Antiquities Service is mentioned in the Petrie Notebooks from his 1883-1886 Delta work: 'Ahmed Negib Inspecteur des Antiquites Mansura' (Notebook 74, scan 31; Notebook 74a scan 3, see above, p. 111). Donald Reid records his path from the same Khedive Ismail school of ancient Egyptian attended by Ahmad Kamal, taught by Heinrich Brugsch, to become one of two inspectors general of antiquities in 1892 (Reid 2002: 189). His 1905 retirement on grounds of ill health fell a year after the Anglo-French rapprochement.

3. Summary biographies for Najama, Fayumi, Qiftawi in Egyptian archaeology

Egyptian nationalist histories share with foreign accounts the representation of the rural population as a mass either without voice, or
assigned a voice that turns out to be that of the urban professional (Gasper
2009). The most precious archival offering may be the rare opportunity to
sketch the beginnings of an outline of lives that have proved essential to
the development of archaeology, but that remain obscured by their place
within this misrepresented mass of individuals. Five examples are chosen
here as the most detailed and prolonged biographies available from the
Petrie archives, always conscious of the risks in, first, biography (see
above), and, secondly, the instinct of dominant forces to install a labour
aristocracy in order to maintain domination (see below).

Muhammad abu Daud of Kafr al-Haram

In November 1884, Ali Jabri had Petrie recruit as one of four dig-supervi-
sor his nephew, then twenty-two years old, Muhammad abu Daud (above,
p. 63). For the next four years, the Journals refer to him often and at
particular critical points, indicating his role as principal site manager. In
1884-1885 he defends the Nabira (Naukratis) excavation against rival
Giza antiquities-hunters, including the case of Muhammad Baraysh (pp.
65-7). In 1885-1886, he is the works supervisor for the excavation of the
Twenty-sixth Dynasty fortress at Dafanna on the north-eastern frontier of
Egypt (p. 281). His central role in these Delta seasons helps to explain why
he alone of the Najama supervisors appears in the photographic archives
as well as the written (pp. 280-1). With his elder brother Said and nephew
Tulba, he joined Petrie and Griffith on their upriver journey in the winter
of 1886-1887, where Petrie learned their ages and genealogy, back to an
ancestral trek of another Said from Ain Jebari in Tunis to Jalu in the
Libyan desert (pp. 68, 132-3). For the spring 1887 clearance at the
Dahshur pyramids, he was named as Antiquities Service official, and in
the same season he was the discoverer of the ancient road-markers across
the strip of desert to Fayum (p. 68). At Hawara in March 1888, he provided
Petrie with a plan of the layout of finds, a critical point in defining
archaeological documentation, and in April 1888 he managed the budget
for pay-day when Petrie fell ill (p. 70). At the high point in his discovery of
antiquities, he masterminded the extraction of Roman Period mummified
bodies with gilt cartonnage and the famous panel portraits over two
seasons of work at Hawara, 1887-1888 and 1888-1889; when Petrie dismissed him in January 1889 over the supervisor levy of a percentage of
wages, the supply of portraits ended (pp. 70-1). Though argued as justice,
that extra-judicial dismissal protected Petrie from the risk of losing control; the later career of Muhammad is not visible in these archives, except
for possible mention of his help on the summer season at Tell Hesy in
Palestine in 1890 (p. 71). The Antiquities Service record for his 1885-1886

official role might offer a starting-point for a longer investigation in Cairo archives.

Makawy Said of Manshiat Abdullah

In 1887, Petrie began his Fayum excavations by a test-dig at the mainly Greek and Roman city-site that had been capital of the province, mounds beside the modern capital Madinat al-Fayum, and he recruited his excavators from 'the village of Menshiet Abdallah at the end of the mounds', taking them on to the main site to be dug that season, the pyramid and cemeteries at Hawara (Petrie 1889: 1, above p. 41). In 1897 a Notebook records the same village as address for Mekowi Said (p. 135). The Notebook name-lists confirm the contribution of Mekowi to all the Fayum excavations of 1887-1891 (p. 231), and record him among the witnesses in the Petrie judgement on Muhammad abu Daud (p. 120). At Maydum he is excavator of a major feature, the great block-superstructure tomb 'ENE of Δ' (p. 160). In three other instances Petrie specified the site area for which 'the lad Mekowi' was responsible (Petrie 1891: v): at Hawara a tomb with Late Period burials richly equipped with amulets, and shabtis of a man named Horwedja; at the Lahun valley temple the foundation deposit; and in the town-site at Lahun the cellar re-used for Eighteenth Dynasty burials including that of a woman identified on her jewellery as 'the lady of the house Maket'. He then appears again in the name-list for Dishasha in 1896-1897 (p. 256), and the Journals for that season explain why Petrie, exceptionally, named his home (p. 79): Mekowi had just returned from military service in Sudan, from which Petrie asked him about General Kitchener, then controversial in England; he was 'cut up' by having just lost his four- or five-year-old boy; and he helped in the dispute between Ali Suefi and his wife Fatima and her apparently disruptive brother. His name has not been found in any later English archives, including the 1910-1911 season when Petrie returned to Hawara. Petrie photographic archives for 1886-1890 and 1896-1897 focus on landscape and antiquities, and the few images of Egyptians are anonymous; it seems unlikely that a visual portrait of Makawy Said will emerge from these sources.

The career of this occasional but leading digger 1887-1891 and 1896-1897 is interrupted by work as an Egyptian soldier on the Anglo-Egyptian colonial adventure that would lead to occupation of Sudan. In its detail this partial biography does not represent a standard or average Fayumi life, but gives a glimpse of the way in which rural Egyptians contributed seasonally to archaeology. In contrast to Muhammad Shaban, Abu Saud son of Ali Jabri, and Muhammad abu Daud, there is probably no point at which this life enters Antiquities Service records as a name. Other official archives in Cairo would need to be scoured for a fuller record, but a more vivid encounter with Makawy Said can probably only be achieved by returning to the social networks of village life and local memory. This life points to a more elusive history of the greater number, for which other sources and attitudes become essential.

Ali Muhammad Swayfi of al-Lahun

Ali Suefi, as Petrie usually writes his name, first appears in the name-lists for work at Maydum in 1890-1891 (p. 228). Thereafter he is found in name-lists for 1891-1892 (p. 228), 1893-1901 (p. 243), 1905-1908, 1910-1911, and 1913-1914 (p. 261). For the 1891-1892 season, Ali Suefi is one of five Fayumi supervisors brought by Petrie from al-Lahun to Amarna in Middle Egypt (p. 71). More information is provided on his life and family than any other Egyptian excavator in the Petrie archive. His closeness to Petrie even caused some jealousy among other excavators at Abadiya in 1898 (p. 76). Petrie brought him from al-Lahun to supervise workers recruited at Qift in 1893-1894 (p. 77). There at one point he received charge of some medical supplies, a privilege unparalleled in the surviving record (p. 141). In the published report on the Naqada 1894-1895 season, Petrie recorded that 'my best lad, Ali Suefi' 'has been kindly been rescued from conscription by the Sirdar' (p. 43). In late 1895 his name and address are given as 'Ali Muhammad Suefi, Nahiet Dum, Nagada' (p. 150), far from al-Lahun, and Petrie refers to 'his wife and baby from their village near Negadeh' (p. 77). Presumably he met his wife during the 1893-1894 Qift or 1894-1895 Naqada season. In December 1896 Petrie mentions his younger brother Mahmud as someone also recruited 'as a small boy years ago', and his youngest brother Yusuf, and regrets that Ali spent all his earnings on his family, and returned south with his wife and baby child, along with Mahmud and 'a destitute little girl – a cousin', despite having an elder brother, so with greater family responsibility (pp. 76-7). Petrie records that the mother of Ali prompted the marriage, that the name of his wife was Fatima, and that she had a brother, who became involved in domestic difficulties of separation and maintenance (p. 78). The Margaret Murray album for 1899-1901 work at al-Araba al-Madfuna includes images of Ali Suefi, his first wife Um Muhammad and his second wife Sara. After this season he left, according to Hilda, 'from momentary foolishness and impracticality', but rejoined the Petries on their next work near his hometown al-Lahun, at Ihnasya in January 1904 (p. 76). That year Hilda also recorded the family tree of his wife Um Muhammad, sister of Hashim Muhammad; her father was Muhammad Hantish, and his brother Abul Hamed (p. 235). In 1908 at Mit Rahina, Ali again brought his wives to settle at the work-site (p. 83). He is still working with Petrie in February 1922, when Hilda reveals in a letter to her son that he is a fisherman with his own boat (p. 83); the Margaret Murray album confirms this in a series of images showing him casting and hauling in his net (p. 283). A more elderly Ali Suefi appears in the Henri Frankfort album from 1922-1923, on the expedition of Guy Brunton at Qau (p. 290).

An unusually high number of specific contexts are recorded as dug by

301

or under the supervision of Ali Suefi. Although these represent only a fraction of his contribution, they illustrate the long duration and the variety of his archaeological work. In chronological order, culled from publications, Journals and Notebooks, these are:

1891-1892 Amarna house (later site survey reference O47.21) (p. 160)
1893-1894 Qift, Foundation Deposits of the temple of Min and Isis (p. 75)
1894-1895 Naqada, principal trainer and supervisor (p. 43)
1896-1897 Bahnasa (Oxyrhynchus), Mamluk *hammam* (p. 75)
1897-1898 reconnaissance for Hu-Abadiya season next year, find of marked modelled pottery (p. 76)
1899-1900 al-Araba al-Madfuna (Abydos) Eighteenth Dynasty tomb of Saiset near the Osiris temple precinct (p. 78); First Dynasty tombs within the temple precinct (p. 180)
1900-1901 al-Araba al-Madfuna (Abydos) training new recruits from Qift in excavation of Middle and New Kingdom burials in Garstang Cemetery E (p. 79)
1905-1906 at least ten tombs at Saft and Suwa (pp. 180, 182)
1909-1910 Maydum, supervision of six men on excavation of far western tombs (p. 164); main excavator on at least four of the tombs (p. 185)
1912 al-Riqqa, identification of cemetery sites (p. 76)
1913-1914 Haraga cemeteries, main excavator on about 50 of the tombs (p. 189)
1919-1920 Madinat al-Ghurab cemeteries, main excavator on about 40 tombs (p. 192)
1922-1925 Qau and Badari, identification of sites, including earliest settlements in the Egyptian Nile Valley and their cemeteries (p. 76)

Hussayn Osman
In 1893-1894 Petrie recruited a local team for his excavations at Qift; an assessment table of 'Good', 'Medium', 'Bad' lists Hassan Osman and Hussein Osman under Good, each annotated 'smiler', with a comment below 'smilers brothers' (p. 137). In the census of Qiftawi excavators by Hilda Petrie in 1903-1904, Hassan is recorded as 29 years old, and Hussein 25, and the accompanying sketch-map indicates that they, alone of the mapped names, came from Qift itself rather than one of the surrounding villages (pp. 234, 238). From the ages, Hussein would have been about 14 or 15 on his first Petrie excavation at his home village. By December 1898 Petrie would refer to Hussein Osman as 'our best and most trusty workman next to Ali', in the story of his dispute with the local judge of Waqf over turkeys acquired at market there (p. 79). The Margaret Murray 1899-1901 album includes one photograph of him at work on the excavation of New Kingdom tombs, another of him carrying sugar cane (pp. 286-7).

In the Notebooks, his name appears as main excavator beside sketches of nineteen tombs in the Naqada area (pp. 174, 177, 178), and name-lists register him for the years 1895-1901 (p. 245). His name is not found in any later lists except as an initial entry subsequently deleted of excavators from Qift provisionally enrolled for 1920-1921 (p. 267). This last entry suggests a continuing interest in archaeology, and presumably the decrease in detail in the records accounts for his absence from post-1901 entries. Indeed, other Notebook entries confirm his prominence at Maydum in 1909-1910, when he directs twelve men on the 'pyramid tunnel' (p. 164, cf. Journal p. 84). Yet his absence from the 1913-1924 tomb-cards may indicate that, unlike his elder brother Hassan, he did not form part of the persistent core of Qiftawi workers on whom the British School of Archaeology in Egypt depended. This family introduces differences into the history of archaeology from the inside, at the point where external biography has written a homogeneous collective of Quftis.

II. Archaeological archives as a structural index

Individual lives may be the essential components of history, but they have not yet added up to explanations either for change, or for lack of change. The same structural labour relations persist despite dramatic differences in the wide spectrum of training practice. At the lowest standard of excavation, a dig-director has no specifically archaeological training, and orders the removal of material from the ground with little or no recording work, and no publication; as Petrie wrote in 1904, this is a crime worse than plunder. Here training is absent at every level. At the middle of the spectrum, training takes place, but entrenches a dividing-line of literacy. This is the position occupied by Petrie; he entrusted Ali Suefi with training recruits from Qift, but reserved for foreigners all written and visual documentation. Finally, at the progressive end, George Reisner trained Egyptian foremen fully in archaeological documentation, from writing a full excavation journal, with architecturally accurate plans, and the highest contemporary standards of field photography. Seventy-two expedition Arabic Notebooks by Said Ahmed Said Diraz and his son Mohamed Said Diraz, both among the foremen from Qift, were preserved in the family by Hassan Diraz of the next generation; in 2006 Peter Der Manuelian located the family in Cairo and found the archives a long-term institutional home with the rest of the American excavation documentation, at the Museum of Fine Arts, Boston (Der Manuelian 2007, cf. Drower 1985: 431). Despite this support and enthusiasm of Reisner for Qiftawi skills, no structural breakthrough resulted. Therefore archival research needs to target historical structure, encompassing but beyond biography.

On a structural approach, the Petrie archive may be used to analyse his career as components resulting in archaeological research and publication. If his goal was clearer historical understanding, Petrie shared this with his contemporaries as well as his successors. The ingredients of his Egyptian archaeology can be traced in the archive alongside their presence

303

or absence, strength or weakness, individually and then together, within Egypt. One method for analysing the production of archaeology is the diagrammatic 'operational chain' introduced by Leroi-Gourhan in archaeology. As a diagram, the 'operational chain' creates a simplified unilinear image in place of the messier life-webs of interconnected factors; however, it can be understood as a heuristic device where a single line stands for a cycle of lesser or greater complexity. In the historical self-reproduction of a discipline such as archaeology, the line of operation evokes one circle in a longer sequence of overlapping links in the full chain. This image echoes an ancient Egyptian vocabulary and imagery of time, where the unending line of unrepeated times (Egyptian *djet*) incorporates successive repeating time cycles (Egyptian *neheh*), uniting twin communicative aspects of the complete and the incomplete (Roeten 2004). Precisely the time-line of life-cycles is the problem of archaeology as neocolonial practice; the archive allows us to conceive one life-cycle as an operational chain, becoming the point of reference for contemporary and successive life-cycles, in the effort to understand why the discipline reached its current condition, and whether and how it might move dialectically out of exclusion into inclusion of the past and present inhabitants of the landscape under study. On the page opposite, the life of Petrie in Egyptian archaeology is presented as a diagram, followed by observations on the presence, history and absences within Egypt, of each component of the cycle.

Notes on the histories of these components in Egypt

1. An interest in the past
Against the normative Eurocentric narratives of Europe Rescuing the East, extensive sources demonstrate interest in the material evidence for the past throughout Egypt. Ancient periods and monuments are prominent in nineteenth-century Arabic-language historiography, from the metropolitan traditions of Rifaa al-Tahtawi and Ali Mubarak (Crabbs 1984; 79, 118; for medieval antecedents, El-Daly 2005) to writers in rural centres such as Muhammad al-Maraghi of Girga (Gran 2004). The European account of Egyptian disinterest leaves us as entirely unprepared as Petrie for the strength of interest in the past in the most rural environment of Egypt, in the person of Umran Khallil of Misid (above, p. 19). Print-publication research needs new initiatives to uncover manuscript and local traditions.

2. Logistical underpinning
The entire infrastructure necessary for any archaeological expedition existed within Egypt already half a century before the arrival of Petrie, in the Maslahat al-Athar 'Antiquities Service', established in 1835 under Mohammad Ali at the recommendation of Rifaa al-Tahtawi on return from the Egyptian educational mission to Paris (Reid 2002: 50-3; Colla 2007:

10. Parallel lives in the archaeology of Egypt

The archaeological life-cycle of Petrie in Egypt 1880-1924 as one line

1. interest in past
↓
2. logistical underpinning of expeditions
(financing; accommodation; supplies; pay for expedition force; transport)
↓
3. survey
↓
3a. recording in graphic form
+/
3b. recording in written form
+/
3c. recording by visual depiction (line-drawing, photography)
↓
4. removing earth
↓
4a. recording in graphic form
+/
4b. recording in written form
+/
4c. recording by visual depiction (line-drawing, photography)
↓
5. selecting finds for off-site study/display
↓
6. preserving finds (including initial packing/transport)
a. conservation
b. secure storage/display
↓
7. publishing finds
↓
8. access to full range of finds
(including academic communication network/conferences/access to library
containing wide range of publications)
↓
9. university teaching/on-site training

118-24). The early decades of the Service were precarious in staff and finance, and only detailed research in Cairo can recover the economic history of the institution from 1835 to its 1858 re-foundation (its finances, local accomodation, supplies, transport/packing, labour payment). Yet already the existence of a Museum from 1835 testifies to a centralised system for retrieving material from sites around the country.

3. Surveying
Two decades before Umran Khallil surprised him with his knowledge and interest, an official at Alexandria 'astonished' Petrie with knowledge of surveying equipment (above, p. 86). This was in December 1880, the first time Petrie arrived in Egypt, and it raises another line of historical research, into the relation between branches of government and knowledge before the military occupation of 1882. Professional surveying skills

305

had been applied from geology to archaeology in Egypt already by the 1850s, on fieldwork in Mit Rahina (Mennefer/Memphis) and Matariya (Iunu/Heliopolis) by an Anglophile Armenian from Istanbul, Yusuf Hekek-yan (Jeffreys 1999; Reid 2002: 59-63). Beside surveys with technical equipment, sites are regularly identified in archaeology by trained eyes in walking the terrain; here, those who know the landscape from birth hold the advantage. Guy Brunton acknowledged the exceptional talents of Ali Suefi in locating sites, even far from his al-Lahun and Naqada homes.

4. Unearthing
From 1858, Mariette employed foremen such as Hamzawy and his son Roubi to direct workforces around the country on clearing sites for the Maslahat al-Athar (David 1994: 110, 169; a photograph of Roubi of Saqqara in David 1999: pl. [4] between pp. 164 and 165). Under Moham-mad Ali and his successors, central government agencies used the corvée, i.e. unpaid labour, for manual labour on irrigation and construction works. In addition, a more or less formalised system of treasure-hunting had long existed, in the eleventh century AD under an *amir matalibin* 'director of seekers' (cf. El Daly 2005: 34-5); Najama bedouin in Giza had provided Mariette with foremen there and at San al-Hagar in the Delta, and offered Petrie the same service (above, p. 60). Najama expertise resulted in the few Arabic notes of find-locations in Petrie Notebook 74e (1886), the ability of Muhammad abu Daud to provide Petrie with a tomb-plan in the 1888 seasons at Hawara, and the career of Muhammad Shaban. More detail may be sought in other sources, in Cairo, and including Arabic, both for the Najama and for other Egyptian contributions to the development of archaeology, starting with Qurna/Luxor and Saqqara, the other most prominent sites of monumental architecture. The decisive turn in the standard of archaeological recording is reached with simultaneous uncov-ering-and-recording. Both survey and uncovering yield controllable infor-mation for others only if they are recorded as they proceed, in maps/plans/diagrams (here summarised as 'graphic form'), descriptions (written form) and/or accurate drawings/ lithography/ photography ('vis-ual form'). Instances of each of these three in non-European archaeology in Egypt may be cited as examples of the material for separate and then combined historical research:

3/4a. Recording in graphic form: Mahmud al-Falaki excavated at Alexandria in 1865-1866 to clarify points for a city-plan (Reid 2002: 153); from the previous decade, the papers of the English-trained Yusuf Hekek-yan demonstrate high standards in survey draughtsmanship (Jeffreys 1999); later the plans for the articles by Ahmad Kamal on excavations in Middle Egypt capture relative position with as much accuracy as any other work in Egypt at the time, including that by Petrie (e.g. Kamal 1911).

3/4b. Recording in written form: descriptions of sites and monu-ments already form a recurrent motif in medieval Arabic historiography

(El Daly 2005: 47-53); the early registers for the Egyptian Museum after 1858 (Dewachter 1985) provide descriptions in French, by Mariette himself, and some drawings, and may rely on accounts from foremen, in forms to be identified; more or less informal museum training under the successors of Mariette may have enabled Ahmad Kamal to compile his excavation reports (see too, for his translations of museum guides, Reid 2002: 202).

3/4c. Recording in visual form: the Hekekyan papers again provide examples of outstanding quality for recording antiquities in the process of being unearthed (e.g. Jeffreys 1999: 166, fig.7); antecedents for such draughtsmanship in Ottoman Egypt are not known to me; photography in Egypt is dominated initially by the commercial studios, such as Kelekian and Abdullah Frères, or European immigrants such as Hippolyte Délié and Emile Béchard, creators of the official *Album* of the Boulaq Museum (Mariette 1872); by the end of the century, Maslahat al-Athar publications included photography of sites and artefacts, and the authorship of those photographs needs further research.

5. Selecting finds for preserving and storing

Here a history remains to be researched and written, on the journey of artefacts from the tuhaf 'treasures' of Mamluk and Ottoman culture to the historical documents of excavation, recorded at the moment of discovery in order to capture the information massed in their position in the ground in relation to other material. One source for the later end of this investigation would be the early Egyptian Museum register, the Inventaire de Boulaq (Dewachter 1985), because it offers in effect the finds register for the Maslahat al-Athar excavations under the directorship of Mariette from 1858 to 1881. Correspondence may reveal more on who decided to leave finds on site, or remove them to secure storage or display (cf. Simpson 1974: 8-9, letters to Mariette from his French supervisor Charles-Edmond Gabet at Qena on work by the foreman Salib at al-Araba al-Madfuna/Abydos).

6. Preserving

a. Conservation: Hilda Petrie and Bernard Grenfell (above, pp. 97, 136) both emphasise the skill needed in uncovering or retrieving material, and even child excavator Yusuf appears as conservator in one Brunton photograph; the possibility to study and appreciate any material today depends entirely on the dexterity of its discoverer, and in this respect all manual excavators have to be considered conservators; for care after discovery, the line of conservation may be continuous or intermittent, but tends to receive less attention in Egypt, as much as in London, until the late twentieth century, making it a difficult history to trace; after the 1952 Revolution, the history of conservation in Egypt led to one of the outstanding achievements in world archaeology, the successful retrieval and reconstruction of perhaps the greatest single find in the country, the royal boat buried beside the Great Pyramid; the conservator was Hag Ahmed Youssef, who began his career on the Giza expedition directed by George Reisner (Hawass 1999: 158).

b. Storage and display: the history of the museum as a research store for later access to finds goes back in Egypt to the Antikakhana founded in 1835 (Colla 2007: 116-20), and refounded after 1858 under the directorship of Mariette as the Egyptian Museum (Reid 2002: 104-7); the museum catalogue proposed by the German Egyptologist Ludwig Borchardt, and carried out under Gaston Maspero in his second directorship after 1899, was an international project including, among Egyptian curators, Ahmad Kamal, and resulting in far the greatest series of publications for any Egyptian collection worldwide; with Ahmad Kamal, Maspero also encouraged the formation of local museums at Asyut and Tanta before the First World War (Reid 2002: 204; for more recent history see Doyon 2008).

7. Publishing

On the histories of printing-press and print-readership in Egypt, see above, pp. 2-4, 29. Under Mohammad Ali and his successors, the Boulaq Press of the Egyptian government published Arabic-language journals and historical monographs (Reid 2002: 54, 112); in the 1860s Mariette planned a lithographic studio at the Egyptian Museum itself, but could not secure funding for the project (David 1999: 164-5); later, both Cairene and European presses produced the publications of the Maslahat al-Athar, covering archaeological fieldwork as well as museum catalogues and guides.

8. Library/archive access

The archaeological library brings full circle the life-line of learning, and its presence is crucial to the chance of the next generation to build on the knowledge of the previous. Histories of monumental and encyclopaedic libraries attracted much attention following the opening of the new Alexandria Library at the end of the twentieth century (e.g. Giard and Jacob 2001). Individual disciplines may require less, but still need efficiently functioning reading-resources; efficiency here means adequate stock, fast retrieval, good reading-space and reliable access. Local standards of the specialised library have long dictated the strength of learning within single European countries and across Europe, and favour the concentration of learning in older and richer universities, in countries with concentrations of capital. Yet the advantages of the good library do not amount to a veto on disciplinary development; Petrie himself seems to have relied more on fieldwork and collecting than on encyclopaedic reading. New digital technology has now transformed access to information in archives and in printed books, removing what has arguably been one of the main differences between the European and the Egyptian resources for Egyptological study.

9. University teaching

Donald Reid has charted the history of archaeology in higher education across the Egyptology School created under Khedive Ismail and Ali Mubarak as Minister for Education, with lectures by Heinrich Brugsch, to the Egyptian University which published the Ahmad Kamal lectures there from 1908 (Reid 2002: 116-18, 203-4). English occupying administrators deliberately restricted higher education, by limited places and high fees, creating less opportunity than Egyptians had enjoyed before 1882 (cf. in medicine Chiffoleau 1997: 54-7).

Archaeological practice could be articulated as a cyclical line in many different ways, and the example above is simply one suggested by the example of Petrie, as read in his publications and archive. The notes on the presence of each ingredient in Egypt can only be initial prompts to new searches in other source-bases. A first reading might identify in the nineteenth-century Egyptian record particular gaps in the study of the past (accurate drawings/lithographs/photographs of excavations/finds) – but should also highlight the shallowness or absences on the European side, where Egyptological libraries and departments could scarcely be said to flourish anywhere before the later nineteenth century, and where photography too was regular practice only at its end. Before closing, two additional factors deserve consideration, turning more to the future from the ground exposed by the archive.

(1) Social mobility

In its conferences and publications, Egyptology remains a discipline of three European languages: English, French and German. With US global power, English has tended to become dominant, but the publication record for French and German excavation remains so much more efficient that the trilingual European practice of the discipline continues in effect. After a century of focus on the written evidence, and on training in the ancient Egyptian language, Egyptology now bears the profile of European and Euroamerican university knowledge, with its narrow demographic base. Several sub-disciplines have flourished, with new separate congresses for studies of specific periods (predynastic, Old Kingdom, New Kingdom), sites (Memphis, Thebes) or areas of written evidence (literature, demotic script). However, even in the most flourishing sectors of the study of ancient Egypt, new dissertations struggle to avoid repetition, reflecting a conceptual stagnation that itself might mirror the narrow band of social and ethnic background for the overwhelming majority of Egyptology graduates. The social profile of Egyptian education is not very different (on education barriers, cf. Saad 2006), but social mobility remains higher than in the USA, Germany or England. More openness and mobility might help preserve a discipline from narrowness in its field of enquiry. Future Egyptian practice of archaeology perhaps has greater chances of returning to the history of social mobility in nineteenth-century Egypt, than have Europeans or Euroamericans.

(2) Foreigners in Egypt

It could be argued that foreign expeditions exhaust a limited supply of oxygen in the thin air of exploring the past in Egypt. If the 'helping hand' turns out to be a major block, non-Egyptians in Egypt need to help identify how they can most productively contribute. What is the role of the capital-concentrations outside Egypt in these developments? Although this might be considered a predominantly financial question, there are other, equally important dimensions to cultural relations. One part of the contribution from abroad would be a new access to archaeological archives as well as collections dispersed for study and display around the world from old excavations as much from trade and collecting activities outside archaeo-logy. In this context, the history of archaeology is crucial because it foregrounds the role of the recent past, including the development of archaeological institutions: journals, libraries, museums, and university departments. The history of archaeology by archaeologists could offer new equal access by exposing its own uneven terrain.

III. Future agendas for Egyptian histories and archaeologies

In his 1934 redraft of one paper as 'Ai Margini della Storia (Storia dei gruppi sociali subalterni)', Antonio Gramsci offered the start of an agenda for studying the historical development of working-class political parties:

> 1) the process of objective formation of subaltern social groups, by the development and transformations observable in the world of economic pro-duction; their quantitative diffusion and their origin in previous social groups, from which they retain for a certain time the mentality, ideology and ends;
> 2) their active or passive adherence to dominant political formations; at-tempts to influence the programmes of those formations to press their own claims, and the consequences of such attempts in determining processes of disintegration and of reneweal or of re-formation;
> 3) the birth of new parties of dominant groups to maintain the consent and control of subaltern groups;
> 4) the formations of the subaltern groups themselves for claims of limited and partial character;
> 5) the new formations asserting the autonomy of subaltern groups but within the old frameworks;
> 6) the formations affirming the integral autonomy (of subaltern groups).

In the following paragraph, Gramsci refers to this as a 'list of phases', in which 'the historian must note down and justify the line of development towards integral autonomy, from the most primitive phases, and must also note every instance of the "spirit of schism" as Sorelli put it' (Gramsci 1975: III (1934), 2288). His focus is the formation and political potential of the Italian working-class parties, above all the Communist Party that he helped to create, and his circumstances were utterly bleak, imprisonment in a country under Fascist rule since 1922. The influential literary Indian research movement that called itself Subaltern Studies cited this paragraph as a research agenda for working-class history (cf. Crehan 2002: 123-4). In the context of the rest of the note Gramsci seems more focussed on one part of that history, the formation of political parties in modern times. Yet, so specific a check-list offers a useful point of departure, because it reminds those of us in Archaeology or Ancient History that we hold little potential on any of these points. The excavation archives need to be handed over to the different disciplines of Modern History for analysis, to the academic and wider readership of the majority source language, Arabic, for context, and to the subjects of the history for reflection, rejection or use in the most important national and local settings involved in these sources.

Bibliography

Abu-Lughod, L. 2001. *Dramas of Nationhood: The Politics of Television in Egypt.* Chicago.

Adams, R. 2003. 'Evaluating development 1980-1997', in M. Riad El-Ghonemy (ed.), *Egypt in the Twenty-first Century*, London and New York: 19-40.

Addison, F. 1949. *The Wellcome Excavations in the Sudan, Vol. I: Jebel Moya.* London.

Alcock, S. 1994. 'Breaking up the Hellenistic world: survey and society', in I. Morris (ed.), *Classical Greece: Ancient Histories and Modern Archaeologies*, Cambridge: 171-90.

Aldred, C. 1971. *Jewels of the Pharaohs: Egyptian Jewellery of the Dynastic Period.* London.

Amélineau, E. 1899-1905. *Les Nouvelles Fouilles d'Abydos*, 4 vols. Paris.

Amin, S. 1973. *Le développement inégal: essai sur les formations sociales du capitalisme periphérique.* Paris.

Armbrust, W. 1996. *Mass Culture and Modernism in Egypt.* Cambridge.

Armbrust, W. 2003. 'Bourgeois leisure and Egyptian media fantasies', in D. Eickelman and J. Anderson (eds), *New Media in the Muslim World: Emerging Public Sphere*. Bloomington.

Asad, T. (ed.) 1973. *Anthropology and the Colonial Encounter*. Atlantic Highlands and Reading.

Ascherson, N. 2000. Editorial, in *Public Archaeology* 1: 1-4.

Ascherson, N. 2004. 'Archaeology and the British media', in N. Merriman (ed.), *Public Archaeology*, London and New York: 145-58.

Attiatallah, H. 1984a. 'Die Rolle der einheimischen Ägyptologen in der Entwicklung der Ägyptologie als Wissenschaft', in *Göttinger Miszellen* 75: 59-71.

Attiatallah, H. 1984b. 'Die Rolle der einheimischen Ägyptologen in der Entwicklung der Ägyptologie als Wissenschaft (Fortsetzung) ', in *Göttinger Miszellen* 76: 73-7.

Baer, G. 1969. 'Submissiveness and revolt of the Fellah', in *id.*, *Studies in the Social History of Modern Egypt*, Chicago: 93-108.

Baer, G. 1982. 'Continuity and change in Egyptian rural society 1805-1882', in *L'Egypte au XIXe siècle*, Paris: 231-46.

Ballerini, J. 1993. 'The in-visibility of Hadji-Ismael: Du Camp's 1850 photographs of Egypt', in K. Adler and M. Pointer (eds), *The Body Imaged*. Cambridge: 147-60.

Bannerji, H. 2001. 'Pygmalion nation: towards a critique of subaltern studies and the "resolution of the women's question" ', in H. Bannerji, S. Mojab and J. Whitehead, *Of Property and Propriety: The Role of Gender and Class in Imperialism*, Toronto: 34-84.

Barthorp, M. 1984. *War on the Nile: Britain, Egypt and the Sudan 1882-1898.* Poole.

Baumgartel, E. 1970. *Petrie's Naqada Excavations: A Supplement*, London.

313

Bibliography

Behrens-Abouseif, D. 2008. *Cairo of the Mamluks: A History of the Architecture and its Culture*. London and New York.

Ben-Srhir, K. 2005. *Britain and Morocco during the Embassy of John Drummond Hay*. London and New York (tr. M. Williams and G. Waterson).

Bernal, M. 1987. *Black Athena: The Afroasiatic Roots of Classical Civilization, Vol. I: The Fabrication of Ancient Greece 1785-1985*. New Brunswick.

Bernal, M. 2001. *Black Athena Writes Back: Martin Bernal Responds to his Critics*. Durham NC.

Bernback, R. 1997. *Theorien in der Archäologie*. Tübingen and Basel.

Berque, J. 1967. *L'Egypte: impérialisme et révolution*. Paris.

Bloom, J. 2001. *Paper before Print: The History and Impact of Power in the Islamic World*. New Haven.

Boinet, A. 1884. *Le recensement général de l'Egypte*. Cairo.

Bourdieu, P. 1984. *Homo Academicus*. Paris.

Bourriau, J. 1981. *Umm el-Ga'ab: Pottery from the Nile Valley before the Arab Conquest*. Cambridge.

Brodie, N., M. Kersel, C. Luke, K. Walker Tubb (eds), 2006. *Archaeology, Cultural Heritage and the Antiquities Trade*. Gainesville.

Brunton, G. 1927. *Qau and Badari I*. London.

Brunton, G. and R. Engelbach, 1927. *Gurob*. London.

Callinicos, A. 1987. *Making History: Agency, Structure and Change in Social Theory*. Cambridge.

Cerquiglini, B. 1989. *Eloge de la variante: histoire critique de la philologie*. Paris.

Chartier, R. 1992. 'Labourers and voyagers: from the text to the reader', in *Diacritics* 22: 49-61.

Chiffoleau, S. 1997. *Médecines et médecins en Egypte: construction d'une identité professionelle et projet médical*. Lyon.

Clackson, S. 2004. 'Papyrology and the utilization of Coptic sources', in P. Sijpesteijn and L. Sundelin (eds), *Papyrology and the History of Early Islamic Egypt*, Leiden: 21-44.

Cole, J. 2000. *Colonialism and Revolution*. Cairo.

Colla, E. 2007. *Conflicted Antiquities: Egyptology, Egyptomania, Egyptian Modernity*. Durham NC and London.

Cooper, D. 2006. 'Truthfulness and "inclusion" in archaeology', in C. Scarre and G. Scarre (eds), *The Ethics of Archaeology: Philosophical Perspectives on Archaeological Practice*, Cambridge: 131-45.

Crabbs, J. 1984. *The Writing of History in Nineteenth-Century Egypt*. Cairo and Detroit.

Crabbs, J. 1990. 'Historiography and the eighteenth-century milieu', in D. Crecelius (ed.), *Eighteenth Century Egypt: The Arabic Manuscript Sources*. Claremont.

Crecelius, D. 1981. *The Roots of Modern Egypt: A Study of the Regimes of Ali Bey al-Kebir and Muhammad Bey Abu al-Dhahab, 1760-1775*. Minneapolis and Chicago.

Crehan, K. 2002. *Gramsci, Culture and Anthropology*. London.

Crowfoot Payne, J. 1987. 'Appendix to Naqada Excavations Supplement', in *Journal of Egyptian Archaeology* 73: 181-9.

Cuno, K. 1988. 'Commercial relations between town and village in eighteenth and early nineteenth-century Egypt', in *Annales Islamologiques* 24: 111-35.

David, E. 1994. *Mariette Pacha 1821-1881*. Paris.

David, E. 1999. *Gaston Maspero 1846-1916. Le gentleman égyptologue*. Paris.

Bibliography

David, E. 2003. *Gaston Maspero. Lettres d'Egypte. Correspondance avec Louise Maspero (1883-1914)*. Paris.

Davis, M. 2001. *Late Victorian Holocausts: El Nino Famines and the Making of the Third World*. London and New York.

Delanoue, G. 1982. *Moralistes et politiques musulmans dans l'Egypte du XIXe siecle (1798-1882)*. Cairo.

Der Manuelian, P. 1999. 'Excavating the Old Kingdom: the Giza necropolis and other mastaba fields', in *Egyptian Art in the Age of the Pyramids*, New York: 138-53.

Der Manuelian, P. 2007. 'Historic discovery in Egypt: the lost Arabic excavation diaries. Giza Archives Project Press Release 1/1/2007', at www.gizapyramids.org, under News.

Dewachter, M. 1985. 'L'original de l'Inventaire de Boulaq', in *Bulletin de l'Institut Français d'Archéologie Orientale* 85: 105-31, pl. 20-1.

Dialismas, A. 2004. 'The Aegean melting-pot: history and archaeology for historians and prehistorians', in E. Sauer (ed.), *Archaeology and Ancient History*, London: 62-75.

Doyon, W. 2008. 'The poetics of Egyptian museum practice', in *British Museum Studies in Ancient Egypt and Sudan* 10: 1-37, available online at http://www.britishmuseum.org/pdf/Doyon.pdf.

Drower, M. 1982. 'Gaston Maspero and the birth of the Egypt Exploration Fund (1881-3)', in *Journal of Egyptian Archaeology* 68: 299-317.

Drower, M. 1985. *Flinders Petrie: A Life in Archaeology*. London.

Drower, M. 2004. *Letters from the Desert: The Correspondence of Flinders and Hilda Petrie*. Oxford.

Dyhouse, C. 1995. *No Distinction of Sex? Women in British Universities 1870-1939*. London.

El Daly, O. 2005. *Egyptology: The Missing Millennium. Ancient Egypt in Medieval Arabic Writings*. London.

El-Desouky, A. 2007. 'Notes on political memory and cultural memory', in A. El-Desouky and N. Brehony, *British-Egyptian Relations from Suez to the Present Day*, London: 163-78.

Engelbach, R. 1915. *Riqqeh and Memphis VI*. London.

Erdogdu, A. 2002. 'Picturing alterity: representational strategies in Victorian type photographs of Ottoman men', in E. Hight and G. Sampson (eds), *Colonialist Photography: Imag(in)ing Race and Place*, London and New York: 107-25.

Eternad, B. 2000. *La possession du monde: poids et mesures de la colonisation (XVIIIe-XXe siècles)*. Brussels.

Fabian, J. 1983. *Time and the Other: How Anthropology Makes its Object*. New York.

Fabian, J. 1992. 'Dilemmas of critical anthropology', in J. Fabian, *Time and the Work of Anthropology. Critical Essays 1971-1991*. Chur.

Fabian, J. 2000. *Out of Our Minds: Reason and Madness in the Exploration of Central Africa*. Berkeley and Los Angeles.

Feuchtwang, S. 1973. 'The discipline and its sponsors', in Asad 1973: 71-100.

Fitton, L. 1995. *The Discovery of the Greek Bronze Age*. London.

Foucault, M. 1975. *Surveiller et punir: naissance de la prison*. Paris.

Freire, P. 1996 [1970]. *Pedagogy of the Oppressed*. London.

Gamblin, S. 2004. 'Luxor: a tale of two cities', in N. Hopkins and R. Saad (eds), *Upper Egypt: Identity and Change*, Cairo: 267-84.

Garcin, J.-C. 1976. *Un centre musulman de l'Haute Egypte medievale. Qus*. Cairo.

Bibliography

Gardner, E. 1888. *Naukratis, Part II*. London.

Gasper, M. 2009. *The Power of Representation: Publics, Peasants, and Islam in Egypt*. Stanford.

Giard, L. and C. Jacob (eds) 2001. *Des Alexandries I. Du livre au texte*. Paris.

Giddens, A. 1971. *Capitalism and Modern Social Theory: An Analysis of the Writings of Marx, Durkheim and Max Weber*. Cambridge.

Goldberg, E. 1992. 'Peasants in revolt – Egypt 1919', in *International Journal for Middle East Studies* 24: 261-80.

Goldsmith, J. and T. Wu. 2006. *Who Controls the Internet? Illusions of a Borderless World*. New York.

Gonzalez-Quijano, Y. 1998. *Les gens du livre: édition et champ intellectuel dans l'Egypte républicaine*. Paris.

Goode, J. 2007. *Negotiating for the Past: Archaeology, Nationalism and Diplomacy in the Middle East, 1919-1941*. Austin.

Gorman, A. 2003. *Historians, State and Politics in Twentieth-century Egypt: Contesting the Nation*. London and New York.

Gorman, A. 2007. 'Foreign workers in Egypt 1882-1914. Subaltern or labour elite?' in S. Cronin (ed.), *Subalterns and Social Protest: History from Below in the Middle East and North Africa*. London and New York: 237-59.

Gosden, C. 1999. *Anthropology and Archaeology: A Changing Relationship*. London.

Gosh, A. 1994. *In an Antique Land*. London.

Gramsci, A. 1975. *Quaderni del carcere* (ed. Gerratana). Turin.

Gran, P. 2004. 'Upper Egypt in modern history: a "Southern Question"?' in N. Hopkins and R. Saad (eds), *Upper Egypt: Identity and Change*, Cairo: 79-96.

Gräslund, B. 1987. *The Birth of Prehistoric Chronology*. Cambridge.

Green, M. 2002. 'Gramsci cannot speak: presentations and interpretations of Gramsci's concept of the subaltern', in *Rethinking Marxism* 14: 1-24.

Griffith, F. Ll., and W.M.F. Petrie 1889. *Two Hieroglyphic Papyri from Tanis*. London.

Habermas, J. 1990. *Strukturwandel der Öffentlichkeit*, reissue with new foreword. Frankfurt am Main. (English translation: *Transformation of the Public Sphere*. 1989.)

Hankey, J. 2007. *A Passion for Egypt: Arthur Weigall, Tutankhamun and the 'Curse of the Pharaohs'*. London.

Hanna, N. 2003. *In Praise of Books: A Cultural History of Cairo's Middle Class, Sixteenth to the Eighteenth Century*. Syracuse.

Harte, N. 1979. *The Admission of Women to University College London: A Centenary Lecture*. London.

Hassan, S. 1930. 'Excavations at Gizeh', in *Ancient Egypt* (1930 issue): 23-4.

Hassan, S. 1932-1960. *Excavations at Giza*, 10 vols. Cairo.

Hathaway, J. 1994. Review of M. Winter, *Egyptian Society under Ottoman Rule, 1517-1798*, London 1992, in *International Journal of Middle East Studies* 26: 299-301.

Hawass, Z. 1999. 'Excavating the Old Kingdom: the Egyptian archaeologists', in *Egyptian Art in the Age of the Pyramids*, New York: 154-65.

Hawass, Z. (ed.) 2003. *Egyptology at the Dawn of the Twenty-first Century: Proceedings of the Eighth International Congress of Egyptologists, Cairo, 2000*. Cairo.

Hayes, W. 1953. *The Scepter of Egypt: A Background for the Study of the Egyptian Antiquities in the Metropolitan Museum of Art, I: From the Earliest Times to the End of the Middle Kingdom*. New York.

Bibliography

Hendrickx, S. 1993. 'Relative chronology of the Naqada culture: problems and possibilities', in J. Spencer (ed.), *Aspects of Early Egypt*, London: 36-69.

Hill, M. and W. Montag (eds) 2000. *Masses, Classes, and the Public Sphere*. London and New York.

Hirschkop, K. 1999. *Mikhail Bakhtin: An Aesthetic for Democracy*. Oxford.

Hollowell, J. 2006. 'Moral arguments on subsistence digging', in C. Scarre and G. Scarre (eds), *The Ethics of Archaeology: Philosophical Perspectives on Archaeological Practice*, Cambridge: 69-93.

Holt, P. 1961. 'The Beylicate in Ottoman Egypt during the seventeenth century', in *Bulletin of the School of Oriental and African Studies, University of London* 24: 214-68.

Holton, S. 2003. *Feminism and Democracy: Women's Suffrage and Reform Politics in Britain, 1900-1918*. Cambridge.

Hoving, T. 1978. *The Search for Tutankhamun: The Untold Story of Adventure and Intrigue Surrounding the Greatest Modern Archeological Find*. New York.

Howe, S. 1998. *Afrocentrism: Mythical Pasts and Imagined Homes*. London.

Hunter, F.R., 1984. *Egypt under the Khedives 1805-1879: From Household Government to Modern Bureaucracy*. Pittsburgh.

Hutton, H. and J. King 1981. *Ten per Cent and No Surrender: The Preston Strike 1853-1854*. Cambridge.

Iversen, E. 1961. *The Myth of Egypt and its Hieroglyphs in the European Tradition*. Copenhagen.

James, T.G.H. 1991. 'The discovery and identification of the alabaster quarries of Hatnub', in *Comptes-rendues de l'Institut de Papyrologie et d'Egyptologie de Lille* 13 (*Mélanges Jacques Jean Clère*): 79-84.

Janssen, R. 1992. *The First Hundred Years: Egyptology at University College London 1892-1992*. London.

Jeffreys, D. 1999. 'Joseph Hekekyan at Heliopolis', in A. Leahy and J. Tait (eds), *Studies on Ancient Egypt in Honour of H.S. Smith*, London: 157-68.

Jenkins, I. 1992. *Archaeologists and Aesthetes in the Sculpture Galleries of the British Museum 1800-1939*. London.

Kahle, P. 1954. *Coptic Texts from Deir el-Balaizeh in Upper Egypt*. London.

Kamal, A. 1911. 'Rapport sur les fouilles exécutées dans la zone comprise entre Déirout au Nord et Déir el-Ganadlah au Sud', in *Annales du Service des Antiquités d'Egypte* 11: 3-39.

Kapitan, T. 1997. 'Historical Introduction', in *id.* (ed.), *Philosophical Perspectives on the Israeli-Palestinian Conflict*. New York: 15-41.

Kemp, B. 2007. 'Abydos', in P. Spencer (ed.), *The Egypt Exploration Society – The Early Years*, London: 131-65.

Khater, A. 1996. ' "House" to "Goddess of the House": gender, class, and silk in 19th-century Mount Lebanon', in *International Journal of Middle East Studies* 28: 325-48.

Kramer, M. 1986. *Islam Assembled: The Advent of the Muslim Congresses*. Princeton.

Labica, G. 2007. 'From imperialism to globalization', in S. Budgen, S. Kouvelakis, and S. Žižek (eds), *Lenin Reloaded: Towards a Politics of Truth*, Durham and London: 222-38.

Laidlaw, S. 2008. 'A technical examination of Petrie's photography', in J. Picton and I. Pridden (eds), *Unseen Images: Archive Photographs in the Petrie Museum*, London: 11-16.

Lefkowitz, M. and G. Rogers (eds), 1996. *Black Athena Revisited*. Chapel Hill.

317

Lichtheim, M. 1988. *Ancient Egyptian Autobiographies chiefly of the Middle Kingdom: A Study and an Anthology.* Freiburg and Göttingen.

Loprieno, A. 1996. 'The "King's Novel" ', in A. Loprieno (ed.), *Ancient Egyptian Literature: History and Forms*, Leiden: 277-95.

Lorimer, D. 1999. Introduction to English re-issue of V. Lenin, *'Left-Wing' Communism – an Infantile Disorder.* Sydney.

Losurdo, D. 2007. 'Lenin and *Herrenvolk* democracy', in S. Budgen, S. Kouvelakis, and S. Žižek (eds), *Lenin Reloaded: Towards a Politics of Truth*, Durham and London: 239-52.

Lucas, G. 2005. *The Archaeology of Time.* London and New York.

McDavid, C. 2004. 'Towards a more democratic archaeology? The Internet and public archaeological practice', in N. Merriman (ed.), *Public Archaeology*, London and New York: 159-87.

MacDonald, S. 2003. 'Lost in time and space: ancient Egypt in museums', in S. MacDonald and M. Rice (eds), *Consuming Ancient Egypt*, London: 87-100.

McInerney, D. 2000. 'Print-capitalism?', in Hill and Montag 2000: 179-201.

McKale, D. 1997. 'Influence without power: the last Khedive of Egypt and the Great Powers, 1914-18', in *Middle Eastern Studies* 33: 20-39.

Mapunda, B. and P. Lane 2004. 'Archaeology for whose interest – archaeologists or the locals?' in N. Merriman (ed.), *Public Archaeology*, London and New York: 211-23.

Mardam-Bey, F. and B. El Hage 2007. *L'Orient des photographes arméniens.* Paris.

Mariette, A. 1872. *Album du Musée de Boulaq.* Cairo.

Marsot, A. Lutfi al-Sayyid 1984. *Egypt in the Reign of Muhammad Ali.* Cambridge.

Marx, K. and F. Engels 1848. *Manifest der Kommunistischen Partei.* London.

Mekhitarian, A. 1985. 'La destruction systématique des tombes thébaines', in *Mélanges offerts à Jean Vercoutter*, Paris: 239-47.

Meskell, L. (ed.). 1998. *Archaeology under Fire: Nationalism, Politics and Heritage in the Eastern Mediterranean and Middle East.* London.

Messiri, S. el-, 1978. *Ibn al-Balad: A Concept of Egyptian Identity.* Leiden.

Milne, G. 2000. *Trade and Traders in Mid-Victorian Liverpool: Mercantile Business and the Making of a World Port.* Chicago.

Mitchell, T. 1988. *Colonising Egypt.* Cambridge.

Montag, W. 2000. 'The pressure of the street: Habermas's fear of the masses', in Hill and Montag 2000: 132-45.

Moon, B. 2006. *More Usefully Employed: Amelia B. Edwards, Writer, Traveller and Campaigner for Ancient Egypt.* London.

Morgan, J. de 1896-1897. *Recherches sur les origines de l'Egypte*, 2 vols. Paris.

Morrell, R. 2002. *'Budgie': The Life of Sir E.A.T. Wallis Budge, Egyptologist, Assyriologist and Keeper of the Department of Egyptian and Assyrian Antiquities at the British Museum, 1892-1924.* Nottingham.

Moser, S. 2006. *Wondrous Curiosities: Ancient Egypt at the British Museum.* Chicago.

Murray, G. 1935. *Sons of Ishmael: A Study of the Egyptian Bedouin.* London.

Murray, M. 1904. *The Osireion at Abydos.* London.

Nasrallah, Y. 2007. 'Egypt, cinema and the national imaginary', in A. El-Desouky and N. Brehony, *British-Egyptian Relations from Suez to the Present Day*, London: 200-8.

Naunton, C. 2006. 'Frankfort photograph albums', in *Egyptian Archaeology* 28: 2.

Naunton, C. 2007. 'The archaeological survey', in P. Spencer (ed.), *The Egypt Exploration Society – The Early Years*, London: 67-93.

Osing, J. 1998. *Hieratische Papyri aus Tebtunis I.* Copenhagen.

Bibliography

Owen, R. 1965. 'The influence of Lord Cromer's Indian experience on British policy in Egypt 1883-1907, in *Middle Eastern Affairs* 4. London.

Owen, R. 2004. *Lord Cromer: Victorian Imperialist, Edwardian Proconsul*. Oxford.

Pappé, I. 2003. *A History of Modern Palestine: One Land, Two Peoples*. Cambridge.

Petrie, W.M.F. 1883. *The Pyramids and Temples of Gizeh*. London.

Petrie, W.M.F. 1885. *Tanis, Part I: 1883-4*. London.

Petrie, W.M.F. 1886. *Naukratis, Part I: 1884-5*. London.

Petrie, W.M.F. 1888. *Tanis, Part II: Nebesheh (Am) and Defenneh (Tahpanhes)*. London.

Petrie, W.M.F. 1889. *Hawara, Biahmu, and Arsinoe*. London.

Petrie, W.M.F. 1890. *Kahun, Gurob, Hawara*. London.

Petrie, W.M.F. 1891. *Illahun, Kahun, Gurob*. London.

Petrie, W.M.F. 1892. *Medum*. London.

Petrie, W.M.F. 1894. *Tell el Amarna*. London.

Petrie, W.M.F. 1895. *The Egyptian Research Account. Report of the First Year, presented to the contributors. 1895, with subscription list and balance sheet*. London.

Petrie, W.M.F. 1896a. *Koptos*. London.

Petrie, W.M.F. 1896b. *Naqada and Ballas. 1895*. London.

Petrie, W.M.F. 1897. *Six Temples at Thebes. 1896*. London.

Petrie, W.M.F. 1898. *Deshasheh. 1897*. London.

Petrie, W.M.F. 1900a. *Dendereh. 1898*. London.

Petrie, W.M.F. 1900b. *The Royal Tombs of the First Dynasty. 1900, Part I*. London.

Petrie, W.M.F. 1901a. *The Royal Tombs of the Earliest Dynasties. 1901, Part II*. London.

Petrie, W.M.F. 1901b. *Diospolis Parva: The Cemeteries of Abadiyeh and Hu. 1898-9*. London.

Petrie, W.M.F. 1904. *Methods and Aims in Archaeology*. London.

Petrie, W.M.F. 1906a. *Researches in Sinai*. London.

Petrie, W.M.F. 1906b. *Hyksos and Israelite Cities*. London.

Petrie, W.M.F. 1907. *Gizeh and Rifeh*. London.

Petrie, W.M.F. 1930. *Ancient Egypt*: 128 [Obituary for Henry Hall].

Petrie, W.M.F., E. Mackay, G. Wainwright, 1910. *Meydum and Memphis (III)*. London.

Piacentini, P. 2005. *La Valle dei Re riscoperta. I giornali di scavo di Victor Loret (1898-1899) e altri inediti*. Milan.

Picton, J., P. Roberts, S. Quirke (eds), 2007. *Living Images: Egyptian Funerary Portraits in the Petrie Museum*. Walnut Creek.

Piquet, C. 2008. *La Compagnie du canal de Suez: une concession française en Egypte (1888-1956)*. Paris.

Pope, J. 2006. 'Ägypten und Aufhebung: G.W.F. Hegel, W.E.B. Du Bois, and the African Orient', in *The New Centennial Review* 6: 149-92.

Porter, B. 2008. *Critics of Empire: British Radicals and the Imperial Challenge*. London.

Quibell, J. 1898a. *The Ramesseum*. London.

Quibell, J. 1898b. *Elkab*. London.

Quirke, S. 2007a. 'Labour at Lahun', in Z. Hawass and J. Richards, *The Archaeology and Art of Ancient Egypt: Essays in Honor of David O'Connor*, Cairo.

Quirke, S. 2007b. 'Interwoven destinies: Egyptians and English in the labour of archaeology, 1880-2007', in A. El-Desouky and N. Brehony (eds), *British-Egyptian Relations from Suez to the Present Day*, London: 246-73.

Rathbone, D. 2007. 'Grenfell and Hunt at Oxyrhynchus and in the Fayum', in P. Spencer (ed.), *The Egypt Exploration Society – The Early Years*, London: 199-229.

Raymond, A. 1974. *Artisans et commerçants au Caire au XVIIIe siècle*. Damascus.

Reeves, N. 1990. *The Complete Tutankhamun: The King, the Tomb, the Royal Treasure*. London and New York.

Reid, D. 1985. 'Indigenous Egyptology: the decolonisation of a profession', in *Journal of the American Research Center in Egypt* 105: 233-46.

Reid, D. 2002. *Whose Pharaohs? Archaeology, Museums and Egyptian National Identity from Napoleon to World War I*. Berkeley.

Roberts, P. 2007. 'An archaeological context for British discoveries of mummy portraits in the Fayum', in Picton *et al.* 2007: 13-72.

Roeten, L. 2004. 'Some observations on the *nHH* and *D.t* "eternity" ', in *Göttinger Miszellen* 201: 69-78.

Rose, J. 2001. *The Intellectual Life of the British Working Classes*. Yale.

Rowland, J. 2007. 'El-Amrah, el-Mahasna, Hu and Abadiyeh', in P. Spencer (ed.), *The Egypt Exploration Society – The Early Years*, London: 167-97.

Ryholt, K. 1997. *The Political Situation in Egypt during the Second Intermediate Period c. 1800-1550 BC*. Copenhagen.

Saad, A. 2006. 'Subsistence education: schooling in a context of urban poverty', in L. Herrera and C. Torres (eds), *Cultures of Arab Schooling: Critical Ethnographies from Egypt*. Albany.

Safty, A. 2009. *Might over Right. How the Zionists took over Palestine*. Reading.

Said, E. 1978. *Orientalism*. New York.

Said, E. 1989. 'Representing the colonized: anthropology's interlocutors', in *Critical Inquiry* 15: 205-25.

Sauer, K. (ed.) 2004. *Archaeology and Ancient History: Breaking down the Boundaries*. London and New York.

Schiffer, M. 1987. *Formation Processes of the Archaeological Record*. Albuquerque.

Schölch, A. 1972. *Ägypten den Ägyptern*. Zurich. (English translation *Egypt for the Egyptians: The Sociopolitical Crisis in Egypt, 1878-1882*, 1981, London.)

Schölch, A. 1976-1977. 'The Egyptian bedouins and the 'Urâbîyûn (1882)', in *Die Welt des Islams* 17: 44-57.

Schwartz, F. 2005. *Blind Spots: Critical Theory and the History of Art in Twentieth-century Germany*. New Haven.

Scott, J. 1985. *The Weapons of the Weak: Everyday Forms of Peasant Resistance*. New Haven.

Scott, J. 1998. *Seeing Like a State: How Certain Schemes to Improve the Human Condition have Failed*. New Haven.

Serpico, M. 2008. 'Introduction', and 'Sedment', in J. Picton and I. Pridden (eds), *Unseen Images: Archive Photographs in the Petrie Museum*, London: 1-10, and 99-180.

Shackel, P. and E. Chambers (eds) 2004. *Places in Mind. Public Archaeology as Applied Anthropology*. New York and London.

Shanks, M. and C. Tilley 1989. *Re-constructing Archaeology: Theory and Practice*. London and New York.

Shaw, G.B. 1984 [1907]. *John Bull's Other Island*. London.

Shaw, I. 1999. 'Sifting the spoil: excavation techniques from Peet to Pendlebury at el-Amarna', in A. Leahy and J. Tait (eds), *Studies on Ancient Egypt in Honour of H.S. Smith*, London: 273-82.

Shaw, S. 1962. *Ottoman Egypt in the Eighteenth Century: The Nizâmnâme-i Misr of Cezzâr Ahmed Pasha*. Cambridge, MA.

Bibliography

Sheehi, S. 2007. 'A social history of early Arab photography or a prolegomonon to an archaeology of the Lebanese image', in *International Journal of Middle East Studies* 39: 177-208.

Simpson, W.K. 1974. *The Terrace of the Great God: The Offering Chapels of Dynasties 12 and 13*. New Haven and Philadelphia.

Skovgaard-Petersen, J. 2003. 'Da pan-islamismen kom til Skandinavien – Om muslimers deltagelse i Den Socialistiske Fredskonference, 1917', in *Kritik* 36: 44-51.

Smith, H. 2007. *The British Women's Suffrage Campaign: 1866-1928*, 2nd edn. London.

Sobhy, G. 1923. 'Customs and superstitions of the Egyptians concerning pregnancy and child-birth', in *Ancient Egypt*: 9-16.

Spencer, P. (ed.) 2007. *The Egypt Exploration Society – The Early Years*. London.

Thomas, T. 2000. *Late Antique Egyptian Funerary Sculpture*. Princeton.

Tomber, R. 2008. *Indo-Roman Trade: From Pots to Pepper*. London.

Tomiche, N. 1982. 'Remarques sur la langue et l'écriture en Egypte 1805-1882', in *L'Egypte au XIXe siecle*, Paris: 299-317.

Toth, J. 1999. *Rural Labor Movements in Egypt and their Impact on the State, 1961-1992*. Cairo.

Trigger, B. 2006. *A History of Archaeological Thought*, 2nd edn. Cambridge.

Trumpler, C. 2008. *Das Grosse Spiel: Archäologie und Politik*. Cologne.

Tsountas, C. 1889. 'Ereuna en te Lakonike kai o taphos tou Vapheiou', in *Ephemeris Archaiologike*: 129-72.

Tvedt , T. 2004. *The River Nile in the Age of the British: Political Ecology and the Quest for Economic Power*. London.

Ucko, P. 1987. *Academic Freedom and Apartheid: The Story of the World Archaeological Congress*. London.

Ucko, P. 1998. 'The biography of a collection: the Sir Flinders Petrie Palestinian Collection and the role of university museums', in *Museum Management and Curatorship* 17: 351-99.

Ucko, P. and T. Wang 2007. 'Early archaeological fieldwork practice and syllabuses in China and England', in P. Ucko, Q. Ling, J. Hubert (eds), *From Concepts of the Past to Practical Strategies: The Teaching of Archaeological Field Techniques*: 22-57.

Ufford, P. 2007. *The Pasha: How Mehemet Ali Defied the West, 1839-1841*. Jefferson.

Vernoit, S. 2006. 'The visual arts in nineteenth-century Muslim thought', in D. Behrens-Abouseif and S. Vernoit (eds), *Islamic Art in the Nineteenth Century: Tradition, Innovation and Eclecticism*: 19-35.

Wallis, H. 1898. *Egyptian Ceramic Art: The MacGregor Collection; A Contribution Towards the History of Egyptian Pottery*. London.

Wallis, H. 1900. *Egyptian Ceramic Art: Typical Examples of the Art of the Egyptian Potter Portrayed in Colour Plates with Text Illustrations Drawn and Described*. London.

Weatherhead, F. 1992. 'Painted pavements in the Great Palace at Amarna', in *Journal of Egyptian Archaeology* 78: 179-94.

Weingarten, J. 1991. *The Transformation of Egyptian Taweret into the Minoan Genius: A Study in Cultural Transmission in the Middle Bronze Age*. Partille.

Wengrow, D. 2006. *The Archaeology of Early Egypt: Social Transformations in North-east Africa, 10,000 to 2650 BC*. Cambridge.

Werner, M. 2005. *Pre-Raphaelite Painting and Nineteenth-century Realism*. Cambridge.

Wiener, M. 1982. *English Culture and the Decline of the Industrial Spirit 1850-1980*. Cambridge.

Wilkinson, T. 1999. *Early Dynastic Egypt*. London and New York.

Willems, H. 1988. *Chests of Life: A Study of the Typology and Conceptual Development of Middle Kingdom Standard Class Coffins*. Leiden.

Wilmore, M. 2006. 'Landscapes of disciplinary power: an ethnography of excavation and survey at Leskernick', in M. Edgeworth (ed.), *Ethnographies of Archaeological Practice: Cultural Encounters, Material Transformations*, Lanham: 114-26.

Wilson, A.N. 2002. *The Victorians*. London.

Wilson, T. 2002. 'A Victorian artist-collector and the museum: the letters of Henry Wallis: Part I', in *Journal of the History of Collections* 14: 139-59.

Winter, M. 1992. *Egyptian Society under Ottoman Rule 1517-1798*. London.

Wynn, L. 2008. 'Shape shifting lizard people, Israelite slaves, and other theories of pyramid building. Notes on labor, nationalism, and archaeology in Egypt', in *Journal of Social Archaeology* 8: 272-95.

Zaman, M. 2002. *The Ulama in Contemporary Islam*. Princeton.

Illustrations and sources

1.1. Excavating in Egypt: Professor Petrie at Thebes, watercolour by Henry Wallis, 1895, UCL Art Collections no. EDC 2674 © UCL Art Collections, University College London.
5.1. Family tree of Ali Jabri and Muhammad abu Daud, as recorded by Petrie in 1887, Petrie Notebook 46 © Petrie Museum of Egyptian Archaeology, UCL.
5.2. Hilda Petrie notes on women at an excavation (1902?), Petrie Notebook 132 © Petrie Museum of Egyptian Archaeology, UCL.
6.1. Names of finders in the record of excavation of Roman Period mummified bodies with panel portraits, 1911, Petrie Notebook 37 © Petrie Museum of Egyptian Archaeology, UCL.
6.2. Panel portrait of an adult woman, from a group burial excavated by Khalifa at Hawara, 1st century AD, UC30088 © Petrie Museum of Egyptian Archaeology, UCL.
6.3. Panel portrait of a child, from a group burial excavated by Khalifa at Hawara, 1st century AD, UC36215 © Petrie Museum of Egyptian Archaeology, UCL.
7.1. Pottery brewing-vessel re-used as coffin for a child, about 2500 BC, excavated by Shahat Ahmad in 1920 at Gurob, UC17865 © Petrie Museum of Egyptian Archaeology, UCL.
8.1. Hilda Petrie sketchmap of villages in the Qift area with names of workforce, Petrie Notebook 134 © Petrie Museum of Egyptian Archaeology, UCL.
8.2. The start of the Hilda Petrie record of the Qift workforce, Petrie Notebook 134 © Petrie Museum of Egyptian Archaeology, UCL.
9.1. Petrie 1881 photograph showing him at the rock-cut tomb where he lived, Petrie Museum archive photograph © Petrie Museum of Egyptian Archaeology, UCL.
9.2. Petrie 1881 photograph of the Great Pyramid from the East, showing the Old Kingdom rock-cut tombs where he lived, Petrie series no. 457, from Petrie Album 5 in the Griffith Institute © the Griffith Institute, University of Oxford.
9.3. Petrie 1881 photograph of Kafr al-Haram from the rock-cut tomb where he lived during his pyramid survey, Petrie series no. 458, from Petrie Album 7 in the Griffith Institute © the Griffith Institute, University of Oxford.
9.4. Petrie 1881 photograph of Kafr al-Batran during the annual Nile flood, as seen from the rock-cut tomb where he lived during his pyramid survey, Petrie series no. 35, from Petrie Album 7 in the Griffith Institute © the Griffith Institute, University of Oxford .
9.5. Petrie 1881 photograph 'Sheikh Seidi and an ancient friend' at Giza, Petrie series no. 428, from Petrie Album 7 in the Griffith Institute © the Griffith Institute, University of Oxford.
9.6. Petrie 1881 photograph 'My friend Sheikh Omar holding a levee in a sunny corner. Gizeh', Petrie series no. 432, from Petrie Album 7 in the Griffith Institute © the Griffith Institute, University of Oxford.
9.7. Petrie 1881 photograph of Ali Jabri, Petrie series no. 386, from Petrie Album 7 in the Griffith Institute © the Griffith Institute, University of Oxford.

9.8. Petrie 1881 sketch of Kafr al-Haram from the rock-cut tomb where he lived, Petrie Notebook 25 © Petrie Museum of Egyptian Archaeology, UCL.

9.9. Boy and girl on the San al-Hagar excavation, 'Ahmed Hafnawi <and> Muhd Hassan (girl)' in Petrie photograph 'Tanis series' no. 105, from a copy in the Petrie Museum archives © Petrie Museum of Egyptian Archaeology, UCL.

9.10. Three boys on the excavation workforce, 'Muhd es Said, Muhd Jafur, Muhd Timsas' in Petrie photograph 'Tanis series' no. 106, from a copy in the Petrie Museum archives © Petrie Museum of Egyptian Archaeology, UCL.

9.11. Dr Alexandre Habra from Zagazig, in Petrie photograph 'Tanis series' no. 157, print in the Egypt Exploration Society Lucy Gura Archive © the Egypt Exploration Society.

9.12. Ibrahim Kamil from Fakus, in Petrie photograph 'Tanis series' no. 159, print in the Egypt Exploration Society Lucy Gura Archive © the Egypt Exploration Society.

9.13. Two boys on the excavation workforce, 'Abd el Hamed abd el Gani <and> Smein Suleiman' in Petrie photograph 'Tanis series' no. 366, from Petrie Album 7 in the Griffith Institute © the Griffith Institute, University of Oxford.

9.14. Muhammad abu Daud in 'Afrangi' pose, in Petrie photograph 'Tanis series' no. 373, Petrie Museum Archive Negative 2718 © Petrie Museum of Egyptian Archaeology, UCL.

9.15. Muhammad abu Daud in 'Beledi' pose, in Petrie photograph 'Tanis series' no. 374, Petrie Museum Archive Negative 2719 © Petrie Museum of Egyptian Archaeology, UCL.

9.16. Undated photograph in the Petrie Museum archives, possibly of Ali Suefi © Petrie Museum of Egyptian Archaeology, UCL.

9.17. 'Ali excavating in Khasekhemui', Margaret Murray album 1899-1900 © Petrie Museum of Egyptian Archaeology, UCL.

9.18. 'Ali buying things from Soudanese', Margaret Murray album 1899-1900 © Petrie Museum of Egyptian Archaeology, UCL.

9.19. 'Um el Mohammed bread making', Margaret Murray album 1899-1900 © Petrie Museum of Egyptian Archaeology, UCL.

9.20. 'Mohd Derwish', Margaret Murray album 1899-1900 © Petrie Museum of Egyptian Archaeology, UCL.

9.21. 'Smeine Abjnad etc digging XVIII pits', Margaret Murray album 1899-1900 © Petrie Museum of Egyptian Archaeology, UCL.

9.22. 'Hosein Osman. XVIII graves', Margaret Murray album 1899-1900 © Petrie Museum of Egyptian Archaeology, UCL.

9.23. 'Sara. Ali's 2nd wife', Margaret Murray album 1899-1900 © Petrie Museum of Egyptian Archaeology, UCL.

9.24. 'Hosein Osman with sugar cane', Margaret Murray album 1899-1900 © Petrie Museum of Egyptian Archaeology, UCL.

9.25. 'The Quftis' band lined up for a welcome back – season beginning and employment', Henri Frankfort 1920s photograph, in the Egypt Exploration Society Lucy Gura Archive © the Egypt Exploration Society.

9.26. 'Ali Suefi and the village guard', Henri Frankfort 1922-1923 album in the Egypt Exploration Society Lucy Gura Archive © the Egypt Exploration Society.

9.27. 'Mohammed Ismaïn', Henri Frankfort 1922-1923 album in the Egypt Exploration Society Lucy Gura Archive © the Egypt Exploration Society.

9.28. Ali Suefi and Guy Brunton, Henri Frankfort 1922-1923 album in the Egypt Exploration Society Lucy Gura Archive © the Egypt Exploration Society.

9.29. 'Mr Brunton and Ali Suefi decide which of the many villagers hoping for pay are to be enrolled', Henri Frankfort 1922-1923 album in the Egypt Exploration Society Lucy Gura Archive © the Egypt Exploration Society.

9.30. 'Mahmud Osman, Starkey, Youssouf, Khallawi en Mohammed Hassan bij Tatters botten onder Sheikh Ibrahim's huis', Henri Frankfort 1922-1923 album in the Egypt Exploration Society Lucy Gura Archive © the Egypt Exploration Society.

9.31. 'Youssouf, bones, parafin', Henri Frankfort 1922-1923 album in the Egypt Exploration Society Lucy Gura Archive © the Egypt Exploration Society.

In addition to the photographs reproduced in this book, all citations from the Petrie Journals are by permission of, and remain copyright of, the Griffith Institute, University of Oxford.

Index

327